AMERICANALAND

MUSIC IN AMERICAN LIFE

A list of books in the series appears at the end of this book.

AMERICANALAND

Where Country & Western Met Rock 'n' Roll

JOHN MILWARD

Portraits by Margie Greve

Manufactured in the United States of America
C 5 4 3 2 1
∞ This book is printed on acid-free paper.

Library of Congress Control Number: 2021936455
ISBN 978-0-252-04391-8 (cloth)
ISBN 978-0-252-05281-1 (e-book)

CONTENTS

ILLUSTRATIONS

AMERICANALAND

INTRODUCTION

Americanaland

Americana is a genre of music that presumes to include country & western, rock 'n' roll, folk, blues, soul, and bluegrass (among other things). Americana is hard to define, but easier to recognize. In the 1990s bands such as Wilco and the Jayhawks and such singer-songwriters as Steve Earle and Lucinda Williams combined elements of rock and country and were said to be playing "alt-country." That's when Jon Grimson, a record promoter, and Rob Bleetstein of the Gavin Report radio tip sheet created a chart to monitor airplay for such records.

"I originally wanted to call it the 'Crucial Country' chart," said Bleetstein, "but [Bill] Gavin thought it was too big a slight on mainstream country." Then Grimson came up with "Americana." "That one stuck with me after I thought about what it meant musically," said Bleetstein, "which was really nothing, so it was our chance to define it as something." The Americana chart only lasted a few years, but the term stuck around. The genre is now more than twenty years old, with its own trade organization (the Americana Music Association was founded in 1999) and Grammy Award category (since 2009).

This is how the Americana Music Association defines Americana: "Contemporary music that incorporates elements of various American roots music styles, including country, roots-rock, folk, bluegrass, R&B, and blues, resulting in a distinctive roots-oriented sound that lives in a world apart from the pure forms of the genres upon which it may draw. While acoustic instruments are often present and vital, Americana also uses a full electric band." Both broad and vague, the term became a useful handle for roots-oriented musicians. "I've been bleeding outside the lines for some time," said Emmylou Harris, who was a country star before she became the queen of Americana. "I like to think I have my own category by now." In recent years, Harris has won Grammy Awards for both Americana and Contemporary Folk.

But Americana was happening long before it had a name. Think of string bands, blues singers, folk musicians, and jazz players passing songs and instrumental techniques from one generation to the next. The modern history begins with the 1927 recordings of Jimmie Rodgers and the Carter Family. Then Hank Williams twisted a yodel into 1949's "Lovesick Blues," and Elvis Presley paired an Arthur Crudup blues ("That's All Right") with a Bill Monroe bluegrass song ("Blue Moon of Kentucky") for his 1954 debut. Ten years later, the Beatles cut country songs by Buck Owens and Carl Perkins and brought those influences into their own tunes. The Byrds, inspired by Bob Dylan and the Beatles, pioneered folk rock and, a few years later, country rock. Dylan turned heads when he went to Nashville to record 1966's *Blonde on Blonde* (and later, *John Wesley Harding* and *Nashville Skyline*) with the city's best musicians. Willie Nelson left Music City to become a Texas "outlaw" who appealed to fans of both country and rock. Guy Clark and Townes Van Zandt went from Texas to Nashville and nurtured a songwriting circle that included Steve Earle and Rodney Crowell. All this inspired recent generations of musicians to make music at the corner of country and rock. That's Americana.

Elvis, to choose one, was far too popular to be considered Americana, which in the contemporary music scene is a niche genre in an era in which rock 'n' roll is itself a minority taste. Chris Stapleton got his start writing hits for mainstream acts such as Kenny Chesney and sang and played guitar with the Steeldrivers, a bluegrass band. Stapleton's 2015 solo debut, *Traveller*, has the musical characteristics of Americana, but when it sold more than three million copies, he became a country star. Similarly, Kasey Musgraves found commercial and Grammy success despite being too pop for country and too modish for Americana. Both artists make music that is likely to appeal to fans of Americana but already play to a broader audience. Conversely, Sturgill Simpson and Mumford and Sons are mainstream acts that got started

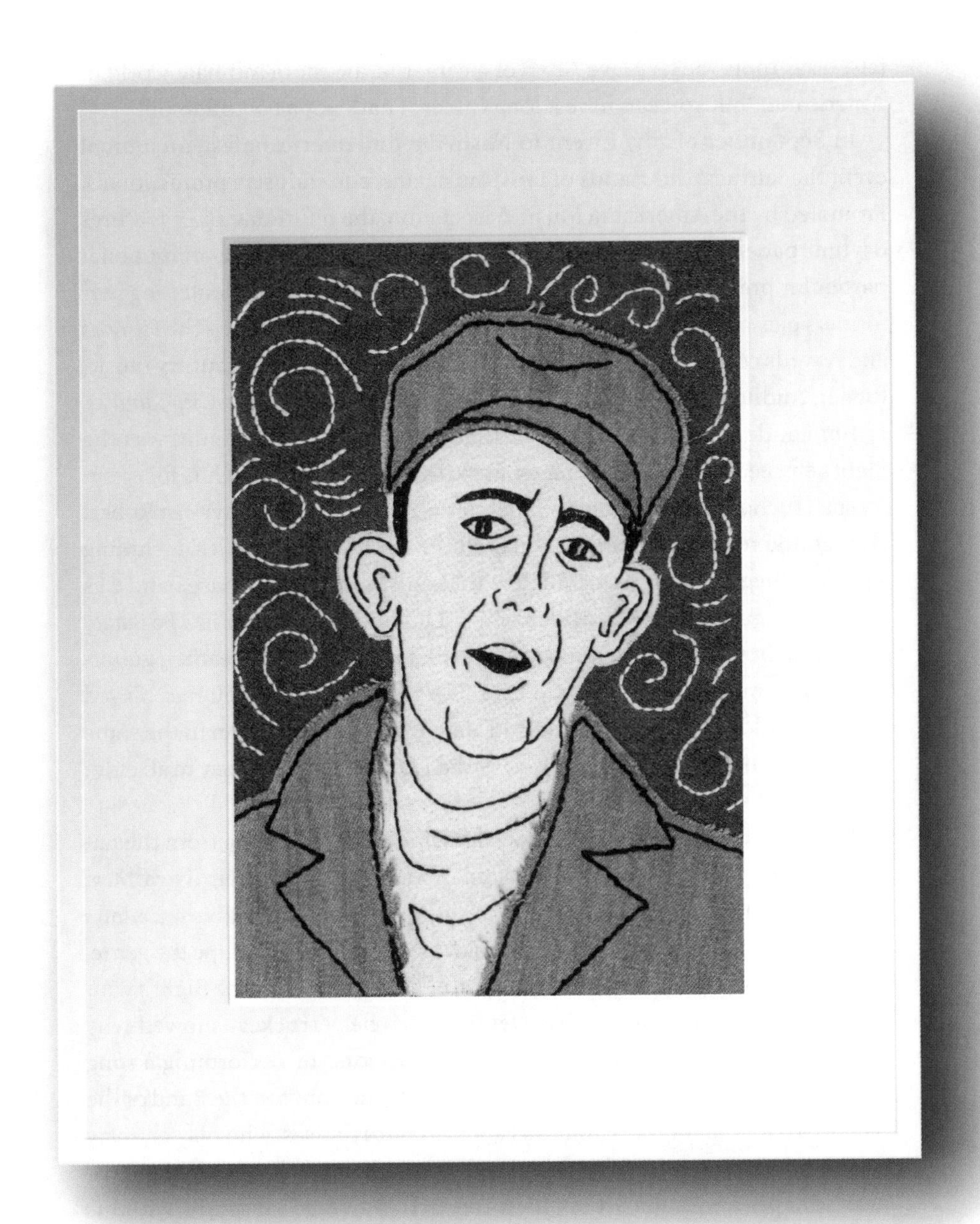

JIMMIE RODGERS

in Americana. Plenty of others stuck around. "You don't get limos and Lear jets," says roots rocker Dave Alvin of a career in the more intimate world of Americana, "but you can have a long career. That's not a bad trade-off."

In September of 2017 I went to Nashville for Americanafest, an annual event that attracts thousands of fans, musicians, and industry professionals. Promoted by the Americana Music Association, the multi-day affair features daytime panels about various aspects of the music and business, promotional parties for press and record-business insiders, and long nights watching performers play at clubs all over town. The centerpiece of the event is the Honors and Awards ceremony held at the so-called Mother Church of country music, Ryman Auditorium, and recorded for later broadcast on *Austin City Limits*.

Jim Lauderdale, wearing an embroidered Nudie-inspired suit, was the night's emcee. Lauderdale is Americana to the core. He's written hits for country stars such as George Strait, collaborated with Grateful Dead lyricist Robert Hunter, and released more than thirty albums in a variety of styles, including a pair of bluegrass albums recorded with Ralph Stanley. The house band was to be led by guitarist Buddy Miller, who is Lauderdale's partner in *The Buddy and Jim Show* on SiriusXM. But because Miller was under the weather, guitarist Larry Campbell stepped up to lead the ensemble. Campbell had played with the Buddy Miller Band in 1980 in New York, where they ran in the same pre-Americana, urban-country circle as did Lauderdale. Now they're all elder statesmen of the genre.

The show opened with Old Crow Medicine Show emerging from the audience while playing "Rainy Day Woman #12 & 35" from their live album celebrating the fiftieth anniversary of a landmark Americana album, Dylan's *Blonde on Blonde*. John Prine, another songwriter who's helped shape the genre, performed his wry country song "In Spite of Ourselves" with the night's winner of the Trailblazer award, Iris DeMent. Drive-By Truckers showed why some call Americana "country music for Democrats" by performing a song about racially motivated shootings, "What It Means," but lost the Band of the Year award to Marty Stuart and His Fabulous Superlatives, who play country music with the intensity of a rock 'n' roll band. Jason Isbell, among the most successful of Americana artists, performed "If We Were Vampires" with his wife Amanda Shires, a singer-songwriter and violinist who won the Best New Artist award. All of these artists live within the pages of *Americanaland*.

Old World rock stars were also on the program, with Ireland's Van Morrison given a Lifetime Achievement award, and the U.K.'s Graham Nash given the Spirit of Americana/Free Speech in Music award. Nash sang "So Sad," an Everly Brothers song, with the Milk Carton Kids, a duo that evokes the tradition of singing siblings. These famous musicians have also been honored at the UK Americana Awards, and Australia holds its own Americana Music Honours. These events draw Americana fans and performers looking to court them. At the end of the Americana Awards show, the players gathered to pay tribute to country singer Don Williams, who had just died, with a communal sing-along of his "Tulsa Time."

The real business of Americanafest takes place at twenty clubs all over town, with different musicians taking the stage hourly. Fans with a plan circulate between venues until the wee hours. My Thursday evening began at the Downtown Presbyterian Church, where singer-songwriter-producer Joe Henry was followed by Shelby Lynne and Allison Moorer, solo singers and sisters who'd just released their first collaborative effort, *Not Dark Yet*. An hour (and a little barbecue) later, I saw Lynne on stage at City Winery singing with the late swamp rocker Tony Joe White. Then it was off to the Cannery Ballroom to catch the end of a set by the Lumineers and to see if Buddy Miller would make his scheduled appearance. Emmylou Harris announced that because Buddy was still feeling ill, the War and Treaty, a gospel duo whom he'd been producing at his home studio, would take his slot. Closing a long day's night were the Drive-By Truckers.

Friday's entertainment began at the 3rd & Lindsey with Jim Lauderdale's band playing honky-tonk tunes and Larry Campbell and his wife Teresa Williams performing songs from their latest album, *Contraband Love* (plus a virtuosic cover of Duke Ellington's "Caravan"). Back at City Winery, I caught Brandy Clark, a singer-songwriter whose sharp set of songs about folks on the edge of respectability made her my favorite new discovery. Energy flagging, I lingered for the start of a midnight set by an Americana star from Australia, Kasey Chambers, and was jolted awake by her songs, powerful voice, and wicked sense of humor. (It turns out that Buddy and Julie Miller added vocals and guitar to her 1998 debut, *The Captain*.)

Promoting musicians is the job of the Americana Music Association (also check nodepression.com for news of contemporary acts). *Americanaland* is concerned with the long history of connections between country & western (and bluegrass) and rock 'n' roll (including folk music and singer-songwriters). This approach is similar to Merriam-Webster's more precise definition of *Americana* as "a genre of American music having roots in early folk and country music."

I've been spare in my coverage of blues music within Americana, and not simply because I wrote a book about the more pertinent interactive history of the blues and rock called *Crossroads: How the Blues Shaped Rock 'n' Roll (and Rock Saved the Blues)*. The blues is in the groundwater of American music and informs everything from jazz and folk to country and rock. "Where I come from in Mississippi," said Marty Stuart, "the blues is underlying everything. Whether you are playing country or gospel or bluegrass, blues is just part of the atmosphere there." Or, as John Lennon from Liverpool said, "The blues is a chair, not a design for a chair, or a better chair . . . it is the first chair."

Our story starts in Bristol, Tennessee, and travels to Alabama, Memphis, Nashville, Greenwich Village, London, Los Angeles, Texas, and points in between. I spent decades as a rock critic for big-city newspapers and magazines and my beat included such "country" artists as Emmylou Harris, Steve Earle, Buddy and Julie Miller, and Shawn Colvin. Middle age found me increasingly drawn to the roots of rock and to the best in vintage blues and country. These days, I sing in a Hudson Valley band whose set list includes songs by the musicians featured in this book, from Jimmie Rodgers and Hank Williams to Merle Haggard and George Jones. Tucked into my LP collection are vintage copies of seminal Americana albums: Dylan's trilogy of Nashville albums, *The Band* and *Music from Big Pink*, The Byrds' *Sweetheart of the Rodeo*, the Flying Burrito Brothers' *Gilded Palace of Sin*, the Grateful Dead's *Workingman's Dead,* and the Nitty Gritty Dirt Band's *Will the Circle Be Unbroken*. The artists who populate these pages are as close as your streaming service, and as you read this story and listen to that fine, fine music, you just might hear the whistle of a train. Next stop, Americanaland.

1

WILL YOU MISS ME WHEN I'M GONE?

This wasn't at all like home. No hearth, no front porch, just a wooden platform in a vacant building in Bristol, a mountain town on the border of Tennessee and Virginia. A recording machine powered by carefully calibrated weights, like a cuckoo clock, was nearby. Sara Carter studied the carbon microphone while Maybelle Carter quietly fingered the strings of her husband's Stella guitar. Then, like back home in Poor Valley, they began to sing "Bury Me Under the Weeping Willow," with Sara taking the lead and Maybelle adding an alto harmony. A long moment later, as if jolted awake by a dream coming true, A. P. Carter added his bass vocal. "When we made the record and they played it back to us," said Maybelle, "I thought, 'Well, it can't be!' You know . . . it just seemed so unreal, that you stand there and sing and then turn around and [they] play it back to you." The next day A. P. was absent, and the women recorded what would become the Carter Family's first hit, "Single Girl, Married Girl."

Ralph Peer spent twelve days in the summer of 1927 recording regional musicians in Bristol, Tennessee; the sessions have been called the big bang of country music because they introduced two seminal acts, the Carter Family and Jimmie Rodgers. The recording and distribution of homespun American music was not new, but the Bristol sessions confirmed that commercial records would soon supplant an oral tradition that had passed songs from one musician (and generation) to the next. Peer already had a history of recording roots music; his stint at Okeh Records produced historic examples of recorded blues (Mamie Smith's "Crazy Blues" in 1920) and "hillbilly" music (Fiddlin' John Carson's "The Little Old Log Cabin in the Lane" in 1923). When Peer moved from Okeh to the Victor Talking Machine Company (soon to become RCA Victor), he negotiated a unique contract in which he took no salary but retained the publishing rights of the songs he recorded. That meant he'd earn a royalty on each record sold. In three particularly lucrative months in 1928, Peer received $250,000.

The Carter Family and Jimmie Rodgers had some things in common—for one, both acts helped turn the guitar into a lead instrument—but were also quite different. "[The Carter Family's] style was something they created out of older styles," said musician and folklorist Mike Seeger, "with the tear between A. P.'s way-back sounds, and Maybelle's guitar pulling them forward. But with Jimmie [Rodgers], he was reaching toward being a creator, trying to get something that would grab people's attention—and that's pop."

The Carters' repertoire was drawn from and inspired by the folk songs brought to America from the British Isles (among other places). Maybelle and A. P. draped Sara's lead voice with church-based harmonies, and the Carter Family's rich vocal sound stood out in an era dominated by string bands. Jimmie Rodgers was a folkie bluesman with a shape-shifting persona suitable for songs that could be randy or pious, silly or sad. Generations of folk musicians grew up singing the songs of the Carter Family. Rodgers's personable voice and guitar informed a long line of troubadours, including Woody Guthrie, Hank Williams, Elvis Presley, and Bob Dylan. "It's arguable," said Steve Earle, a contemporary embodiment of that tradition, "that we just wouldn't have this consistent, lasting genre of music based on one guy singing and accompanying himself on a guitar. . . . I think [Jimmie Rodgers] invented the job."

The Carter Family and Rodgers took different paths to Bristol. The Carters were borne of the passions of Alvin Pleasant Carter, known as A. P., who played the fiddle and collected folk songs as he traveled around Appalachia selling fruit trees. When A. P. married Sara Dougherty in 1915, he found both a mate and a musical partner who played guitar and autoharp and who sang with a voice of uncommon splendor. They were joined by Sara's cousin Maybelle Addington, who created a unique guitar style (the so-called Carter scratch)

THE CARTER FAMILY

by using her thumb to pick a melody on the bass strings while her fingertips created rhythms on the upper strings. “We’d get together and, you know, flump around [on our instruments], and sing,” said Sara. “Maybe go to a neighbor’s home once in a while. . . . It was just our natural way of playing—we don’t know any music, we just played by ear.” The Carters couldn’t read music, but they sure knew songs.

At an early performance by the Carter Family, Maybelle met A. P.’s brother Ezra, whom everybody called Eck. “I’d gone to Sara and A. P.’s to do a show at a schoolhouse,” said Maybelle. “A. P.’s brother was . . . going with the schoolteacher there at the school. Well, he was supposed to take her home, but he didn’t.” When Bristol beckoned, A. P. borrowed his brother’s Essex sedan after agreeing to weed Eck’s corn patch; Maybelle was eight months pregnant.

Jimmie Rodgers was born in 1897 in Meridian, Mississippi, the son of a railroad worker. His mother died when he was a child, and he ran away twice in hopes of becoming an entertainer; at fourteen, he began to learn about the blues and playing guitar while working as a water boy for a black railroad crew. Rodgers became a brakeman on the New Orleans and Northeastern Railroad, but his health began to fail, and he was diagnosed with tuberculosis. At the age of twenty-eight Rodgers decided to sing for a living or die trying; one early gig found him touring with a medicine show and singing in blackface.

In Asheville, North Carolina, Rodgers recruited the Tenneva Ramblers to perform with him as the Jimmie Rodgers Entertainers. The group arrived in Bristol on August 3, 1927, but Peer recognized that Rodgers was a bright star in a mediocre string band and recorded him solo. Peer left Bristol with six tunes by the Carter Family and a pair by Rodgers (“The Soldier’s Sweetheart” and “Sleep, Baby, Sleep”) and paid the artists fifty dollars per song against a 2½-cent royalty. He encouraged them to create original material that could be copyrighted by Peer’s Southern Music Company, a move that would bring him revenue not only from their releases but more money when other artists recorded the songs. In order to maximize his influence, Peer also managed the Carter Family and Jimmie Rodgers.

The Carters went home to Poor Valley, nestled beneath Clinch Mountain, and presumed that little would change; but the success of “Single Girl, Married Girl” prompted Peer to schedule another session in early 1928, this time in Camden, New Jersey. Rodgers, whose first release went nowhere, was more proactive, checking into a Manhattan hotel room in November 1927 and informing Peer that he was ready to record more tunes. They cut a twelve-bar blues called "T for Texas" that featured a catchy yodel that prompted Peer to retitle the song "Blue Yodel."

Rodgers's background earned him the nickname "the Singing Brakeman," but it was the bluesy yodel that became his commercial hook. "Blue Yodel" was a monster hit, and subsequent songs bore titles like "Blue Yodel No. 4 (California Blues)" and "Blue Yodel No. 8 (Mule Skinner Blues)." Rodgers's yodel was not unlike the sob that operatic tenor (and Victor recording artist) Enrico Caruso created by changing registers during his recording of "Vesti la Giubba" from the opera *Pagliacci.* A more likely source was Riley Puckett, a blind singer and guitarist who played with Gid Tanner and the Skillet Lickers and who recorded "Sleep, Baby, Sleep," a yodel-laden tune that Rodgers had cut in Bristol.

Rodgers's intimate vocals anchored his records in a manner that, like hits by Bing Crosby, influenced generations of popular singers. As befits an icon, he appealed to almost everyone, including innumerable country singers and such bluesmen as B. B. King and Chester "Howlin' Wolf" Burnett, who turned Rodgers's yodel into a howl. Robert Johnson sang the songs of Jimmie Rodgers alongside his own. "If you believe that rock 'n' roll brings about a nexus of black music and white music," said Steve Earle, "then Jimmie Rodgers is one of the people who made that happen."

Rodgers was a prolific songwriter, both by himself ("Waiting for a Train" and almost all of his thirteen Blue Yodels) and in collaboration with others. By contrast, A. P. Carter didn't write songs so much as recognize a good one when he heard it. Returning home from his travels with tunes and stray lyrics, A. P. would work over the words and (with the help of Sara and Maybelle) craft melodies that could be copyrighted as new songs. The Carter Family's "I'm Thinking Tonight of My Blue Eyes" is a telling example of the porous nature of American roots music in the first half of the twentieth century.

Maybelle and A. P. are said to have modeled the tune after "The Prisoner's Song," a 1925 release by Vernon Delhart. The Carter Family's recording was a major hit in 1929; Roy Acuff heard a gospel group put different lyrics to the same melody and used those words for the 1936 song that launched his career, "The Great Speckled Bird." Sixteen years later Hank Thompson cut "The Wild Side of Life," in which the same tune carried new, broken-hearted lyrics about a man spotting his ex-wife in a honky-tonk. "The Wild Side of Life" stayed at the top of the country charts for fifteen weeks. Then songwriter J. D. Miller used the same melody to create an "answer song" that became the #1 hit that introduced the world to Kitty Wells, "It Wasn't God Who Made Honky Tonk Angels."

Peer's output at Victor also included tracks by black musicians (known as "race records") by such southern blues musicians as Tommy Johnson, Furry Lewis, and Sleepy John Estes. He also recorded such seminal ensembles as Will Shade's Memphis Jug Band and Gus Cannon's Jug Stompers. Bluesmen like Son House and Skip James recorded for Paramount Records in 1931 but remained virtually unknown until they became rediscovered stars of the blues revival of the 1960s. That group also included Mississippi John Hurt, a guitarist and singer who recorded for Okeh Records in 1929 and whose repertoire of blues and folk tunes was not unlike those of Rodgers and the Carter Family.

Roots music was also of interest to folklorists who recorded music not for profit but to document regional styles before they disappeared. In 1933 John Lomax, an author and musicologist, made field recordings for the Library of Congress with his son Alan. The pair discovered and recorded Huddie Ledbetter at the Louisiana State Prison in Angola. Ledbetter, who'd already served time for murder, was in prison for stabbing a white man. Released two years later, he would soon come to be known as the folk singer Lead Belly. Alan would subsequently establish his own relationship with the Library of Congress and in 1941 would record McKinley Morganfield, already known as Muddy Waters, at Stovall Plantation.

Singing into Lomax's microphone, Waters performed "Country Blues," which was his version of Robert Johnson's "Walking Blues," which was Johnson's rewrite of Son House's "My Black Mama." A. P. Carter could relate to the way Delta blues musicians created new songs using familiar guitar licks and lyrical fragments. And Sara Carter would understand how Waters felt when Lomax played back the recording to him. "Man, you don't know how I felt that Saturday afternoon when I heard that voice and it was my own voice," said Waters. "Later on he sent me two copies of the pressing and a check for twenty bucks, and I carried that record up to the corner and put it on the jukebox. Just played it and played it and said, 'I can do it, I can do it.'" By the late 1940s, Waters would be in Chicago reshaping his delta music into a whole new style of big-city blues.

Jimmie Rodgers couldn't wait around to become famous; living with tuberculosis, he already knew his days were numbered when he traveled to Bristol. If

Peer personified the modern record man, Rodgers was like a pop star. Recording 111 songs in just five years, Rodgers was an avid self-promoter, quick to sign autographs and talk up deejays and reporters while he was on concert tours. He sat for numerous photo shoots in a variety of outfits and snappy hats, filmed a promotional movie short for Columbia Pictures called *The Singing Brakeman*, recorded with superstar colleagues such as the Carter Family and jazzman Louis Armstrong, and toured with showbiz cowboy and humorist Will Rogers to benefit the Red Cross. In a word, Rodgers was the Bono of his time.

But time was short for one of the biggest stars of his day. In May 1933 Rodgers traveled to New York for what would be his last recording session. A cot was brought to the studio so that he could lie down between takes. In four sessions held over the course of a week, Rodgers recorded eleven songs; the words of the last one, "Years Ago," spoke to being sad to leave Mississippi. The next day, Rodgers and his private nurse took a trip to Coney Island; feeling distress, he returned to the Taft Hotel, where five years earlier he had stayed while hustling a second chance with Ralph Peer. Rodgers died late that night. The body was brought back to Mississippi by rail, and as the night train pulled into Meridian, the mournful cry of the locomotive's whistle welcomed the brakeman home.

Jimmie Rodgers inspired a school of emulators. Gene Autry spent the late 1920s releasing virtual copies of Rodgers's "Blue Yodels" and was quick to cut a tribute song, "The Death of Jimmie Rodgers." Autry soon found his own mellifluous style and became Hollywood's premiere singing cowboy. Ernest Tubb was another fan; Carrie Rodgers gave Tubb one of her late husband's guitars and helped him obtain a contract with RCA. Like Autry, Tubb didn't click until he established his own sound, in his case with 1940's "Walking the Floor Over You." Future country stars like Lefty Frizzell and Johnny Cash grew up idolizing Rodgers. The first tune Doc Watson learned to play on guitar was the Carter Family's "When the Roses Bloom in Dixieland," but he started using a flat pick after listening to Jimmie Rodgers.

Others didn't imitate Rodgers so much as interpret his songs in new ways. Bill Monroe and his brother Charlie recorded in the 1930s as the Monroe Brothers. When that group broke up, Bill formed the Blue Grass Boys. Monroe, who played mandolin, had learned the syncopations of blues and jazz from a black guitarist named Arnold Schultz; these rhythmic touches became his special sauce. Monroe's group used fast tempos and high-pitched vocal harmonies to create a lively string-band style that came to be called bluegrass. Monroe became known as the "Father of Bluegrass" with the mid-1940s lineup that included guitarist Lester Flatt and Earl Scruggs, who used a unique three-fingered technique to pick his banjo. But in 1939, when Monroe and the Blue Grass Boys successfully auditioned for the *Grand Ole Opry* program in Nashville, they played Jimmie Rodgers's "Mule Skinner Blues." "Charlie and I had a country beat," said Monroe, "but the beat in my music—bluegrass music—started when I ran across 'Mule Skinner Blues' and started playing that. We don't do it the way Jimmie sang it. It's speeded up, and we moved it up to fit the fiddle, and we have that straight time with it—driving time."

On the day in 1940 when Monroe recorded "Mule Skinner Blues," the Blue Grass Boys also cut "I Wonder If You Feel the Way I Do" by Bob Wills and His Texas Playboys, who in 1938 counted fourteen members including three fiddles, two saxophones, a trumpet, and a drummer. The band did big business in the Southwest and kept the dance floor hopping with its big-band style of country music. Wills recognized that a Jimmie Rodgers tune could kill with a big beat, rhythmically bowed fiddles, jazzy improvisations on the pedal steel, and smoothly swinging vocals (delivered most famously by Tommy Duncan).

Willie Nelson, a Texas teenager who played music in a combo with his sister Bobbi and her husband Bud Fletcher, staged a Bob Wills concert not far from his childhood home in Abbott. Nelson figures that about five hundred people came to the show; the gate receipts barely covered the band's guarantee and left nothing for the young promoter, whose group was the opening act. "He hit the bandstand at eight and didn't leave it for hours," said Nelson of Wills. "He would play continually, there was no time wasted between songs. . . . His band watched him all the time, and he only had to nod or point the bow of his fiddle to cue band members to play a solo. He was the greatest dance hall bandleader ever."

Wills ruled a Southwest music scene full of talent. The Maddox Brothers and Rose, a popular swing band that called its version of the Rodgers song "New Muleskinner Blues," traveled the rodeo circuit to play the local bars. "Right across the street from us would always be Woody Guthrie," said Rose Maddox. "I was a kid. He looked tall and skinny." Guthrie, the enduring archetype of the socially conscious folk singer, took up music as a teenager and led a life of wanderlust that included three wives and eight children. During the late 1930s he performed on KFVD, a radio station in Los Angeles, and debuted songs that would appear on his 1940 RCA release, *Dust Bowl Ballads*. He also wrote a column called "Woody Sez" for a Communist newspaper, *People's World*, a sideline that ultimately cost the "fellow traveler" his radio job.

At the request of Alan Lomax, Guthrie traveled to New York to perform at "A 'Grapes of Wrath' Evening for the Benefit of the John Steinbeck Committee for Agricultural Workers." Lomax subsequently recorded hours of Guthrie's conversation and songs for the Library of Congress. "The first hint of his real importance didn't come from him or me," said his third wife, Marjorie Guthrie. "It was Alan Lomax who said to me, 'Don't throw anything away. Save everything.' And I looked at him to say, 'Why?' And he said, 'Woody is going to be very important.'"

At the benefit, Guthrie met a folk singer who worked for Lomax: Pete Seeger. "I learned a lot about songwriting from Woody," said Seeger, a Harvard dropout who was the son of composer and musicologist Charles Seeger. "I learned something that was awful important. And that was: don't be so all-fired concerned about being original. You hear an old song you like but you want to change it a little, there's no crime in that." This explains why Guthrie borrowed the melody of the Carter Family's "John Hardy Was a Desperate Man" for his own "Tom Joad" and used the tune of the Carters' "When the World's on Fire" for "This Land Is Your Land," his wry response to Irving Berlin's "God Bless America." Guthrie had less success teaching Seeger how to hop a freight train. "Woody said, 'Wait on the outskirts of town,'" said Seeger, "'and when the train is picking up speed, and it's still not going too fast, you can grab a hold of it and swing on.' Getting off the first time I didn't know how to do it and I fell down and skinned my knees and elbow and broke my banjo."

In the early 1940s Seeger and Guthrie performed on Lomax's radio program *Back Where I Came From* alongside Josh White, Burl Ives, and Lead Belly. The pair also belonged to the Almanac Singers, a coterie of leftist musicians who lived together at 130 West 10th Street in New York's Greenwich Village. To make the rent on the three-story "Almanac House," the singers anticipated the arrival of Village folk clubs by passing the hat at hootenannies held in the basement.

The legacy of the Carter Family was in its deep repertoire. Peer continued to record the Carters into the 1930s, introducing such songs as "Keep on the Sunny Side," "Wildwood Flower," "Lonesome Valley," "Worried Man Blues,"

and "Will the Circle Be Unbroken?" These songs provided fundamental lessons for folk musicians from Guthrie and Seeger to Bob Dylan and Joan Baez. "The first time I heard ["Gold Watch and Chain"]," said Emmylou Harris, "I thought about my grandparents and cried . . . I found the music very haunting." Listen to a singer-songwriter like Gillian Welch, and you're hearing the distant echo of the Carter Family.

To find these songs, A. P. traveled widely. Brownie McGhee, a guitarist who would form a blues duo with harmonica player Sonny Terry, recalled the excitement when A. P. rolled into Kingsport, Tennessee, driving the red Chevrolet that he'd bought with record royalties. He met black musicians (and learned their songs) with the help of an African American guitarist named Lesley Riddle. "I was his tape recorder," said Riddle, who took about fifteen trips with A. P. "He'd take me with him and he'd get someone to sing him the whole song. Then I would get it, then I'd learn it to Sara and Maybelle." Along the way, Maybelle absorbed Riddle's instrumental techniques. "You don't have to give Maybelle any lessons," he said. "You let her see you play something, she'll get it."

Her husband's travels left Sara alone for long periods of time, and she had an affair with his cousin, Coy Bays, fifteen years her junior. Poor Valley was scandalized, and the Bayses relocated to New Mexico, where Coy's mother intercepted letters from a forlorn Sara. She and A. P. divorced, and while she became an increasingly reluctant performer, hard times conspired to keep the Carter Family together. When record sales plummeted during the Great Depression, radio became vital to the careers of the Carters and other roots musicians. The big action was on the shows with national network affiliates such as *National Barn Dance* on WLS in Chicago and the *Grand Ole Opry* on WSM in Nashville. But there was another route to a wide audience, and in 1938 the Carter Family began performing on XERA, a powerful border radio station located near Del Rio, Texas. The venture was bankrolled by Doctor John Romulus Brinkley, who'd made his fortune promoting an operation that sought to cure male impotence by grafting goat glands onto a man's testicles.

"Good Neighbor Get-Together" was the name of the Carter Family's show, and its theme song was "Keep on the Sunny Side." The Carters recorded two shows per day for six months of the year. Compared with the weekly barn dance shows, with live audiences adding visceral big-city excitement, the Carters' daytime program was far more intimate. One J. R. Cash, listening from his boyhood home in Dyess, Arkansas, could hardly imagine that one day he'd marry Maybelle's daughter, June, who was already part of the act. One day in February 1939 Sara dedicated "I'm Thinking Tonight of My Blue Eyes" to "Coy Bays in California." "For the pleasures we both seen together," she sang, "I am sure, love, I'll never forget." Coy heard the broadcast and traveled to Texas, where he and Sara were married. Though the original Carter Family would continue performing for another four years, including a stint at WBT, a fifty-thousand-watt radio station in Charlotte, North Carolina, the familial circle was broken beyond repair.

Sara left the music business and lived a quiet life with Coy in northern California. Returning to Poor Valley, A. P. ran a grocery store that was a community center as much as a business. He later worked at a fire tower on the top of Clinch Mountain that looked over the countryside that had given him so many songs. Maybelle began performing with her three daughters (Helen, Anita, and June) as The Carter Sisters and Mother Maybelle. Driving long distances between small-time shows, they'd rehearse in the car, and on the radio they'd occasionally hear an old Carter Family song that increasingly sounded like something from a distant past.

The postwar years were a tumultuous time in popular music, with big bands supplanted by solo singing stars such as Frank Sinatra and small combos led by, for example, Louis Jordan and Nat King Cole. One can imagine Elvis Presley from Tupelo, Mississippi, noticing how much hits by hillbilly acts like Red Foley ("Tennessee Saturday Night") and Tennessee Ernie Ford ("Shot-Gun Boogie") had in common with race records by Roy Brown ("Good Rockin' Tonight") and Joe Liggins ("Pink Champagne").

The music trade magazine *Billboard* struggled to classify roots music made by white and black musicians. For a time in the 1940s, both hillbilly and race records were listed as "American Folk Records." Recordings were subsequently segregated into "Race Records" and "Hillbilly Records." Finally, in June 1949, *Billboard* created two charts that encompassed the roots of Americana: "Country & Western" and "Rhythm & Blues." Industry insiders had another term for the kind of pre-rock 'n' roll records that appealed to white people: "cat music."

If such sounds made Maybelle and her daughters feel old fashioned, they could certainly relate to Merle Travis, a popular yet deeply traditional Appalachian artist who in 1947 released an influential recording called *Folk Songs of the Hills*. Travis had had such popular hits as "Smoke! Smoke! Smoke! That Cigarette," but this collection put a spotlight on the guitar playing that had made him a superstar among musicians. His style came to be called "Travis picking," a syncopated form of fingerpicking in which alternating bass notes are struck by the thumb while melodies are played with the index finger. Travis picking is essentially the flipside of the Carter scratch, and it was in part derived from the playing of Arnold Shultz, the same African American musician who'd influenced Bill Monroe.

When the Carters had a radio program at WNOX in Knoxville, they met Chester "Chet" Atkins, a staff guitarist who'd perfected a version of Travis picking that used three fingers to pick the melody atop the bass notes. Maybelle was quick to appreciate the instrumentalist whom some considered too jazzy for country music, and he was soon traveling with an act now dubbed "The Carter Sisters and Mother Maybelle and Chet Atkins and His Famous Guitar." "Maybelle was kind of like a second mama to me," said Atkins. "We never had a cross word. She was just a gentle soul." Atkins was at home in a family of women. "I'd lay my head in one of 'em's lap and try to go to sleep," he said. "It wasn't all bad, I tell you."

By the time America had suffered through the Great Depression and World War II, the big bang in Bristol was ancient history. Country & western music now lived at the *Grand Ole Opry* and in beer-soaked honky-tonks, and Hank Williams was starting to write the songs that would make him country's singular star. At the same time, Muddy Waters was electrifying the blues in Chicago, Pete Seeger and the Weavers were bringing a repertoire of folk songs to urban nightclubs, and R&B musicians were recording tunes that appealed to a young and occasionally white audience. Even the formats were changing, with thick 78 rpm records replaced by 45 rpm singles and 33⅓ rpm long-playing albums.

There was little to nothing in record stores by Rodgers or the Carter Family, a particular hardship for Jim Evans and his quest to collect all 111 songs of Jimmie Rodgers. Evans created a fan club and obliged other collectors by reproducing increasingly rare Rodgers songs on blank discs. The label that owned the recordings, RCA, warned Evans that his "bootlegs" were illegal and soon released *Yodelingly Yours—Jimmie Rodgers: A Memorial Album to a Great Entertainer, Volume One* (1949). In the early 1950s RCA reissued twenty-four Rodgers songs to relatively slim sales; then, in 1955, Webb Pierce's cover of "In the Jailhouse Now" spent twenty-one weeks at the top of the country charts and confirmed that Rodgers had become an enduring legend.

In 1952 the past met the present in Harry Smith's *Anthology of American Folk Music*, an eccentrically curated ramble through what critic Greil Marcus called "the old, weird America." Smith had become obsessed with collecting rural music while living a bohemian life as a visual artist and experimental filmmaker. He made history by creating a unique portrait of American music using eighty-four songs from his collection of ten thousand 78s. It is significant that he drew no distinctions between black musicians who recorded race records and country pickers who played hillbilly music. The *Anthology* included songs by Blind Lemon Jefferson, Clarence Ashley, Blind Willie Johnson, and Dock Boggs, as well as four by the Carter Family (including "Single Girl, Married Girl"). Smith included no songs by Jimmie Rodgers, perhaps because he considered them too popular to be included in a collection of the old and the obscure.

The *Anthology* was marketed as three sets of two LPs labeled "Ballads," "Social Music," and "Songs." Moses Asch of Folkways Records had sent letters of inquiry to the labels that had released these mostly forgotten songs but received no replies, so technically the *Anthology* was a bootleg recording that became the Holy Grail to musicians drawn to the roots of Americana. (The package wasn't entirely licensed until the Smithsonian released it on compact disc in 1997.) "We knew every word of every song on it," said Dave Van Ronk, a central figure in the Greenwich Village folk music scene, "including the ones we hated." The *Anthology* also reintroduced performers lost to history, with musicians such as Furry Lewis, Mississippi John Hurt, and Sleepy John Estes finding an unexpected third act playing at urban coffeehouses, college campuses, and folk festivals.

"I'm glad to say that my dreams came true," said Smith, accepting a special Grammy Award for the *Anthology* in 1991. "I saw America changed through music." And in the 1950s the changes would come fast, with country music intermingling with blues and R&B to create what would become the next big bang. You can hear a hint of rock 'n' roll in the biggest country hit of 1950, Hank Snow's "I'm Moving On," a powerful boogie that stayed at #1 for twenty-one weeks and was later recorded by the Rolling Stones. Snow loved the man from Meridian so much that he named his son Jimmie Rodgers Snow. Meanwhile, after a couple of rejections due to the presence of a suspiciously sophisticated guitarist, the Carter Sisters and Mother Maybelle and Chet Atkins and His Famous Guitar joined the *Grand Ole Opry*. "I owe everything to the Carters," said Atkins, who would soon be regarded as Nashville's preeminent guitarist. "I don't know what the hell would have happened to me if I hadn't run into 'em."

2
THE LOST HIGHWAY

Hank Williams was the greatest country artist in history. He put the poetry into hillbilly music and influenced innumerable country, rock, and Americana songwriters. His sad story also anticipated the tragic tales of such artists as Gram Parsons and Townes Van Zandt. Don Helms played the steel guitar for Williams, using a metal bar to carve instrumental figures within Hank's heartbreak tunes. Helms learned to go high when Hank's voice went low and to drop down when Hank went up. When Helms's group, the Alabama Rhythm Boys, first met its new boss in 1943, Hank took them to a pawnshop.

"Hank said, 'Jake, have you got any more of those blackjacks back there?'" recalled Helms, whose group was renamed the Drifting Cowboys. "'Give me five of them.' And he passed these clubs out to us guys and said, 'Boys, if you're gonna play with me you're gonna need these." Hank spoke from experience; he'd already saved his skin by breaking a Gibson guitar over the head of a rowdy tough at Thigpen's Log Cabin.

The sound of classic country was born in the rural honky-tonks that promised dim lights, thick smoke, and loud, loud music. "When you paid and got in," said Helms of visiting a roadhouse in a so-called dry country, "you'd pick a table, slap your bottle on it, and throw your [switchblade] in the floor. The thing was still vibrating when they brought you a bucket of ice and some glasses." Chicken wire was sometimes strung across the stage to protect the musicians from flying bottles.

Hiram Williams was born in the backwoods of Alabama in 1923. A deformity in his spinal column (spina bifida) was left untreated and pained him all his life. His father, Alonzo Williams, had lost his mother to suicide at the age of six. While serving in the army in World War I, he either fell off a truck or was hit with a wine bottle during a fight over a woman. Whatever the case, a brain aneurysm landed him in a Veterans Administration hospital; Hank and his sister Irene grew up in the care of their mother Lillian, who would forever occupy a central role in her son's life.

Lillian ran a boarding house in Georgiana where Hank took to the streets to shine shoes and sell newspapers. It was there that he met Rufus Payne, a black musician known as "Tee-Tot" (derived in jest from "teetotaler") because he carried a flask filled with whiskey and tea. Though Tee-Tot worked as a janitor and deliveryman, he considered himself a troubadour; he sang blues and gospel and sometimes used the neck of a bottle to fret the strings of his guitar. Williams pestered Tee-Tot for guitar lessons and absorbed the way he sang the blues atop a good, steady beat. In 1951 he told the *Montgomery Advisor*, "All the training I ever had was from him."

When Lillian moved the family to Montgomery, Hank busked outside the studios of WSFA. The station soon gave him his own fifteen-minute radio show, which earned him $15 per week and helped him get gigs at local honky-tonks, where Lillian was on hand to handle the business. Liquor was already a problem for the young talent. Backstage at a concert, Williams met Roy Acuff, of whom he'd said, "It's Roy Acuff and then God!" Said Roy to Hank: "You've got a million-dollar voice, son, but a ten-cent brain."

In 1944 Hank moved to Mobile, took a job on the docks, and courted a married woman named Audrey Mae Sheppard. Lillian saw Audrey as competing for Hank's allegiance, but the women were actually on the same page, because Audrey preferred a hillbilly singer to a working stiff. Audrey, whose husband was a soldier on the European front, pushed Hank to make her part of the act in spite of the fact that she could scarcely hold a note. Meanwhile, Lillian worked her maternal magic. "I booked Hank solid for sixty days," she said. "Then the third week he had been 'out of the music business,' I went to

Mobile and put him back in it. When Hank saw the datebook for those shows, he gave me the sweetest smile I've ever seen and said, 'Thank God, Mother. You have made me the happiest boy in the world.'"

Hank and Audrey (after a quick divorce) were married at the end of 1944 by a justice of the peace at his gas station in Andalusia. Hank now had two women whispering in his ear. He'd found his professional footing with his WSFA show and a busy schedule of live gigs making him the hottest country act in southern Alabama. But local success was for losers, and Audrey pushed Hank toward Nashville and a crucial association that would focus his songwriting and turn him into a recording star.

Fred Rose was everything Hank wasn't. He'd been a professional pianist and songwriter for decades, performing on the radio in Chicago and writing more than a dozen songs for America's favorite singing cowboy, Gene Autry. Rose also liked to drink, and the bottle let him down until he became a Christian Scientist and embraced sobriety. Settling in Nashville, he played piano at WSM and was bankrolled by Roy Acuff to launch Acuff-Rose, country music's first major publishing company. Rose signed Williams to a publishing contract with the encouragement of singer Molly O'Day, who recorded four of his tunes. Rose soon gave Williams a chance to sing his own songs; *Billboard* said that his first single, "Calling You," showed that he had "real spiritual qualities in his pipes." But Hank truly hit stride with "Honky Tonkin'," a bouncy track without drums that rode on the "crack" backbeat created by the interplay of the bass fiddle and the muted strings of an electric guitar. Ten years later a similar "boom-chicka-boom" rhythm would become the signature sound of Johnny Cash.

Williams and Rose made a perfect pair, with the musically savvy publisher lending a sympathetic ear to the work of an inspired original. Rose would suggest a chord change here or excise a whiskey reference there but recognized that Hank's appeal rested on simple melodies and everyday language. Unlike many behind-the-scenes players, Rose didn't take undue advantage. He only shared songwriting credit when he significantly contributed to a song, as on "Kaw-Liga," where he switched up the chord progression and came up with the lyrical conceit of a romance between a couple of wooden Indians.

Williams flourished with Rose's encouragement and was soon producing such enduring hits as "Move It On Over" and "I Saw the Light," a spiritual tune inspired by the early morning sight of an airport beacon as the Drifting Cowboys drove home from a gig. "When a hillbilly sings a crazy song," said

Williams, "he feels crazy. When he sings, 'I Laid My Mother Away,' he sees her a-laying right there in the coffin. He sings more sincere than most entertainers because the hillbilly was raised rougher than most entertainers. . . . You got to have smelt a lot of mule manure before you can sing like a hillbilly."

Hank's stark and reedy voice was as unaffected as his lyrics. He put a yodel into some of his songs, but he was no Jimmie Rodgers. "Characteristic of Williams," said Henry Pleasant, who wrote about the art of singing, "is the rapid yodeling alternation of falsetto and normal voice within the phrase or even within the time span of a single note, the effect being that of a birdlike warble, its function at once ornamental and expressive." "Lovesick Blues" is a brilliant example of this technique. It also said something about the difference between Williams and Rose. The song came from a mid-1920s Broadway musical that flopped (*O-oo Ernest*) and bore lyrics by Irving Mills, who also put words to Duke Ellington's "It Don't Mean a Thing (If It Ain't Got That Swing)." Emmett Miller, a blackface vaudevillian who sang (and yodeled) in a bluesy style that influenced Jimmie Rodgers, cut the song in 1925. Williams sang "Lovesick Blues" to a rapturous response from audiences, but when he played the structurally unorthodox tune for Rose, he declared it a stinker. "I'll tell you one damn thing," said Williams. "You might not like the song, but when I walk off the stage and throw my hat back on the stage and the hat encores, that's pretty hot."

"Lovesick Blues" turned out to be the biggest country hit of 1948, selling two million copies and spending sixteen weeks at #1, but with his reputation as an unreliable drunk, Williams was still shunned by the conservative and hugely influential *Grand Ole Opry* program. The *Opry* debuted on Nashville's WSM in 1925 and was dominated by fiddlers and string bands until Roy Acuff became its marquee star with his sentimental, tear-stained vocals. In 1941 the program found a permanent home in the Ryman Auditorium, an austere tabernacle used by Evangelical preachers that was built in 1892 by Thomas Ryman as penance for the fortune he'd made running saloons and riverboat casinos. Because the *Opry*'s syndicated Saturday night broadcast reached a coast-to-coast audience and had an additional network affiliation with NBC, appearing on the program was considered the key to a successful career.

Aiming to win a spot on the *Opry*, Williams relocated to Shreveport, Louisiana, and performed on the KWKH show that booked talented up-and-comers, the *Louisiana Hayride*. Six years later, Elvis Presley would appear on the *Hayride* to sing his first single for Sun Records, "That's All Right." Merle

HANK WILLIAMS

Kilgore was fourteen years old when he carried Hank's guitar on the night of his *Hayride* debut. (Years later, Kilgore would write "Ring of Fire" with June Carter Cash; the song became one of Johnny Cash's biggest hits. Kilgore also managed the musical career of Hank Williams Jr.)

"Hank had the same look in his eyes that Elvis had," said Kilgore. "That 'I know something you don't know' look. Hank was cocky. That first night [August 7, 1948, with Hank fifth on the bill], the Bailesses were on before him and he said, 'How did they do?' I said, 'Real good. I hate that you have to follow 'em.' He said, 'I'll eat 'em alive.'" Between the success of "Lovesick Blues" and the excitement Williams was generating on *Louisiana Hayride*, the *Opry* gave in within a year. To seal the deal, Fred Rose pledged that Hank would stay sober (which didn't happen) and gave two *Opry* principals part of the writer's share of his song "Chattanooga Shoe Shine Boy," which soon became a #1 hit. Williams finally made his *Opry* debut on June 18, 1949.

Williams was introduced as "the lovesick boy," and the string bean of a singer (six foot one, 150 pounds) was all elbows and angles as he strode onto the celebrated stage wearing a fringed cowboy suit, a broad white hat, and shiny boots. Nobody recognized him, but the bubbly steel guitar lick that introduced "Lovesick Blues" lit the fuse, and when Hank began to sing—"I got a feelin' called the blues"—the place exploded, with flashbulbs popping and women swooning at the feral sound of his yodel and the way he swung his hips behind his flat top guitar. Legend has Hank called back for no fewer than six encores, but the details are irrelevant, for by the time Williams returned later in the program to sing "Move It On Over," he'd become not just a hillbilly star but a giant of American roots music.

Williams's career went into orbit, with concert appearances alongside other stars organized by the *Opry* and a daily radio show (often pre-recorded) on WSM. He wrote whenever he could. "One Sunday morning we left Nashville to go to Birmingham to do a matinee and a night," said Helms, "and he said, 'Hand me that tablet up there.' And he wrote down, 'Hey, good lookin', what you got cookin', and before we got to Birmingham it was finished." Hank would bring songs and fragments to Rose in anticipation of recording sessions, and he created an alter ego (Luke the Drifter) for sentimental songs and spiritual recitations that sold nowhere near his usual numbers.

The songs of Hank Williams are distinguished by the pared-down poetry of his lyrics; the vast majority of the words he used consist of single syllables, with a smaller number containing two, and once in a blue moon, three syllables. Consider the lyrics of "I'm So Lonesome I Could Cry," which Williams initially earmarked for Luke the Drifter. Fred Rose thought otherwise, and an American standard was born. Savor this single couplet: "The silence of a falling star / Lights up a purple sky." Songwriters study the artful concision of Williams's best song. "Hank's recorded songs were the archetype rules of poetic songwriting," said Bob Dylan. "Even in words—all the syllables are divided up so they make perfect mathematical sense. You can learn a lot about the structure of songwriting by listening to his records."

Harlan Howard, a songwriter whose copyrights include "Heartaches by the Number" and "I Fall to Pieces," examines the first verse of Williams's "Cold, Cold Heart" with the acumen of a poetry professor. He notes that the eight lines of the first verse are held together with fifteen *r* phonemes, six of them in its first two lines: "I try so hard my dear to say / that you're my every dream." "Nobody notices this," said Howard. "That's the idea, but once those words are put together this way, they won't come apart. One follows the other as day the night." How did Williams, whose reading rarely went beyond comic books, achieve such verbal acuity? Willie Nelson's theory is that Williams wasn't a "songwriter" as much as a "song-singer" who sang his works-in-progress until they sounded just right.

Hank Williams emerged at a time when hillbilly hits were being covered for the pop market. Bing Crosby enjoyed wartime success with a Jimmie Davis song, "You Are My Sunshine," but the floodgates really opened when Jerry Wexler, a reporter at *Billboard*, encouraged Patti Page to record "Tennessee Waltz," which ended up selling nearly five million copies. Wexler subsequently steered Mitch Miller, the A&R director of Columbia Records, to the Hank Williams song "Cold, Cold Heart." "I was sort of a tune pimp," said Wexler, who would soon become a principal at Atlantic Records, one of the major independent record labels of the 1950s.

"When I heard the song," said Miller of "Cold, Cold Heart," "I thought it was made to order for Tony [Bennett]. I thought the last four lines were particularly poetic, and so I played Hank Williams's record for Tony, with the scratchy fiddle and everything, and Tony said, 'Don't make me do cowboy songs!'" After Bennett's rendition of the "cowboy song" hit the top of the pop charts, Miller was granted first dibs on new Acuff-Rose songs once they'd had their run on the country & western chart. Miller (and Hank) soon struck gold when Frankie Laine and Jo Stafford recorded a duet of "Hey, Good Lookin'" and Rosemary Clooney cut "Half as Much."

Miller, a classically trained musician who famously passed on the chance to sign Elvis Presley, had a genuine appreciation for Williams. "He had a way of reaching your guts and your head at the same time," said Miller. "No matter who you were, a country person or a sophisticate, the language hit home. Nobody I know could use basic English so effectively." Tony Bennett never understood the appeal of "Cold, Cold Heart," but Williams got a kick out of seeing his song at the top of the *Billboard* pop charts and carried a copy of the page in case he wanted to show off.

The spoils of success bought matching Cadillacs for Hank and Audrey and the remodeling of their home outside Nashville, but their marriage was full of friction, with endless arguments about his drinking and her spendthrift ways. When Hank indulged in sexual liaisons on the road, Audrey retaliated with affairs of her own. And if the band was hauling Williams back to Nashville at the end of a particularly brutal bender, they knew to bring him, not home, but to a suburban sanatorium. "Oh no, I ain't going there," cried Williams when he awoke to find himself being hustled into a small stone cottage equipped with cot, a toilet, and barred windows. "It's that damn hut!"

Williams found unlikely solace with the Carter Sisters and Mother Maybelle. Anita Carter shed a tear in the wings of the *Opry* the night Hank debuted a song inspired by Audrey, "Cold, Cold Heart." He asked the teenager out on a date and ended up taking the whole family out to dinner. Hank took to calling Maybelle "Mama," and when visiting her and Eck at their home, would crumble freshly baked corn bread into a glass of milk. When both Williams and the Carters were in New York to appear on the *Kate Smith Show*, Hank and Anita duetted on his "I Can't Help It If I'm Still in Love with You." To celebrate Anita's nineteenth birthday he took her to see Peggy Lee at the Copacabana; when Lee sang one of Williams's songs, Hank asked Anita to dance. "I was embarrassed to death," she said. "His knees were coming up even with his ears. He was dancing like a Texas oilman. People just stopped and stared, until Peggy Lee announced who he was."

The hillbilly star also stuck out in Hollywood. Williams was signed to a movie contract with MGM, the studio associated with his record label, but cameras never rolled. Ralph Gleason, who would later help launch *Rolling Stone*, wrote a profile of Williams for the *San Francisco Chronicle* in 1952, and his prose suggested the cultural divide the singer had experienced in Hollywood. During the interview Hank threw back a handful of pills and talked about his first instrument ("When I was about eight years old, I got my first git-tar. A second-hand $3.50 git-tar my mother bought me") and of meeting Tee-Tot ("I was shinin' shoes and sellin' newspapers and followin' this ole Nigrah around to get him to teach me to play the git-tar").

That evening, Gleason saw a show twenty miles outside of Oakland, California. "When you got to San Pablo," he wrote, "it looked like every place else only a little raunchier." Gleason didn't like the band, but Williams sang all the hits. "And he had that *thing*," he noted. "He made them scream when he sang. . . . There were lots of those blondes you see at C&W affairs, the kind of hair that mother never had and nature never grew and the tight skirts that won't quit and the guys looking barbershop neat but still with a touch of dust on them." That was Hank's crowd, not the swells at the Copacabana.

Williams ruled the honky-tonk but was also competing with a new country star, Lefty Frizzell, who was having hits with a softer singing style that put a little pop into his country shuffle. Frizzell's biography reads like a melodramatic country song, with an impoverished Texas boyhood brightened by singing Jimmie Rodgers songs on a $2 guitar. Married at sixteen, Frizzell became a local star in Roswell, New Mexico; he had a daily radio show and played the Cactus Garden until he and three others were arrested for the statutory rape of a fourteen-year-old girl. Frizzell spent six months in prison, and left having written one of his biggest hits, "I Love You a Thousand Ways."

Hard drinking, womanizing, and bad business bedeviled Frizzell's career. Jim Beck, the talent scout who first recorded Frizzell, added his name as the co-writer of his first hit song, "If You've Got the Money (I've Got the Time)." When Frizzell was signed to Columbia Records by Don Law, who'd recorded the influential bluesman Robert Johnson, Beck and Art Satherly had him sign a contract that gave them each one third of the financial pie. Not even a slew of hit records could ameliorate that bad deal. Still, by the end of 1951 he had posted three #1 records ("I Love You a Thousand Ways," "I Want to Be with You Always," and "Always Late with Your Kisses") compared with a pair for Williams ("Cold, Cold Heart" and "Hey, Good Lookin'"). "No one could handle a song like Lefty," said Merle Haggard. "He would hold on to each word until he finally decided to drop it and pick up the next one. Most of us learned to sing listening to him."

Williams and Frizzell toured together in 1951. Their relationship was initially tepid, but Hank later conceded, "It's good to have a little competition. Makes me realize I gotta work harder than ever." In truth, Frizzell's songs were trifles compared to those of Williams, though Hank could never sing in the mellifluous style that made Lefty famous. Their double bill made for honky-tonk heaven, but the place to be would have been the late-night jam sessions where the liquor flowed and the legends traded Jimmie Rodgers songs.

Heavy drinking took a toll on both Williams and Frizzell, whose hits dried up by the mid-1950s. Frizzell scored one more classic, "Saginaw, Michigan" (1964), but at the time of his death in 1975 at the age of forty-seven he was an influential yet largely forgotten figure. Williams took a more direct highway to hell, and when Audrey filed for divorce on January 10, 1952, he went into a dramatic, heart-breaking free fall. Discharged from the *Opry* for missing gigs and general misbehavior, Williams broke up his band and, following major back surgery, moved into an apartment with Ray Price, a young singer from Texas with whom he'd written the song "Weary Blues from Waitin'." Williams hosted endless parties that attracted every freeloader in Nashville. He'd sit amid the hubbub, drink himself into incoherence, and scribble out lyrics on a tablet. Price used the Drifting Cowboys for his own gigs.

The divorce from Audrey was contentious and threatened Hank's pride, cash flow, and relationship with his son Hank Jr., who was born just days before his father made his debut at the *Opry*. In *Hank Williams: The Show He Never Gave*, a film by David Acomba, actor and folk singer Sneezy Waters re-creates a roadhouse performance during which Hank describes his marriage to Audrey as a three-act musical. Act 1 consisted of a couple of giddy love songs, "Hey, Good Lookin'" and "Rooty-Tooty," while Act 2 contained the more cautionary "Half as Much" and "Your Cheating Heart." The story ended with "Alone and Forsaken."

One day, on his way to visit the Carters, Williams thought he saw June and Audrey in a car and tried to run the vehicle off the road. Maybelle rebuffed Williams when he tried to explain, saying, "Don't call me 'Mama.'" A few months later June Carter drove Audrey to the home she retained after the divorce. Hank was waiting in the driveway. As an angry Williams brandished a pistol, June ran interference while Audrey ran into the house. A scuffle ensued, the gun discharged, and June dropped to the ground. Williams jumped into his car and fled. The bullet had missed June by inches, and she spurned his attempt to apologize. “I realized he was crazy,” said June. “We knew he was going to die, and he was going to die soon.”

Hank’s first concert after his back surgery was in Richmond, Virginia. Desperate for a drink, he mixed tomato juice with rubbing alcohol and became violently ill. Price opened the show and had to add songs in order to give his friend time to get sober. “I introduced him,” said Price, “warning the audience that he’s recently undergone some serious surgery, trying to prepare them. So, what does Hank do? He walks straight to the microphone and immediately says, ‘Y’all don’t believe him, do you? Don’t think I’ve had an operation.’ And then he starts to take his clothes off, ready to show the sellout crowd his scar and God-knows what else.” The headline in the next day’s *Richmond Times-Dispatch* was “Hank Williams Hillbilly Show Is Different: Star Makes Impression of Unexpected Kind.” The next night, Williams dedicated “Mind Your Own Business” to the writer of the review.

Recording sessions could be tortured, but Williams still came up with great material. One Friday in June 1952, he recorded both “Settin’ the Woods on Fire,” a tune that anticipated the rhythms of rockabilly, and “Jambalaya (On the Bayou),” a song that proved to be among his most popular and that also became a #2 pop hit for Jo Stafford. (In order to write the lyrics of “Jambalaya,” Williams consulted a page listing Cajun foods spelled out phonetically.) Chet Atkins, who was on the session, recalled the third song of the day. “We recorded ‘I’ll Never Get Out of This World Alive,” said Atkins, “and after each take, he’d sit down in a chair. I remember thinking, ‘Hoss, you’re not just jivin’,’ because he was so weak that all he could do was just sing a few lines, and then just fall in the chair.”

Williams had a charlatan doctor on retainer to supply him with amphetamines, Seconal, chloral hydrate, and morphine. Audrey was gone, but Williams did not lack for women, getting one pregnant and pursuing a young knockout he’d met in Shreveport. The plan was for Hank to marry Billie Jean Jones during a concert at the Municipal Auditorium in New Orleans, but fearful that Audrey would disrupt the ceremony, the lovebirds traveled to the countryside, where a justice of the peace declared them man and wife. Back in New Orleans, the show went on with a wedding “rehearsal” at the matinee and another nuptial at the evening concert. A honeymoon trip to Cuba was scuttled after Hank got too drunk on champagne to make the trip. In the first eight weeks of his marriage to Billie Jean, he was admitted to the North Louisiana Sanitarium three times.

In the end, there was nothing left for Hank Williams but to climb into his blue Cadillac convertible. On December 30, 1952, he loaded his guitar and songbooks into the car. Charles Carr, a college student, was paid $400 to drive Hank from Montgomery to gigs in Charleston, West Virginia, and Canton, Ohio. Williams rode shotgun and sang a couple of tunes, including Red Foley's "Midnight." The travelers stopped for the night in Birmingham and took two hotel rooms. Three women soon materialized, and Hank asked one where she was from. "Heaven," she replied. "Well, in that case," said Williams, "you're the very reason I'm going to hell."

The next morning, Williams bought a bottle of booze and hit the road, stopping for a meal in Chattanooga, where he played Tony Bennett's "Cold, Cold Heart" on the jukebox and left the waitress a $50 tip. Snow began to fall; already running late, he booked air passage to Charleston, but after takeoff the storm forced the plane to return. The New Year's Eve show in Charleston was cancelled and the Cadillac left Knoxville at 10:30 p.m. for Canton, stopping around midnight to gas up in Bristol, Tennessee, where Jimmie Rodgers and the Carter Family had made history. Williams stretched out on the back seat, covered himself with a blanket, and folded his hands over his chest. Hours later, Carr reached into the back seat to rearrange the blanket and touched a cold, cold hand.

Hank Williams put the heartbreak into American roots music and died on a dark highway while "I'll Never Get Out of This World Alive" was high on the charts. Later that day, in Canton, a spotlight shone on a microphone at center stage while, behind the curtain, Don Helms's steel guitar led the band in "I Saw the Light." Then it was on with the show. Lillian secured the now-famous Cadillac, which Hank Jr. later drove when he was in high school. Audrey was in litigation for years over her late husband's estate. The "death car" ultimately became the centerpiece of the Hank Williams Museum in Montgomery, where his funeral was held on the first Sunday of 1953. Three thousand people were in the auditorium and thousands more filed past a silver coffin, where Hank lay in a Nudie suit; his ankles had been broken so that he could be buried in his boots. Helms played the steel guitar while Ernest Tubb, Roy Acuff, and Hank Snow sang their goodbyes. Williams was interred in a hillside plot that later welcomed Audrey. "Your Cheating Heart" was released after his death and spent six weeks at the top of the country charts. And the moon went behind the clouds to hide its face and cry.

3
SUNRISE

On December 4, 1956, Carl Perkins was at Sun Studio at 706 Union Avenue in Memphis searching for a song to follow the hit of a lifetime, "Blue Suede Shoes." To beef up Carl's trio Sam Phillips hired his latest discovery, Jerry Lee Lewis, who had yet to release a record, to play the studio's spinet piano. Nothing clicked until Perkins cast "Matchbox" (a version of Blind Lemon Jefferson's "Match Box Blues") in the new style people were calling rockabilly. Then history walked through the door in the form of Elvis Presley.

Presley was Sun's biggest star until Phillips sold his contract to RCA. Elvis was now the King, with hits such as "Heartbreak Hotel" and "Hound Dog," and *Love Me Tender* already in movie theaters. But Sun was where he'd crossed country & western with rhythm & blues to create rock 'n' roll. Phillips summoned Sun's hottest new act, Johnny Cash, to the studio and alerted the *Memphis Press-Scimitar* to the gathering of what would become known as the Million Dollar Quartet. Jack "Cowboy" Clement didn't have to be told to roll tape. Elvis was soon at the piano surrounded by Cash and Jerry Lee with Carl hunched over an acoustic guitar. Elvis's latest flame sat atop the piano. The southern singers jammed on gospel tunes, country songs, and Chuck Berry's "Brown-Eyed Handsome Man."

ELVIS PRESLEY

"It was like everything I had worked to achieve in that one little room," said Sam Phillips of the gathering of four men who'd helped create rock 'n' roll. "It was a time when black and white were fusing musically," said Carl Perkins, speaking of his own musical education. "There was a little circle in West Tennessee, where we combined the blues influence coming up from Mississippi, and the bluegrass from out of Kentucky, but I don't think none of us ever quite knew what it was. It didn't have a name; we called it feel-good music"—which is to say, not exactly blues or country but the roots of rock 'n' roll.

Sam Phillips grew up poor on a farm in Florence, Alabama, and worked in radio before (and after) going into the record business. In the early 1950s his Memphis Recording Services recorded early sides by such influential blues artists as B. B. King and Howlin' Wolf, as well as one of the very first rock 'n' roll records, "Rocket 88," by Jackie Brenston and His Delta Cats. This was an ensemble from Clarksdale, Mississippi, led by its piano player, Ike Turner (the group was actually known as Ike Turner's Kings of Rhythm). A significant wrinkle in the recording of "Rocket 88," a jump blues written about an Oldsmobile, was that guitarist Willie Kizart played through a damaged amplifier whose speaker cone was held in place by wads of newspaper. The result was the kind of fuzzy tone that electric guitarists would later obtain using distortion pedals. The musicians were surprised when Phillips didn't object to the oddball sound, but capturing something unique, even if it was by accident, was a key to his aesthetic.

Because Phillips had yet to launch his own record label, Chess Records released "Rocket 88," and it became one of 1951's biggest rhythm & blues hits. Ike Turner also played piano when Phillips recorded B. B. King's breakthrough hit, "Three O'Clock Blues." King promoted his music career by working as a singing deejay on Memphis's WDIA, the first radio station in the nation programmed for an African American audience. The call-and-response pattern between King's voice and his lead guitar on "Three O'Clock Blues," a technique pioneered by T-Bone Walker (best known for writing and recording "Stormy Monday Blues"), came to define the sound of urban blues and, later, the blues-rock of British guitarists like Eric Clapton and Peter Green.

But Phillips was even more enamored with another blues singer who'd moved from the Mississippi Delta to Memphis. "When I heard Howlin' Wolf," noted Phillips, "I said, 'This is for me. This is where the soul of man never dies.'" It didn't take long for Phillips to get Wolf in the studio. "He would sit there with these feet planted wide apart," said Phillips, "playing nothing but the French harp, and I tell you, the greatest thing you could see to this day would be Chester Burnett doing one of those sessions in my studio." No one who's heard "Moanin' at Midnight" or "How Many More Years," both recorded at Sun, would question the word of Sam Phillips.

Elvis Presley was the first member of the Million Dollar Quartet to reach Memphis. He was born in Tupelo, Mississippi, to Gladys and Vernon Presley; his identical twin brother, Jesse Garon Presley, was stillborn. Vernon, who worked odd jobs, once spent eight months in prison for altering a check issued by his landlord and sometime employer. "We were broke, man, broke, and we left Tupelo overnight," said Presley. "We just headed for Memphis. Things had to be better." The thirteen-year-old carried the $12.95 guitar he'd received when his parents couldn't afford to buy him a bicycle.

The Presleys moved into Lauderdale Courts, a public housing complex, and Elvis picked up guitar tips from a neighbor, Jesse Lee Denson. He studied his hillbilly favorites (Roy Acuff, Ernest Tubb, and Jimmie Rodgers), soaked up race records on WDIA, and went to hear both black and white gospel quartets. "I also dug the real low-down Mississippi singers," said Presley, "mostly Big Bill Broonzy and Big Boy Crudup, although they would scold me at home for listening to them. 'Sinful music,' the townsfolk in Memphis said it was. Which never bothered me, I guess."

The enigma of Elvis Presley is how a shy kid mocked by his classmates for being a mama's boy became such a musical provocateur. There were visual clues in the sideburns he grew as a teenager, the way he styled his hair with Vaseline and rose oil, and the flashy clothes he bought at Lansky Bros., a Beale Street store that catered to the black community. He first showed up at Sun Studio in August 1953 to make a recording as a gift for his mother, but this was a young man who clearly wanted to be noticed and who likely knew all about Sam Phillips.

Presley certainly made an impression on Marion Keisker, who ran a second tape while Presley recorded "My Happiness" and "That's When Your Heartaches Begin." "The reason I taped Elvis was this," said Keisker: "Over and over I remember Sam saying, 'If I could find a white man who had the Negro sound and the Negro feel, I could make a billion dollars.' This is what I heard in Elvis, this . . . what I guess they now call 'soul,' this Negro sound. So I taped it. I wanted Sam to know."

Phillips took the bait and recruited guitarist Scotty Moore to rehearse with the young singer. They tried a variety of country and pop tunes along with string bassist Bill Black, and Moore reported to Phillips that he wasn't particularly impressed. Phillips nonetheless brought them into the studio, where the session foundered until, according to Moore, "Elvis picked up his guitar and started banging on it and singing 'That's All Right, Mama,' jumpin' around the studio, just acting the fool." Phillips liked what he heard and worked the trio until they had a master take of a blues song written by Arthur "Big Boy" Crudup.

Attempts to record the flip side went nowhere until, once again, serendipity saved the day. "Bill jumped up," said Moore, "started clowning with his bass and singing 'Blue Moon of Kentucky' in falsetto, mimicking Bill Monroe [the bluegrass pioneer who'd written the song]. And Elvis started banging on his guitar. And the rhythm thing jelled again." In both cases, the musicians succeeded by acting the fool, which is to say that in order to cut records that drew on both the black and white music of the South, Elvis, Scotty, and Bill had to get out of their own skins.

"'That's All Right' is in the R&B idiom of negro field jazz, 'Blue Moon of Kentucky' more in the country field," wrote Bob Johnson in the *Memphis Press-Scimitar*, "but there is a curious blending of the two different musics in both." The record became a regional hit, and subsequent singles from Sun struck a similar balance by pairing R&B numbers with pop or country tunes; Presley's next release was "Good Rockin' Tonight," a 1947 hit for Roy Brown, and "I Don't Care If the Sun Don' Shine," a pop hit for Patti Page that had also been recorded by one of Presley's favorite singers, Dean Martin. Live gigs ensued, and Moore said that Presley would get so nervous that his legs would shake. When his gyrations prompted girls to scream, he realized that he was onto something good.

Presley's life changed overnight, with recording sessions at Sun sandwiched between live appearances. In 1955 he was on a package tour that included the Louvin Brothers, Mother Maybelle and the Carter Sisters, and headliner Hank Snow, whose Machiavellian manager, Colonel Tom Parker, was already moving in on the new star. He called Maybelle "Mama," and she would replace the buttons that popped off during his performances. "We worked many a show with safety pins in our skirts," said Helen, explaining that her mom would repurpose buttons from her daughters' clothing to help Elvis avoid a wardrobe malfunction.

Presley had a crush on Anita Carter, who was married, and once feigned a heart attack to get her attention. "The thing is," he said, "I don't know anybody else like you and your sisters. Would you look for someone for me that's like you all?" Anita replied that she couldn't be the one to find his true love. "Well," said Elvis, "I guess I'm going to have to find one on my own and raise her to suit myself."

Elvis Presley's Sun singles galvanized musicians throughout the South. "He was the first boy I heard on record playing the songs the way I always done," said Carl Perkins, who was born to poor sharecroppers near predominantly black Tiptonville, Tennessee. Perkins picked cotton after school and on long, hot summer days. A weekly pleasure was listening to the *Grand Ole Opry*. After he struggled with a homemade cigar-box instrument his father bought him a battered Gene Autry guitar, and John Westbrook, a black field worker whom he called Uncle John, taught him to play the blues. "Get down close to it," said Westbrook. "You can feel it travel down the strings, come through your head and down to your soul where you live. You can feel it. Let it vib-a-rate."

In addition to country heroes like Jimmie Rodgers and the Carter Family, Perkins was drawn to the blues of Big Bill Broonzy and T-Bone Walker and to the bluegrass of Bill Monroe. By the age of fourteen Perkins was playing local gigs at the Cotton Boll and the Sand Ditch with his brother Jay (younger brother Clay soon joined them on bass). When he heard Presley's recording of "Blue Moon of Kentucky," a song already in the trio's repertoire, Perkins went to Memphis to get an audition with Sam Phillips, who reluctantly agreed. "We were set up and picking before he could get back to the control room," said Perkins; liking what he heard, Phillips told him to come back with some new songs.

Perkins found regional success with a country ballad, "Turn Around," that sounded a lot like a Hank Williams song. He also went on tour with Presley, who took him to Lansky's to jazz up his wardrobe. "When I'd jump around they'd scream some," said Perkins, "but they were gettin' ready for him. It was like TNT, man, it just exploded. All of a sudden the world was wrapped up in rock." While on tour with Sun's newest act, Johnny Cash, Perkins was inspired to write his greatest hit. Cash told him about a fastidious man in the army who'd get ornery if anybody stepped on his shoes; Perkins saw kids in the audience doing the same fool thing. He wrote the lyrics of "Blue Suede Shoes" on a brown paper bag, added a nursery-rhyme introduction—"Well, it's one for the money!"—and cut the record in three takes. "Blue Suede Shoes,"

CARL PERKINS

along with Presley's early sides, essentially defined rockabilly, which writer Nick Tosches called "hillbilly rock-and-roll. It was not a usurpation of black music by whites because its soul, its pneuma, was white, full of redneck ethos."

"Blue Suede Shoes" was the first Sun record to sell a million copies; it hit the top of the country charts, #2 on the pop charts, and #3 on the rhythm & blues charts. "When the song was popular," said Perkins, who took to wearing its signature footwear, "somebody would always come up with a camera and want a picture of them stepping on the shoe." The song's success caused the Perkins family to lose its $32-a-month public housing apartment.

The Perkins Brothers Band was booked to appear on the *Perry Como Show*. That was high cotton for a kid who had actually picked cotton. After a March 21, 1956, show in Norfolk, Virginia, the brothers piled into their new Lincoln for the overnight drive to New York. Before sunrise, near Dover, Delaware, the car crashed into the back of a pickup, killing the truck driver and flipping the Lincoln into a watery ditch. Perkins suffered a severe concussion, three broken vertebrae in his neck, and a broken collarbone. His brother Jay fractured his neck and sustained extensive internal injuries, dying two years later. Perkins ultimately did the *Perry Como Show*, but it was too late; his moment had passed. Elvis had by then enjoyed his own 1956 hit with "Blue Suede Shoes" and sang it on television no fewer than one, two, three times.

The fourth of seven children, J. R. Cash was three when his family moved to Dyess, Arkansas, as participants in a New Deal program that let poor families earn ownership of a twenty-acre plot by working the land. Cash was picking cotton by the age of five, and the family sang together in the field and at church and would always tune in to the *Grand Ole Opry*. His mother taught him the rudiments of guitar and sent him to a voice teacher who was stunned when the indifferent student sang a song of his own choosing, Hank Williams's "Lovesick Blues." The instructor told him to not let anyone mess with the way he sang. In 1944 his older brother Jack died when a saw-blade accident all but split him in half. Cash was haunted by Jack's death for the rest of his life.

John Cash (he was required to change his legal name from "J. R.") enlisted in the Air Force in 1950 and served as a radio operator in Germany, where he played guitar in a combo that performed songs by the usual suspects (Rodgers, the Carters, and Hank Snow). Back in the United States, he married Vivian Liberto, the girlfriend he'd left behind (after dating for three weeks). The

JOHNNY CASH

newlyweds moved to Memphis, where Cash sold appliances door-to-door and liked to end his day by paying a visit to Gus Cannon, who once led Cannon's Jug Stompers, a Memphis combo popular in the late 1920s and 1930s. Cash would sing along with Cannon, whose "Walk Right In" would become a #1 hit for the Rooftop Singers in 1963.

Cash also played music with guitarist Luther Perkins and bassist Marshall Grant. He pitched himself to Sam Phillips as a gospel singer but piqued his interest with an original song he'd written in Germany, "Hey Porter." Phillips encouraged Cash's combo (plus drummer J. M. Van Eaton) to pump up the tempo. (Phillips also suggested that Cash call himself "Johnny.") This was the same advice he gave to Cash when the singer wanted to record "Folsom Prison Blues" as a recitation instead of the up-beat cry against confinement that became one of Cash's greatest hits. In order to amplify the percussive sound of his strum, Cash looped a piece of paper through the strings of his guitar. The song, with its famously nihilistic lyric ("I shot a man in Reno just to watch him die") hit the top of the country charts, and its boom-chicka-boom rhythm became Cash's signature sound. (Gordon Jenkins, a songwriter and arranger, successfully sued Cash over the song's similarity to his own "Crescent City Blues"; curiously, Jenkins didn't act until the song became a hit for the second time on Cash's 1968 album *Live at Folsom Prison*.)

Johnny Cash and the Tennessee Two toured hard and were quick to learn of the rigors and rewards of the road. Women were easy to meet, and amphetamines would keep a musician awake until another pill put him to sleep. Cash and Perkins talked about how to handle these temptations. "I walk the line," said Cash; Perkins said that that was a good title for a song. When Cash cast the lyric as a spiritual ballad, Phillips once more encouraged him to pick up the pulse. The song was a hit, but all the same, Cash cheated on his wife and was soon addicted to bennies.

Sun Records wasn't the only place where rock 'n' roll was born. In Chicago, Chess Records, the label that released the Howlin' Wolf tracks cut by Sam Phillips, spiced up its roster of blues artists with two seminal rockers, Chuck Berry and Bo Diddley. Berry, who grew up in St. Louis listening to blues and country music, pitched himself to Leonard Chess at the suggestion of Muddy Waters. Chess liked a country-tinged tune called "Ida Red," which Berry had adapted from a 1938 song by Bob Wills and the Texas Playboys,

CHUCK BERRY

but wanted a snappier title. The song became "Maybellene" and was cut at Berry's first recording session in May 1955 along with "Wee Wee Hours," "Thirty Days," and "You Can't Catch Me." During those few hours, Berry, like Elvis at Sun, found rock 'n' roll on the corner of country and R&B. A critical difference is that Berry was also a gifted songwriter who would quickly create one of the greatest catalogs in all of rock 'n' roll. Bo Diddley, whose given name was Ellas McDaniel, also wrote enduring hits including "I'm a Man," "Mona," and "Who Do You Love?" McDaniel's secret ingredient was the "Bo Diddley beat," his take on the clave rhythm common to African (and Caribbean) music.

Buddy Holly (born Charles Hardin Holley) grew up in west Texas playing country music but was quick to follow Elvis into rock 'n' roll. Opening for Presley shows in Lubbock won Holly a recording contract with Decca; in January 1956 he went into a Nashville studio with Owen Bradley, who dismissed Holly's band in favor of studio pros. When two singles went nowhere, Decca dropped his contact. Holly's next stop was Clovis, New Mexico, where producer Norman Petty had recorded "Party Doll," a rock 'n' roll hit for fellow Texan Buddy Knox. Holly and his band cut a demo of "That'll Be the Day" (a tune from the Nashville sessions) with Holly accentuating the punchy rhythm with his electric guitar. Brunswick Records liked the demo so much that it was released as a single, and in the fall of 1957 it hit #1 in both the United States and the United Kingdom. Holly's next release, "Peggy Sue," reached #3 on the pop charts and was a #2 R&B hit (the flip side was a soft-pop evergreen, "Everyday"). Over the course of the next year Holly recorded a heap of hits including "Oh, Boy!," "It's So Easy," "Not Fade Away," and "Maybe Baby."

Buddy Holly and the Crickets codified the classic rock band format of lead and rhythm guitars, bass, and drums, and his influence was profound. British singer and guitarist Richard Thompson cites the "singability" of his songs. "I can remember every word of every Buddy Holly song, perhaps more than any other writer," said Thompson. "Just making all that flow and the words blending into each, it's just beautiful." Bob Dylan spoke of Holly when he won the 2016 Nobel Prize in Literature. "Buddy played the music that I loved," said Dylan in his Nobel Lecture, "the music I grew up on: country western, rock 'n' roll, and rhythm and blues. Three separate strands of music that he intertwined and infused into one genre. One brand. And Buddy wrote songs—songs that had beautiful melodies and imaginative verses. And he sang great—sang in more than a few voices. He was the archetype."

In the late 1950s, two archetypes climbed aboard a tour bus to headline a rock 'n' roll package tour. Chuck Berry and Buddy Holly, both writing hit songs at a feverish pace, were feeling lucky, and they walked to the back of the bus to shoot craps.

The country establishment in Nashville hated rock 'n' roll. Like many American parents, it considered the music to be both crude and juvenile. But what really hurt was that rock had left country music in the dust, commercially speaking, with Nashville particularly galled that hits by Elvis Presley and Carl Perkins were simultaneously topping the country, pop, and R&B charts. "It has already been suggested that country artists with r&b-styled material, or r&b-styled delivery, be excluded from the best-selling country charts," wrote Paul Ackerman in *Billboard*. "They will be dropped when the kid with the 89 cents feels it time for a change."

The antipathy toward rock 'n' roll was due, at least in part, to the music's clear link to the blues and R&B created by black America. What's more, the sexy panache of the young rockers made country artists seem a little old hat. "Most of the record-buying public regarded us as hillbillies," said George Jones, whose career got rolling in 1956. "Even in Nashville there were folks who looked down on those of us on Sixteenth Avenue South, where we recorded three-chord songs that were played on tiny AM stations scattered mostly in the rural South."

Not every country artist suffered at the hands of rock 'n' roll. Ray Price, who'd shared a Nashville apartment with Hank Williams, topped the charts for twenty weeks in 1956 with "Crazy Arms." Price had had a musical epiphany while recording the tune that knocked Presley's "Heartbreak Hotel" off the top of the country charts. "We were having trouble getting a good, clean bass sound," said Price. "So instead of going with the standard 2/4 beat, I said, 'Let's try a 4/4 bass and a shuffle rhythm, and it cut. It cut straight through." The rhythm, which became known as the "Ray Price Shuffle," favored a walking bass line and western-swing fiddles reminiscent of Bob Wills. Roger Miller played drums with Price's band, the Cherokee Cowboys, and wrote their 1958 hit "Invitation to the Blues." In the 1960s Miller found great success with witty, original songs such as "Dang Me" and "King of the Road." Willie Nelson became a Cherokee Cowboy after Price recorded one of his early evergreens, "Night Life." "I took Willie out on the road as my bass player," said Price, "and after a few gigs, he said, 'I bet you didn't know I'd never played the bass before.' I said, 'I knew the first night.'"

Price had another hit in 1956, "You Done Me Wrong," which he wrote with another Texan, George Jones. Jones got his Gene Autry guitar when he was nine, played honky-tonks as a teenager, and met Hank Williams at a Beaumont radio station. Jones recorded his first single, "No Money in This Deal," for Starday, the small label that had hit pay dirt with Lefty Frizzell. "I wanted to sound like Hank Williams, but I phrased like Lefty," said Jones. "I made five syllables out of one." Jones found his own voice on "Why, Baby, Why," which won him a spot on the *Grand Ole Opry*. "A country singer making it to the Opry in 1956," said Jones, "was like an athlete making it to the Olympics."

Still, Jones wasn't making enough money to carry his own band, so he traveled from town to town to quickly rehearse (if he was lucky) with a group of local musicians. Along the way, his vocals evolved into artistry. "It makes you sad," said Jones, "because you're singin' all these sad words, about how a man can do a woman and a woman can do a man, until you're just like the people in the song, and you're living it and their problems become your problems, until you're lost in the songs and it just takes everything out of you." That's one reason why Jones typically took a bottle into the recording studio.

Elsewhere on the country charts, the Louvin Brothers continued a tradition of singing siblings that went back to the Blue Sky Boys and the Delmore Brothers. The Louvins grew up on a tiny cotton farm in southern Appalachia, singing songs their mother taught them from the *Sacred Harp* hymnal and avoiding their violent father. They sang gospel before recording their first secular song ("The Getting Acquainted Waltz") with Chet Atkins. The brothers would soon record songs that continue to be performed by Americana artists including "If I Could Only Win Your Love," "When I Start Dreaming," and "You're Running Wild."

Ira, a head taller than Charlie, played mandolin alongside his brother's guitar; they harmonized with familial ease. "We knew when to switch when something came along that was too high for me," said Charlie. "In one line of a song we'd sometimes change parts twice." Though their vocals were harmonious, Ira's heavy drinking caused friction. Headlining a 1955 tour with Elvis Presley, who was already a hard act to follow, a cantankerous Ira called the rocker's music low-rent garbage. The Louvins faded when a pair of their fans, the Everly Brothers, produced close-harmony songs that spoke to teenage concerns.

Ike Everly was a coal miner from Kentucky who learned finger-style guitar from Kennedy Jones, who'd picked up the technique from Arnold Schultz, the same black guitarist who had tutored Bill Monroe; Jones had also influenced the playing of Merle Travis. Ike and his wife Margaret moved with their two sons, Phil and Don, to Shenandoah, Iowa, where the parents hosted a radio show that soon featured "Little Donnie and Baby Boy Phil." In 1955 the family moved to Nashville, where Chet Atkins helped Phil and Don get a deal with Columbia Records, which dropped them after one flop single. Atkins then steered them to Wesley Rose of Acuff-Rose Publishing, the firm where Rose's recently deceased father Fred had famously mentored Hank Williams.

Rose signed the siblings to a publishing deal, got them a contract with Cadence Records, and crucially, introduced them to a pair of songwriters, Felice and Boudleaux Bryant, who played them "Bye Bye Love," a song that had already been rejected by thirty artists. The Everly Brothers cut the tune (Atkins played guitar) and then went on a tent-show tour of Louisiana and Mississippi with Bill Monroe. "Driving back to Nashville," said Phil, "when we got within radio distance, they had this pop station on in the car—and it was playing our record. That was, like, big juju." "Bye Bye Love" topped the country charts, hit #5 on the R&B list, and reached #2 on the pop chart. The duo followed up with other multiformat hits by the Bryants, including "Wake Up Little Susie," "All I Have to Do Is Dream," and "Love Hurts." The country duo, suddenly pop stars, were featured on a seventy-eight-city package tour alongside Chuck Berry, the Drifters, and Buddy Holly and the Crickets.

Colonel Tom Parker courted both Elvis and Sam Phillips, who recognized that Elvis needed a major label to make him a truly national star. Name your price, said Parker; Phillips came up with a number that he thought would never be met, $35,000. But RCA paid $40,000, the extra $5,000 going to cover royalties owed to Elvis by Sun. Within weeks, Presley was in RCA's Nashville studio cutting "Heartbreak Hotel" with Chet Atkins in the band. Phillips used his newfound cash to promote the Carl Perkins smash "Blue Suede Shoes."

Meanwhile, in Ferriday, Louisiana, a boogie-woogie pianist named Jerry Lee Lewis figured it was high time he auditioned for the man who'd discovered Elvis. His father Elmo was a farmer who also produced 100-proof whiskey in a fifty-gallon still, a lucrative sideline that had twice landed him in jail. During his second incarceration, when Jerry Lee was three years old, a drunk driver ran over his older brother, Elmo Jr.; prison guards accompanied the father to his son's graveside funeral, where, with his hand in cuffs, he threw a flower onto the child's coffin.

Elmo Lewis, an amateur musician, recognized that young Jerry Lee showed promise, and he took out a mortgage on the farm to buy a $250 Starck piano. Lewis would pound the keys alongside his cousins Mickey Gilley and Jimmy Swaggart and was soon playing music with his family at the Assembly of God, where parishioners sometimes fell to the floor and spoke in tongues. Jerry Lee called Jimmie Rodgers "a natural born blues singer" and Roy Acuff "the worst singer [he] ever heard." He was drawn to the Big House, a black honky-tonk run by Will Haney that booked such traveling musicians as Charles Brown, Fats Domino, and Ray Charles. Jerry Lee lurked near the door, and when he had the chance, would sneak inside to hide under a table. "It's where I got my juice," he said.

Jerry Lee married Dorothy Barton, the daughter of a traveling evangelist, when he was sixteen and knew in an instant that he'd made a mistake. He escaped to Southwestern Bible Institute in Waxahachie, Texas, and found late night fun in Dallas. But what got him kicked out of school was his boogie-woogie take on "My God Is Real" at a student talent show. Back in the honky-tonks, Jerry Lee met Paul Whitehead, a fifty-year-old blind pianist who also played trumpet and accordion. "Mr. Paul knew every song in the world," said Lewis. "And we played 'em all." One night, he heard Whitehead perform the song that would change his life, "Whole Lot of Shakin' Going On." That was when Lewis asked Elmo to accompany him to Memphis to meet Sam Phillips. To finance the trip, Elmo cleaned out the henhouse and sold four hundred eggs.

At Sun Studio, Jerry Lee bragged that he could play piano the way Chet Atkins played guitar. "We sat down at the little spinet piano," said Jack Clement, who was minding the store while Phillips was out of town, "and sure enough, he played somethin' that sounded like Chet Atkins. 'So what else do you do?' I said. 'Well, I sing.' So I got him to sing, but it was all country stuff. . . . So I told him if he could come up with some rock 'n' roll we could probably do somethin'." Lewis's cousin, J. W. Brown, angling to play bass in Jerry Lee's band, put him up in the home he shared with his wife and two children, including his thirteen-year-old daughter Myra. "I did notice," said Jerry Lee, "that she wasn't no kid." Phillips called Lewis into the studio as soon as he heard his audition take on Ray Price's "Crazy Arms."

JERRY LEE LEWIS

The song, recut after thumbtacks were stuck into the hammers of the piano to juice up the sound, was Lewis's first chart record but not a big hit. His next session focused on a Clement shuffle called "It'll Be Me." "I felt like we ought to get off of it," said Clement, "and one of 'em piped up and said, 'Hey, Jerry, why don't you do that thing you did the other night?' So all I did was walk back into the control room and turn on the machine. We didn't run it down or nothin'." Jerry Lee closed his eyes, imagined himself back at the Big House, and knocked out "Whole Lot of Shakin' Going On" in a single take, pausing in the middle of the tune to "wiggle it around just a little bit."

Lewis's aggressive boogie-woogie piano was far more explosive than the affable piano rock of Fats Domino. A more pertinent comparison was to Little Richard (Richard Wayne Penniman), who went nowhere as a rhythm & blues singer until 1955, when Specialty Records sent him to New Orleans, where the studio players took a swing at the dirty ditty that Richard sang between takes of the planned material. With a "wop bob a loo bob a lop bam boom," Richard ripped into "Tutti Frutti," the most riotously risqué rock 'n' roll song until the release of "Whole Lot of Shakin' Going On."

Johnny Cash, Carl Perkins, and Jerry Lee Lewis went on a month-long tour of Canada in a fleet of cars loaded with musicians and equipment. Cash topped the bill. Lewis, known only (if at all) for his version of "Crazy Arms," felt like a failure. "He came off one night in Calgary moaning, 'This business ain't for me, people don't like me,'" said Perkins. "John and I told him, 'Turn around so they can see you, make a fuss.' So the next night he carried on, stood up, kicked the stool back and a new Jerry Lee Lewis was born.... Four nights later, he was top of the bill." By tour's end, "Whole Lot of Shakin' Going On" was selling like happy hour drinks; then radio stations began pulling the record for being too sexually suggestive.

Judd Phillips, Sam's brother, took Jerry Lee to New York to audition for *The Steve Allen Show*, a tough sell given that the now-controversial record had yet to break nationally. Allen tapped the top of the upright piano with a pencil as Jerry Lee played his song, and he won the gig when he hammed it up during the "shake it for me one time" lyric. Comedian Milton Berle was backstage during rehearsal. After seeing how Lewis kicked away his piano stool, Uncle Miltie suggested that Allen throw it back onto the stage. That's exactly what happened on July 28, 1957, an appearance that sent "Whole Lot of Shakin' Going On" to the top of the country charts and into the top five of the pop and R&B charts.

Six million copies later, Jerry Lee was Sun's biggest star; Cash and Perkins felt lost in the shuffle. Perkins's records sold only modestly after "Blue Suede Shoes," and though Cash continued to thrive, he was frustrated that Phillips wouldn't let him record a gospel album. Both Cash and Perkins eventually signed with Columbia Records, but only after Phillips stockpiled enough material by Cash to keep releasing records into the 1960s.

After seeing Lewis on *The Steve Allen Show,* Otis Blackwell, a black New York singer-songwriter and himself a pianist, sent him "Great Balls of Fire." Blackwell had struck gold when Presley had had hits with two of his songs, "Don't Be Cruel" and "All Shook Up" (he also wrote the jazz-blues standard "Fever"). Blackwell, who never met Presley, had agreed to Colonel Parker's condition that the songwriter relinquish half of both his publishing and writer's royalties. The Colonel applied the same unorthodox 50–50 split to his own management contract with Elvis.

"Great Balls of Fire," with lyrics that would again make Bible-thumpers call rock 'n' roll the Devil's playground, was huge in the United States (#1 on the country chart, #2 for pop, and #3 for R&B) and also a hit in the United Kingdom. The money came in sacks, and like Jimmie Rodgers and Hank Williams, Jerry Lee spent it like the day after tomorrow. Lewis bought his parents a house and matching Cadillacs and drove Myra to high school in his own fancy car. "One night," said Lewis, "we parked out in front of the house. . . . After we got through, she started crying, 'Now I've done this,' and it wasn't the first time, 'you'll never marry me, will you?' I said, 'Sure.' And I lived up to my bargain." Neglecting to divorce his second wife, Jerry Lee wed Myra, whose parents were enraged on discovering that their thirteen-year-old was now married. Her father, J. W. Brown, whipped his daughter, and continued to play bass with his new son-in-law.

Jerry Lee's concerts were now played before big crowds, and he starred in package tours with Chuck Berry, Fats Domino, and Buddy Holly. (Holly asked Lewis for romantic advice when he was thinking of marrying his Manhattan girlfriend, Maria Elena Santiago.) Before a concert at the Brooklyn Paramount promoted by Allen Freed, Berry and Lewis argued about who should close the show. Freed chose Berry. Lewis capped his typically riotous set with "Great Balls of Fire," except this time he reached into his jacket for a Coke bottle filled with gasoline. Wild-eyed, shaking his curly locks, Lewis baptized his instrument, tossed a match into its belly, and pounded the ivories as flames engulfed the piano. Walking off the stage, Lewis looked at Berry and said with more mirth than malice, "Follow that, nigger."

Sam Phillips encouraged his new star to leave Myra at home when he toured the United Kingdom but Jerry Lee would have none of it, and he took his extended family to witness his emergence as a truly international star. The entourage was met at London's Heathrow Airport, where Myra identified herself to a reporter as Jerry Lee's wife. Lewis, thinking fast, said that she was fifteen. Soon enough, reporters learned that it was the rocker's third marriage; a dispatch from Memphis also revealed the wed-while-already-married angle. The salacious story hit the British tabloids like a match to a petrol-soaked piano. A thirteen-year-old child bride! Bigamy! Great balls of sinful fire! When the tour opened to a half-empty hall in North London, boos were mixed with salacious catcalls. The tour, cancelled after two dates, buckled under the weight of rock 'n' roll's first great scandal. The stink followed Lewis back to the United States. Records were returned, and airplay dried up. When he left for England, Jerry Lee was taking in $10,000 per night. Now, he was lucky to get $250.

The Million Dollar Quartet grew up poor, loved Hank Williams, lost brothers, and made music that mixed black and white. They went to church, found their unique voices, and arrived at Sun Studio full of big dreams. Against all odds, they all hit it big and became men of the world, which turned out to invite a ton of trouble. Perkins drank too much, Cash gobbled down pills, Lewis was scorched by scandal, and Elvis lived alone in a crowd of sycophants.

Lewis didn't even know that he had broken any rules. His mother was fifteen when she married his father, and country kin can be thick as thieves. Roy Orbison, who had a rockabilly hit called "Ooby Dooby" during his brief stay at Sun, stayed at Sam's house with his fifteen-year-old girlfriend. Elvis was asked about Jerry Lee before he left for army duty in Germany. "He's a great artist," said Presley. "I'd rather not talk about his marriage, except that if he really loves her, I guess it's all right." In Europe, Elvis fell in love with fourteen-year-old Priscilla Beaulieu, the daughter of a U.S. Air Force officer. The unorthodox courtship—Beaulieu followed Elvis back to Memphis and attended Immaculate Conception High School—avoided tabloid scrutiny. They married in Las Vegas when Priscilla turned twenty-one. "He hid her in his house," said Lewis, "and then he acted like he wasn't doin' nothin'. . . . When I got married to my thirteen-year-old cousin, I blew it out and told the whole world."

Parents and preachers already hated how black music had morphed into rock 'n' roll, but Jerry Lee's downfall suggested that the art of hillbillies could be equally sinful. Johnny Cash came off a little differently; he was married with three young daughters. But he also had a roving eye. Cash met June Carter in 1956 at the *Grand Ole Opry*. "Hello," said the married man to the married woman, "I'm Johnny Cash, and I'm going to marry you someday." In the meantime, another woman had caught his eye. "From the time I met Johnny Cash," said Billie Jean Horton, "I wanted him, but I was married to a man that I loved and I had three kids and Johnny had three."

Billie Jean had married Hank Williams in a concert arena in New Orleans and after his death wed country singer Johnny Horton, who'd hit it big with "North to Alaska." Horton appeared at the Skyline Club in Austin (where Hank had played his last gig). Driving home to Shreveport on November 5, 1960, Horton died when his car collided with a truck. Cash arrived to offer solace, and before long, he and Billie Jean became lovers. "There was a little bit of drugs before, I think," said Billie Jean, "but when Johnny Horton died, that put him over the top. I lived with Hank Williams, the king of the dope, and I was afraid Johnny was going to destroy himself if he didn't get off those pills." Cash, still married, asked for her hand; she hesitated, and then said no.

If the Bristol sessions were the big bang of country music, the arrival of rock 'n' roll was the Manhattan Project of Americana. The fact that Elvis Presley, Chuck Berry, Jerry Lee Lewis, Buddy Holly, the Everly Brothers, and Carl Perkins took the same songs to the top of all three charts—country, pop, and R&B—was nothing less than revolutionary. Never again would the genres' borders be quite so porous. That mélange of styles is the essence of Americana music, except unlike today, it was universally popular. In later years country artists would occasionally cross over to the pop charts, and vice versa, but such songs were always exceptions. But at this moment of creation, the genres were fluid, an abstract painting of black and white, country and blues. Popular music would never be the same.

Then the first generation of rockers hit the wall. Elvis went into the army and came home to great celebrity but would never again seem so wild. Jerry Lee was washed up, a lion in exile. Chuck Berry went to prison (after two trials) for transporting a fourteen-year-old girl over state lines for "immoral purposes." Little Richard released raucous rockers like "Slippin' and Slidin'" and "Lucille" but then gave up rock 'n' roll to preach the Gospel. Buddy Holly wanted to avoid a long winter ride in a tour bus with a broken heater, so he chartered a plane to take him from Clear Lake, Iowa, to his next show in Minnesota. The flight ended in a cornfield crash. The next morning, when the wreckage was discovered in seven inches of snow, the pilot and his passengers were long dead. Holly's horn-rimmed eyeglasses weren't found until the spring thaw. In his 1972 hit song "American Pie" Don McLean said this was "the day the music died," but that's not true. It only changed.

Peter Guralnick would write a two-volume biography of Elvis Presley in the 1990s (*Last Train to Memphis* and *Careless Love*), but twenty years earlier, he speculated that "if Elvis Presley had simply disappeared after leaving the little Sun studio for the last time, his status would be something like that of a latter-day Robert Johnson: lost, vulnerable, eternally youthful, forever on the edge, pure and timeless." But Elvis didn't disappear; Colonel Parker made sure of that. Still, the blunt-force impact of mid-fifties rock 'n' roll was history; now the music scene was dominated by teen idols and the folk revival. Sam Phillips drank with his friend Audrey Williams at the house she'd bought with Hank and put his money into radio stations and a new hotel chain, the Holiday Inn. His musical moment had passed. "Everything was all happening one day," said Jack Clement, "and then it's not."

4
BLOWIN' IN THE WIND

Bobby Zimmerman pushed against the stage at the Duluth National Guard Armory. Buddy Holly, twenty-two, was playing a Fender Stratocaster, and he and the Crickets were dressed in black jackets, gray slacks, and ascots. Zimmerman, a senior in high school, said that it was as if "there was a halo around Buddy's head." Truth be told, these were not the real Crickets because Holly's band and producer Norman Petty had argued over songs, money, and Buddy's move to New York to live with his wife, Maria Elena Santiago, whom he had met during a visit to the Manhattan office of Peer-South Publishing (yes, that Ralph Peer). Holly's new bass player was Waylon Jennings, a Texas deejay and musician. Before joining the "Winter Dance Party," Jennings visited Holly at his Greenwich Village apartment just north of where the folkie musicians hung out in Washington Square.

The January 31, 1959, concert also featured Ritchie Valens ("La Bamba"), Dion and the Belmonts ("I Wonder Why"), and J. P. Richardson, a.k.a. the Big Bopper, who was riding high with "Chantilly Lace" and who had just written a future George Jones smash, "White Lightning." But Bobby's eyes were on the man rocking the sunburst Strat as everybody jammed on Chuck Berry's "Brown-Eyed Handsome Man." Two nights later, Holly, Valens, and Richardson died in the crash of a four-seat Beechcraft Bonanza. For Zimmerman it was tragic, if not as twisted as the death of his first musical hero, Hank Williams.

Bobby was crazy about Elvis and the other early rock 'n' rollers, especially Little Richard. In his first high school band, the Golden Chords, he pounded the piano and sang songs such as Richard's "Jenny Jenny." His second group never had a name but added blues and R&B to his repertoire. "Late at night I used to listen to Muddy Waters, John Lee Hooker, Jimmy Reed, and Howlin' Wolf blastin' in from Shreveport," he said. "Listened to all those songs, then tried to figure them out." The radio show was called *No Name Jive*, and Zimmerman ordered records from one of its sponsors, Stan's Rockin' Record Shop.

Playing in another band, the Rock Boppers, Zimmerman took on his first stage name, Elston Gunn (inspired by Elvis and televisions's Peter Gunn). Early in the summer of 1959, Gunn played a couple of gigs in Fargo, North Dakota, with the Shadows, one of whom would soon become pop star Bobby Vee ("Take Good Care of My Baby"). "We gave Bob Zimmerman a chance to work with us," said Vee, "and he played great—in the key of C." By the fall, when he enrolled in the University of Minnesota, he had another new name, Bobby Dillon (after *Gunsmoke*'s Marshall Dillon). Eventually he'd decide that *Bob* sounded stronger than *Bobby* and that *Dillon* looked cooler spelled with a *y*. Bob Dylan had also traded his electric guitar for an acoustic Gibson and a teenager's rock 'n' roll for a college kid's folk music.

"I first met Bob in the Ten O'Clock Scholar," said John Koerner. "Bob just drifted in. He and I both played the same sort of guitar things." Koerner and Dylan traded tunes by Jimmie Rodgers and Lead Belly and soon afterward Dylan's latest favorite, Odetta. Paul Nelson, who began his career as a music critic co-editing the *Little Sandy Review*, saw the pair perform in the University of Minnesota neighborhood called Dinkytown. "In 1959," he said, "Bob and Koerner were playing the standard repertoire, adequate guitarists and singers, but plenty of other kids were as good. Dylan seemed to learn so incredibly fast. If you didn't see him for two weeks, he made three years' progress."

College campuses helped nurture the folk revival. In the early 1950s, folk music reached a mass audience through the Weavers, who played upscale nightclubs and enjoyed major hits, including some that Pete Seeger had first heard sung by Lead Belly ("Goodnight, Irene," "The Midnight Special"). But the group's popularity plummeted when Seeger and fellow Weaver Lee Hays were found to have associations with the Communist Party and were called to testify before the House Un-American Activities Committee. Both refused to name names and the Weavers, already being monitored by the FBI, lost lucrative concert gigs and were essentially banned from radio and television.

But their influence lingered, and in 1955 the Weavers filled Carnegie Hall for a reunion concert. At about that time, Seeger played a California concert and sold a copy of his self-published *How to Play the 5-String Banjo* to David Guard, a student at Stanford University. Guard soon formed a collegiate folk combo called the Kingston Trio. After a long run at San Francisco's Purple Onion, the Kingston Trio broke nationally with a nineteenth-century ballad, "Tom Dooley"; the 1957 hit inspired such other folk groups as the Highwaymen, the New Christy Minstrels, and the Rooftop Singers, who revived Gus Cannon's "Walk Right In." It was these largely apolitical groups that inspired the 1960s television show *Hootenanny*.

In Chicago, Jim McGuinn jammed with another folk group, the Limelighters, who were booked into the Gate of Horn. McGuinn made such an impression that he was offered a spot in the band, which he joined a few months later, after graduating high school. McGuinn would tour with the Chad Mitchell Trio and Bobby Darin before becoming a founding member of the Byrds. Other Byrds earned their wings in similar fashion, with Gene Clark performing with the New Christy Minstrels, Chris Hillman playing in a California bluegrass group called the Scottsville Squirrel Barkers, and David Crosby, the son of a Hollywood cinematographer, singing in coffeehouses with the Balladeers.

"There were little pockets of musicians," said David Grisman of traditional acoustic players in New York, Boston, Chicago, the Bay Area, and Los Angeles, "and all these people were aware of each other." Over the years they formed bands, guested on each other's recordings, and cultivated the acoustic foundation of Americana. Few of these musicians became household names—Grisman's friend Jerry Garcia is a notable exception—but all contributed to a vibrant musical scene. Club 47, the center of the Boston-Cambridge scene, featured touring acts and local talents such as Eric Von Schmidt, a blues guitarist and graphic artist, and Debbie Green, a talented folksinger. The musicians saw themselves as continuing a tradition. "We'd go out and find these ancient records," said Tom Rush, "and the guitars sounded out of tune, and you couldn't understand the words. But it was more powerful than anything you'd hear anywhere else."

Joan Baez, a student at Boston University, was the daughter of an astrophysicist born in Mexico and a mother from Scotland. Baez was introduced to folk music at a Pete Seeger concert and began performing in Boston after absorbing Debbie Green's repertoire. She became a breakout star when she sang with Bob Gibson at the first Newport Folk Festival in 1959. All told, it took Baez just nine months to go from first playing Club 47 to recording her debut album.

Albert Grossman, who managed Odetta and Bob Gibson and ran the Gate of Horn in Chicago, booked Baez in hopes of becoming her manager. Baez instead chose the more genteel Manny Greenfield, who steered her to Vanguard, a label that specialized in folk and classical music, though she retained Grossman to negotiate her contract. Around that time, Grossman was at his Chicago club when Dave Van Ronk, on the advice of Odetta, arrived for an impromptu afternoon audition after hitchhiking from New York. "'Do you know who works here?'" said Grossman after Van Ronk played a few songs to an empty club. "Big Bill Broonzy works here. Josh White works here. Brownie McGhee and Sonny Terry play here a lot. Now tell me, why should I hire you?" A deflated Van Ronk returned to New York, where he would become a folk star known as the Mayor of McDougal Street.

Meanwhile, in Minneapolis, Bob Dylan was busy being born. "From Odetta," said Dylan, "I went to Harry Belafonte, the Kingston Trio, little by little uncovering more as I went along. Finally, I was doing nothing but Carter Family and Jesse Fuller songs. Then later, I got to Woody Guthrie, which opened up a whole new world." Dylan couldn't help but notice the new folk star whom some called the "barefoot Madonna." "The sight of her made me high," said Dylan of Baez. "All that and then there was her voice. A voice that drove out bad spirits."

In January 1961 Dylan caught a ride to New York. It proved to be a brutal winter, but Dylan had been raised in the windswept cold of the Iron Range, and a big city shrouded in snow was a perfect stage for an ambitious young folkie to create a new image to go with his made-up name.

Jerry Lee Lewis walked through commercial hellfire after marrying Myra Brown. He continued to record for Sun, but nothing sold; his one modest hit was a 1961 cover of Ray Charles's "What'd I Say," a roadhouse gospel song cut from the same suggestive cloth as Jerry Lee's own hits. His life had become an endless hustle of inconsequential gigs fueled by pills and booze. The one blessing was his son, Steve Allen Lewis, born in 1959 and named after the television host who'd given Jerry Lee a break.

Three years later, Lewis was on the road when Myra, now seventeen, found Steve Allen facedown in the brackish water of a backyard swimming pool. A distraught Lewis soon left for a tour of England. "They were screaming for me this time," said Lewis, who nonetheless was criticized in the tabloids for touring so soon after burying his boy. A couple of years later Jerry Lee cut *Live at the Star-Club Hamburg*, a raucous disc recorded at a venue that had hosted a residency by the Beatles. A hit in Europe, the album never came out in the United States, where the gigs were grim. "He started havin' a lot of goons around," said his drummer, Tarp Tarrant. "They were buyin' him dope. . . . They were totin' a lot of money for him, 'cause everything was always cash with Jerry. Guns. Hell, man, we had guns galore."

Alcohol broke up the Louvin Brothers (along with rock 'n' roll in general and the Everly Brothers in particular). "Satan is Real," they sang, while Ira, whose high-lonesome tenor echoes throughout Americanaland, hit the bottle. One drunken fight with his third wife ended with gunfire. "If the son of a bitch don't die," said Faye Cunningham, "I'll shoot him again." Ira's beleaguered younger brother finally went solo in 1963. A year later, a drunken driver killed Ira and his fourth wife. "It's been thirty years since we were separated," said Charles, "and still, if I'm playing a Louvin Brothers song, when I get to the harmony part, I move off to one side of the mike. It's a habit I can't break." The Everly Brothers also began to fade after a dispute with Acuff-Rose left them estranged from the writers of many of their hits, Felice and Boudleaux Bryant. The brothers wrote their biggest single, 1960's "Cathy's Clown," but while their influence lingered, the hits soon stopped.

A struggling Carl Perkins played an early-sixties gig in a small Tennessee club. As he slipped off his guitar at the end of a set, his fingers got caught in the blades of an onstage fan; Perkins passed out while his fingers were cut to ribbons. "That tunnel of light they talk about," said Perkins. "That happened to me. It just opened up in the most beautiful colors." Perkins regained consciousness to discover that his wife had begged the surgeon not to amputate his disfigured fingers. His left pinky was dead, but months of squeezing a rubber ball put the rockabilly back into his other fingers. The bourbon that used to calm his nerves before a show now soothed deeper pain. In 1964 his old friend Johnny Cash asked Perkins to join his touring band, but it wasn't exactly like the old days. Perkins said that he and Cash would sit in the back of a motor home and "get so drunk—me and my whiskey and he on his pills—that we couldn't see each other and we'd start crying. We'd sit there and talk about our dead brothers and get to feeling sorry for ourselves."

June Carter joined the Cash show in 1962 on a bill in Des Moines with Patsy Cline and George Jones. The married Cash let it be known that the married Carter was off-limits to the boys in the band. Family life remained a challenge for Cash. "When I was six years old, it was like my daddy always came home," said Rosanne Cash. "But when I was eight, somebody else came home. He was distracted and depressed and antsy." One night in Carson City, Nevada, police put a naked, unconscious Cash in a jail cell with a drunken lumberjack. When his cellmate woke up spoiling for a fight, Cash sang a spiritual and then "Folsom Prison Blues." "Me and you are a couple of drunks," said the pacified prisoner, "but you sure sound like Johnny Cash."

"I'd watched Hank Williams die," said June Carter. "I was part of his life—I'm Hank Jr.'s godmother—and I grieved. So I thought, 'I can't fall in love with this man, but it's just like a ring of fire.'" Their tortured relationship inspired the lyrics she wrote for a song that was first recorded by her sister Anita and then became Cash's biggest hit of the early 1960s, "Ring of Fire." Jack Clement, who'd recorded Cash at Sun, was enlisted to make sure the recording had just the right rhythm; Cash requested the mariachi horns that he'd heard in a dream.

Cash gave up the pretense of marriage in 1964 and rented a house in Nashville that he shared with Waylon Jennings. "We were the original 'Odd Couple,'" said Jennings, who'd recorded briefly for A&M Records before being signed to RCA by Chet Atkins. "I was supposed to clean up, and John was the one doing the cooking. . . . He'd be stirring biscuits and gravy dressed in one of his thin black gabardine shirts, and the flour rising in clouds of white dust all over him." They hid their respective drug stashes in the air conditioner (Jennings) and behind the television set (Cash).

June and Maybelle Carter lived nearby and would periodically clean the men's house and cook a real meal. Cash bonded with Maybelle and soon added the entire Carter clan to his road show. Musicians active in the folk revival had already rediscovered Maybelle, who'd been moonlighting as a practical nurse to make ends meet. In 1963 she traveled to Los Angeles to play the Ash Grove with the New Lost City Ramblers (she also joined them at the

Newport Folk Festival). Meeting her at the airport, the Ramblers cringed as her historic Gibson guitar dropped down the baggage chute in a plastic case.

"I will never forget standing up there onstage at the Ash Grove," said the band's John Cohen, "and watching Maybelle. The way she moved her hands in simple little elegant, graceful gestures, making this incredible sound come out of that Gibson. It reminded me of the way my grandmother used to crochet—she used the same skilled, graceful movements, repeated over and over."

On New Year's Day in 1958, Johnny Cash's itinerary included a concert at California's San Quentin State Prison. Merle Haggard was in the audience not because he was arrested after a drunken attempt to rob a tavern that he thought was closed but because he then broke out of the local jail. It was his final act of juvenile delinquency, and the Cash concert helped scare him straight. "The next day down in the yard," said Haggard, who was known to play guitar, "the players . . . came to me, and they all wanted to learn that Luther Perkins lick [from 'Folsom Prison Blues']. It was like seeing Muhammad Ali or something." On his release Haggard got to work making music; during a brief 1962 run playing bass for Buck Owens, Haggard suggested that he call his band the "Buckaroos."

Alvis Edgar Owens was one of four children born to Texas sharecroppers, and as a young boy he took the name of the farm's donkey, Buck. The family struggled during the Depression, and in 1937, when Buck was eight, headed west. They ended up outside Phoenix and worked at various dairy and fruit farms. "I remember always saying to myself that when I get big," said Buck, whose childhood suppers could be cornbread and milk, "I'm *not* going to go to bed hungry."

By the age of sixteen Buck had dropped out of school and was performing in local honky-tonks, preferring to earn $5 for playing a smoky club than for picking produce in the hot sun. While he was performing with Mac's Skillet Lickers, he met and married singer Bonnie Campbell. In 1951, with a young son, the couple relocated to Bakersfield, California, where Buck played with Bill Woods and the Orange Blossom Playboys. (The marriage didn't last; Bonnie later wed Bakersfield's other major star, Merle Haggard.) Owens also worked sessions in Los Angeles, playing on records by Tommy Collins, Faron

Young, and Wanda Jackson. After a handful of small-label releases, he was signed by Capitol Records.

Buck's first success came in 1959 with a shuffle reminiscent of Ray Price called "Second Fiddle"; his next single, "Under Your Spell Again," reached the top ten; the song also became a hit for Price. At about this time Owens met Don Rich, a fiddle player who became integral to his music. "I'm driving and singing," said Owens, "and Don starts singing harmony with me. I say, 'Hey!' He sounded like me. . . . If you listen to all the cuts you'll think he's singing melody and I'm singing harmony. You can't tell." Owens and Rich also used twangy Telecaster guitars to knit an instrumental weave of similar richness. "Don and I made a sort of synergy where one and one don't make two," said Owens. "The two of us together made three."

The hits kept on coming, including songs by Harlan Howard ("Above and Beyond") and others that Howard wrote with Owens ("Foolin' Around," "Under the Influence of Love"). Owens aimed to create what he called "freight train" songs: tunes with simple, memorable lyrics set atop beefy rhythms that owed more than a little to rock 'n' roll. Beginning with "Act Naturally" (1963) Owens had more than twenty #1 country hits, and he was the first to admit that he wasn't reinventing the wheel.

"My songs are quite alike, like Chuck Berry," said Owens, who admired Berry's songs and who'd recorded his own version of "Maybelline." "Once in awhile I'd throw in a left-field song. But basically, if you listen to 'I Don't Care' and 'My Heart Skips a Beat' and 'Tiger by the Tail,' I just changed the song and chord progression a little bit, and it sold to them over and over again." It was music built for the honky-tonk. "Buck was wild and rowdy," said Loretta Lynn. "The music was loud—too loud for me. He said, 'You'll never see nobody leave if the music's loud. If it's soft, people'll walk out.' So after that I played loud the way he did. When I got to the fourth or fifth song, if a fight didn't break out in Texas, I'd think I was doing something wrong."

Buck Owens bought his own honky-tonk (the Crystal Palace), invested in real estate and radio stations, and never went to bed hungry. Neither did Harlan Howard, who moved from Bakersfield to Nashville after hitting it big with "Heartaches by the Number." "I got two hits out of the Army," said Howard. "'Heartaches by the Number,' because everything in the Army is by the number, and I turned 'above and beyond the call of duty' into 'Above and Beyond the Call of Love.' You take things that are part of your life and turn 'em into love songs."

Howard liked talking shop at Tootsie's Orchid Lounge, located across the alley from the Grand Ole Opry, where he'd drink with such songwriters as Roger Miller, Hank Cochran, Waylon Jennings, and Willie Nelson. For years Jennings and Nelson labored as radio disc jockeys to support their work as musicians. While working at KVAN in Oregon, Nelson asked the advice of Mae Axton, the co-writer of Elvis Presley's "Heartbreak Hotel." "If I could write half as well as you," said Axton, "I would be the happiest woman in the world. . . . either come to Nashville or go home to Texas if you want to make it as a songwriter."

Nelson at first chose Dallas but headed to Nashville in 1960 after a week in which he wrote "Night Life," "Funny How Time Slips Away," and "Crazy." Nelson moved his family into Dunn's Trailer Court, where, according to former resident Roger Miller's "King of the Road," there were "trailers for sale or rent, rooms to let, fifty cents." Before long, Faron Young took Nelson's "Four Walls" to the top of the country charts; Young declined the songwriter's offer to sell him the tune for $500 and kindly lent him the money. At about that time, Hank Cochran (brother of Eddie "Summertime Blues" Cochran) helped Nelson sign a writer's contract with Pamper Music, a publishing firm that was half-owned by Ray Price, who would make "Night Life" a hit.

Price's version of "Night Life" reflected the "Nashville sound" that had come to dominate country music, a style that typically replaced the fiddles and steel guitars of 1950s country with lush strings and background singers. Conceived as an "adult" alternative to rock 'n' roll, the "countrypolitan" style also gave Buck Owens a counterintuitive avenue to country success. Though Chet Atkins had little success producing Nelson for RCA, it boded well for the songwriter's future that "Night Life" could be both a mellow country hit for Price and a long-time staple in the repertoire of blues singer and guitarist B. B. King.

Patsy Cline came to be the ultimate embodiment of the Nashville sound. Cline achieved regional success on *Town and Country Time*, a Washington, DC, radio show hosted by country star Jimmy Dean and His Texas Wildcats. But her mid-1950s recordings went nowhere until she cut "Walkin' After Midnight," a bluesy shuffle that featured Don Helms on steel guitar. After she performed the song on a 1956 episode of the television show *Arthur Godfrey's Talent Scouts*—the producers insisted that she swap her usual cowgirl outfit for an evening gown—Cline won the competition, and the song sailed to #2 on the country chart and just missed reaching the pop Top 10. But Cline failed to find a follow-up hit until producer Owen Bradley signed her to Decca Records in 1960.

Cline's first recording for the label was "I Fall to Pieces," a song written by Hank Cochran and Harlan Howard that topped the country charts and was also a pop hit. Like "Walkin' After Midnight," the song was a savvy blend of pop and country that found Cline employing a vocal technique known as "back phrasing." "From the songwriter's viewpoint," said Howard, "Patsy Cline was the greatest reader of lyrics that I've ever worked with. She understood that certain lines in a song are just there to be sung. They're not emotional lines. Patsy had the knack to hold back on those lines, then when she got to the really juicy part of the song, she'd give it everything she had."

Willie Nelson recorded "Crazy" on his 1962 debut album. One night at Tootsie's, Nelson played his recording on the jukebox and piqued the interest of Hank Cochran and Cline's husband, Charlie Dick. Though the hour was late, they decided to wake up Patsy. A nervous Nelson stayed in the car and left the pitch to Cochran. "[Patsy] went out there and drug his ass in [the house] and had him sing it to her," said Cochran. But Cline thought that "Crazy" was too much of a pop song; Owen Bradley had to twist her arm to give it a shot. But first she had to ignore Nelson's version. "No one should try to follow my phrasing," said Nelson. "I'll lay back on the beat or jump ahead . . . I believe in taking my time. When it comes to singing a song, I've got all the time in the world."

Cline had a similarly distinctive approach, and "Crazy," one of the best-selling country songs of all time, made her a legend. "She understood the lyrics on the deepest possible level," said Nelson. "She sang it with delicacy, soul, and perfect diction." Cline transcended genres, and generations, with a catalog of songs still cherished by Americana artists. "Even though her style is considered country," said Lucinda Williams, "her delivery is more like a classic pop singer."

Patsy was a singular stylist not unlike Ray Charles, who'd become a star by fusing gospel with rhythm & blues before releasing his own take on countrypolitan, *Modern Sounds in Country and Western Music* (1962). Other black artists had found success with country songs, including Solomon Burke, who had a 1961 hit with a Faron Young song from 1952, "Just out of Reach." But the Charles record was something more: a complete set of country songs featuring his own soulful interpretation of the Nashville sound. Charles had heard plenty of country music growing up in Florida. "I can't recall a single Saturday

RAY CHARLES

night in those years when I didn't listen to the *Grand Ole Opry* on the radio," said Charles, who was particularly fond of Hank Williams and Hank Snow. "I could do country music with as much feeling as any other Southerner," said Charles. "And why not? I had been hearing it since I was a baby."

Although it feared that a country album would alienate his black audience, ABC Records, which had signed Charles away from Atlantic, had little leverage because his contract guaranteed artistic control. Charles considered a list of 250 country songs before choosing four by Hank Williams ("Half as Much," "You Win Again," "Worried Mind," "Hey, Good Lookin'"), an Everly Brothers hit ("Bye Bye Love"), a Cindy Walker tune ("You Don't Know Me") that had been sung by Eddy Arnold, and "I Can't Stop Lovin' You," which was a 1958 hit for its writer, Don Gibson. Charles's version of that song spent five weeks atop the pop charts; it's perhaps telling that while it was also a #1 R&B hit, the song failed to scale the country chart.

Charles saw a natural affinity between country music and the blues. "The words to country songs are very earthy like the blues," he said. "They're not as dressed up, and the people are very honest and say, 'Look, I miss you, darlin', so I went out and I got drunk in this bar.' That's the way you say it. Whereas in Tin Pan Alley, it will go, 'Oh, I missed you darling, so I went to this restaurant and I sat down and I had dinner for one.' That's cleaned up now, you see? But country songs and the blues is like it is."

Modern Sounds in Country and Western Music confirmed Charles's status as an American roots-music star, and as such, a seminal figure in Americana. Cline's greatest hits assured her similar standing, but her temporal stardom ended on March 5, 1963, when she died, just like Buddy Holly, in a small plane felled by stormy weather. Friends in Nashville knew the flight was long overdue, and early the next morning Roger Miller found himself at the crash site. "I came up over this little rise," he said, "and my God, there they were. It was ghastly. The plane had crashed nose down."

When Bob Dylan arrived in New York in 1961, he knew where to go. "Greenwich Village was a universe unto itself," said musician and composer David Amram. "It felt like an oasis where people from all over the world came to commune . . . a place where they could fit in because the village was actually a joyous community of misfits." Dylan fit right in and feasted on the musical smorgasbord. "Washington Square was a place where people you knew or met congregated every Sunday and it was like a world of music," said Dylan. "There could be 15 jug bands, 5 bluegrass bands, an old crummy string band, and folk singers of all kinds and colors, singing John Henry work songs.... That is what New York was like when I got there."

Musical Sundays in Washington Square had flourished during the 1950s. In the middle of the decade, Dave Van Ronk heard Tom Paley playing an intricate finger-picking style of guitar that inspired Van Ronk to switch from playing in a jazz combo to becoming a solo performer specializing in blues and ragtime (Paley would soon form the New Lost City Ramblers). Dylan landed at the Café Wha, where he blew harmonica behind Fred "Everybody's Talking" Neil, cadged a hamburger in the kitchen, and cruised the other clubs where baskets were passed to collect tips for the performers. One afternoon, Dylan stopped in an empty club to watch jazz pianist Thelonious Monk "playing stuff that sounded like Ivory Joe Hunter." Dylan told the pianist, "I play folk music up the street. 'We all play folk music,'" said Monk.

During his first week in the city Dylan caught a bus at the Port Authority to visit Woody Guthrie at Greystone Park Psychiatric Hospital in Morristown, New Jersey. He brought along a pack of Woody's favorite Raleigh cigarettes. Guthrie, suffering from Huntington's Disease, was losing control of his muscles and could no longer play guitar. Dylan sang him his old songs such as "Tom Joad" and "Pretty Boy Floyd" while mentally ill patients howled in the hallway. "His influence on me was never in inflection or in voice," said Dylan. "What drew me to him was that hearing his voice I could tell he was very lonesome, very alone, and very lost out in his time." After the visit, Dylan wrote his first significant original composition, "Song to Woody."

One day at the Folklore Center, a music store run by Izzy Young that was at the center of the Village folk scene, Dylan met Van Ronk, who was trying out one of the shop's Gibson guitars. Dylan asked Van Ronk how one could get a job at the Gaslight café; the singer inquired about the stranger's experience mopping floors. Dylan, persisting, used the Gibson to sing "Nobody Knows You When You're Down and Out." The vicar of the Village mellowed and invited Dylan to come by the Gaslight and sing a few songs during his set.

Musicians far from the mainstream enriched (and were educated by) the Village folk scene. "Everything I needed was in New York," said Judy Collins, who moved to the city from Colorado. "I lived in the center of the folk music revival." Native New Yorker John Sebastian enjoyed an early apprenticeship with Lightnin' Hopkins after the Houston bluesman performed on the same television show as Sebastian's father John, a harmonica virtuoso who played classical music. "Lightnin' would stay with me in New York when he came to play at the Village Gate or some other places in Midtown," said Sebastian of their relationship. "It became all about getting Lightnin' to the gig, carrying his guitar, and getting him his pint."

John Herald sang and played guitar with the Greenbriar Boys, a bluegrass group that formed at the University of Wisconsin and that, in 1960, had the chutzpah to perform at the Old Time Fiddlers' Convention in Union Grove, North Carolina. It was during this trip that Herald and another band member, Ralph Rinzler, met a blind guitar player, Doc Watson, who had spent much of the previous decade playing electric guitar in a rockabilly band. "Ralph and I went down to Doc's house [in western North Carolina] with a tape recorder and got him to play [acoustic] guitar," said Herald, "and he played breaks like we never heard in our lives. And I'd ask, 'Can you play it hotter?' and it would just get hotter and hotter." The musicians cherished these visits. "I was learning from Doc," said Herald, "and since I didn't want to practice in their little living room, I'd go sit under the steps to their house." Hearing the distant guitar, Watson would insist that the shy New Yorker come inside.

"Ralph told me once," said Watson, "'Doc, if you play the ethnic music, the old-time music we call it, you can get your foot in the door. Then you can expand the repertoire to play some of these other things.'" To that end, Watson reacquainted himself with a lifetime of songs. "My first acquaintance with finger style was the old Carter Family style where Maybelle did the thumb lead and the fingers for the rhythm part," said Watson. "Later on, I began to fool around doing a vamp with my thumb and doing the lead with my fingers. Merle Travis inspired me to do that."

A few years later, Rinzler briefly managed Bill Monroe and His Blue Grass Boys and helped expose the group to fans of the folk revival. Rinzler shared an apartment in Nashville with another northerner, Bill Keith, who'd taken up the banjo while studying nineteenth-century French literature and mathematics at Amherst College. After learning the basics from Seeger's *How to Play the 5-String Banjo*, Keith became frustrated when trying to re-create complex fiddle melodies on the instrument. To solve this problem, he found chord fingerings up the neck that accommodated arpeggios and fluid, fast-picked melodies. Keith's innovations proved to be a vital link between Earl Scruggs's work with Bill Monroe in the late 1940s and the music of such modern banjo players as Tony Trischka and Bela Fleck.

In early 1963 Keith was in Nashville to help Earl Scruggs write a banjo instructional, and on the weekends he joined backstage jam sessions at the *Grand Ole Opry*. Bill Monroe was quick to hire Keith but had one problem. "There's only one Bill in the Blue Grass Boys," said Monroe, who subsequently called Keith by his middle name, Brad. "Before he came along, no banjo player could play those old fiddle numbers right," said Monroe. "You have to play like Brad could play or you would be faking your way through a number." Keith lasted only nine months with the group; bad pay and arduous travel prompted him to give notice before an engagement at the Ash Grove in Los Angeles. Keith tutored a talented teenager, Ry Cooder, to take his place for the second week and soon joined a group more attuned to his bohemian sensibilities, the Jim Kweskin Jug Band.

The Greenbriar Boys recorded with Joan Baez and had their own contract with Vanguard. In September 1961 the group played New York's premiere folk club, Gerde's Folk City. Opening the show was the new kid in town, Bob Dylan. Robert Shelton reviewed the show for the *New York Times*, and the headliners were likely chagrined by the headline: "Bob Dylan: A Distinctive Folk-Song Stylist." "If not for every taste," wrote Shelton, "his music-making has the mark of originality and inspiration, all the more noteworthy for his youth. Mr. Dylan is vague about his antecedents and birthplace, but it matters less where he has been than where he is going, and that would seem to be straight up."

Coincidentally, Dylan had been hired to play harmonica for a recording session with Carolyn Hester, signed by Columbia Records in search of its own Joan Baez. Dylan arrived at the studio with a copy of the *Times* under his arm, but he needn't have bothered; John Hammond, Hester's producer, had already read the review, and he asked for a few minutes with the young musician. Dylan was well aware of Hammond's history with such artists as Count Basie, Charlie Christian, and Billie Holiday. "It seemed like eons ago since I'd been in . . . southeast Minneapolis listening to the *Spirituals to Swing* album and the Woody Guthrie songs," said Dylan. "Now, incredulously, I was sitting in the office of the man responsible for the *Spirituals to Swing* album and he was signing me to Columbia Records."

Dylan had been in New York for less than a year, soaking up repertoire and starting to write his own songs. Only two originals appeared on his 1962 debut, *Bob Dylan*: "Song to Woody" and the playful "Talkin' New York." The album included blues by Jesse Fuller ("You're No Good") and Blind Lemon Jefferson

BOB DYLAN

("See That My Grave Is Kept Clean") and a Blind Boy Fuller tune that Dylan had learned from Eric Von Schmidt, "Baby, Let Me Follow You Down." The album was cut in three afternoon sessions for less than $2,000. "Half of the cuts on it were renditions of songs that Van Ronk did," said Dylan. "It's not like I planned that, it just happened. Unconsciously I trusted his stuff more than I did mine."

His artistic growth was explosive. His girlfriend Suze Rotolo encouraged an interest in politics and social justice, which prompted him to write topical material. As a result, his second album, *The Freewheelin' Bob Dylan*, on which he's pictured strolling on Jones Street with Rotolo, included such topical tunes as "A Hard Rain's A-Gonna Fall" (written during the Cuban Missile Crisis) and "Masters of War." The collection also featured one of his sweetest ballads ("Girl from the North Country") and a song that would become an anthem of social justice, "Blowin' in the Wind." Dylan saw himself as a part of the folk tradition and was more confident writing lyrics than creating melodies. "I tend to base all my songs on old songs," he said, "like the old folk songs, the old blues songs; they are always good. They always make sense."

When he first signed Dylan, John Hammond sent him home with a copy of what would prove to be a very influential collection, Robert Johnson's *King of the Delta Blues Singers*. Hammond had tried to recruit Johnson to play 1938's "Spirituals to Swing" concert at Carnegie Hall only to discover that the bluesman was dead, said to have been poisoned by a jealous husband. Dylan took the LP over to Van Ronk's apartment, where his friend dismissively identified the recorded antecedents to some of Johnson's "original" songs. "I did see what he meant," said Dylan, "but Woody had taken a lot of old Carter Family songs and put his own spin on them, too." Back at home, Dylan listened to the album repeatedly and wrote down the lyrics to see how they scanned.

Dylan was also touched by a production of Bertolt Brecht's *Threepenny Opera*, and in particular, the song "Pirate Jenny." "I took the song apart and unzipped it," said Dylan. "It was the form, the free verse association, the structure and disregard for the known certainty of melodic patterns to make it seriously matter, give it its cutting edge." That song, with music by Kurt Weill, gave him the insight and courage to write such unorthodox tunes as "Mr. Tambourine Man" and "It's Alright Ma (I'm Only Bleeding)." Similarly, he said, "If I hadn't heard the Robert Johnson record when I did, there probably would have been hundreds of lines of mine that would have been shut down." Suddenly, it was all systems go. Van Ronk remembers the first time

Dylan sang "A Hard Rain's A-Gonna Fall" at the Gaslight. "I had to get out of the club," said Van Ronk. "I couldn't speak—to Bobby or anybody else for that matter. I remember being confused and fascinated that night because, on one hand, the song itself excited me, and on the other, I was acutely aware that it represented the beginning of an artistic revolution."

Dylan's career caught fire alongside his songwriting. After the release of his first album he agreed to be managed by Albert Grossman, who'd relocated to New York, where he was the mastermind behind a popular folk group. Grossman had auditioned both Van Ronk and Carolyn Hester before casting Peter Yarrow, Noel Paul Stookey, and Mary Travers as Peter, Paul, and Mary. The idea was to create a hipper Kingston Trio and to jazz up folk music with humor, social consciousness, and a sexy woman. Peter, Paul, and Mary's 1962 debut album sold more than two million copies and earned Pete Seeger a nice payday by including his "Where Have All the Flowers Gone." Dylan, fiercely loyal to Hammond, resisted Grossman's interest in voiding his contract with Columbia but was quick to take $1,000 of his manager's cash to buy himself out of his publishing deal with Leeds Music, for which he'd received a $100 advance. Grossman then arranged for Dylan's songs to be published by Witmark and Sons, with whom the manager had his own deal to receive half of the publishing income of any artist he brought to the company. All was in order by the time Peter, Paul, and Mary's second album made a hit out of "Blowin' in the Wind."

"They were kindred spirits," said Rotolo of Dylan and his manager. "Albert never denied who he was, but he had that way of observing and not being forthcoming. Bob never gave a straight answer. . . . He was creating his own legend and his own fiction of himself." The two changed each other's lives. "You could look at Albert's passport pictures," said Vinny Fusco, who worked for Grossman, "[and] there was B.D. and A.D.—Before Dylan and After Dylan."

Hammond sent copies of Dylan's albums to another Columbia artist, Johnny Cash, who was particularly impressed by "Blowin' in the Wind." Cash sent a letter of appreciation to Dylan, who replied that he'd been a fan since hearing "I Walk the Line." At about that time, folk music's bright young knight met the queen. "When I heard him sing 'With God on Our Side,' I took him seriously," said Joan Baez. "I never thought anything so powerful could come out of that little toad . . . I realized he was more mature than I had thought. He even looked a little better." Baez would soon invite Dylan to join her onstage; they'd warm up backstage singing songs by the Everly Brothers. "When he was on tour with me and we were getting close," said Baez of their romance, "it was very sweet between us. I was very nurturing, and he was incredibly vulnerable and endearing."

On April 28, 1963, Baez and Dylan participated in the March on Washington. Martin Luther King delivered his historic "I Have a Dream" speech; Dylan sang "Only a Pawn in Their Game" and "Blowin' in the Wind." Dylan was now a public figure. "He came on my radio show," said singer Oscar Brand, "and he said nothing but lies about his life. . . . I don't think many of us really believed he was that Dust Bowl character he pretended to be. Nobody really cared very much one way or another, because everybody was faking something and afraid in our own way. But he didn't know that." To Dylan's chagrin, a profile in *Newsweek* let the biographical cat out of the bag.

Bob and Joan had become the figureheads of folk. Pete Seeger and the folk music establishment considered them saviors who could attract and influence a whole new generation of fellow travelers. "To the old left," said Brand, "Dylan was the second coming." Said Theodore Bikel: "I think of that highlight of the 1963 Newport Folk Festival, that stunning, stirring ringing out of 'We Shall Overcome'—as the apogee of the folk movement. There was no point more suffused with hope for the future." But the times, as Dylan would sing on his third album, were a-changing.

5

TURN! TURN! TURN!

"[America] is where the music came from that influenced me as a child," said John Lennon. "And we had all the Doris Day movies and the Heinz beans.... I was brought up on Americana." To the boys who would become the Beatles, America meant music and cowboys. Ringo Starr loved how Gene Autry would ride his horse Champion while singing "South of the Border." George Harrison discovered Jimmie Rodgers's "Waiting for a Train" in a family record collection that also included 78s by Hank Williams.

Then came Elvis Presley. "We'd never heard American voices singing like that," said Lennon. "They'd always sung like Sinatra or enunciated very well, and suddenly there was this hillbilly, hiccupping on the tape echo, and the bluesy background.... My whole life changed." Paul McCartney liked Elvis, but he flipped for Richard Penniman. "Little Richard was this voice from heaven or hell, or both," said McCartney. "This screaming voice seemed to come from the top of his head. I tried to do it one day and found I could. You had to lose every inhibition to do it."

But it was Buddy Holly (along with Gerry Goffin and Carole King) who inspired Lennon and McCartney to start writing their own songs. "Practically every Buddy Holly song was three chords," said Lennon, "so why not write your own?" Harrison saw Holly as a musical role model. "First of all," said Harrison, "he sang, wrote his own tunes and was a guitar player, and he was very good. Buddy Holly was the first time I heard A to F-sharp minor. Fantastic—he was opening up new worlds there." Many years later, McCartney purchased the publishing rights to Holly's songs.

But in the beginning, John, Paul, and George were smitten by "skiffle," a synthesis of folk and blues that developed in the U.K. at virtually the same time Elvis was helping create rock 'n' roll. Skiffle emerged from Lonnie Donegan's vocal performance during the otherwise instrumental program of the Chris Barber Jazz Band. Donegan's "Rock Island Line," a Lead Belly tune recorded with only guitar, string bass, and washboard percussion, became an international hit in 1956 and spawned an English skiffle fad that put guitars in the hands of such future rock stars as Jimmy Page, Keith Richards, and Eric Clapton, as well as John, Paul, and George. "I liked Elvis at the time, and Buddy Holly," said Richards, "and [my classmates] didn't understand how I could possibly be an art student and be into blues and jazz. . . . For me, it reflected an incredible explosion of music, of music as style, of love of Americana."

Lennon formed the Quarrymen to play skiffle in 1957; McCartney joined within months, and they were soon joined by Harrison, who passed his audition by playing the guitar instrumental "Raunchy" on the top deck of a municipal bus. By 1960 the group had a local following in Liverpool, but the musicians truly gelled during five trips to Hamburg, Germany, to play extended residencies at clubs in the city's red light district. The group was now called the Beatles, a name that evoked Buddy Holly's band, the Crickets. On its final trip to Germany, in 1962, the quartet included Starr, a drummer poached from another Liverpool band, Rory Storm and the Hurricanes.

The Beatles' lengthy stays in Hamburg amounted to rock 'n' roll boot camp, with the group playing every night for up to eight hours. Malcolm Gladwell cited this experience in his book *Outliers*, in which he maintained that it takes ten thousand hours of "deliberate practice" to become world-class in any field. "Paul would be doing 'What'd I Say' for an hour-and-a-half [and we'd be] lying on the floor and banging our guitars and kicking things, always drunk," said Lennon of a typical performance at the Kaiserkeller. "And all these gangsters would come in, like the local Mafia, and send a crate of champagne on stage . . . and we had to drink it or they'd kill us. They'd say, 'Drink it and then do "What'd I Say."'"

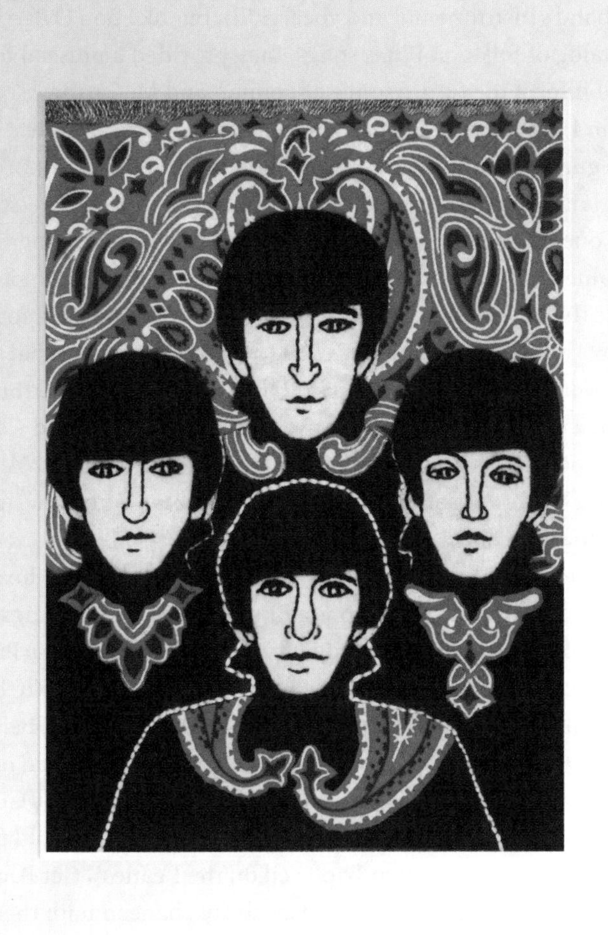

THE BEATLES

Deliberate or not, the long hours sharpened the band's instincts and abilities. Over the course of an evening, the Beatles would perform songs by Elvis Presley, Carl Perkins, Little Richard, Chuck Berry, Buddy Holly, Eddie Cochran, the Coasters, and Jerry Lee Lewis. Such performances didn't merely hone the band's instrumental and vocal skills, but like Bob Dylan absorbing a deep catalog of folk and blues songs, they provided a musical foundation that would inform the future songs of Lennon and McCartney.

While in Hamburg the Beatles were tempted by sex, amphetamines, and American guitars. Lennon purchased a blonde Rickenbacker 325; on returning to England, Harrison traded his Futurama guitar for a Gretsch Duo Jet similar to one played by Nashville's Chet Atkins, whose playing had taught him the value of using a variety of chord voicings. Gigs at Liverpool's Cavern Club made the Beatles local stars. "If the Beatles ever wanted 'a sound,'" said McCartney, "it was R&B—that was what we used to listen to, what we used to like, what we wanted to be like. Black. That was basically it. Arthur Alexander. It came out white because it always does—we're white and we were just young Liverpool musicians." The band's debut album included "Anna (Go to Him)," a 1962 hit for Alexander, a southern black man who grew up listening to country music.

The Beatles played a package tour of the United Kingdom headlined by Little Richard, who'd returned to playing the rock 'n' roll songs that he'd abandoned in a religious pique. "Right from the start," said Billy Preston, the sixteen-year-old keyboardist in Richard's band, "I fell in love with the Beatles. . . . They didn't get any meals from the promoter, but Richard, being the big American headliner, got steaks and chops and a fabulous spread nightly, so I made sure they [the Beatles] were well fed and watered." In 1969 George Harrison went to a Ray Charles concert and discovered that his old friend was in the band. Preston subsequently played on the Beatles' "Get Back," a tune about the days before their music and celebrity changed both them and the world. But six years earlier, the Beatles were little more than a rumor in the land that had given them a repertoire.

By the time the Beatles played on *The Ed Sullivan Show* on February 9, 1964, Bob Dylan was the preeminent folk singer of his generation. Dylan's record sales were dwarfed by those of Peter, Paul, and Mary, but he was the face of folk with a growing repertoire of original songs. Dylan's first album was dominated by folk and blues standards, but *The Freewheelin' Bob Dylan* and *The Times They Are A-Changin'* included original songs that were both political ("A Hard Rain's A-Gonna Fall," "Only a Pawn in Their Game") and personal ("One Too Many Mornings," "Boots of Spanish Leather"). Dylan published some of his topical songs in *Broadside*, a mimeographed magazine that featured song lyrics and passionate debates about the state of folk music. Political activists loved these songs, but Dylan hated being called a protest singer. "All my songs are protest songs," he said. "Every single one of them. That's all I do is protest."

In February 1964 Dylan took a road trip across the country that included a couple of concerts and concluded with an appearance with Joan Baez at a folk festival in Monterey, California. They stopped in North Carolina to pay an unannounced visit to poet Carl Sandburg and went to Mardi Gras in New Orleans, which inspired Dylan to start writing "Mr. Tambourine Man." During the long drive, songs by the Beatles dominated the radio hit parade. "He [Dylan] practically jumped out of the car," said his road manager, Victor Maymudes, about the first time they heard "I Want to Hold Your Hand."

"They were doing things nobody was doing," said Dylan. "Their chords were outrageous, just outrageous, and their harmonies made it all valid. Everybody else thought they were for the teenyboppers, that they were gonna pass right away. But it was obvious to me that they had staying power. I knew they were pointing to the direction where music had to go. I was not about to put up with other musicians, but in my head the Beatles were *it*."

Dylan didn't want to be in a band, but he did want to rock. "I played all the folk songs with a rock 'n' roll attitude," said Dylan. Musician Peter Stampfel heard Dylan sing the folk standard "Sally Gal" at Gerde's Folk City. "His singing style and phrasing were stone rhythm and blues!" said Stampfel. "He fitted the two styles together perfectly, clear as a bell, and I realized for the first time that my two true loves, traditional music and rock music, were in fact one." Still, when he went into the studio in June to record what would become *Another Side of Bob Dylan* in a single ten-hour session, he arrived not with a band but with his guitar, his harmonicas, and a couple bottles of wine.

But the songs were different. "There aren't any finger-pointing songs in here," Dylan told Nat Hentoff, who attended the session while preparing a profile for the *New Yorker*. "Me, I don't want to write for people any more—you know, be a spokesman. From now on, I want to write from inside me, and to do that I'm going to have to get back to writing like I used to when I was ten—having everything come out naturally." Some in the folk community were disappointed that songs like "All I Really Want to Do" and "My Back Pages" ditched social commentary for more personal concerns.

"The political folkies were very black and white," said Izzy Young, who'd known Dylan since his arrival in New York. "They had all decided he was on their side—oh boy! He's one of us! Then he sings a couple of songs that aren't about some dying coal miner, and now—oh no! He's not one of us!" The editor of *Sing Out!*, Irwin Silber, sounded the alarm: "You seem to be in a different kind of bag now, Bob—and I'm worried about it. I saw at Newport [in the summer of 1964] you had somehow lost contact with people. . . . Your new songs seem to be inner-directed now, inner-probing, self-conscious. . . . You're a different Bob Dylan than the one we knew. The old one never wasted our precious time."

Those puzzled by Dylan's evolution either hadn't been paying attention or were unaware of the myriad influences that had shaped him. At Newport that summer, Dylan sat on the floor and swapped songs with another festival headliner, Johnny Cash. He made a tape recording of two songs for Cash: the just-recorded "It Ain't Me, Babe" and "Mama, You Been on My Mind." Cash gave Dylan a Martin guitar and recorded a hit version of "It Ain't Me, Babe" with June Carter.

Later that summer, the Beatles were touring the United States following the July release of their first movie, *A Hard Day's Night*. In the preceding year they had become a musical and social phenomenon, lobbing multiple songs to the top of the charts while leading an invasion of such British rock groups as the Rolling Stones and the Animals, who had a huge hit by adding a rock feel to "House of the Rising Sun," a song that Dylan had taken from Dave Van Ronk's repertoire for his debut album. The Beatles were well aware of Dylan. Lennon said that he started "A Hard Day's Night" with Dylan in mind before it evolved into a Beatles song, and his influence was clearly evident in the more intimate language of Lennon's "Norwegian Wood" and "You've Got to Hide Your Love Away." The Beatles absorbed Dylan's music the way Harrison echoed the rockabilly guitar of Carl Perkins ("I Don't Want to Spoil the Party"), and Lennon and McCartney aimed for the compositional rigor of Buddy Holly ("Every Little Thing").

Dylan was a star in the Village, but he'd never seen anything like the crowds gathered behind police barricades surrounding the Delmonico Hotel in midtown Manhattan. When he gained entrance and met the Beatles, worlds collided, with the Fab Four wearing collarless mod suits and Bob in blue jeans and motorcycle boots. Dylan asked if they wanted to get stoned and was shocked to discover that they'd never smoked marijuana (pills, they knew). Dylan figured the Beatles had to be pot smokers because he understood the background vocals on "I Want to Hold Your Hand" as "I get high, I get high" instead of "I can't hide." Neither Dylan nor the Beatles went to college, but on this occasion the era's five most influential musicians were like university students careful to hide the smell of turning on.

Back in London, the Beatles threw a party for Carl Perkins after the last date of a U.K. concert tour during which he opened for Chuck Berry. "We wound up—John, Paul, George and Ringo—sitting on the couch and me on a floor with a guitar," said Perkins. The Beatles invited Perkins to a recording session at Abbey Road. "It was a magic time," said Perkins. "I was in the studio when they cut [my] 'Honey Don't,' 'Matchbox,' and 'Everybody's Trying to Be My Baby.' And then they did a version of 'Blue Suede Shoes' that was never recorded." Nearly ten years after the country boy had found fame at Sun Records, Perkins enjoyed a publishing windfall that allowed him to buy his parents a farm.

"I first saw the Beatles on television in New York," said Jim McGuinn, who at the time was working with Bobby Darin. "It was the clip with all the screaming girls. I loved the music! I got it right away and started playing folk songs with a Beatle-beat down in Greenwich Village." He also started growing his hair. Relocating to Los Angeles, McGuinn played the Troubadour, where he met Gene Clark, another Beatles freak who'd toured with the New Christy Minstrels. They were soon joined by David Crosby, who added a harmony voice and a business connection to Jim Dickson, who'd been making demo recordings of Crosby. Dickson agreed to manage the band that called itself the Jet Set and recruited a new member, Chris Hillman, an L.A. bluegrass player who switched from mandolin to bass guitar. (The Dillards, a bluegrass band in the same California scene, won national attention by playing music as "The Darlings" on *The Andy Griffith Show*. Douglas Dillard later formed Dillard & Clark with Gene Clark.)

Dickson put the Jet Set to work at a studio owned by World Pacific Records. "We learned faster than any other garage band you ever saw," said Crosby. "[Dickson] would sit down and make us listen to tapes . . . we'd come back and try more, and eventually we got pretty good at it." McGuinn recalled: "A lot of bands have to work on the road for years to get the kind of sound we recorded together in about eight or nine months." For the musicians, this studio time was akin to the experience that the Beatles found in the clubs of Hamburg; a crucial difference was that while they learned how to make records, the band lacked the in-person panache of the Beatles and left a legacy of erratic live shows.

In the summer of 1964, the Jet Set went to see *A Hard Day's Night*. "I can remember coming out of that movie so jazzed that I was swinging around stop-sign poles at arm's length," said Crosby. "I knew right then what my life was going to be. I wanted to be that." After seeing the film, McGuinn bought the twelve-string Rickenbacker model that George Harrison played. The band also changed its name to the Byrds, with the unique spelling mirroring that of the Beatles. Dickson had by then come into possession of an unreleased song that Dylan had recorded during the *Another Side* sessions, "Mr. Tambourine Man." The band recast the song in 4/4 time and cut all but one verse, but had doubts about its potential until Bob Dylan stopped by the studio and said, "Wow, man. You can dance to that!"

Back in New York, Tom Wilson, Dylan's record producer, had the Animals in mind when he experimented with adding electric instruments to "House of the Rising Sun." "We tried by editing and by overdubbing to put like a Fats Domino early rock and roll thing on top of what Dylan had done," said Wilson. "That's where I first consciously started to try to put these two different elements [folk and rock] together." Wilson would soon jump-start the career of Simon and Garfunkel by overdubbing a band onto the original acoustic take of "The Sounds of Silence."

In January 1965 the Byrds cut "Mr. Tambourine Man" with Columbia staff producer Terry Melcher, the son of Doris Day. Uneasy with the band's musicianship, Melcher hired members of the "Wrecking Crew," an elite group of studio musicians who recorded with the Beach Boys and producer Phil Spector. While the Byrds provided vocals—McGuinn and Clark typically sang in unison with Crosby adding a harmony—McGuinn was the only one to play an instrument, and it was the ringing, sustained tone of his twelve-string that evoked the "jingle jangle" referred to in Dylan's lyrics.

"Mr. Tambourine Man" topped the charts in both the United States and the United Kingdom; critics dubbed this new sound "folk rock." The group's debut album fleshed out this new style with three more Dylan songs ("All I Really Want to Do," "Spanish Harlem Incident," and "Chimes of Freedom"),

THE BYRDS

three originals by Gene Clark (including the enduring "I'll Feel a Whole Lot Better"), and "The Bells of Rhymney," a Pete Seeger song about an Irish mining disaster that McGuinn had already recorded with Judy Collins.

The Byrds inspired others to pursue folk rock, with the Turtles making the Top 10 with Dylan's "It Ain't Me, Babe" and Sonny and Cher, a couple of showbiz bohemians, hitting with such vaguely Dylanesque songs as "I Got You, Babe" and "Laugh at Me." Soon to come was Barry McGuire's "Eve of Destruction," the Spinal Tap of protest songs. While the Byrds became the talk of Los Angeles by playing to Hollywood hipsters at Ciro's, the city was also home to a very popular folk-pop quartet, the Mamas and the Papas ("California Dreaming"), and Buffalo Springfield ("For What It's Worth"), a rock band that included two bright stars, Neil Young and Stephen Stills.

The Lovin' Spoonful was the most successful folk-rock band from the East Coast. John Sebastian had grown up in Greenwich Village and played in the Even Dozen Jazz Band with Maria Muldaur on vocals, David Grisman (mandolin), and Stefan Grossman (guitar) before forming the Lovin' Spoonful. The name came from a lyric in Mississippi John Hurt's "Coffee Blues." The rediscovered songster was a favorite in Village coffeehouses. "I remember working with the Spoonful at the Night Owl Café," said Sebastian, "and we'd be playing to maybe six beatniks. Then I'd go to see John at the Gaslight and the place would be filled with all these beautiful college girls that we couldn't get down to our little club."

That changed when the Spoonful produced a run of hits that included "Do You Believe in Magic?," "Daydream," and "Summer in the City." The band's jug-band roots were reflected by the fact that Sebastian played not only the guitar and harmonica but the autoharp. Their appreciation of country music was apparent in "Nashville Cats," a tuneful tribute to the musicians of Music City. "Nashville cats," say the lyrics, "been playin' since they're babies. Nashville cats, get work before they're two."

Amidst this bounty of bands, Dylan was a singularly influential singer-songwriter who was still searching for a sound. Lennon and McCartney wrote their own songs but got an invaluable assist in the recording studio from producer George Martin. Dylan's gift was in his compositions and performances, and he believed that making good records depended on capturing the magic of the moment. Still, Dylan saw a model of what he wanted in *So Many Roads*, an urban blues album that John Hammond Jr. (the son of the man who'd signed him to Columbia) had cut with members of a band that he'd discovered in Canada, Levon and the Hawks.

When Dylan went into the studio in January 1965, he and producer Wilson spent the first day recording Dylan by himself; a second session was held with a small band. Some songs, such as "Love Minus Zero/No Limit," were recorded both solo and with the band; in that case, the group performance made the final cut. By contrast, "Mr. Tambourine Man" didn't work with the group. It was completed with Dylan accompanied only by the electric guitar of Bruce Langhorne. "I remember that we didn't do any rehearsal," said Langhorne, "we just did first takes and I remember that, for what it was, it was amazingly intuitive and successful."

Bringing It All Back Home underscored the expansive nature of Dylan's latest songs, with the second side of the LP including not only "Mr. Tambourine Man" but such loquacious epics as "Gates of Eden" and "It's Alright Ma (I'm Only Bleeding)." But it was two blues-rock songs that signaled something new. "Subterranean Homesick Blues" consisted of four fast-talking verses that tumbled out of Dylan's mouth like silver on a hot skillet of guitars, drums, and harmonica. "You don't need a weather man to know which way the wind blows," he sang, just one of the couplets from the song that would resonate with the political protesters of the 1960s. It is noteworthy that he didn't model the song after something by Woody Guthrie or the Carter Family. "It's from Chuck Berry, a bit of 'Too Much Monkey Business,'" said Dylan, "and some of the scat songs of the '40s." "Subterranean Homesick Blues" was (barely) Dylan's first Top 40 single, peaking at # 39.

"Maggie's Farm" mated a blues-based melody with rat-a-tat lyrics about the injustice of working like a slave. Rhythm & blues singer Solomon Burke covered the tune in a manner that suggested the frustrated fury of civil rights demonstrators. Sam Cooke, touched by Dylan's "Blowin' in the Wind," was a bit chagrined that a white man had written such a profound civil rights anthem. Cooke added the tune to his nightclub repertoire and then wrote a socially conscious masterpiece of his own, "A Change Is Gonna Come."

In the spring of 1965 Dylan toured the United Kingdom. He was trailed by documentary filmmaker D. A. Pennebaker, whose *Don't Look Back* showed a high-strung Dylan indulged by his entourage and quick to ridicule reporters and celebrity fans like Donovan. Joan Baez is seen singing Hank Williams with Dylan in a hotel room but was not welcomed onto his concert stage. The film captures the end of their romance but ignores a dead-end recording session in which Dylan tried to record "If You Gotta Go, Go Now" with John Mayall's Bluesbreakers and its hot new guitarist, Eric Clapton. After one ramshackle take, drummer Hughie Flint said, "You haven't worked much with bands, have you?"

Back in the United States, Dylan made another stab at electric music, extracting the lyrics for a new song from a twenty-page prose poem. His new recruit on electric guitar was Mike Bloomfield, a Chicagoan making his name with the Paul Butterfield Blues Band. "The first thing I heard was 'Like a Rolling Stone,'" said Bloomfield. "I figured he wanted blues, string bending, because that's what I do. He said, 'Hey, man, I don't want any of the B. B. King stuff.' He had heard records by the Byrds that knocked him out. He wanted me to play like McGuinn." New York musician Al Kooper brought his guitar to Dylan's recording session but put it away as soon as he heard Bloomfield play his Telecaster. Kooper settled behind a Hammond organ, and although he was a neophyte on the instrument, improvised his way onto "Like a Rolling Stone." As the tape rolled, the Byrds' version of "Mr. Tambourine Man" was at the top of the charts. In July, a week before Newport, Dylan released the song that *Rolling Stone* would later call rock's greatest single.

Arriving in Newport, Dylan looked more like a Beatle than a folk singer. "There was a clear generation and cultural gap widening as the weekend went on," said Joe Boyd, who was working at the festival and had been Tom Rush's roommate at Harvard. "The year before, Dylan had been a pied piper in blue jeans. This year he was in a puffed polka-dotted dueling shirt and there were rumors that they were smoking dope. The old guard—Seeger, Lomax, [Theodore] Bikel—were very upset. They had gotten to the point of having all their dreams come true two years before, having this gigantic mass movement of politically active kids. And suddenly they could see it all slipping away in a haze of marijuana smoke and self-indulgence. As far as they were concerned, Grossman was the money changer at the gates of the temple."

The friction between the old and the new was evident at a Friday afternoon workshop called "Blues: Origins and Offshoots," which included performances by Mance Lipscomb, Son House, and, closing the show, the Butterfield Blues Band. The emcee for the program was Alan Lomax, who in the early 1940s had traveled through the Mississippi Delta and recorded House and

Muddy Waters for the Library of Congress. "Today you've heard some of the greatest blues musicians in the world playing their simple music on simple instruments," said Lomax, looking at a stage now filled with microphones, drums, and amplifiers. "Let's find out if these guys can play at all."

The band left no doubt. "We were boogying and totally blown out by the Butterfield Band," said Maria Muldaur. "I had heard a lot of blues, but... I'd never heard real Chicago electric blues like this, and we loved it." But at show's end, the talk wasn't about the music as much as it was about the fistfight. "Lomax walked down off the stage," said Paul Rothchild, who was producing the Butterfield band's debut album and mixed their sound at Newport. "And Albert [Grossman]... walked up to him and said, 'What kind of fuckin' introduction was that?' And Lomax said, 'What do you know about blues?' Albert said, 'I don't have to know anything about blues to know that was a terrible introduction.'... And before anyone knew what was happening there were these two giants, both physically and in the business, wrestling around in the dust!"

Bloomfield rejected Lomax's doctrinaire definition of the blues. "What we played was music that was entirely indigenous to the neighborhood, to the city that we grew up in," said Bloomfield. "There was no doubt in my mind that this was folk music; this was what I heard on the streets of my city, out the windows, on radio stations and jukeboxes in Chicago.... That's what folk music meant to me—what people listened to." After the scuffle, Lomax demanded that Grossman be banned from the festival grounds. The board demurred because three of Grossman's clients (Dylan, the Jim Kweskin Jug Band, and Peter, Paul, and Mary) had yet to play and just might leave with their manager. Meanwhile, Dylan held a late-night rehearsal that included Bloomfield, Al Kooper, and Butterfield's rhythm section (drummer Sam Lay and bassist Jerome Arnold). "We just learned the tunes right there," said Bloomfield. "He sang and we played around him. But he never got with the band so that we could groove together.... He always seemed to be fighting the band."

On the festival's last night, Dylan took the stage with a sunburst Fender Stratocaster like the one played by Buddy Holly. Dylan and the band, which now included pianist Barry Goldberg, then played the most famous three-song set in the history of popular music. Books and countless articles have tried to explain why (and if) the crowd at Newport booed Dylan's first live performance with a band. The truth remains murky; many complained of a lousy sound mix that buried Dylan's vocals; others cited a blues-band rhythm section that never gelled with the material. Fans also felt shortchanged by a set that consisted of "Maggie's Farm," "Like a Rolling Stone," and "Phantom Engineer," an early version of what became "It Takes a Lot to Laugh, It Takes a Train to Cry."

Tumult reigned backstage during Dylan's set; the volume outraged Pete Seeger, who was said to have wanted to take an axe to the power cords. Dylan's hasty exit, and the rowdy crowd he left behind, prompted Peter Yarrow to beg him to return to the stage and sing an acoustic tune. He reluctantly obliged and used Johnny Cash's guitar to play "Mr. Tambourine Man" and an elegiac "It's All Over Now, Baby Blue." But Dylan was no longer the puckish folk singer who'd charmed Newport; he was now the most influential Americana artist since Hank Williams.

Dylan's friends in the folk world were either dismissive or jealous. "We had been playing for tips and sleeping on floors," said Dave Van Ronk, "and when one of us suddenly could get a suite at the top of the Plaza, naturally that hurt." Some griped that that they, too, would be stars with the right connections and record contract. "Yeah, sure you could," said Van Ronk. "All you had to do was write 'A Hard Rain's A-Gonna Fall'—for the first time. That was what Bobby did, and none of the rest of us did that. Even if everyone didn't admit it, we all knew that he was the most talented of us."

Four days after his controversial appearance at the Newport Folk Festival, Dylan returned to a New York studio and in three days, with new producer Bob Johnston behind the recording console, cut the album that would make him a rock star, *Highway 61 Revisited*. The title itself reflects Dylan's musical journey. "Highway 61, the main thoroughfare of the country blues, begins about where I began [Duluth]," said Dylan. "I always felt like I'd started on it, always been on it and could go anywhere, even down into the deep Delta country.... It was my place in the universe, always felt like it was in my blood." With Bloomfield and Kooper leading the band, Dylan looked to pair his literary lyrics with the kind of brawny folk rock he'd created on "Like a Rolling Stone." Easier said than done. "We did 20 alternative takes of every song," said Bloomfield. "It was never like, 'Here's one of the tunes, and we're gonna learn it and work out an arrangement." It didn't matter. Dylan knew a good take when he heard it.

Tony Glover observed Dylan working in the studio. "After finishing [another] rollicking, hard-driving, rock and roll version [of 'It Takes a Lot to

Laugh, It Takes a Train to Cry'']," said Glover, "and while the group took a lunch break, Dylan reworked the tune alone at the piano and came back with the sweeter, bluesy version which appeared on *Highway 61 Revisited*. The juxtaposition of these extremely variant versions made a lasting impression." Dylan followed his vision to the end; dissatisfied with numerous takes of "Desolation Row," he recorded it as an acoustic duet with a visitor from Nashville, Charlie McCoy, who contributed Flamenco-flavored guitar fills.

Ten years after absorbing the Memphis music of Elvis and Cash, and four years after meeting Woody Guthrie, Dylan had joined them as American icons. So many artists covered his tunes in 1965 that Dylan's publishing income was said to be greater than the combined royalties of Richard Rodgers, Lorenz Hart, Oscar Hammerstein, George Gershwin, and Cole Porter. As an influential international star, Dylan stood alongside the Beatles, who were touring America on the release of a second film, *Help!* When the Beatles spent a week in Los Angeles they rented the Beverly Hills mansion of Zsa Zsa Gabor. One day, the Byrds joined them for an LSD party during which twelve-string guitars were played amid enthusiastic chatter about Ravi Shankar and John Coltrane. (George Harrison had already sent the Byrds a note of appreciation for the guitar lick he'd taken from "The Bells of Rhymney" for his "If I Needed Someone.") That same week, the Beatles also accepted Colonel Tom Parker's invitation to visit Elvis Presley at his Bel Air home.

Presley was now quite different from the artist who'd rocked the world in the mid-1950s. Though he'd made some great singles since getting out of the army in early 1960 ("Stuck on You," "Little Sister," "Can't Help Falling in Love") and had just enjoyed a hit with a song he'd recorded in 1960, "Crying in the Chapel," Presley mostly cranked out formulaic movies and mediocre soundtracks; he'd already released three in 1965 (*Girl Happy*, *Tickle Me*, and *Harum Scarum*). In a pop world that revolved around the Beatles, Dylan, Motown, and the burgeoning counterculture, Presley was a King without a kingdom. Still, the Beatles tumbled out of a limousine foggy with pot smoke like giggly kids excited to meet their original hero.

Details of the meeting are sketchy. Elvis greeted the Beatles in a red shirt and gray trousers and sat on a white couch playing bass guitar to a recording of "Mohair Sam," a current hit for Charlie Rich, who'd gotten his start at Sun Records. Elvis drank 7-Up while the Beatles had scotch and Coke; George smoked a joint and talked about Hinduism with Larry Geller, Presley's spiritual advisor and hairstylist. John and Paul were said to have played "I Feel

Fine" on acoustic guitars with Elvis on bass and Ringo thumping on a table. Beatles manager Brian Epstein gambled at roulette with Colonel Parker and pitched him the idea of having Elvis tour the United Kingdom.

"Long live ze king," said John as the Beatles said goodbye. "He was our greatest idol," said Paul, "but the styles were changing in favor of us." Pete Seeger might have had a similar feeling after Bob Dylan made a rock 'n' roll racket on a Newport stage built by acoustic folk music. On the pop charts, Dylan's "All I Really Want to Do," the second single by the Byrds, was beaten into the Top 20 by Cher's cover of the same song. Desperate for a hit, McGuinn thought of "Turn! Turn! Turn!," a Pete Seeger song that he'd recorded with both the Limelighters and Judy Collins. Seeger wrote the chorus—"To everything (turn, turn, turn), there is a season (turn, turn, turn)"—and, like a true folklorist, found his verses in the biblical book of Ecclesiastes. And in this season of folk rock and the British Invasion, it was only natural for McGuinn to open his band's second (and last) #1 record with the reverberating sound of the twelve-string Rickenbacker that he'd bought after falling for the Beatles.

6
WHITE LINE FEVER

Merle Haggard, inmate A-45200, was released from San Quentin State Prison on November 3, 1960, and caught a bus to Bakersfield. Haggard had spent three years in lockup; when he got caught drinking moonshine he spent a week in solitary, and used a Bible for a pillow. Now Haggard hustled music gigs at local clubs like the Blackboard and the Lucky Spot. Working in Las Vegas, Haggard met Johnny Cash, whom he'd seen play a 1958 concert at San Quentin; Cash offered the ex-con a Benzedrine and a sip of wine. Haggard also heard Wynn Steward perform "Sing a Sad Song," which in 1964 would become his first hit for a small label owned by his manager, Fuzzy Owens. Within a year, Haggard was on Capitol Records.

Haggard grew up in a renovated boxcar in the Bakersfield suburb of Oildale. His father died of a brain hemorrhage when he was eight; at fourteen, Haggard hitchhiked to Texas in a failed attempt to meet his favorite singer, Lefty Frizzell; months later, he saw him play at Bakersfield's Rainbow Gardens. "His songs hit me right in the heart," said Haggard. "It was strange; it was like listening to my own voice." Haggard absorbed the influence of Frizzell's soft, melodious style before finding what writer David Cantwell calls a voice that's "relaxed, warm and rugged; intensely felt, unmistakably masculine, and unabashedly Okie-accented; but smooth, too, for all that, and tending toward what we might fairly term pretty. Haggard's a crooner."

Bonnie Owens, Buck's ex-wife, was singing with Haggard when she took him to meet Liz Anderson. "If there was anything I didn't wanna do," said Haggard, "it was sit around some danged woman's house and listen to her cute little songs." Minutes after arriving, he picked up a guitar to learn what would become his next hit, "(My Friends Are Gonna Be) Strangers." That tune gave his band a name, the Strangers. Another Anderson song, "The Fugitive," based on the popular television show, hit #1 in 1967 and encouraged Haggard to plumb his own past to write songs like "Sing Me Back Home," "Mama Tried," and "Branded Man."

Haggard became the biggest act in Bakersfield this side of Buck, who continued to crank out buoyantly rocking tunes to great success. Haggard was different, more apt to sing about the troubled aftermath ("Tonight the Bottle Let Me Down") than the party itself. He wrote about hard work ("Working Man Blues") and couples facing tough times ("If We Make It Through December"). Bonnie, who became the second of his five wives, witnessed the birth of the songwriter. "It's amazing to me the things that came out of Merle's mouth when he's writing," said Owens. "He'd later say, 'Bonnie, I don't ever remember saying these words. It's like God put 'em through me." Sometimes, God spoke fast. In Dallas, Haggard asked Bonnie to fetch him a late-night hamburger. By the time she returned, he'd scribbled the words to "Today, I Started Loving You Again" on a paper bag. He then sang the song and made Bonnie cry.

Haggard forged the lean sound of these songs with the Strangers and such hired hands as James Burton, a master of the Telecaster who'd played guitar for the *Louisiana Hayride* as a teenager, created the unforgettable guitar lick of Dale Hawkins's 1957 hit "Susie Q" and was Ricky Nelson's lead guitarist for more than a decade. At about the time Burton played on such Haggard tunes as "Swinging Doors" and "Life in Prison," he turned down an offer from Bob Dylan to tour the world in his first electric band.

Dylan might have been hip to Haggard, but he more likely knew Burton from his work with Nelson because songs from the country charts were largely unknown to those listening to the Beatles and the Byrds. Two exceptions were Roger Miller, who enjoyed pop success with such sharp-witted hits as "Dang Me" and "Chug-a-Lug," and Buck Owens, who was introduced to the rock audience when the Beatles covered his "Act Naturally" on the soundtrack to *Help!* (the song was also the flip side of "Yesterday"). Johnny Russell wrote

MERLE HAGGARD

"Act Naturally," but he acceded to Owens's demand that he be given the publishing rights before he recorded the song. Russell later sued to regain his lucrative copyright. Owens, meanwhile, took a little flack when he and the Buckaroos began performing a Beatles medley at live shows; this prompted his 1965 pledge to *Music City News* that "I Shall Sing No Song That Is Not a Country Song."

Buck Owens's fondness for the Beatles should hardly be a surprise because country and folk were increasingly prominent in the band's mid-sixties music. Consider "Yes It Is." "That's me trying a rewrite of 'This Boy,'" said John Lennon, "but it didn't work." With its close harmonies and melancholy lyric, "Yes It Is" is not unlike a ballad by the Everly Brothers. *Rubber Soul* (1965) included other songs with American roots: Lennon's "Run for Your Life" recalled Elvis Presley's "Baby Let's Play House," while McCartney's "I'm Looking Through You" mixed acoustic and electric instruments in consummate folk-rock style. One night banjoist Bill Keith of the Kweskin Jug Band listened to *Rubber Soul* with Doc Watson. "Man!," said Watson. "Those boys have been doing their homework!"

Haggard and Owens created a repertoire that would prove highly influential for Americana artists. So did Loretta Lynn, who arrived in Nashville in the early 1960s. Born Loretta Webb in Butcher Hollow, Kentucky, she was a coal miner's daughter and one of eight children. She married Oliver "Doolittle" Lynn when she was fifteen, and the couple relocated to the state of Washington when she was seven months' pregnant with the first of six children. Doo gave his wife a $17 Harmony guitar for her eighteenth birthday and encouraged her to sing in a local honky-tonk. "He thought I was something special," said Lynn, "more special than anyone else in the world, and never let me forget it." In 1960 Lynn recorded a song of her own, "I'm a Honky Tonk Girl." She and Doo lived in their car while promoting the song at local country stations; when it reached the Top 20 they drove to Nashville, where Lynn played the *Opry* and was signed to Decca by Owen Bradley.

"I remember my first recording session for [Decca]," said Lynn, "I was so scared I just stood in the background and was even afraid to speak to the musicians. . . . Owen would put up a screen, so I couldn't see nobody; I'd just sing to myself. He said he did the same thing for Brenda Lee." Early on, Lynn cut records in the honky-tonk style of Kitty Wells, but she soon found her own unique voice. In the country music world dominated by men, Lynn wrote songs such as "Don't Come Home A-Drinkin' (With Lovin' on Your Mind)" that showed a distinctively feminine perspective.

"The way most of my songs got started," said Lynn, "was I'd hear a good line, or make one up." One night, she recalled, "a little girl came back stage and said her husband didn't bring her to the show—he brought his girlfriend. . . . I peeked out and there she was, painted up like you wouldn't believe. I looked 'round to the little girl that was talking to me. And she didn't have no makeup at all. And I said, 'Honey, she ain't woman enough to take your man.' I went straight to my dressing room and wrote 'You Ain't Woman Enough (To Take My Man)' in ten minutes."

Musicians quickly learn that the real money in the music business is in songwriting; Willie Nelson struggled as a recording artist but bought a family compound outside Nashville with the earnings from tunes recorded by Patsy Cline ("Crazy") and Faron Young ("Hello Walls"). But country music remained stubbornly far from the coastal mainstream. "The country music jamboree was as ambitious, colorful, star-laden, uneven, beautiful and banal as a circus," wrote Robert Shelton in the *New York Times* in 1964 about a show at Madison Square Garden that featured George Jones, Buck Owens, Bill Monroe, and Ernest Tubb. "There was a bit of noise, a lot of nostalgia, but enough good music-making for this circus to be one that country music fans will long remember." That same year, a young woman from the mountains of east Tennessee arrived in Nashville, won a publishing deal, and had a few minor hits. But it wasn't until Dolly Parton started singing duets with Porter Wagoner that the world would meet the woman who would become one of the most successful songwriters in country music history.

With Newport in the rearview mirror and *Highway 61 Revisited* about to be released, Bob Dylan needed a band. Guitarist Mike Bloomfield, happy to stick with the Butterfield Blues Band, wasn't interested, and James Burton preferred session work and playing in the house band on television's *Shindig!* Mary Martin, who worked for Albert Grossman, suggested the Hawks, a Toronto group that had backed Ronnie Hawkins, a rockabilly singer from Arkansas. Hawkins had paired Levon Helm, a drummer from his home state, with a quartet that he'd cultivated in Canada. Dylan was a fan of the album some of the Hawks had recorded with John Hammond Jr.

By the summer of 1965 the quintet had left Hawkins and were playing on the Jersey shore and calling themselves Levon and the Hawks. Guitarist Robbie Robertson of the Hawks traveled to New York to meet Dylan; they broke the ice at a Manhattan music store where Robertson suggested that Dylan try a Fender Telecaster, which tended to stay in tune better than a Stratocaster. Dylan settled on a black Tele with a white pick guard. Back at Grossman's office, Dylan and Robertson played acoustic guitars. "That was the first time I really heard Bob Dylan," said Robertson. "Sitting on a couch with him singing in the room. And that was the first time I said to myself, 'There's something to this; it kind of rambles a bit, but there is something about it.' I was playing a little loud, and I could see from his attitude that he wanted it to be rough."

Grossman had concerts booked at New York's Forest Hills Tennis Stadium and the Hollywood Bowl, with Al Kooper and bassist Harvey Brooks already recruited to accompany Dylan; Robertson and drummer Levon Helm agreed to play the dates, leaving the other Hawks to hold down the Jersey gig. Dylan opened the Forest Hills concert with an acoustic set that ended with the concert debut of "Desolation Row." During intermission, he gave the group a pep talk. "I don't know what it'll be like out there," said Dylan. "It's gonna be some kind of carnival. . . . So just go out there and keep playing no matter how weird it gets."

New York was as restive as Newport; Kooper thought people booed "because they'd read that they were supposed to." Robertson couldn't believe that electric guitars were even an issue. "It was like, jeez," said Robertson, "somebody's bought a television!" The old-school folkies howled; others saw Dylan as a pop star and sang along to "Like a Rolling Stone." Los Angeles, home of the Byrds, gave the electric set a much better reception. When Grossman booked a full national tour, Robertson and Helm wouldn't commit unless Dylan hired the other Hawks: Rick Danko on bass, Richard Manuel on piano, and Garth Hudson on a variety of keyboards. Since Al Kooper had already passed on the full tour, Dylan agreed, and rehearsed with the Hawks in Toronto.

Dylan's idiosyncratic songs were a far cry from the blues and R&B they'd performed with Ronnie Hawkins. "I'd watch where he was going all the time," said Danko, "and he really liked the fact that I could anticipate the way he broke meter." Though Robertson found the rehearsals inadequate, when the tour got under way Dylan and his protégés developed a fierce new sound. "It was like thunder," said Robertson, "with this Elmer Gantry speaking, talking these words, singing them, preaching them. He was no longer doing his nasally folk thing; he was screaming his songs through the rafters."

"It was so in your face," said Angus Wynne, who booked Dylan for shows in Austin and Dallas. "You couldn't really understand the words—quality concert sound systems were nonexistent back then—but you could feel the energy. It was like being knocked over by this huge burst of sound." Dick Alderson was the tour's sound engineer. "There were hardly any monitors at all," he said, "so you could never really hear yourself. . . . We were in territory that nobody had ever been in. No one had played those kind[s] of halls before." Except for the Beatles, of course, who were typically drowned out by the excited squeals of teenage girls.

With tour dates scheduled around weekends, Dylan and his band went into Columbia's Manhattan studio to begin recording a follow-up to *Highway 61 Revisited*. The first completed recording was a single that flopped, "Please Crawl out Your Window"; other tracks were left unfinished except for "One of Us Must Know (Sooner or Later)," which would appear on Dylan's next album, *Blonde on Blonde*. Frustrated by the slow progress, Dylan took Bob Johnston's suggestion of trying to record in Nashville. Before Dylan's arrival, Johnston spent two days recording Simon and Garfunkel's "Homeward Bound" and "I Am a Rock."

Charlie McCoy, who'd accompanied Dylan on "Desolation Road," played about four hundred recording sessions in 1966. Tasked to hire the musicians, he enlisted two members of his weekend group, Charlie McCoy and the Escorts: guitarist Wayne Moss and drummer Kenneth Buttrey. He also called pianist Hargus "Pig" Robbins, who'd been accidentally blinded at the age of four. All had extensive recording résumés; McCoy had played harmonica on Roy Orbison's "Candy Man," while Moss had played guitar on Orbison's "Pretty Woman." Joe South, a guitar player who'd have later solo success with 1969's "Games People Play," also played the sessions. Dylan brought along Al Kooper to be his interface with the southern musicians. "He'd teach me a song," said Kooper, "and I'd play it over and over again, and he'd write the lyrics. He had a piano in his room. Then I'd go to the session an hour before him, and teach the band the songs that I knew."

When Dylan arrived at Columbia's Nashville studio on February 14, 1966, he told Johnston that he needed time to polish his first batch of songs. "Johnston came to us," said McCoy, "and said, . . . 'He's not finished writing a lyric, so go ahead and do your dinner and get on back because I don't know when he's gonna be ready.' So we all left and came back, and then sat around for eternity." On this night, the musicians signed two three-hour session cards before playing a single note. Then, in the wee hours, three songs were recorded: "Fourth Time Around," "Visions of Johanna," and "Leopard Skin Pillbox Hat."

The next night turned into a nocturnal challenge when Dylan wrestled with the lyrics to "Sad-Eyed Lady of the Lowland," which at eleven minutes and twenty-two seconds would occupy the fourth side of what became one of rock's first double albums. Kris Kristofferson, a Rhodes Scholar and U.S. Army captain who'd taken a job as the studio's janitor in an attempt to launch a career in music, recalled an opened Bible on a music stand. "I saw Dylan out in the studio at the piano," he said, "writing all night long by himself. And wearing shades." Recording commenced at around four a.m., ten hours after the start of the session. "After five or six minutes," said drummer Buttrey, who was twenty years old, "we started looking at the clock. We'd build to a peak, and bang, there goes another harmonica solo, and we'd drop down into another verse. About ten minutes of this thing, and we were cracking up at what we were doing. I mean, we peaked five minutes ago." It was far from a typical night in Nashville. "It was one of those deals," said McCoy, "[where you think,] '*Please* don't let me make a mistake.'" "This," according to Kooper, "is the definitive version of what 4 a.m. sounds like."

Reuniting with the Hawks for more concerts, Dylan played his new recordings for Robertson. "He was really impressed by the Nashville [musicians]," said Robertson. "He said, 'I just went in there—these guys didn't know me, they didn't know this music—I went in there, and they just all get in a huddle, and they figure it out so quickly and come up with an arrangement, a whole idea for the song." Robertson joined Dylan on his next trip to Nashville, where he impressed the studio pros with an especially raucous guitar solo on "Obviously Five Believers."

Dylan might have taken his time with words, but musical ideas were executed with alacrity. When Dylan played the bluesy "Rainy Day Women #12 & 35," Johnston said that he imagined a Salvation Army horn section. McCoy unpacked his trumpet, and though it was after midnight, scared up a trombone player. For "I Want You," the last tune recorded for the album and a subsequent hit single, guitarist Moss created the sixteenth-note obbligato that runs throughout the song. All told, Dylan was in the studio for nearly seventy hours. "The time we spent on *Blonde on Blonde* was for us like an eternity," said McCoy. "Most Nashville artists at the time would record a whole album in three [three-hour] sessions."

Dylan later said that the Nashville musicians had captured what he was looking for: "that thin, that wild mercury sound." But when the folk-singer-turned-rock-star headed out on a world tour, Levon Helm was no longer behind the drums. "We'd look at one another and try to figure out if we were playing great music or total bullshit," said Helm, who went home to Arkansas. "I began to think it was a ridiculous way to make a living; flying to concerts in Bob's thirteen-seat Lodestar, jumping in and out of limousines, and then getting booed." Mickey Jones, who drummed with Johnny Rivers, got the gig.

Touring the world, Dylan and the Hawks found their own wild mercury sound. "By the time we did Australia and Europe," said Robertson, "we had discovered whatever this thing was. It was not light, it was not folky. It was very dynamic, very explosive, and very violent." This was not the ramshackle sound of the Newport performance and not at all like the folk rock of the Byrds; instead, this was a rough blueprint for the kind of singer-songwriter rock that would inspire artists from Bruce Springsteen and John Mellencamp to Steve Earle and Lucinda Williams. Dylan was also starting to spiral out of control.

"He was what you call a real road dog," recalled Rick Danko. "You never got to sleep [in his company]." There were amphetamines to keep you up, pot to get you high, pills to put you to sleep, and by some accounts, a snort or two of heroin for a change of pace. Cinematographer D. A. Pennebaker, who'd fashioned *Don't Look Back* from the 1965 British tour, was again shooting film, this time as a hired gun for an ABC television special. Robertson would often share a hotel suite with Dylan, and guitars were always nearby.

"In those hotel rooms," said Robertson, "I also found that Bob probably knew more songs than anybody walking the earth." When Dylan and his entourage settled into a London hotel, the music world came to pay its respects. Paul McCartney dropped by with a copy of "Tomorrow Never Knows," a new Beatles song that reflected McCartney's interest in electronic music. "It was a little bit 'An Audience with Dylan' in those days," said McCartney, who after a bit of a wait played the record for Dylan. "I remember his saying, 'Oh, I get it, you don't really want to be cute anymore.' And I was saying, 'Yeah, that's it.'" Singer Marianne Faithfull observed the encounter. "Paul was obviously terribly proud of it," she said. "He put it on the record player and stood back in anticipation, but Dylan just walked out of the room."

Johnny Cash also paid a visit. "Bob and Johnny were on a wavelength that actually matched, high-voltage madness," said Robertson. Cash bounced in his chair. Rattled by a knock at the door, he bolted from the room. "'If it's June, tell her I'm not here,'" he said, according to Robertson. "And with that he disappeared into the other room and hid in the closet, yelling, 'I'm not here.'" When the coast was clear, Dylan picked up a guitar and Cash sang along as he played Hank Williams's "I'm So Lonesome I Could Cry."

The Beatles and other rock royalty attended Dylan's concert at the Royal Albert Hall and were quick to defend him against those who still had a problem with the show's electric half. But it was Dylan's widely bootlegged concert at the Free Trade Hall in Manchester that would give the world a taste of the music that had caused such a commotion (the live recording was officially released in 1998). "The concerts were incandescent because the singer was living for art," wrote critic Paul Williams, "was literally burning himself out, not to please the audience and certainly not out of obligation, but for the sheer joy of doing it, traveling with intrepid companions out into unknown aesthetic realms, shining lights into unexplored darkness." At the end of the Manchester set, Dylan confronted his combative audience with the acerbic "Ballad of a Thin Man." "Something is happening here and you don't know what it is," bellowed Dylan, prompting an audience member to scream the most famous heckle in rock 'n' roll history: "Judas!" Dylan was both hurt and defiant. "I don't believe you," he cried, "you're a liar!" Turning to the band, he said, "Play it fuckin' loud!" and closed the show with an especially scathing version of "Like a Rolling Stone."

How does it feel? How does it feel to be on top of the world? Pennebaker filmed two men who would know, Dylan and John Lennon, in the back of a limousine; years later Lennon would say that they were high on heroin. What we see is a barely coherent Dylan mumbling about the Beatles' publishing deal before vomiting on the floor. "Come, come, boy," said Lennon. "Pull yourself together." At Dylan's Mayfair hotel, Lennon and Pennebaker carried him up to his room. "We laid him down on his bed," said Pennebaker, "and he looked really weird. We sat on his bed and I just looked at him. He looked dead. We went downstairs and back outside, and John said, 'Well, I think we just said good-bye to old Bob.'" But Bob didn't go away; he went home to Woodstock, New York.

But there was no rest for the weary. Dylan was late delivering his first book, ABC wanted its television special, and Albert Grossman was booking another round of U.S. concerts. Reunited with his new wife, the former Sara Lownds, and first-born child, Jesse, Dylan struggled to keep all these balls in the air. On the morning of July 29, 1966, he steered his Triumph 650 Bonneville motorcycle over a hilltop before descending steep Striebel Road. "I was drivin' right straight into the sun," said Dylan, "and I looked up into it even though I remember someone telling me a long time ago when I was a kid never to look straight at the sun." But Dylan was no Icarus, getting too close to the sun; he was a strung-out pop star fresh from touring the world and hanging with Cash and the Beatles, and he was now flying over the handlebars of his Triumph.

7
SOMETHING IN THE AIR

"Of course it was a drug song," said David Crosby of the Byrds about "Eight Miles High." "We were stoned when we wrote it. We can justifiably say that it wasn't a drug song because it was written about the trip to London. But it was a drug song and it wasn't a drug song at the same time." "Eight Miles High" (like Dylan's "Rainy Day Woman #12 & 35") was banned by many radio stations because of its presumed drug references, but you didn't have to listen to the words to tune in, turn on, and drop out; McGuinn's lead guitar, played in a modal scale, was enough to suggest a hit of LSD. "The Rick by itself is kind of thuddy," he said of his Rickenbacker twelve-string. "It doesn't ring. But if you add a compressor, you get that long sustain. With compression, I found I could hold a note for three or four seconds, and sound more like a wind instrument. Later, this led me to emulate John Coltrane's saxophone on 'Eight Miles High.' Without compression, I couldn't have sustained the riff's first note."

McGuinn's distinctive guitar was the instrumental signature of the Byrds, and his political instincts made him the leader of an unruly flock. Gene Clark, who made his bandmates jealous by buying a Ferrari with the proceeds of his original songs, quit the Byrds over his fear of flying. David

Crosby always irritated McGuinn and Chris Hillman, but the three found folk-rock grace on 1967's *Younger Than Yesterday*. Clarence White played guitar on Hillman's "Time Between," one of a number of the group's early songs (including "Hey Mr. Spaceman" and a cover of Porter Wagoner's "Satisfied Mind") that showed an affinity for country music. Hillman knew White from his days with the Kentucky Colonels: the world-class picker was now a successful session musician.

At the Monterey Pop Festival (1968), Crosby annoyed McGuinn by introducing "He Was a Friend of Mine" with a rant about the Warren Commission's investigation into the assassination of President John F. Kennedy. Crosby then sat in for an absent Neil Young during the Buffalo Springfield's festival performance. Los Angeles had other hit bands, including the Beach Boys and the Mamas and the Papas, but Buffalo Springfield was the only act with the hipster credentials of the Byrds. The Springfield had problems of its own; after Stephen Stills's "For What It's Worth" became a counterculture anthem, group comity was in short supply, and Young quit the band.

Crosby, too, wasn't long for the Byrds. First the group refused to release his song about a ménage à trois, "Triad" (the song was recorded by the Jefferson Airplane). Then Crosby refused to sing on "Goin' Back," a folk-rock ballad by Gerry Goffin and Carole King. Tempers flared, Crosby stormed out of the studio, and McGuinn and Hillman kicked him out of the Byrds with a $10,000 settlement for his share of the band's name. It was about this time that Jim McGuinn changed his name to Roger after becoming associated with Subud, an international spiritual movement with roots in Indonesia.

Crosby licked his wounds in Coconut Grove, Florida, where he shopped for a sailboat and revisited haunts from his folkie days, including a club called the Gaslight South. "Joni [Mitchell] was singing one of those songs," said Crosby, "like 'Michael from Mountains,' 'Both Sides Now,' one of those songs, and it just slapped me up against the back wall. . . . I'd never heard anybody that good, playing [guitar] tunings like that. I didn't know anybody who could write songs that well or sing like that and I immediately had a crush on her as well."

Mitchell's path to Coconut Grove began in rural Canada, where Roberta Joan Anderson was born to a schoolteacher mother and a Royal Canadian Air Force lieutenant. She contracted polio at the age of nine and taught herself guitar by studying a Pete Seeger songbook; the lingering effects of her illness encouraged her to employ alternate tunings. Leaving college, where

JONI MITCHELL

she studied art, Anderson played music in Toronto and met another Canadian musician, Neil Young. After Mitchell played "Both Sides Now" for Young, he offered his coming-of-age tune, "Sugar Mountain," which inspired her to write "The Circle Game." She met and married folk singer Chuck Mitchell; they lived in Detroit and played coffeehouses. Tom Rush, a folk singer from Cambridge, Massachusetts, crashed on their couch and left with a song for his next album, Joni's "Urge for Going."

The marriage ended in early 1967 and Mitchell moved to New York, where she played some of her songs for Al Kooper. "One song especially killed me," said Kooper, "'Michael from Mountains.' I thought it would be great for Judy Collins." Collins liked the song and helped get Mitchell and another Canadian singer-songwriter, Leonard Cohen, slots at the 1967 Newport Folk Festival. Collins then recorded two of Mitchell's songs ("Michael from Mountains" and "Both Sides Now") and a pair of Cohen's ("Sisters of Mercy" and "Hey, That's No Way to Say Goodbye") on her album *Wildflowers*.

At the Café Au Go Go in Greenwich Village Mitchell met Elliot Roberts, an agent at the William Morris Agency. "I went up to her after the show," said Roberts, "and said, 'I'm a young manager and I'd kill to work with you.' She said she was going on tour, and if I wanted to pay my own expenses, I could go with her." Roberts quit his job; a month later, Mitchell asked him to be her manager. Meanwhile, Rush contacted Mitchell looking for more songs. She sent a tape that included "The Circle Game," writing in an accompanying note, "It sucks and you're going to hate it."

Rush titled his album *The Circle Game* and included a third Mitchell song, "Tin Angel," alongside original compositions from two other little-known singer-songwriters, James Taylor ("Something in the Way She Moves" and "Sunshine Sunshine") and Jackson Browne ("Shadow Dream Song"). Browne had a publishing deal with Elektra and had made demos of thirty songs, including "These Days" and "Jamaica, Say You Will." Taylor had met Rush at Elektra's New York office and pitched his songs in person. All told, the two albums by Collins and Rush introduced four singer-songwriters who would become stars in the 1970s and collectively influence generations of Americana musicians.

This new crop of songwriters wrote from personal experience and was as strongly influenced by contemporary music as by traditional folk songs. But to varying degrees Bob Dylan touched them all. "When I heard 'Positively 4th Street,'" said Mitchell, "I realized that this was a whole new ballgame;

now you could make your songs literature." "I heard Bob Dylan," said Cohen, "listened to him carefully, and thought 'He has already done it.' It was exactly what I wanted to do: write as well and simply as possible and lay it at the feet of the people." "He turned the world on its ear and opened the door for a lot of us," said Taylor. "He and the Beatles were the biggest influences on my lyrics." When asked how he went from writing a rock 'n' roll song like "Hey Schoolgirl" to "The Sounds of Silence," Paul Simon said, "I really can't imagine it could have been anyone else besides Bob Dylan."

Mitchell played three sold-out shows at the Troubadour in Los Angeles and was quickly signed to Reprise with Crosby to produce her first album. "He was going to protect the music and pretend to produce me," said Mitchell; the strategy was to record Mitchell as a solo artist and eschew typical folk-rock arrangements. Mitchell would make more musically adventurous albums than *Song to a Seagull* (1968), but the collection firmly established her status as a singular singer-songwriter.

Mitchell moved into a house in Laurel Canyon, a neighborhood in the Hollywood Hills that was thick with songwriters and musicians. Cass Elliot of the Mamas and the Papas was the scene's social director. "She was very important not only as an individual artist and a great singer," said Jackson Browne, who'd played with the Nitty Gritty Dirt Band as a teenager and then recorded with Nico of the Velvet Underground, "but also for knowing . . . who should be working with or singing with whom." Elliot played musical matchmaker for Crosby and his friend Stephen Stills. "David and I were messing around," said Stills, "and she came up to me and says, 'Do you think you need a third voice?' And I said, 'Yeah.' She said, 'OK, don't say anything, especially to Crosby." The third voice belonged to Graham Nash, a member of the British pop group the Hollies, who declined to record his new songs, including "Marrakesh Express." Crosby, Stills & Nash became a folk-rock supergroup, and Nash and Mitchell soon shared a very fine house with two cats in the yard.

Jerry Lee Lewis looked out at the audience from a Los Angeles stage. "Oh, beware, my lord, of jealousy," said the Killer. "It is the green eyed monster which doth mock." Jerry Lee was playing Iago in a rock 'n' roll adaption of Shakespeare's *Othello* called *Catch My Soul*. "I never worked so hard in my life," said Lewis of his unlikely side project. "I mean two hours and forty-five minutes running up and down stairs—it was a mess." During the play's six-week run, Lewis was surprised to see that a song he'd reluctantly cut in Nashville, "Another Time, Another Place," had risen to #4 on the country charts.

In an astonishing turn of events, rock 'n' roll's bad boy became a major country star, with seventeen Top 10 country hits between 1968 and 1977, including four chart toppers. Compared to most of the competition in that genre, Lewis's records had a stripped-down sound and featured a voice that was as distinctive as those of George Jones and Merle Haggard. Jerry Lee still punctuated his songs with piano glissandos and never stopped performing his rock 'n' roll hits in concert, but he caught a second wind by focusing on the country side of the musical hybrid that he and Elvis had created at Sun Records.

Lewis's country hits were largely unknown to rock fans because there was little crossover from the country to the pop charts. Glen Campbell was a notable exception, hitting first with "Gentle on My Mind" by folk musician John Hartford, who was a regular on *The Smothers Brothers Comedy Hour*. But it was the more pop-oriented Jimmy Webb who wrote Campbell's biggest hits ("By the Time I Get to Phoenix," "Wichita Lineman," "Galveston"); Webb also penned pop hits for the Fifth Dimension ("Up, Up, and Away") and Richard Harris ("MacArthur Park"). More often than not, however, country and rock fans had little in common.

In 1968 one artist bridged that gap: Elvis Presley. With Presley's movie and soundtrack career running out of gas, Colonel Parker arranged for him to star in a Christmas television special. Parker imagined a show filled with seasonal carols, but producer Steve Binder had a different idea after seeing Presley casually jamming in his dressing room. By show time, Binder had convinced Presley to play before a studio audience with a small band that included his original guitarist (Scotty Moore) and drummer (D. J. Fontana). Dressed in a tight black leather suit, Presley seemed to rediscover his own legend as he played a set that included "That's All Right," "Jailhouse Rock," and "Don't Be Cruel."

"We didn't rehearse it," said Binder of the onstage jam session. "The beauty of it for me was that . . . he forgot he was doing a show with Scotty and Bill, and they were just playing again." The performance on what came to be called the "Comeback Special" inspired Presley to record new material in Memphis, and he returned to the pop charts with "In the Ghetto," "Suspicious Minds," and "Burning Love." The next year, Presley was booked to perform fifty-seven shows at the International Hotel in Las Vegas. That's when James Burton got an unexpected phone call. Burton told his wife to take a message, but she said this might be important. He chatted briefly with a member of Presley's entourage before Elvis got on the phone to say that he used to watch *The Ozzie and Harriet Show* to see Burton play guitar. "We talked for two hours," said Burton, who had turned down the offer to tour with Bob Dylan but took the job of Presley's bandleader.

George Jones had hits throughout the 1960s, but one of pop music's great vocalists was all but unknown beyond the country audience. Jones had hit duets with Melba Montgomery, starting with "We Must Have Been out of Our Minds," and solo hits such as "The Race Is On" and "A Good Year for the Roses." But washing down amphetamines with booze had become a drag on his career. During one multiday bender his first wife Shirley hid the car keys. "It might have taken an hour and half or more for me to get to the liquor store," said Jones of riding his lawnmower into town, "but get there I did."

One night Jones went to dinner at the house of a couple who had opened his shows, Don Chepel and his wife Tammy Wynette. Jones had drinks while the contentious couple prepared dinner, and he lost his temper when Chepel cursed out his wife. Chepel asked what business it was of his. "Because I love her," said Jones, "and she's in love with me, aren't ya, Tammy?" Tammy nodded and took her three children to a hotel. Jones soon had a new wife and duet partner; they shared a tour bus with the inscription "Mr. and Mrs. Country Music."

Newcomers to Nashville struggled to be heard. "When I came to Nashville," said Kris Kristofferson, "the people I hung out with were serious songwriters, none of whom were successful. Willie was the hero of the soulful set—the people who were in the business because they loved the soul of country music." While working as a janitor at Columbia studios, Kristofferson slipped a tape of his songs to June Carter Cash that got lost in a pile of her husband's ignored demos. When the former army captain took a job as a commercial helicopter pilot in southern Louisiana, he wrote "Help Me Make It Through the Night" while perched atop an oil platform in the Gulf of Mexico. Kristofferson tried once more to pitch his music to Cash, this time by landing a helicopter outside his home in Henderson, but the touring country star missed his aerial ballet. Finally, in 1969, after Kristofferson had tunes recorded by Ray Stevens and Jerry Lee Lewis, Cash cut his "Sunday Mornin' Comin' Down," which became a #1 country hit and was named the song of the year by the Country Music Association.

It turns out that Cash might have missed the helicopter in his yard even if he had been at home. "I was always sick," he said, "and Maybelle [Carter] was always trying to take care of me. She saw me at my very worst and never pointed it out to me except to say loving things like 'I hope you'll take care of yourself because we really need you.'" Maybelle and June would scour the house for pills. In October 1967 Cash was again arrested for drug possession; then, after driving a tractor into the lake on his property, he crawled into a cave to die. Instead, he emerged to go cold turkey in a locked bedroom; June, Maybelle, and Eck surrounded his bed and prayed. They kept him fed and heard him ransacking the room looking for pills. After nearly a month of nightmares and stomach cramps Cash emerged, and if he was not exactly a new man, there was a spring in his step. Within months, he recorded a hit live album, *At San Quentin*, and proposed to June while onstage in London, Ontario. They were married in 1968.

As for Kristofferson, with his literary airs and bohemian instincts, one could imagine him hanging with the hipsters in Laurel Canyon. But few in Hollywood knew of "Me and Bobby McGee" when Roger Miller recorded the song in 1969. Bob Neuwirth, a pal of Dylan's, heard the tune sung by Gordon Lightfoot at the office of his manager, Albert Grossman. "That very night, I was having dinner with Janis [Joplin]," said Neuwirth. "I went down and picked her up, and while she and her girlfriend were getting ready, I played the song on her guitar. She goes, 'What is that song, man? Teach it to me!' So I did." Kris and Janis later had an affair. It was brief, but they are forever bound by her reading of his song. Joplin died of a drug overdose in October 1970; "Me and Bobby McGee" was her only #1 hit.

Willie Nelson, a songwriter with a decade of experience and a catalog of albums on RCA, continued to search for his singular voice. He cut tunes by Kristofferson and James Taylor ("Fire and Rain") alongside his own songs and tunes by Hank Williams and Merle Haggard. Then Nelson found a valuable partner when he broke the neck of his electric guitar and bought a rosewood Martin acoustic that his guitar tech outfitted with the electronics of his old instrument. He named his new nylon-stringed guitar Trigger after Roy Rogers's trusty palomino. "I had the sound I'd been looking for," said Nelson. "I heard it as a human sound, a sound close to my own voice. Didn't take long for me to pick a hole in it. That's 'cause classical guitars aren't meant to be picked. But that hole, along with the aluminum amp—aged by just the right amount of beer that'd been spilled inside—seemed to deepen its soulful tone." Nelson was at a Nashville Christmas party in 1969 when he learned that his house was on fire. By the time he got home, volunteer firefighters were dousing the flames, and they cried out in alarm when Nelson ran into the burning building to retrieve two totems that would define his future: Trigger and a trash bag filled with primo Columbian pot.

What exactly happened that July morning in 1966 when Bob Dylan tumbled off his Triumph motorcycle? Questions remain. Sara Dylan was following in a car to bring her husband home after leaving his bike at the repair shop, but instead of calling an ambulance for transport to a hospital in nearby Kingston, she drove her husband to the home of Doctor Ed Thaler in Middletown, more than an hour away. Dylan was subsequently seen with a neck brace, but his convalescence at Thaler's home led many to believe that he was really in recovery from his drug-fueled twenty-four-hour days. "The turning point was back in Woodstock," said Dylan. "A little after the accident. Sitting around one night under a full moon I looked out into the bleak woods and said, 'Something's gotta change.'"

That had already happened. Dylan was now a father, and he and Sara were raising their family in an Arts and Crafts house called Hi-Lo-Ha on the edge of the Byrdcliffe Arts Colony in Woodstock, New York. His tour plans were thwarted by his recuperation, though by early 1967 he was once more working on *Eat the Document*, a willfully incomprehensible film that was ultimately rejected by ABC. "Tarantula," an opaque prose poem, was published to critical disregard in 1971. The twin failures suggested that Dylan was not working in his artistic wheelhouse. Still, while secluded from the outside world, 1967 turned out to be one of the most productive years of Dylan's musical life.

Robbie Robertson, who like the other Hawks was still on retainer, came to Woodstock to work on *Eat the Document*. Rick Danko, Richard Manuel, and Garth Hudson soon followed and moved into a secluded, nondescript house in nearby West Saugerties that was painted pink. The bachelors shared chores, with Manuel cooking, Hudson doing the dishes, and Danko responsible for taking out the trash and keeping logs on the fire. Robertson and his wife-to-be, Dominique Bourgeois, had already settled into a cabin on the grounds of Albert Grossman's home. Dubbed "The Duke" by Ronnie Hawkins, Robertson was the musician closest to Dylan; he also bonded with Grossman, who taught him about the business of music.

Before long, the band started having informal musical sessions with their boss, first in the so-called Red Room of Dylan's home and then in the basement of the house that came to be called Big Pink. Dylan began by surveying his past via a wide variety of folk, country, and blues songs. "With the covers Bob was educating us a little," said Robertson. "The whole folkie thing was still very questionable to us—it wasn't the train we came in on. He'd be doing this Pete Seeger stuff and I'd be saying, 'Oh God. . . . ' And then . . . he'd come up with something like 'Banks of the Royal Canal,' and you'd say, 'This is so beautiful!'" After a world tour that was a high-decibel firestorm, playing this music was a far more intimate exercise. "[He'd] pull out some old song," said Robertson, "and he'd prepped for this. He'd practiced this, and then . . . [he'd] show us."

Dylan's students were attentive, and by the time the sessions moved to Big Pink, Hudson had cobbled together a studio in the basement. Dylan would arrive in the late morning, put up a pot of coffee, and sit down at a typewriter to knock out whatever came into his caffeinated head. The others assembled by noon and descended to the basement to bang out a loose-limbed take of Johnny Cash's "I Walk the Line" or maybe one of his obscure Sun tracks like "Belshazzar." Casual fun sometimes led to new compositions. "Bob would be running through an old song," said Robertson, "and he'd say, 'Maybe there's a new song to be had here.'"

The songs Dylan played in the basement suggested a latter-day version of Harry Smith's *Anthology of American Folk Music*. They included an old blues ("Goin' Down the Road"), another that he'd done on his debut album ("See That My Grave Is Kept Clean"), and songs by Hank Williams ("My Bucket's Got a Hole in It"), John Lee Hooker ("I'm in the Mood"), Bobby Charles ("See You Later, Alligator" rendered as "See You Later, Allen Ginsberg"), the Carter Family ("Wildwood Flower"), Ian Tyson ("Four Strong Winds"), Eric Von Schmidt ("Joshua Gone Barbados"), and Elvis Presley ("I Forgot to Remember to Forget"). Some of the takes were rickety, others spot-on; all were imbued with wit and a sense of fun. Many were recorded without drums; others found Manuel or Robertson behind the kit. Hudson operated a tape recorder set within easy reach of his keyboards.

"We played in a circle," said Robertson, "like mountain musicians sittin' where they can hear each other, someone singing lead and someone singing a harmony, maybe, and you would just play at that volume." If the instruments got too loud, everybody turned the volume down. The atmosphere was key. "You know," Dylan said, "that's really the way to do a recording—in a peaceful, relaxed setting, in somebody's basement, with the windows open and a dog lying on the floor." The dog in question was Hamlet, who had proved too unruly for the Dylan household and moved to Big Pink to live with Danko.

New songs soon began to tumble out of Dylan's typewriter. "It amazed me," said Hudson, "how he could come in, sit down at the typewriter, and write a song." He gave some lyrics to Richard Manuel, who put music to "Tears of Rage," and to Rick Danko, who co-wrote "This Wheel's on Fire." Dylan wrote all of "I Shall Be Released," and all three of these songs would be on *Music from Big Pink*, an album by the boys in the band that was recorded after Levon Helm rejoined his old group in Woodstock. Robertson couldn't help but be impressed by Dylan's songwriting. "Bob just made me think I could write these stories and not feel like every song I was writing was 'Once upon a time,'" said Robertson. "I'd have songs that I thought would only work if Jimmie Rodgers sang them, songs I'd be embarrassed to play to people. Bob broke down a barrier, and I wasn't embarrassed after that."

The original songs Dylan recorded in the basement included at least an album's worth of superior material that would have provided a stark contrast to the most influential album of 1967, the Beatles' *Sgt. Pepper's Lonely Hearts Club Band*. One can only imagine the impact if Dylan had done properly produced studio recordings of "I Shall Be Released," his two new co-writes, and "You Ain't Going Nowhere," "Too Much of Nothing," "Quinn the Eskimo (The Mighty Quinn)," "Nothing Was Delivered," and "Crash on the Levee (Down in the Flood)." And that doesn't include more prosaic tunes prized by Dylan aficionados such as "Goin' to Acapulco" and "Sign of the Cross," a consideration of Christianity that included a recitation that Hank Williams might have cut as Luke the Drifter. Dylan wasn't oblivious to the outside world. "It was the Summer of Love," said Dylan, "so we did our thing and wrote 'Million Dollar Bash.'" He also composed "Clothes Line Saga" in response to a big hit of the day, Bobbie Gentry's "Ode to Billy Joe."

Grossman kept tabs on the sessions and had sixteen Dylan songs copyrighted in hopes of generating lucrative cover versions. The object was to create "mailbox money," which is to say revenue for Dwarf Music, the new publishing company that Grossman had established for Dylan. (It wouldn't take long for the songwriter to learn that Grossman owned 50 percent of Dwarf.) Dylan had spent the summer writing new songs that reflected his roots in folk, blues, country, and rock. He'd also inadvertently pointed to the future. “Listening back to the Basement Tapes now,” said British folksinger Billy Bragg, “it seems to be the beginning of what is called ‘Americana.’”

The songs were circulated to the usual suspects, with Peter, Paul, and Mary releasing “Too Much of Nothing,” and another of Grossman’s clients, the duo Ian and Sylvia, recording three songs (including “Tears of Rage”). The Byrds released a single of “You Ain’t Going Nowhere” in April 1968, months before it was included (along with “Nothing Was Delivered”) on their country-rock album *Sweetheart of the Rodeo*. The tapes also circulated in London, with Manfred Mann making “The Mighty Quinn” into a worldwide pop hit and Brian Auger and the Trinity with Julie Driscoll reaching #5 on the U.K. charts with “This Wheel’s on Fire.” Fairport Convention, England’s premiere folk-rock group, which included Richard Thompson and Sandy Denny, crowded into the office of Dylan’s U.K. representative to hear all the songs before choosing to record “Million Dollar Bash.”

Joe Boyd, who’d worked behind the scenes at Newport the night Dylan went electric, was now living in London and producing Fairport Convention. “There was something fascinating and intimidating about the relentless confidence of Dylan at that time,” said Boyd. “Those guys . . . sat up there in Woodstock and they felt no necessity to broadcast it. There was a feeling that you could be as cool as you want at the Scotch of St. James or in Laurel Canyon or Greenwich Village, but up here in Woodstock, in this basement room, we are doing shit we know is the best.”

But in late 1967 the biggest surprise was that Dylan also recorded an album of songs that got nowhere near the basement of Big Pink. Some speculate that it was the death of Woody Guthrie on October 3 that inspired Dylan’s new collection. “Every artist in the world was in the studio trying to make the biggest-sounding record they possibly could,” said producer Bob Johnston, referencing the influence of *Sgt. Pepper’s*. “So what does [Dylan] do? He comes to Nashville and tells me he wants to record with a bass, drum and guitar.” The *Blonde on Blonde* rhythm section of Charlie McCoy on bass and Ken Buttrey on drums was booked, and Dylan arrived with three polished songs: “The Drifter’s Escape,” “I Dreamed I Saw St. Augustine,” and “Ballad of Frankie Lee and Judas Priest.” “The songs were written out on paper,” said Dylan, “and I found the tunes for them later. I didn’t do it [that way] before, and I haven’t done it since.” Johnston, McCoy, and Buttrey were stunned that Dylan got three final takes in one three-hour session.

Just two more sessions were required to complete *John Wesley Harding*, one of Dylan’s most stylistically coherent collections of songs. His language was pared to the bone and filled with biblical allusions; Ben Cartwright's *Bible in the Lyrics of Bob Dylan* cites more than sixty biblical references in the thirty-eight-minute album. Yet songs such as "All Along the Watchtower" and "Dear Landlord" were as elegantly plainspoken as something by Hank Williams. The last session tipped toward country rock with Pete Drake contributing pedal steel guitar to "Down Along the Cove" and "I'll Be Your Baby Tonight." But the album was hardly standard Nashville fare. "Some of it is country," said Johnston. "Some of it is like the '29 dust-bowl days of Woody Guthrie."

Dylan originally thought that Robertson and Hudson would add some overdubs to the recording, but back in Woodstock, everybody agreed that there was poetry in the album's simplicity. If the basement sessions had prepared Dylan for this artistic sprint—*John Wesley Harding* was released in late December—it had also transformed the Hawks from a hard-edged bar band to an ensemble thick with voices and instrumental textures. While Dylan was at work in Nashville, Grossman had the group cut some demos. When the results failed to win over Columbia Records, Grossman hired John Simon, who'd recently produced Simon and Garfunkel and Leonard Cohen, to work with the group.

"I realized quickly that these guys were different from other artists I worked with," said Simon, "and that they had a deep respect, bordering on reverence, for the roots of American music." They also had three distinctive lead voices—Helm's southern twang, Manuel's soulful moan, and Danko's country honk—that could blend into a unique harmonic union, with Manuel on top, Danko in the middle, and Helm down below. The instrumental work was equally seamless, with Robertson contributing subtle rhythms and spiky guitar solos and Hudson adding rich keyboard accompaniment. At the dawn of 1968 Simon took the group into a Manhattan studio.

"The guys were accustomed to playing in close proximity to each other in the basement," said Simon. "So we put the baffles away and re-grouped 'in the open.' Besides, they didn't need the protection of separation, in which, if someone made a mistake, that mistake wouldn't 'bleed' into the other microphones. They didn't make mistakes." In two sessions the quintet recorded "Tears of Rage," "We Can Talk About It Now," "Chest Fever," "This Wheel's on Fire," and "The Weight." Capitol Records loved the music but wouldn't let the group call itself The Crackers, an epithet used to refer to poor white southerners. So they took the name that everybody called them in Woodstock: The Band.

8
SWEETHEART OF THE RODEO

Chris Hillman of the Byrds met Gram Parsons of the International Submarine Band in line at a Beverly Hills bank. The Byrds had fired David Crosby, and Roger McGuinn wanted to add keyboards and make a concept album about the history of American music. "I asked Gram if he could play some McCoy Tyner type of piano," said McGuinn, "because I was into John Coltrane." Parsons played some rudimentary rock 'n' roll piano and won the gig when he picked up the guitar.

"He started singing a Buck Owens song, 'Under Your Spell Again,'" said Hillman, "and I immediately started singing harmony with him on it. I thought, 'Oh my God, he knows who Buck Owens is! . . . I used to write little songs for the band in that vein, but the rest of the band always shouted me down. Then Gram joined and I had an ally." Instead of becoming a profit-sharing "official" Byrd, Parsons was put on salary; he didn't care because he was already living large on the payments from a trust fund. Hillman and Parsons then convinced McGuinn to have the Byrds make a country record in Nashville. To get in the mood, McGuinn bought a Nudie suit and listened to country radio in his Cadillac.

Parsons was born to a wealthy southern gothic of a family. His father was a World War II pilot; the fortune came from his mother's father, a citrus mogul who owned large tracts of real estate. His father committed suicide on Christmas Day when Parsons was twelve; his alcoholic mother, who remarried, died of cirrhosis on the day he graduated from high school. Parsons saw Elvis Presley at the age of ten and played in a teenage rock band at the Derry Down, a club owned by his stepfather. Parsons sang folk music with the Shilohs and spent the summer of 1965 playing coffeehouses in Greenwich Village and meeting Dave Van Ronk, Fred Neil, and Stephen Stills. Matriculating at Harvard University, he skipped classes and listened to Merle Haggard, George Jones, and the Louvin Brothers. The International Submarine Band lived together in the Bronx before relocating to Los Angeles.

They opened for such local stars as the Doors and Love and recorded an album called *Safe at Home* for a label run by Lee Hazelwood, who'd hit it big with Nancy Sinatra's "These Boots Are Made for Walking." But before *Safe at Home* was released, Parsons and the Byrds went to Nashville to record *Sweetheart of the Rodeo*, a collection that amounted to an Americana hit parade. It included two selections from Dylan's basement tapes ("You Ain't Goin' Nowhere" and "Nothing Was Delivered") and songs written by or associated with Merle Travis ("I Am a Pilgrim"), George Jones ("You're Still on My Mind"), Woody Guthrie ("Pretty Boy Floyd"), Gene Autry ("Blue Canadian Rockies"), Merle Haggard ("Life in Prison"), the Louvin Brothers ("The Christian Life"), and William Bell ("You Don't Miss Your Water"). (Bell, who co-wrote the Albert King blues classic "Born Under a Bad Sign," won the Americana Grammy for his 2016 album *This Is Where I Live*.) The record also included two of Parsons' finest original songs, "Hickory Wind" and "One Hundred Years from Now."

When the Byrds were in Nashville, Columbia pulled strings to get them booked on the *Grand Ole Opry*; for the occasion, the group got haircuts and McGuinn went without his trademark granny glasses. Still, when the Byrds played a recent Merle Haggard hit, "Sing Me Back Home," the audience reacted as if they were setting fire to draft cards. "I wanted to crawl off the stage," said Lloyd Green, who played pedal steel on *Sweetheart* and accompanied the Byrds on country's sacred stage. "I didn't believe they'd get such rude, redneck treatment." Matters got worse when Parsons, during the live broadcast, scuttled a second planned Haggard song to play his own "Hickory Wind." *Opry* officials were not amused.

Back in Los Angeles the Byrds completed *Sweetheart* with sidemen more accustomed to cutting country records. "[When recording] with Buck Owens we had to get at least three songs done in our three-hour period," said pianist Earl Ball. "Then I'd go over and record with the Byrds, where if you got one song all night you were doing good. And Don Rich [Buck's guitarist and arranger] was insistent about everybody being in tune, and everybody having the intros together. . . . I'd get over to the Byrds and the first thing they'd do was get high and try to tune their guitars." Pedal steel player Jay Dee Maness noted, "I learned something important from that record. That steel guitar can fit into any kind of music." Pete Drake learned the same thing when George Harrison flew him to London to play pedal steel on *All Things Must Pass*.

Lee Hazelwood, meanwhile, threatened to sue Columbia because he still had Parsons under contract. (When the International Submarine Band's LP was finally released, it sank without a trace.) Here the truth gets murky. Some say that McGuinn and Parsons both recorded lead vocals for some selections with an eye toward picking the best. Others say that McGuinn replaced Parsons's lead vocals because of the legal imbroglio and that the settlement came in time to retain three of them, including "Hickory Wind." There's another interpretation. "McGuinn was reluctant to have Gram sing an entire Byrds album when he was the newest member of the group," said producer Gary Usher. "The album had just the exact amount of Gram Parsons on it that McGuinn, Hillman, and myself wanted."

The Byrds flew to the United Kingdom for a concert at the Royal Albert Hall before a planned tour of South Africa. The after-show party was especially memorable when Mick Jagger and Keith Richards proposed driving to Stonehenge to watch the sun come up. "Wandering around out there in the dark with the Stones was like a Middle Earth fantasy trip," said Chris Hillman, "except that Gram was so enamored with Mick and Keith that he was behaving like a schoolgirl with a crush on the teacher." The Stones told Parsons that it was wrong to play South Africa because of racial apartheid. But something more than politics might have prompted Parsons to miss the flight to Johannesburg. Carlos Bernall, the band's road manager, who ended up substituting for Parsons on guitar, said the reason was that "he couldn't have things exactly how he wanted. . . . He wanted a steel guitar on a lot of his tunes and things that the band wasn't prepared to jump into overnight." Parsons stayed in England with his new best friend, Keith Richards.

GRAM PARSONS

"He taught me the mechanics of country music," said Richards, "the Nashville style as opposed to the Bakersfield style. . . . He started to turn me on to certain classic tracks and [a] certain style of playing things—George Jones, Merle Haggard, Jimmie Rodgers." Parsons also showed Richards "Nashville" tuning, in which the lower four strings of the guitar (low E through G) are replaced with strings that are tuned an octave above standard tuning. At about this time Richards also soaked up valuable expertise from guitarist Ry Cooder, who played sessions with the Rolling Stones, adding a slide guitar solo to "Sister Morphine" and mandolin to the band's version of Robert Johnson's "Love in Vain." It was Cooder who introduced Richards to the open-G guitar tuning that he used on such songs as "Honky Tonk Women" and "Brown Sugar." In the early 1970s Cooder made albums like *Into the Purple Valley* and *Paradise and Lunch* that were infused with American roots music. In the late 1990s Cooder played on and helped promote *The Buena Vista Social Club*, an internationally successful album that introduced a venerable ensemble of Cuban musicians."

McGuinn fired Parsons from the Byrds before the release of *Sweetheart of the Rodeo*, which, selling fewer than fifty thousand copies, was the group's least successful album. His replacement was Clarence White, the guitar virtuoso who'd already played on the group's albums. "Clarence White's brother, Roland, got me my first job with Lester Flatt's band," said Marty Stuart, who joined the group as its mandolin player in 1972, when he was fourteen. "For a while, I lived with Roland and his family, and in his house he had a stack of Byrds records. I said, 'What's that about?' and he said, 'My brother Clarence recorded with the Byrds.'"

"I remember buying *Sweetheart of the Rodeo* in 1973," continued Stuart. "It was already in the discount bin. I was blown away, because it was the first time I had heard folk and gospel and bluegrass and rock 'n' roll and country come together in one place." *Sweetheart* similarly moved Gillian Welch, who bought the album while in college in the late 1980s. "It was my gateway record," said Welch, a singer-songwriter who would become a star of Americana. "It's like the spokes of a wheel and, in many respects, my record collection radiates out from this record."

On January 20, 1968, The Band backed Bob Dylan at the Woody Guthrie Memorial Concert at Carnegie Hall, but this wasn't the thunderous ensemble that had stunned folk fans. Rather, it was a performance born in the basement of Big Pink, with tangy vocal harmonies, atmospheric keyboards, and the occasional cry of an electric guitar. Dylan sang three Guthrie tunes on a program that also featured Pete Seeger and Judy Collins; it was his first public appearance since being secluded in Woodstock. Coming just weeks after the release of *John Wesley Harding*, the performance served to introduce both the country-dad Dylan and a group about to complete its debut album.

The Band and producer John Simon traveled to Los Angeles to record at Capitol's Los Angeles studio. "I wanted to discover the sound of The Band," said Robertson. "So I thought, 'I'm gonna do this record and I'm not gonna play a guitar solo on the whole record. I'm only going to play riffs, Curtis Mayfield kind of riffs. I wanted the drums to have their own character. I wanted the piano not to sound like a big Yamaha grand. I wanted it to sound like an upright piano." As for the vocals, said Robertson, "I didn't want screaming vocals. I wanted sensitive vocals where you can hear the breathing.... I like voices coming in one at a time, in a chain reaction kind of like the Staple Singers did."

That kind of sound required an attention to detail, a specialty of Garth Hudson, who Simon said was "many levels above the organists and pianists in other rock groups." Hudson introduced "Chest Fever" with a solo sprung from Bach's Toccata and Fugue in D minor; on "The Weight," he fed his Rock-Si-Chord electric keyboard through a wah-wah pedal to make the sound rise and fall within the vocal harmonies. Hudson used a telegraph key to add a playfully percussive element to "This Wheel's on Fire." Meanwhile, at Robertson's suggestion, Helm tuned his drums to accentuate the deep, woozy meter of "Tears of Rage." "You make the drum notes bend down in pitch," said Helm, noting that Ringo Starr used the same technique. "You hit it, it sounds, and then it hums as the note dies out. If the ensemble is right, you can hear the sustain like a bell, and it's very emotional. It can keep a slow song suspended in an interesting way."

And then there was the material. "Robbie had obviously learned a lot from being in such close proximity to Bob," said Simon, "particularly in the story songs and the freewheeling imagery." Musically, however, Robertson drew from a wider menu of styles and chords. Simon said that the group's three voices "gave Robbie as a songwriter a rich vocal palette to utilize. His use of the guys' individual distinctive vocal qualities reminds me of Duke Ellington's use of the special colors of his horn soloists." Those different hues are clearly evident on "The Weight." "The characters that appear in the lyric—Luke, Anna Lee, Crazy Chester—were all people we knew," recalled Helm. "The music was the sum of all the experiences we'd shared for the past ten years, distilled through the quieter vibe of our lives in the country." And the vocals reflect that history, with Helm and Danko singing individual verses and Manuel joining them on the chorus.

Manuel took the majority of lead vocals, including soulful turns on his own "Lonesome Susie" and the song he wrote with Dylan, "Tears of Rage," a grief-stricken ballad that was a willfully offbeat choice to open *Music from Big Pink*. "They were seasoned veterans whose debut album sounded more like a band in its prime," said Simon. "The songs were more like buried treasure from American lore than new songs by contemporary artists. The reason for this is they were playing out of what I call their 'Appalachian scale,' a pentatonic, five-note scale like the black keys on the piano. That was the palette from which those melodies came."

The album contained one cover song, "Long Black Veil," a country ballad by Danny Dill and Marijohn Wilkin that sounded as old as the hills but was actually a country hit for Lefty Frizzell in 1959. Robertson said that country music wasn't in the mix during their days with Ronnie Hawkins. "When we were up in Woodstock," he said, "something happened. . . . All of a sudden this bluegrass music, this mountain music became something that we would do in our living room. We would do it with guitar, mandolin, and Rick sometimes would play acoustic bass. It was a nice setup and Richard would just sing and maybe play along on a tambourine and Garth would sometimes play accordion. Then, that actual setup of instrumentation kind of entered into what we were doing on other kinds of things that weren't necessarily even mountain music."

Music from Big Pink, released on July 1, 1968, was as different from the music of the day as moonshine at a pot party. Al Kooper gave it a rave review in *Rolling Stone* that concluded, "There are people who will work their lives away in vain and not touch it." *Time* magazine put The Band on its cover with the headline, "The New Sound of Country Rock." Eric Clapton travelled to Woodstock to meet the musicians, dreamed of joining the group, and then broke up his popular blues-rock power trio, Cream. "These guys were the real thing," said Clapton, "and I was touring with this band of psychedelic loonies."

Dylan first heard *Big Pink* at a listening party in Albert Grossman's living room. "When 'The Weight' came on," said Robertson, "he said, 'This is fantastic. Who wrote that song? That was so good. You did it man, you did it.'" Dylan, who'd taken up painting, had already given his friends a naïve image for the album's cover that depicted not five but six musicians plus a pachyderm. Some consider the sixth musician to be Dylan in that he had a hand in three of its songs, but I choose to think that it's the producer of the recording, John Simon, and that Dylan is actually the elephant in the room. (Dylan and Grossman's Dwarf Music published all the songs on *Big Pink*.)

The Band kept a low profile in Woodstock while *Music from Big Pink* made waves among rock 'n' roll tastemakers. There were no plans for the group to tour, but that didn't stop promoters from offering increasingly larger paydays. But there would be no shows. First, Helm and Manuel were involved in a multivehicle accident that involved a Woodstock police car. Then Manuel burned his foot firing up a barbecue grill using gasoline, and Danko broke his neck in another car accident. In the meantime, Hudson kept to himself, and Robertson took care of business.

"He alone of them was organized enough to present this mountain lion energy they all had," said Libby Titus, who grew up in Woodstock and was at the center of the town's social scene. "He knew how to call it in and turn it into art that could be put on record. He suffered later for this quality, but I saw him as a great young man." Titus also noted that Dylan and his musical pals had attracted "charming and attractive vultures" to Woodstock. "As The Band was trying to continue their career," she said, "a major heroin scene began to surround the picture. They were very dangerous times for all of us."

Gram Parsons wasted little time after being fired from the Byrds and enlisted bass player Chris Ethridge by telephone from the United Kingdom. Back in Los Angeles, he approached Richie Furay, who had played with Buffalo Springfield and who invited Parsons to a rehearsal of a new country-rock band he was forming with Jim Messina called Poco. Meanwhile, Chris Hillman quit the Byrds after discovering that fiscal mismanagement had left the group with only $20,000. Hillman and Parsons were soon sharing a house in the San Fernando Valley and putting together a band of their own; they tried but failed to poach Clarence White from the Byrds.

At night the pair hit the local clubs, where they were excited to discover the gospel-tinged rock and soul being played by Delaney and Bonnie (Bramlett) with such friends as guitarist J. J. Cale and pianist Leon Russell. "[Gram] had this sort of 'wasted boy in Hollywood' charisma about him," said singer-songwriter Tom Russell. "He had a real soulful voice, and he'd done his homework. He could do Louvin Brothers songs, or Hank Williams . . . all day long. Gram used to go out to cowboy country bars in Encino in his cape and long hair and almost get killed until he'd sing a George Jones song. And he'd do the same in hippie bars."

Parsons already had a name for the new band, the Flying Burrito Brothers, and Hillman's history with the Byrds helped secure a deal with A&M. Parsons encouraged his mates (who in addition to Ethridge included pedal steel player "Sneaky" Pete Kleinow) to splurge on specially designed Nudie suits. Hillman decorated his with a burning yellow sun, while Parsons designed a head-turner that depicted pills, marijuana leaves, pinup girls, and a throbbing red cross. (The suit is now on display at the Country Music Hall of Fame.) Parsons and Hillman kept busy writing songs in the bachelor pad they dubbed Burrito Manor.

"We drove to a modern cowboy's ranch with wagon wheels paving the driveway," said Mercy Peters, who was accompanied by Pamela Des Barres. Both women were members of Frank Zappa's tongue-in-cheek girl group, the GTOs (Girls Together Outrageously). "We entered the house and shy Chris Hillman and the cat in the Nudie suit greeted us with a grocery bag full of grass, and Gram was so down-home dazzling with sensuous southern hospitality, it just slayed me. These are the first words I recall him speaking to me: As he leaned over his pile of records, and put on an old George Jones album, a tear fell from his eye, and he [said], 'This is George Jones, the king of broken hearts.'"

Parsons's writing sessions with Hillman produced an enduring country shuffle ("Wheels") and an up-tempo rocker ("Christine's Song"); both songs featured vocals modeled on those of the Everly Brothers. "They were harmonies," said Hillman, "first and thirds. Gram would sing the harmony to me, and we'd switch on the chorus, where I would sing the harmony and he would sing the lead." Kleinow added unorthodox fuzz-toned licks on the pedal steel guitar. (During his tenure with the Burritos, Kleinow kept his day job producing stop-motion animation for *The Gumby Show*.) Parsons helped Hillman complete "Sin City," a ballad that reflected his sour state of mind. ("I was going through this horrible divorce," said Hillman, "where my wife had been going out with the road manager. . . . Our manager had robbed us and I quit the Byrds and there was my life. 'This whole town is filled with sin.'") Parsons also put lyrics to two melodies that Ethridge had written in high school. Hillman believes that Gram's very best vocals were on these two songs, "Hot Burrito #1" (often referred to as "I'm Your Toy") and "Hot Burrito #2."

Parsons hated the term *country rock*; he called his work "Cosmic American Music," and an essential part of his musical gumbo was rhythm & blues. That's why it's significant that the Burritos' first album, *The Gilded Palace of Sin*, included two songs written at the corner of country and R&B, "Do Right Woman, Do Right Man" and "Dark End of the Street" (both by Dan Penn and Chips Moman). "We were consciously welding the two," said Hillman. "That was the merging of the black and white blues. The crying out, taking those R&B songs and putting a light country & western arrangement to them."

Penn, born in Alabama, fronted an R&B band called Dan Penn and the Pallbearers (the group traveled in a hearse) while engineering recording sessions in Muscle Shoals. He wrote songs with Lindon "Spooner" Oldham, who played keyboards on Arthur Alexander's 1961 debut, "You Better Move On" (the first national hit recorded in Muscle Shoals) and Percy Sledge's "When a Man Loves a Woman." When Aretha Franklin sat behind the piano to record the gospel-tinged "I Never Loved a Man (The Way I Love You)," Oldham slipped behind an electric keyboard and created the distinctive lick—Penn called it "the three-fingered dumb hum"—that introduced one of the most memorable records of the soul era. After Penn and Oldham wrote their first big pop hit, "I'm Your Puppet" (1966) recorded by James and Bobby Purify, Penn moved to Memphis to try his hand at record production.

Penn hit pay dirt when he produced "The Letter" by the Box Tops (he and Oldham wrote the group's follow-up hit, "Cry Like a Baby"). He also bonded with Lincoln Wayne "Chips" Moman, a Georgia-born guitarist whom he'd met at a Wilson Pickett session and whose nickname referenced his fondness for playing poker. After doing session work in Los Angeles and touring with rockabilly star Gene Vincent, Moman settled in Memphis, where he worked at Stax Records and produced the company's first big hit, "Gee Whiz" by Carla Thomas. He later established American Sound Studios, where he produced Elvis Presley's comeback album, *From Elvis in Memphis* (1969).

In the summer of 1966 Penn and Moman were playing cards with disc jockeys visiting Memphis for a convention. Taking a break, they tried to fulfill an ambition. "We were always wanting to come up with the best cheatin' song," said Penn. Less than an hour later, they'd arguably hit the mark with "Dark End of the Street," which became a #10 R&B hit for James Carr and was subsequently recorded by everyone from the Burritos to Aretha Franklin and Linda Ronstadt. The pair wrote "Do Right Woman, Do Right Man" after Moman invited Penn to his home, where his wife served quail for dinner. First made famous by Aretha Franklin, the song, like "Dark End of the Street," has been covered by singers of both country and soul. The two tunes embody the essence of Americana. The Flying Burrito Brothers also recorded "To Love Somebody," a soulful 1967 pop hit for the Bee Gees that was written with an eye toward having it recorded by Otis Redding. Otis died before that could happen but others who cut the song included Nina Simone, Roberta Flack, and Janis Joplin.

The country–soul connection was artfully underscored in the early 1970s by soul singer Al Green, who was encouraged to sing country music by Audrey Williams. "I met Miss Audrey," said Green, who visited her Nashville home, "and asked, 'Waddya want to do?' 'First,' she says, 'I wanna get a bottle of champagne.'" Williams played a selection of her country favorites, including some by her late husband. Green subsequently recorded slow, poignant versions of Kristofferson's "For the Good Times," Williams's "I'm So Lonesome I Could Cry," and Willie Nelson's "Funny How Time Slips Away." "Every R&B record you hear is not necessarily an R&B song," said Green. "It might have derived from country music."

The Flying Burrito Brothers peaked with the release of *The Gilded Palace of Sin*, which despite lackluster production remains a milestone of country rock and, by extension, Americana. Unfortunately, the Burritos were a poor live band. "I cannot recall one performance where I wasn't embarrassed," said Kleinow, including a showcase at the Whisky-A-Go-Go where Parsons and Ethridge were too stoned to play and A&M executives left in disgust. "I was the taskmaster, and I should have gotten it together," said Hillman. "That first line-up was bad onstage."

On their first national tour the Burritos floundered in front of rock audiences who had little interest in country music. A surfeit of pills, pot, and cocaine didn't help, and a snowstorm in the Northeast caused the band to miss its highly promoted New York City debut at The Scene. The Burrito Brothers returned to Los Angeles with good reviews for their debut album (including a thumbs-up by Dylan in *Rolling Stone*) but minimal sales and a six-figure financial debt to its record company. The group (except Parsons, who never worried about money) made ends meet by playing local clubs and the occasional out-of-town gig.

Hillman moved to bass when Ethridge left the group, and Bernie Leadon, who would soon be a founding member of the Eagles, became the band's guitarist. (Leadon's younger brother Tom was in Florida playing in Tom Petty's band, Mudcrutch. "We started listening to the first Flying Burrito Brothers album and just loved it," said Leadon. "Nobody in Florida was doing anything like that.") Longbranch Pennywhistle, a duo consisting of future Eagle Glenn Frey and J. D. Souther, opened for the Burritos at the Troubadour. "Glenn Frey was just in awe of Gram," said Hillman. "He learned about stage presence and how to deliver a vocal."

"I always thought that what I was trying to do at the time was modern country music," said Souther. "I'd been listening to the Flying Burrito Brothers, the Byrds, Poco, Dillard & Clark. Those guys had listened to Buck Owens and Merle Haggard, and those guys had listened to Hank Williams and George Jones, and *those* guys had listened to the Louvin Brothers and the Carter Family." One lesson of that history was that bad behavior didn't preclude good music. "Gram was very self-destructive," said musician Walter Egan. "To see him as a person, as opposed to a performer or a singer, was disappointing. To hear him sing was amazing."

Parsons was now living at the Chateau Marmont and developing a taste for heroin. The comity of the Burritos was gone; Parsons and Hillman struggled to write anything, let alone songs as strong as those on their debut. Parsons was increasingly unreliable on stage; Leadon said that his acoustic guitar was little more than a prop. Matters worsened in the fall of 1969 when Parsons was distracted by the arrival of the Rolling Stones in Los Angeles to prepare for an American tour and the release of *Let It Bleed*.

"Gram was one of the few people who helped me sing country music," said Mick Jagger. "[Especially] the idea of country music being played slightly tongue in cheek." He was also said to inspire the Stones to record "Country Honk," a down-home take on "Honky Tonk Women." Parsons started wearing makeup and miming Jagger's stage moves, and he already shared dangerous habits with Richards. "Gram was as knowledgeable about chemical substances as I was," said Richards. "He could get better coke than the mafia." One night the two motored to Joshua Tree State Park, dropped LSD, and wandered the desert while scanning the sky for UFOs. Another time, they flew to Las Vegas to catch a show by a mutual hero, Elvis Presley.

During the winter of 1970 the Burritos struggled to complete their second album, *Burrito Deluxe*, a mediocre effort best known for including a then-unreleased Jagger-Richards song, "Wild Horses." Jim Dickson, who'd helped launch the Byrds, produced the album. "I think the Burritos had used up their creative surge that had resulted in all the songs on that first album," said Leadon. "They had shot their wad." In June Hillman finally fired Parsons when he showed up late and loaded for a gig at the Brass Ring in the San Fernando Valley.

But Parsons was already gone. The previous December, he'd begged the Rolling Stones to let the Burrito Brothers play at their free show at the Altamont Speedway. Organized on the fly, with the Hell's Angels handling security, Altamont drew three hundred thousand people and is seen as the apocalyptic counterpoint of the peaceful Woodstock Festival of the preceding August. Jefferson Airplane played both events. "Woodstock was a bunch of stupid slobs in the mud," said Grace Slick, "and Altamont was a bunch of angry slobs in the mud." The Burritos played in the afternoon; the Stones waited for nightfall. "When we went through the backstage area it was full of people," said Stones drummer Charlie Watts. "A lot of them were fucked up and the Angels made a razor-sharp line for us to walk through. I felt very worried as we walked to the stage. It was an event waiting to happen."

And it did. As the Rolling Stones played, the crowd pushed toward the stage, and Meredith Hunter, a black man, was seen to pull a gun. A Hell's Angel promptly stabbed him to death; the Stones played "Under My Thumb" as Hunter bled out into the California dirt. The rock stars fled to a waiting helicopter with Parsons close behind. The other Burritos were left to their own devices as Parsons and the Stones flew back to San Francisco. The entourage, shaken by the violence, gathered at the Huntington Hotel. "Gram was there, leaning against the wall," says Pamela Des Barres, "wearing black leather and eye makeup, nodding out. Keith was wearing cowboy clothes. It looked like they were turning into each other."

9
AMERICAN TUNE

Merle Haggard looked out the window of his tour bus and saw an exit sign along Interstate 40 for Muskogee. Haggard's family had come from this part of Oklahoma, and he poked his drowsy drummer, Roy Edward Burris, to wager that people didn't smoke marijuana in Muskogee. Haggard and the Strangers were quick to think of other things that would raise rural eyebrows such as Roman sandals, shaggy hair, and LSD. Burris said it took about fifteen minutes to write the song that Haggard debuted the next night at Fort Bragg, North Carolina. "Soldiers started comin' after me on the stage," said Haggard, "and I didn't know what was going to happen next until they took the mike and said we'd have to do it again before they'd let us go. I had never had this strong of a reaction before."

Haggard recorded "Okie from Muskogee" in July 1969. Four months later it was a divided nation's #1 country song. "We wrote it to be satirical originally," said Haggard, who joked that Muskogee might be the only place where he hadn't smoked pot. "But then people latched on to it." The song made Haggard a player in the late-sixties culture wars and helped fortify a wall between rock and country music just as the Byrds and the Flying Burrito Brothers were taking their latest music to the Fillmore.

Politics was not new to country music. In 1944 Jimmie Davis rode the popularity of his song "You Are My Sunshine" to the governorship of Louisiana. Davis called for racial segregation at the same time Woody Guthrie and Pete Seeger gave modern folk music its leftist pedigree. When rock 'n' roll became the music of teenage America in the 1950s and of the counterculture of the 1960s, country music offered a more traditional sanctuary. "Many Americans have sought reassurance that the older comfortable and predictable world they once knew is still intact," said Bill Malone in *Country Music, U.S.A.*, published in 1968. "In the realm of popular culture, country music seemed a safe retreat to many because it suggested 'bedrock' American values of solidity, respect for authority, old time religion, home-based virtues, and patriotism."

President Richard Nixon saw the connection between "Okie from Muskogee" and his Southern Strategy, which would turn the region Republican. In 1970 (and for the next three years), he declared October Country Music Month, and the Country Music Association produced an album that paired various songs with excerpts from the president's speeches. On December 21, 1970, Elvis Presley arrived unannounced at the White House and left a note of introduction at the front gate. It said, in part, that Presley had done "an in-depth study of Drug Abuse and Communist Brainwashing techniques." Hours later, Elvis was ushered into the Oval Office after the Secret Service confiscated the World War II Colt 45 that he wanted to give to the president. Presley told Nixon that the Beatles were a bad influence on youth and said that he could help the cause if he were given a "Federal Agent at Large" badge from the Bureau of Narcotics and Dangerous Drugs. Then the two men posed for the photo seen around the world. The King left with cuff links bearing the presidential seal and an honorary badge worth its weight in tin.

In 1972 Johnny Cash went to the White House to lobby for prison reform. Nixon asked him to sing "Okie from Muskogee" and Guy Drake's "Welfare Cadillac." "I don't know those songs," replied Cash. "But I got a few of my own I can play for you." With the press watching, Cash sang an anti-war song ("What Is Truth?") and a song about a Native American who enlisted and "forgot the white man's greed" ("The Ballad of Ira Hayes"). When Haggard himself performed at the White House in 1973, he found that the political swells had little interest in anything but "Okie from Muskogee."

Nixon took to the stage of Nashville's *Grand Ole Opry* in 1974 in the midst of the Watergate scandal. The Ryman Auditorium, rich in history, had hosted its last show the night before his arrival; Nixon helped inaugurate the slick new $15 million theater at a suburban amusement complex called Opryland. George Wallace, the segregationist governor of Alabama who'd run against Nixon in the presidential election, was in the front row as the president sat at the piano and played "Happy Birthday" for his wife Pat. Nixon then praised country music for its embrace of traditional values, led the audience in singing "God Bless America," and exited to a bluegrass rendition of "Hail to the Chief."

One hundred forty-six days later, Nixon left the White House in disgrace. The shuttered Ryman Auditorium, though recognized as a historic site, was threatened with demolition and left to deteriorate for decades. In 1991 Emmylou Harris and the Nash Ramblers recorded *At the Ryman* before a small audience; for safety's sake, no one was allowed to sit beneath the unstable balcony. Subsequent renovations revived the Ryman, which officially reopened with a 1994 broadcast of Garrison Keillor's *A Prairie Home Companion*.

Haggard followed "Okie from Muskogee" with the equally combative "The Fightin' Side of Me." Haggard was one of the best singers and songwriters in country music, but his "love-it-or-leave-it" politics led many to be oblivious to his gifts. Haggard was hardly the only country artist championing conservative values. Tammy Wynette's "Stand by Your Man" (1968) is both her biggest hit and one of the most oft-recorded songs in country music history; it's been used in films as diverse as *Five Easy Pieces* and *The Blues Brothers*. Written in fifteen minutes by Wynette and producer Billy Sherrill, the tune is known to everyone and debated endlessly. The song's subservient lyrics rankled feminists, and its repute lingered; campaigning for her husband in 1992, Hillary Clinton said that she wasn't "some little woman 'standing by my man' like Tammy Wynette." Today, "Stand by Your Man" remains a cultural totem that can be considered both campy and sincere.

In 1972 Wynette and George Jones performed for George Wallace during his presidential race (Haggard declined to lend his support). Country music slipped back into the White House in 1978 when Jimmy Carter of Georgia invited Willie Nelson to perform. After the show, as Nelson was settling into the Lincoln bedroom, there was a knock on the door, and the president's son Chip suggested a trip to the roof to enjoy a panoramic view of the nation's capital. As they admired the American monuments, Chip, who knew a thing or two about Willie, fired up a joint.

The Band never recorded its own music at Big Pink, their famous home in the Catskills. Their second album was made at a rich man's home with a pool house to use as a recording room and a nearby bathroom that was ideal for adding echo. *The Band*, a quintessentially Americana album, was a group of songs that naturally blended country, blues, ragtime, and gospel. One pictures it being recorded in a comfy cabin surrounded by whispering pines; instead, it was made at the Hollywood Hills pad of Sammy Davis Jr.

As John Simon assembled a portable studio, Helm visited a local pawnshop and bought a $130 set of antique drums with wooden rims. "You can feel the wood in this record," said Robertson, describing the album's organic sound as well as Helm's new tools. "We took great care with every instrument," said producer Simon, "to make it sound different for every song, and appropriate for every song." Afternoon rehearsals would refine and polish the arrangements; recording would typically commence at night.

Songs were defined by details, and because the members were multi-instrumentalists, colorful variety was at their fingertips. "With 'Rag Mama Rag,' said Robertson, "we had the basic thing and then, 'Oh, what about if Garth played the piano on this, what about if we do the intro on violin and 'cause you're [referring to Rick Danko] playing violin, you can't play the bass. It's a ragtime thing so what about this tuba [played by Simon] taking the place of the bass.' So we would start to add up the bits and pieces. 'What about if Richard played the drums on it in that kind of funny style he had.' It's ideas coming until you get the character. All of a sudden it's like, 'Oh . . . we're starting to get a match here.'"

And then there was the special sauce. "We called Garth 'H. B.'" said Helm. "This stood for 'Honey Boy,' because at the end of the day, after the other instruments were put away, Garth was still in the studio sweetening the tracks, stacking up those chords, putting on brass, woodwinds, whatever was needed to make the music sing. Garth made us sound like we did." The vocals were recorded live alongside the instruments and not overdubbed separately. Other groups would assemble songs from separate sessions; during the recording of *Sgt. Pepper*, for example, Paul McCartney played his bass guitar in isolation. The Band recorded as a unit.

"Everybody played a major role in our balance and musicianship," said Robertson, who wrote all the songs, including three collaborations with Manuel and one with Helm. "Mostly [Richard] would get a music thing going," said Robertson of songs such as "Whispering Pines" and "When You Awake," and "we would finish that up together." Robertson wrote lyrics that seemed to spring from the past. "I could relate to farmers in the Depression getting together in unions better than I could relate to going to San Francisco and putting flowers in your hair," said Robertson. "The way I get the most effect out of something is to come in from another door."

When Robertson decided that the narrator of one song would be a Confederate soldier, it was clear that the drummer from Arkansas would sing "The Night They Drove Old Dixie Down." Robertson did some research at the Woodstock library and took Helm's advice to "make General Robert E. Lee come out with all due respect." The drummer found his own way into singing the tune. "Instead of keeping full time rhythmically," said Helm, "we found if we halved the beat we could lay the lyrics in a different place, and the pulse would be easier to move to, more danceable."

The album was originally set to be called *Harvest* in reference to the last track, "King Harvest (Has Surely Come)." The song had verses about a beleaguered union man and a farmer praying for a bountiful crop, with a coiled guitar solo by Robertson that was not at all like the wailing improvisations he played with Ronnie Hawkins and Bob Dylan. "It was like you have to hold your breath while playing these kinds of solos," said Robertson of the instrumental passage that concluded the tune. "You can't breathe or you'll throw yourself off."

To get the album done, the group took what Manuel called "high-school fat girl diet pills." By the time The Band flew to San Francisco to make its concert debut at Bill Graham's Winterland, Robertson, who'd suffered over each detail of the recording, was utterly exhausted. With the show just hours away, a hypnotist was summoned to his bedside. "The tall, silver-haired hypnotist, Pierre Clement, [was] rubbing Robbie's forehead," said Simon. The Band finally reached the stage after midnight and played an abbreviated set. "The hypnotist did help him get over it," said photographer Elliott Landy. "He said, 'Every time I snap my fingers, you'll feel better,' and it worked. Robbie says there was this cacophony of sound on stage, with all the instruments and amplifiers—and yet, every time the hypnotist snapped his fingers—he heard it."

The Band mesmerized concert audiences with its delicate ensemble work. "My drums were on a riser, stage right," said Helm, "next to Garth's organ, also on a riser in the middle of the stage. Richard's grand piano was stage left. These were sight lines we'd worked out years before so we could

THE BAND

see one another's eyes to know where the music was going. Robbie stood between me and Garth; Rick between Richard and Garth. It was right and tight." Musicians were especially impressed. "Me and a bunch of guys from New Orleans would listen to that second album all the time and it would just tickle us that Robbie was from Canada," said Malcolm "Dr. John" Rebennack. "The music sounded to me like a cross between Memphis and New Orleans, it was really in the pockets of those places without ever, like, copying the original stuff."

Fairport Convention, a British folk rock band, recognized that The Band presented them with a personal challenge. "Fairport had been an American folk-rock band playing that style of music, even though they were English," said the group's producer, Joe Boyd. "Knowing their sensibilities and their knowledge, they could never be The Band. So the next logical thing was to say, 'Hey, we're good, so we can do with our own culture what they did for American culture.'"

"The Band had such a soulful rhythm section in Rick Danko and Levon Helm," said Nick Lowe, who played bass with the British pub-rock band Brinsley Schwarz. "No one knows how to play soulfully any more. Many people can play earnest . . . earnestness is what people today mistake for soulfulness." He also appreciated the history. "Bob Dylan," said Lowe, "a Jewish bloke from a northern state, a bunch of farm blokes from Canada, and Levon from 2,000 miles away in the South, a white black man. . . . There is North America right there! Certainly as far as white popular music can be portrayed. Was there ever anything better or more representative of North America?"

Happy Traum met Bob Dylan in Greenwich Village and was later a neighbor in Woodstock. "It was very family oriented," said Traum, "dinners together, hanging out and playing a lot of music. He would come down to our house and say, 'Hey, you want to hear this new song I wrote?' What were we gong to say, 'No'? I remember some of the songs from *John Wesley Harding*. Very few people were let into that world—a couple of artists and a couple of stonemasons—we were very careful not to abuse the privilege."

The year 1968 was a tumultuous time, with multiple assassinations, persistent racial tensions, the escalation of combat in Vietnam, and anti-war demonstrations fated to explode outside the Democratic Convention in Chicago. Dylan wrote little music, perhaps wrung dry after a very prolific 1967. (Tracks recorded at Big Pink appeared on the first well-known illegal bootleg, *Great*

White Wonder [1969].) But even without new music Dylan was heard all over the radio, with Manfred Mann hitting the Top 10 with "The Mighty Quinn" and Jimi Hendrix releasing the definitive version of "All Along the Watchtower." Dylan songs were also central to The Band's *Music from Big Pink* and the Byrds' *Sweetheart of the Rodeo*.

Dylan was a public figure enjoying a private life. "He was hiding from the world," said Elliot Landy, "savoring the magical experience of having young children." Fans came to Woodstock in hopes of meeting the Bard; one day a hippie and his old lady had to be thrown out of Hi-Lo-Ha's master bedroom. The aggrieved homeowner bought a gun. "I used to think that myself and my songs were the same thing," he said. "But I don't believe that any more. There's myself and there's my song." Dylan was also angry that Albert Grossman owned 50 percent of Dwarf Music (the songwriter's next publishing company, Big Sky Music, would have the same split with his manager) and pointedly ignored him at the Woody Guthrie tribute. Dylan would eventually fire his manager; lawsuits lingered until a final settlement in 1987 required Dylan to pay Grossman's estate $2 million.

Grossman was busy managing Janis Joplin, The Band, Paul Butterfield, and a Bearsville music operation in Woodstock that would oversee the release of albums by Jesse Winchester (produced by Robbie Robertson with a sound similar to that of The Band) and Bobby "See You Later, Alligator" Charles, whose brief time in Woodstock inspired him to write a quintessential Americana song, "Small Town Talk." Dylan was shaken when his father died of a heart attack at the age of fifty-six. Over the years his relationship with his parents had been strained, but he was also known to call home back when he all but claimed to be an orphan. Dylan, now himself a father, returned to Hibbing for the funeral. "Now there's no way to say what I was never capable of saying before," said the son of Abe Zimmerman.

George Harrison and his wife Pattie Boyd traveled to Woodstock in November and stayed at Grossman's house. "He hardly said a word for a couple of days," said Harrison of Dylan. When guitars emerged, they wrote "I'd Have You Anytime," which Harrison would use to open his first post-Beatles album, *All Things Must Pass* (1970). Dylan played two new songs for Harrison: "I Threw It All Away" and "Lay, Lady, Lay," which was originally written (but not used) for the film *Midnight Cowboy*. The Beatle said that the visit's high point was when The Band arrived for Thanksgiving dinner.

Dylan returned to Nashville in January 1969 intending to expand upon the sound that had characterized *John Wesley Harding* with a band that included guitarist Charlie Daniels, pedal steel player Pete Drake, and Norman Blake, an acoustic guitar virtuoso who played with Johnny Cash. Producer Bob Johnston was now a veteran of Dylan sessions. "No one ever counted off for [Dylan]," said Johnston. "He'd start tapping his foot. . . . I told everybody that I ever came in contact with, 'Just keep playing. Don't stop.'" After tracking four songs in the first day, Dylan returned to the Ramada Inn and wrote three more. "The songs reflect more of the inner me than the songs of the past," said Dylan. "The smallest line in this album means more to me than some of the songs on any of the previous records."

Still, no one was going to mistake casual compositions like "Country Pie" ("Listen to the fiddler play") and "Peggy Day" ("By golly, what more can I say?") for "All Along the Watchtower" ("'There must be some way out of here,' said the joker to the thief"). In a way, Dylan was emulating two of his songwriting heroes, Hank Williams and Buddy Holly, but their personable poetry had emerged fully formed. By contrast, Dylan had become famous for songs with lyrics that could be both complex and poetic; now, he was willfully trying to be simple. His best songs nonetheless hit their mark; "I Threw It All Away" reeked of measured regret, while "Tonight I'll Be Staying Here with You" was playfully ribald. But the biggest shock of *Nashville Skyline* was Dylan's baritone croon. Dylan said the change occurred because he quit cigarettes (for a minute), but others recognized this voice from his coffeehouse days in Minnesota.

Nashville Skyline reunited Dylan with the rhythm section of Ken Buttrey and Charlie McCoy. Searching to create the right drum part for "Lay, Lady, Lay," Buttrey asked Dylan what he heard. The response: "Bongos." Johnston answered the same question with "Cowbell." Thinking it would never work, but aiming to please, Buttrey found a cowbell and a cheap set of bongos, which he tuned to a higher pitch by heating the skins with his cigarette lighter. Then he recruited Kris Kristofferson to hold the bongos in one hand and the cowbell in the other. "We started playing the tune and I was just doodling around on the bongos and the cowbell," said Buttrey. "Come chorus time I'd go to the set of drums. . . . It was the very first take, and to this day it's one of the best drum patterns I ever came up with."

With little more than twenty-five minutes of music, Dylan was short of a new album. He dropped by a Nashville recording session to see his friend Johnny Cash, who'd made a big comeback that included a new recording of his 1955 hit "Folsom Prison Blues." When the pair went out to dinner, Johnston, who was also Cash's producer, quickly set up the studio like a Greenwich Village cafe, with tables and chairs and microphones for two singers. When the diners returned, "they looked at each other and went out and got their guitars and started singing," said Johnston. "People started yelling out song titles. . . . They were laughing and having fun."

The impromptu session, with backing by Cash's band, including Carl Perkins on electric guitar, was essentially an Americana jam. It included songs by Cash ("Big River," "I Walk the Line"), Elvis Presley (Arthur Crudup's "That's All Right"), Perkins ("Matchbox"), Jimmie Rodgers ("Blue Yodel No. 4"), and a touch of gospel ("Just a Closer Walk with Thee"). Johnston's notion of fashioning an album from the superstar session was abandoned due to its more-than casual execution. Nonetheless, the music was widely bootlegged, and was officially released in 2019 as *Travelin' Thru*. One song, the pair's duet on Dylan's "Girl from the North Country," became the lead track of *Nashville Skyline*.

Rock critics, still a new breed in 1969, didn't know what to make of the album. Paul Nelson, who had known Dylan in Minneapolis, took kindly to his unexpected turn. "*Nashville Skyline*," he wrote in *Rolling Stone*, "achieves the artistically impossible: a deep, humane, and interesting statement about being happy." Others weren't as nice. Writing in *Fusion*, Tom Smucker said, "It's cast in the reactionary, Wallace-for-President, traditionally repressed cultural form of country music." In the *Village Voice*, Robert Christgau chided Dylan for working with Johnny Cash, "an enthusiastic Nixon supporter," and described country music as a "naturally Conservative . . . intensely chauvinistic, racist, majority-oriented and anti-aristocratic in the worst as well as the best sense."

Dylan returned to Nashville in June 1969 to appear on the premiere episode of ABC television's *Johnny Cash Show*, which was recorded at the Ryman Auditorium. Dylan sang "I Threw It All Way" and was then joined by the host for "Girl from the North Country"; in the same episode Joni Mitchell sang "Both Sides Now" and, with Cash, "Long Black Veil." The program featured regular appearances by Cash's traveling troupe including Perkins, Mother Maybelle, and June Carter Cash singing with her husband. Subsequent episodes featured an eclectic mix of country and pop musicians including Loretta Lynn, Linda Ronstadt, Merle Haggard, Neil Young, Tammy Wynette, Louis Armstrong, and Eric Clapton's band, Derek and the Dominos. All told, the program celebrated the depth and diversity of American music.

Cash's show became a magnet for Nashville songwriters looking to pitch their songs. "When I told Mickey Newbury I'd been fired [as a janitor]," said Kristofferson, "he said, 'Great!' So we became like the mascots of *The Johnny Cash Show*. . . . There was [*sic*] all kind of stars coming in who'd never been to Nashville. . . . Can you believe anyone having the audacity . . . to subject people [to our songs] when they [were] in a make-up chair?" Johnny and June would often invite the out-of-towners to their home in nearby Hendersonville. "Joni Mitchell sang 'Both Sides Now,'" said Cash of one such gathering, "Graham Nash sang 'Marrakesh Express,' Shel Silverstein sang 'A Boy Named Sue,' Bob Dylan sang 'Lay Lady Lay,' and Kristofferson sang 'Me and Bobby McGee.'"

The Johnny Cash Show ran from June 1969 to March 1971, and its fifty-eight installments anchored a career resurgence that also included a second live prison album, *At San Quentin*, and a #1 country single (Kristofferson's "Sunday Mornin' Comin' Down"). But the program, with its Americana-like mix of music from multiple genres, wasn't the only television show that featured country music. In 1968 Glen Campbell hosted a summer replacement show for *The Smothers Brothers Comedy Hour*, a popular program that had become a political hot potato due to its pointed criticism of the Vietnam War. (Both Cash and the Smothers Brothers had to fight their respective networks in order to book Pete Seeger.) Campbell, who was on a hit parade hot streak, was eventually given his own show.

The next year, CBS debuted another summer replacement, *Hee Haw*, which was co-hosted by Roy Clark and Buck Owens and presented country music alongside comedy bits modeled after those of another hit show, *Laugh-In*. *Hee Haw*'s depiction of rural America echoed the stereotypes of popular sitcoms like *The Beverly Hillbillies* and *Green Acres*; the program featured the Buckaroos as its house band and a posse of women called Hee Haw Honeys. Buck and Roy performed a regular musical feature called "a-pickin' and a-grinnin.'"

In a year that saw the moon landing and the Woodstock Festival, *Hee Haw* put country music in a hick frame apt to give pause to rock fans who had sampled the genre through *Sweetheart of the Rodeo*, *The Gilded Palace of Sin*, and *Nashville Skyline*. Owens later said that the show killed his recording career. "I couldn't justify turning down that big paycheck for just a few weeks work twice a year," he said, referring to the program's biannual shooting schedule. "So I kept whoring myself out to that cartoon donkey." Merle Haggard and the Strangers made seven appearances on the first season of *Hee Haw*, and in December 1969 celebrated the fellowship of the holiday season by performing "Okie from Muskogee."

10
TROUBADOURS

"The Troubadour was the first place I went to when I got to L.A.," said Don Henley, the drummer for Shiloh, a country-rock band from Texas. "The first night I walked in I saw Graham Nash and Neil Young, and Linda Ronstadt was standing there in a little Daisy Mae kind of dress.'" Glenn Frey had moved to Los Angeles from Detroit. On his first day there, Frey said, "I saw David Crosby sitting on the steps of the Country Store in Laurel Canyon, wearing the same hat and green leather bat-cape he had on for [the cover of] *Turn! Turn! Turn!*" Crosby, observed Jackson Browne, "had this legendary VW bus with a Porsche engine in it, and that summed him up—a hippie with power."

Fairport Convention's first American show was at the Troubadour in 1970. "Linda Ronstadt cheered them on from the audience," said Joe Boyd, the band's producer. "When they ran out of encores, they invited her to join them. 'I don't know any English songs,' she shouted. 'That's OK, we know all yours,' said Simon [Nicol]. Pushed onstage, she sang the first acapella notes of 'Silver Threads and Golden Needles,' then heard Fairport enter on cue, recreating her arrangement perfectly. When Richard [Thompson] took an expert James Burton-esque solo, she almost fainted in astonishment."

The Troubadour was ground zero for musicians playing various combinations of rock and folk. *Crosby, Stills & Nash* dominated turntables in the summer of 1969 the way *Sgt. Pepper's Lonely Hearts Club Band* had during 1967's Summer of Love, but whereas the Beatles LP famously exploited the recording studio, the CS&N album succeeded on the earthier strength of vocal harmonies. "Suite: Judy Blue Eyes," a Stills song about his girlfriend, Judy Collins, showcased both his inventive use of alternate guitar tunings and the vivid interplay of the group's three distinctive voices. They had their own Albert Grossman in David Geffen, a New York hustler who left the mailroom of the William Morris Agency to become Laura Nyro's booking agent and half-owner of her publishing company, Tuna Fish Music. When Nyro's artful songs turned to gold through pop hits for the Fifth Dimension, Barbra Streisand, and Blood, Sweat, and Tears, Geffen sold the company for more than $4 million. In the same year he untangled the individual commitments of Crosby, Stills, and Nash and got them a contract with Atlantic Records.

Before the trio hit the road, however, they decided to add Stills's old foil from Buffalo Springfield, Neil Young, who'd just released his first solo album and who shared manager Elliot Roberts with Joni Mitchell. Crosby, Stills, Nash, & Young played their second gig at the Woodstock Festival in August 1969. As a proviso for including the band in the subsequent film, Geffen insisted that its recording of Joni Mitchell's "Woodstock" be heard over the opening credits. Hugely successful on the concert circuit, the group never made a better and more influential record than its debut.

"The beginnings of the singer-songwriters school," said Jackson Browne, "were the first albums by Neil [Young] and Joni [Mitchell]. After that you started to get songs that only the songwriter could have sung—that were part of the songwriter's personality." This was a new kind of folk music, not with traditional songs passed between generations but new tunes expected to be as individual as a fingerprint. By the release of her third album, *Ladies of the Canyon*, Mitchell had evolved from a highly literate folk singer into the creator of uniquely artful songs that employed unusual guitar tunings (and soulful piano playing) to accompany lyrics that were both personal and poetic.

"Joni writes about her relationships so much more vividly than I do," said Neil Young. "I guess I put more of a veil over what I'm talking about." Indeed, in the case of Young's "Only Love Can Break Your Heart," he wasn't writing about himself at all but about the dissolution of Mitchell's relationship with Graham Nash. Young was quick to establish a wider stylistic turf than the

NEIL YOUNG

pensive songwriter suggested by 1969's *Neil Young*. Later in the year he released *Everybody Knows This Is Nowhere*, a collection born of sessions with a band that would come to call itself Crazy Horse. Rock songs like "Cinnamon Girl" and the extended guitar jams of "Down by the River" and "Cowgirl in the Sand" established an electric style that would become the yin to the yang of his acoustic songs. Young would flip this coin throughout his career, and thereby embrace the two poles of Americana music.

The two Canadians ruled Los Angeles, but a new arrival from New England by way of London made the biggest splash of 1970. James Taylor had played music in Greenwich Village with a band called the Flying Machine; when he relocated to London in 1968, the band's guitarist, Danny Kortchmar, told him to call his friend Peter Asher. Half of the duo Peter and Gordon, who'd had a hit with a Lennon-McCartney song, "A World Without Love," Asher was now working for the Beatles' record label, Apple. Taylor was signed to Apple after auditioning in Paul McCartney's living room. Asher produced Taylor's self-titled debut—work paused when the Beatles needed the studio to record "Hey Jude"—but it attracted little notice, partly due to disorganization at Apple. Taylor and Asher relocated to Los Angeles, where they recorded *Sweet Baby James* for Warner Brothers. That album stayed in the Top 40 for more than a year and included a Top 5 single, "Fire and Rain," that established Taylor as the era's preeminent singer-songwriter.

"My style at that time was very intimate," said Taylor. "To criticize it, I think it was very self-centered, very autobiographical, and you could call it narcissistic. But the upside of that was that it was very accessible, and I think people liked that. It was just guitar and voice with some embellishments, and it was miked very close." In a word, Taylor's music was "mellow," not a term typically associated with a heroin addict. Taylor was a junkie when he became involved in a romantic relationship with Joni Mitchell, who was already working on her most intensely personal album.

Mitchell recorded *Blue* at the same time Taylor was producing *Mudslide Slim and the Blue Horizon*, an album that strained to re-create the easygoing bonhomie of *Sweet Baby James*. *Blue* was altogether original, a mature and artful collection that mixed romantic reveries ("All I Want," "Carey") with ballads about the emotional costs of love ("River," "A Case of You"). These were not folk tunes but art songs that reverberated with Mitchell's personality. "I was at my most defenseless during the making of *Blue*," said Mitchell. "I guess you could say I broke down but I continued to work. In the process of breaking down . . . everything became transparent." Paradoxically, *Blue* managed to be both entirely personal and altogether universal. But the intimacy burned Mitchell when *Rolling Stone* chronicled her love affairs with other famous musicians and dubbed her "Old Lady of the Year." "The ultimate irony," said writer Penny Stallings, "is that it is shy, circumspect Joni herself who's to blame for making her life an open record."

Taylor didn't write the biggest hit on *Mudslide Slim*; "You've Got a Friend" was penned by Carole King, who (with lyricist Gerry Goffin) wrote songs in the early sixties for acts such as the Chiffons ("One Fine Day"), Little Eva ("The Locomotion"), and the Drifters ("Up on the Roof"). When Jerry Wexler was collecting material for Aretha Franklin he gave the couple an idea for a song title, "natural woman," and they wrote a song that became one of Franklin's defining performances, "(You Make Me Feel Like) A Natural Woman."

As a solo singer-songwriter, King produced lyrics that were far less artful than those of Mitchell; the words to "You've Got a Friend" scan like a well-written greeting card. But the magic was in the music, and *Tapestry*, King's 1971 album, became one of the best-selling albums of all time and sealed her transition from Brill Building tunesmith to California earth mother. "My production values were . . . learned listening to James Taylor albums and Neil Young albums," said King. "I was able to get naked in my sound. I became more honest by listening to those records and by working with those people." (*Tapestry*'s personnel included Taylor on guitar and vocals plus two players who also worked on his albums, drummer Russ Kunkel and guitarist Danny Kortchmar.) Joni Mitchell sang on *Tapestry*, but following the release of *Blue*, she fled the City of Angels for the rural isolation of British Columbia, where she composed the tunes for her next release, *For the Roses*. Taylor would subsequently marry a more conventional singer-songwriter, Carly Simon.

Back at the Troubadour, Kris Kristofferson turned heads when he opened for Linda Ronstadt, and the handsome singer-songwriter was soon making movies. Ronstadt, meanwhile, was trying to reignite a career that had stalled after the success of "Different Drum" (1967), a song by Michael Nesmith (of the Monkees) that she'd recorded with the Stone Ponies. "One night I was on my way to the bathroom and this band Shiloh came on and started doing an exact version of 'Silver Threads and Golden Needles,'" said Ronstadt of a song that she'd recorded after hearing it done by the Springfields, a British folk trio that launched the career of Dusty Springfield. Ronstadt recruited Shiloh's singing drummer, Don Henley, and paired him with Glenn Frey, a guitarist who played in Longbranch Pennywhistle with her boyfriend, J. D. Souther. Joining Frey and Henley were guitarist Bernie Leadon of the Burrito Brothers and bassist Randy Meisner from Rick Nelson's Stone Canyon Band, Nelson's own venture into country rock. The quartet accompanied Ronstadt on her self-titled 1971 album, which included "Rock Me on the Water," a song by another Troubadour regular, Jackson Browne. Due to various commitments, however, all four actually only accompanied Ronstadt at one concert, though the venue was as emblematic of southern California as was the Troubadour: Disneyland.

Late on a Sunday night in the spring of 1971, John Prine was waiting to get paid after a gig at Chicago's Earl of Old Town. The phone rang behind the bar, and Prine took a call from Steve Goodman, a folkie friend who'd just finished a weekend opening for Kris Kristofferson at the Quiet Knight. Don't go anywhere, said Goodman, because Kristofferson had heard him sing a Prine song and wanted to meet the writer. But that wasn't all. On his flight to Chicago, Kristofferson had run into pop star Paul Anka, who'd recorded one of his songs; Anka was playing at a nightclub in the Loop and was on the way to Old Town in a limo. "When Steve brought Kris down to see me," said Prine, who admired Kristofferson's work, "he could have had the Cowardly Lion and the Tin Man with him . . . Anka was just one more show-biz guy."

Prine was new to this world. In high school he'd taken guitar lessons at the Old Town School of Folk Music; his older brother introduced him to the finger-style playing of Mississippi John Hurt and Elizabeth Cotten. (Cotten, best known for her rendition of "Freight Train," was "discovered" in the 1950s when she was working as a maid for Pete Seeger's father, Charles.) Prine also played country songs by Hank Williams and Lefty Frizzell. He was posted in Germany upon being drafted into the army, but the war in Vietnam couldn't help but creep into his thoughts. Back in Chicago, he played at an open mike night at the Fifth Peg and silenced the crowd with "Sam Stone," an original song about a veteran who'd become a junkie. "I started shuffling my feet and looking around," said Prine. "And then they started applauding, and it . . . was like I found out all of a sudden that I could communicate." Prine was soon playing three nights a week and quit his day job as a mailman.

"We had an early wake-up ahead of us," said Kristofferson, "and by the time we got there Old Town was nothing but empty streets and dark windows.

And the club was closing. But the owner let us come in, pulled some chairs off a couple of tables, and John unpacked his guitar and got back up to sing." Kristofferson and Anka, who a decade earlier had hired Jim McGuinn before he formed the Byrds, quickly forgot about the late hour. "It must've been like stumbling onto Dylan when he first busted on the Village scene," said Kristofferson.

Anka, looking to expand into artist management, bankrolled a trip to New York for Goodman and Prine to pursue record deals. Coincidentally, Kristofferson was playing at the Bitter End; when he invited Prine to sing a couple of songs, he chose the two that had made him a local hero in Chicago, "Sam Stone" and "Hello in There," about the isolated lives of the elderly. Jerry Wexler of Atlantic, who was in the audience, invited Prine to come by his office. "He offered me a $25,000 recording contract," said Prine. "I hadn't been in New York 24 hours." During their stay in Manhattan, Goodman and Prine collaborated on a wry country song, "You Never Even Call Me by My Name," that became a hit for David Allen Coe. Goodman, who died in 1984 of leukemia, signed a deal with Buddha Records; Arlo Guthrie, Woody's son, had a 1972 hit with Goodman's most celebrated song, "City of New Orleans."

Prine wrote with the observant eye of a short story writer. "In my songs, I try to look through someone else's eyes," said Prine, "and I want to give the audience a feeling more than a message." Prine said his principal influences were Bob Dylan (his "Donald and Lydia" was modeled on Dylan's "The Lonesome Death of Hattie Carroll") and Chuck Berry. "He [Berry] told a story in less than three minutes," said Prine, "and he had a syllable for every beat.... Some people stretch the words like a mask to fit the melody. Whereas guys who are really good lyricists have a meter that the melody is almost already there."

Arif Mardin, an engineer with a history of hits, produced Prine's debut in Memphis. Prine was called "the next Dylan," a sobriquet ascribed to, among others, Loudon Wainwright III, Bruce Springsteen, and Steve Forbert. Other singers were quick to cover his tunes; Bette Midler sang "Hello in There" on *The Divine Miss M*, and "Angel of Montgomery" became a concert standard for Bonnie Raitt after she recorded it for *Streetlights*. Back in New York to play his own show at the Bitter End, Kristofferson invited Prine to the apartment of his girlfriend, Carly Simon. "So we come over and we're sitting at Carly's place," said Prine, "and there's a knock on the door, and in walks Bob Dylan." It turns out that Wexler had sent Dylan a copy of Prine's debut. "So he showed up at the Bitter End," said Prine, "and played harmonica behind me on 'Donald and Lydia' and 'Far from Me.' It was like a dream."

Dylan had worked with Wexler when he sat in on sessions for *Doug Sahm and Band*, which included the Dylan song "Wallflower." Sahm, who at the age of eleven witnessed the very last show by Hank Williams, was as Americana as a musician could be. He grew up in Texas playing country, blues, R&B, and almost anything that crossed the border from Mexico. In 1964 he responded to the British Invasion by forming the Sir Douglas Quintet and recording such effervescent hits as "She's About a Mover" and "Mendocino." Sahm was the sort of rootsy musician who appealed to Wexler. So was Willie Nelson, whom Wexler met in 1972 at the Nashville home of songwriter Harlan Howard.

"[Willie] got on the stool late at night when the party had thinned out," said Howard, "and he sang like a total album with a gut string and a stool. He just went from one song to the other and Wexler . . . flipped out." Wexler was looking for new turf. The soul era was fading and Ahmet Ertegun was filling Atlantic's roster with rock acts like Led Zeppelin, CSN&Y, and the Rolling Stones. So Wexler signed pre-Americana acts like Prine, Sahm, and now, Nelson. Chet Atkins at RCA considered Waylon Jennings to have more commercial potential than Nelson and gave him more creative freedom. So Willie left RCA for Atlantic, and for the first time brought his own band into the recording studio.

Wexler heard something in Nelson that Nashville had missed. "Your phrasing reminds me of Ray Charles and Sinatra," Wexler told Nelson. "Like you, they're great proponents of rubato—elongating one note, cutting off another, swinging with an elastic sense of time only the jazz artists understand." Wexler produced Nelson's two albums for Atlantic, *Phases and Stages* (1972) and *Shotgun Willie* (1973); the latter was recorded in Muscle Shoals, but Nelson really ran the show. "I witnessed what I would later recognize as Wexler teaching Willie that he could largely control his own musical destiny," said Chet Flippo, who was in the studio reporting for *Rolling Stone*. But Nelson's records failed to sell in the numbers that rock albums did, and Atlantic soon abandoned trying to market country records. But Willie had enjoyed a tangy taste of freedom, and his music would never be the same.

Dolly Parton was another country musician at a crossroads in the early 1970s. Parton's first hit was "Dumb Blonde" (1967), and though she didn't write the song, and was whip smart, she knew the power of image. "If I'm going to look like this," said Parton of her big hair, bigger breasts, and wardrobe more saucy than chic, "I must have a reason. . . . It makes me different a little bit, and ain't that what we all want to do, be a little different?" Porter Wagoner brought Parton into his organization to make recordings, do live concerts, and appear on his syndicated television show. The first of their string of hit duets was a contemporary folk song written by Tom Paxton, "The Last Thing on My Mind."

Parton's solo singles were less successful until Wagoner had her record Jimmie Rodgers's "Mule Skinner Blues," which hit #3. After that, it was Dolly bar the door, with original songs like "Coat of Many Colors" (written on the tour bus) and "My Tennessee Mountain Home" establishing Parton as a solo star and the best female songwriter in country music this side of Loretta Lynn. After releasing "Jolene" in 1973, Parton decided to go solo. The song that she wrote about Porter, "I Will Always Love You," hit the top of the charts in 1974 but did little to console Wagoner. He sued Dolly for breach of a management contract and eventually settled out of court for a reported $1 million.

Parton wasn't shy about business. She was thrilled to learn that Elvis Presley wanted to record "I Will Always Love You" until she learned that as part of the deal Presley would own half of the publishing royalties. "I said, 'Well, in that case, I don't guess Elvis is going to be recording "I Will Always Love You,"'" said Parton. "Everybody said, 'You've got to be out of your damn mind.'" Parton's wisdom paid off when Whitney Houston made the song an international hit on the soundtrack of the 1992 film *The Bodyguard.*

"I got turned on to bluegrass in around 1960," said Jerry Garcia. "My grandmother was a big *Grand Ole Opry* fan. This was in San Francisco, a long way from Tennessee. . . . I heard Bill Monroe hundreds of times without knowing who he was." Garcia gained fame as the lead guitarist of the psychedelic rock band the Grateful Dead and was known as Captain Trips. But he was schooled in the roots of Americana. "Bluegrass bands are hard to put together because you have to have good musicians to play," said Garcia. Robert Hunter tried to keep up on mandolin, but he gave up and made a career of writing songs with Garcia. By the time Garcia's group had evolved into Mother McCree's Uptown Jug Band, the lineup included future members of the Dead: blues singer Ron "Pigpen" McKernan, drummer Bill Kreutmann, and teenage guitarist Bob Weir. The Grateful Dead played an Americana mix of blues, folk, country, and Chuck Berry; they famously performed improvisatory music at "acid test" LSD parties hosted by novelist Ken Kesey.

JERRY GARCIA

The Dead, stars of the counterculture, didn't sell many records until they found a new old-fashioned sound. "After hearing Dylan's country," said Garcia of *Nashville Skyline*, "it was soon, 'Hey, we can pull good ole country music into our act!'" Garcia took up the pedal steel guitar and played it on a Crosby, Stills, Nash, & Young song, "Teach Your Children." "Crosby and those guys were hanging around a lot," said Garcia, "and nothing turns you on to singing more than three guys who can really sing good. They'd start singing, and we'd think, 'Wow! Why don't we try making a simple record?'" The results were *Workingman's Dead* and *American Beauty*, a pair of Americana albums that included such songs as "Uncle John's Band," "Casey Jones," and "Friend of the Devil." The hippie musicians also adored the sound of Bakersfield. "We used to go see those bands and think, 'Gee, those guys are great,'" said Garcia. "Don Rich was one of my favorites. . . . So we took kind of the Buck Owens approach on *Workingman's Dead*."

The Dead's concert repertoire came to include tunes by such Americana icons as Merle Haggard, Buddy Holly, Bo Diddley, and Bob Dylan. Garcia also played pedal steel with the New Riders of the Purple Sage and banjo with an ensemble called Old & in the Way that included Vassar Clements on fiddle and David Grisman (whom Garcia had met at a Bill Monroe concert) on mandolin. Before meeting Garcia, Grisman had played in the Even Dozen Jug Band (with John Sebastian and Maria Muldaur) and Earth Opera, a psychedelic rock band that also included Peter Rowan, another influential roots musician. Rowan belongs to an elite club of players who (like Lester Flatt and Earl Scruggs) spent time with Bill Monroe and His Bluegrass Boys. Others include banjo player Bill Keith, guitarist Del McCoury, and fiddlers Richard Greene and Byron Berline.

"Bluegrass music has been perfected," said Grisman, "and you can't play better than Bill Monroe, Flatt & Scruggs, and The Stanley Brothers." Grisman's strategy was to make music that also embraced string band music, jazz fusion, and the gypsy jazz of guitarist Django Reinhardt. Garcia gave Grisman the nickname "Dawg," and it became a shorthand term to describe his eclectic music, which included an album cut with Reinhardt's primary accompanist, violinist Stephane Grappelli. The New Grass Revival, led by mandolin player Sam Bush, also pursued a progressive style of bluegrass; in 1979 the group toured as the opening act and backing band for Leon Russell, the rock pianist who'd already cut his own country album, *Hank Wilson's Back*. In 1981 Bela Fleck joined the group on banjo.

Other rock bands of the era, including Creedence Clearwater Revival, were influenced by country. "There was definitely a message on that album," said John Fogerty of Creedence's *Willie and the Poor Boys*. "I was using country and blues music the way Jimmie Rodgers or Woody Guthrie might have." Fogerty, who name-checked Buck Owens on the Creedence hit "Lookin' out My Backdoor," later recorded a one-man-band album, *The Blue Ridge Rangers*, that included songs by Hank Williams, George Jones, and Merle Haggard. Tracy Nelson, who sang in the band Mother Earth, covered the Americana waterfront on two solo albums, one devoted to blues (1965's *Deep Are the Roots*) and the other to country (1969's *Mother Earth Presents Tracy Nelson: Country*). But it took the Nitty Gritty Dirt Band, who'd had a hit with Jerry Jeff Walker's "Mr. Bojangles," to create an Americana classic: *Will the Circle Be Unbroken* (1972). The triple album was not only a virtuosic portrait of American roots music but it challenged the yawning generation gap with its unlikely collaborations between long-haired hippies and traditional country artists.

The project got started when the Dirt Band's banjo payer, John McEuen, who'd studied the virtuosic recordings of Earl Scruggs, learned that his musical hero was coming to the group's concert at Vanderbilt University in Nashville. Scruggs, who'd raised eyebrows in conservative country circles by speaking out against the war in Vietnam, had heard his kids playing the band's records and was happy to hear them playing acoustic instruments. When Scruggs agreed to record with the Dirt Band, his involvement drew Doc Watson to the project. The cast grew to include guitarists Merle Travis and Maybelle Carter and singers Roy Acuff and Jimmy Martin. Supplementing the Dirt Band were Nashville players like Norman Blake and Vassar Clements. Bill Monroe declined to participate; beyond his disdain for hippies, Monroe was still perturbed that Scruggs had left his Blue Grass Boys in 1948.

Personal moments animated the picking party. Doc Watson told Merle Travis that he'd named his son Merle (a gifted guitarist) after his own favorite picker. Maybelle Carter arrived carrying the 1929 Gibson flattop that she'd bought shortly after the Bristol sessions and called her young patrons "the dirty boys." Like everybody else, they addressed her as "Mother." The repertoire consisted mainly of songs associated with the invited guests—such classics as "Keep on the Sunny Side" and "I Am a Pilgrim"—and most tracks were cut in one or two takes.

Roy Acuff, known to be wary of longhairs playing country music, arrived at the studio and asked to hear what had been recorded. Poker-faced during the playback, he asked what the young men called that music. "Uh, well, it's kind of Appalachian, old timey, American folk," said the band's manager, Bill McEuen, who also looked after the career of another banjo player, comedian Steve Martin. "Hell!" said Acuff. "It ain't nothing but country music! Good country music! Let's go make some more, boys!" But it wasn't all sweetness and light. "Acuff made a couple of nasty remarks about Earl Scruggs in front of him," said band member Jeff Hanna. "We were sitting around a big table and Acuff says something about people changin', and then he turns and looks at Earl in a real snide sort of way." Later, Scruggs was driving in a car with banjoist McEuen. "You know, John," he said, "that Acuff really burns my ass. He thinks he invented country music."

Over the years, *Will the Circle Be Unbroken* has sold millions of copies. For many, including Bruce Springsteen, it was the first country album that they'd ever bought. A few years after its release, John McEuen and his friend Marty Stuart paid a visit to Maybelle Carter to give her a "gold record," explaining that it signified that the collection had by then sold five hundred thousand copies. "Well," said the woman who'd traveled to Bristol all those years ago, "I never knew that many people had even heard those old songs." Then, remembering her manners, Mother Maybelle said, "Would you boys like some lemonade?"

Jackson Browne had his songs cut by Tom Rush and the Byrds but struggled to sign a record contract of his own. Even David Geffen couldn't get a deal for Browne. "I said, 'You'll make millions with him,'" said Geffen, recalling his pitch to Atlantic's Ahmet Ertegun. "And he said, 'You know what? I got millions. Do you have millions?' I said no. He said, 'Start a record company and you'll have millions. Then we can all have millions.'" So with seed money from Atlantic, which handled distribution, Geffen (and Elliot Roberts) started Asylum Records.

Asylum's contracts were unique: The label would pay for the recording costs and day-to-day living expenses of its artists, who would earn a royalty from the first record sold but also relinquish half of the publishing income. Geffen was intimately involved in the careers of his artists. He sent Jackson Browne out on the road opening for Laura Nyro in advance of recording his debut album. Browne also introduced Geffen to the musicians who soon named themselves the Eagles; after buying out the existing recording contracts of

Glenn Frey and Don Henley, Geffen financed a stay in Boulder, Colorado, so that the band could woodshed far from the glare of the Troubadour.

"We did four sets a night for a month," said Randy Meisner, "playing as many originals as we'd written, and just about every other song we knew—loads of Beatles and Chuck Berry, some Neil Young. It tightened the group up pretty well. We learned how to play with each other." The band's producer of choice was Glyn Johns, the longtime engineer for the Rolling Stones who'd helmed records by the Steve Miller Band. Johns flew to Aspen to hear the band. "They were doing Chuck Berry stuff and they were bloody awful," said Johns. "Though I knew they could sing, I turned it down."

Geffen cajoled Johns into coming to Los Angeles and listening to a rehearsal, but he remained unimpressed until the band took a break. "Somebody picked up an acoustic guitar and they sat down and sang a song in four-part [harmony]," said Johns. "I said 'This is what this band is all about.'" Johns recorded the first Eagles album at Olympic Studio in London, and its lush production, rich with ringing guitars and clearly articulated harmonies, firmly established the group's sound. "Take It Easy," an unfinished Jackson Browne song that Frey completed, opened the album. It was the group's first (of many) hit singles to evoke a hedonistic California dream that made the "two girls for every boy" lyric of Jan and Dean's "Surf City" sound positively quaint.

Browne, who included "Take It Easy" on his second album, scored his own hit, "Doctor, My Eyes," on his 1972 debut, *Saturate Before Using*; the collection also included "Rock Me on the Water" and "Jamaica, Say You Will." Browne toured with Joni Mitchell, who had signed with Asylum to release her artful *For the Roses.* When Geffen challenged Mitchell to write a hit single for the album, she came up with the modestly successful "You Turn Me On, I'm a Radio" about, of all things, a country music station. Mitchell and Browne were the cream of the southern California singer-songwriter crop, but they were hardly the biggest stars in town.

"Joni and Jackson and Don Henley may have represented a new social order," said Mark Volman, who'd taken an unlikely turn from singing with the Turtles to playing with Frank Zappa's Mothers of Invention, "but they only represented a minimal part of the real record industry. Probably the most commercially successful L.A. artists of the whole period were Bread and Three Dog Night. I love Jackson Browne but he never wrote an 'American Pie.'" The Eagles were built to compete. "We'd watched bands like Poco and the Burrito Brothers lose their initial momentum," said Glenn Frey, "and we were determined not to make the same mistake. Everybody had to look good, sing good, play good, and write good. We wanted it all. Peer respect, AM and FM success, No. 1 singles and albums . . . and a lot of money."

"The Eagles were made to sell a million records," said Elliot Roberts. "They were made as a bridge between the avant-garde and commercial, between the Dead and Chicago." A commercial success from day one, with "Peaceful Easy Feeling" and "Witchy Woman" becoming hit singles, the Eagles have always had a tortured relationship with music critics. "Another thing that interests me about the Eagles is that I hate them," wrote Robert Christgau, in 1972. "Do I hate music that has been giving me pleasure all weekend, made by four human beings I've never met? Yeah, I think so." Part of the issue for Christgau was how the Eagles related to traditional country music: "It's no accident, either," he continued, "that the Eagles' hip country music excises precisely what is deepest and most gripping about country music—its adult working-class pain, its paradoxically rigid ethics—and leaves sixteen tracks of bluegrass-sounding good feelin'."

Like the Eagles, Linda Ronstadt, who also recorded for Asylum, got a generally cool critical reception, though no one disputed the quality of her voice. Ronstadt benefited from the guidance of producer-manager Peter Asher, and because she wasn't a songwriter, her albums included material by artists like Neil Young, Randy Newman, Lowell George of Little Feat, and J. D. Souther, who also co-wrote some of the Eagles' biggest hits. Ronstadt also championed less familiar songwriters such as Anna McGarrigle ("Heart Like a Wheel"), Karla Bonoff ("Someone to Lay Down Beside Me"), and Warren Zevon ("Poor, Poor Pitiful Me") and had hits with rock songs by Buddy Holly ("That'll Be the Day"), the Rolling Stones ("Tumbling Dice"), and Chuck Berry ("Back in the U.S.A."). She sang country songs by Willie Nelson ("Crazy"), Hank Williams ("I Can't Help It [If I'm Still in Love with You]"), and Dolly Parton ("I Will Always Love You"). In a word, her repertoire was Americana.

Ronstadt covered the title song of the Eagles' second album, *Desperado*, whose songs imagined the band as a gang of outlaws but brought less commercial success than had their debut. The Eagles bristled at their producer's reluctance to put more crunch into their country rock. The dispute came to a head during the production of the band's third record, *On the Border*, when Bill Szymczyk replaced Johns. "I saw through the Eagles as far as their acoustic, cowboy elements went," said Szymczyk. "I saw them as rockers who were dying and screaming to get out."

David Geffen was himself restless, and in 1972, just two years after forming Asylum Records, he sold it to Atlantic's parent company, Warner Communications, whereupon it was merged into Elektra/Asylum Records. Some of his artists, especially the hit-making Eagles, weren't happy with Geffen or his $7 million payday. "Asylum was an artist-oriented label for about a minute," said Henley, "until the big money showed up, then my, how things changed." A few years earlier, Henley had been elated when Ronstadt offered him $200 per week to go on tour.

By 1971, as a solo performer and the Y in CSN&Y, Neil Young was already a rock star. If Joni approached her songs as a painter, Neil was more like a sketch artist. His most enduring contribution to the CSN&Y repertoire was "Ohio," a howling rocker dashed off in response to student protesters' being killed by the National Guard at Kent State University. Now Young had something different in mind. "I was saying, 'OK, let's get really, really mellow and peaceful,'" he recalled. "'Let's make music that's just as intense as the electric stuff but which comes from a completely different, more loving place."

Young and Elliot Roberts travelled to Nashville in February for an appearance on *The Johnny Cash Show*. At a dinner party they met record producer Elliot Mazer, who didn't know much about Young beyond the fact that his girlfriend wouldn't stop playing Young's *After the Goldrush*. He asked Mazer to arrange a Saturday night recording session after Cash's show. The last-minute request taxed Mazer's Rolodex, but he attracted musicians who would play with Young for years, including bassist Tim Drummond, pedal steel guitarist Ben Keith, and drummer Ken Buttrey.

"More than any artist I've worked with," said Mazer, "you could sense when it was gonna be the take. Neil'll teach the band the song, but he'll hold back until he knows everything's together." According to Buttrey, Young all but writes his own drum parts with the strum of his guitar. "His rhythm playing is just perfect," said Buttrey. "It'll feel like he's slowing down, but it's just the Neil Young feel. No drummer should ever hold Neil to a certain tempo because if you put a metronome on it, you kill the Neil Young feel."

Neil got Linda Ronstadt and James Taylor to help him sing "Heart of Gold." "We wound up on our knees around this microphone," said Ronstadt. "I was just shrieking this high harmony, singing a part that was just higher than *God*." Taylor played banjo on "Old Man" and said, "I don't think I've played [a banjo] before or since. Neil likes to be present in his own life, as in-the-moment as he can be. And that's how he plays, that's how he writes, that's how he sings. He's present."

Harvest, Young's most popular album, made him an icon of (North) Americanaland. "This song put me in the middle of the road," said Young of "Heart of Gold," his only #1 hit. "Traveling there soon became a bore so I headed for the ditch." Bob Dylan, known to stray outside the lines, couldn't help but notice. "The only time it bothered me that someone sounded like me was when I was living in Phoenix, Arizona, in about '72," said Dylan. "The big song at the time was 'Heart of Gold.' I always liked Neil Young, but it bothered me every time I listened to 'Heart of Gold.' I think it was up at number one for a long time, and I'd say 'Shit, that's me. If it sounds like me, it should as well be me.'"

11
GRIEVOUS ANGELS

Gram Parsons felt right at home at Nellcote, a mansion in the south of France that was home to Nazis during World War II and, in 1970, Keith Richards of the Rolling Stones, who'd left the United Kingdom as tax exiles. A mobile recording truck was parked in the driveway, and couriers from Marseilles brought Richards (and his significant other, Anita Pallenberg) a steady supply of heroin. The other Stones found nearby accommodations and gathered in the spectral basement to record *Exile on Main Street*, as dark and rootsy an Americana album as could be made by a band of British rock stars.

"Engineers and technicians slept over," said Dominique Tarle, a photographer who documented sessions that ran from April until November. "Illegal power lines from the French railway system juiced their instruments, and when the temperature hit 100, they rehearsed with their pants off." The Stones worked deep into the night; Keith spent his days indulging his excesses and singing country songs with Parsons and, occasionally, Mick Jagger. "The three of us would be plonking away on Hank Williams songs while waiting for the rest of the band to arrive," said Richards. "Gram had the biggest repertoire of country songs you could imagine. He was never short of a song."

With his own career stalled, Parsons figured that if he couldn't be a Rolling Stone, then Keith could produce his solo album for the band's new record label. Excluded from the recording sessions, Parsons mostly got drunk and argued with the woman who'd soon become his wife, Gretchen Burrell. Richards, preoccupied with the writing and recording of *Exile*, the last truly great Rolling Stones album, gave little thought to making a record with Parsons. "Mick, I think," said Tarle, "was a little afraid [of a Parsons project]. And if there is no room for Mick, there is no room also for the Rolling Stones."

"A lot of *Exile* was done how Keith works," said drummer Charlie Watts, "which is, play it 20 times, marinate, play it another 20 times. He knows what he likes, but he's very loose." As the Stones cut eighteen tracks of swampy blues, rock, country, and gospel, the scene spun out of control. One September afternoon burglars stole nine of Richards's guitars, Bill Wyman's bass, and a saxophone belonging to Bobby Keys. Jagger, newly married to Bianca Pérez-Mora Macías, finally lost patience. "[Producer] Jimmy Miller was not functioning properly," said Jagger. "I had to finish the whole album myself, because otherwise there were just these drunks and junkies." Amid this turmoil, Parsons and Burrell were exiled from Nellcote. Gram would never again see Keith.

Back in the United States, Chris Hillman told Parsons about a special singer whom the Burritos had encountered at a club in Washington, DC. "I got this call," said Emmylou Harris, "this long, drawled-out voice. Gram was in Baltimore, which is about a fifty-mile drive. He wanted to hear me, and to hear how we sounded together, and would I pick him up? I said, 'Hell, no!'" Instead, Parsons and Burrell took a train to Washington, and Harris brought them to her gig at Clyde's. "We went down to the cellar," said Harris, "sat among the beer crates, and worked up 'I Fall to Pieces' and 'That's All It Took.' It was a rainy night and only about five people were in the audience. We just did the two numbers, then chatted and exchanged phone numbers. Gram said he would be in touch."

Harris didn't wait by the phone. "I was the jaded, cynical, old 25-year-old," said Harris, a high school valedictorian who dropped out of college to play music. "I'd had a baby and a broken marriage and I'd worked as a waitress and I'd been on food stamps." Harris had recorded a folk album in the Joni Mitchell–Judy Collins vein and knew little about country music. When Parsons got a record deal with Warner Brothers, he sent her a plane ticket and an album by the Louvin Brothers. "It really turned my head around," said Harris. "I love the Everly Brothers, but there's something purer and more raw about Charlie and Ira Louvin. It makes your hair stand up. . . . It got me into duets." Harris had found her métier. "It's always intriguing, the infinite combinations human voices can make together," she said. "There's a wonderful feeling singing with somebody else. I suppose it is like what Fred Astaire and Ginger Rogers felt. You aren't conscious, you aren't really thinking, you're just moving with a certain amount of abandon."

Since Keith Richards wasn't going to produce his record, Parsons asked Merle Haggard. They met at Haggard's house in Bakersfield and got acquainted while playing with his model trains. "I thought he was a good writer," said Haggard, who turned down the job. "He was not wild though. That's what was funny to me. All these guys running around in long hair talk about being wild and Rolling Stones." Parsons hired key members of Elvis Presley's band: guitarist James Burton, keyboardist Glen D. Hardin, and drummer Ronnie Tutt. (At the label's insistence, he also paid part of their premium-scale salary.) Parsons was so nervous the first day of recording that he got too drunk to perform. Barry Tashian, an old friend from Boston on board to play rhythm guitar, recognized a change.

"One day his voice would be pretty shaky," said Tashian. "Other times he seemed very, very good. He shook a lot. I was ignorant about what he was putting himself through. Today I realize what the problem was. He was very sick. He had a lot of . . . devils." The presence of Harris, who would crochet between vocal takes, had a calming influence on Parsons. "When I looked at her," he said, "she had fantastic eye contact. Anything you were doing would be in perfect harmony as long as you would look at her. If you raise your eyebrows and go up on a note, she goes right up with you in perfect pitch."

The album, *GP,* was released in 1973. Parsons and Harris reprised the duet from their first meeting, "That's All It Took," and blended beautifully on "We'll Sweep Out the Ashes in the Morning." Parsons's fragility was evident in the performance of two of his original songs, "A Song for You" and "She" (written with Chris Ethridge of the Burritos). Far more traditional than *The Gilded Palace of Sin*, the album was less country rock than real country, and it failed to find an audience in either camp. "I was the audience that he wanted to reach," said Harris. "I hadn't really heard [country]. I couldn't get past . . . country music being politically incorrect. I grew up with rock and roll and folk and was a huge Bob Dylan fan." Sid Griffin, who'd later play in the Long Ryders and write books about Parsons and Dylan, recognized a kindred spirit. "When I heard *GP*, I realized he was the guy," said Griffin. "We hadn't produced any hip white Southerners who played any kind of anti-Vietnam dope-smoking music. Gram was our boy."

To promote the album, Parsons assembled a band (he couldn't afford Presley's men) that he called the Fallen Angels. Phil Kaufman, whom Parsons had met through the Stones, was the tour's road manager. "We had the most disorganized rehearsals," said Harris. "It was like we didn't work up a single song. I mean, we'd play them, but we didn't finish one." The tour's opening night in Colorado was a musical mess. "After that we decided we had better really rehearse," said Harris. "We went back to the hall and picked about twelve songs and we decided on beginnings and endings and breaks."

The album didn't crack the Top 200, but it attracted influential fans. "Gram's first solo record was an *event* in my little circle of musicians," said Steve Earle. "When I heard that Gram and company were coming to Texas, I was off like a prom dress, down the I-10 to the big city. It was loose but it was tough. Gram's hair was frosted and his fingernails were painted red. He sang through his nose with his eyes closed while the band played catch-up for most of the night. I saw and heard Emmylou Harris for the first time. I left a little bit in love and absolutely certain of what I was going to be when I grew up."

The group crossed paths in Houston with Neil Young, who came to their show with his opening act, Linda Ronstadt, and invited everybody back to his hotel for a party. "That was the first time Linda and Emmylou sang together," said Jock Bartley, guitarist in the Fallen Angels. "It was an amazing moment. Emmylou's voice was angelic, fragile, and high, while Linda's was bigger, deeper, and more forceful. When they put those voices together it was magical. And you could see it in their faces. They were as blown away as everyone else." Gretchen Parsons had become so jealous of the intimate on-stage eye contact between her husband and Harris that she had to be sent home. When the band played Oliver's in Boston, a young writer approached Parsons with a poem that he thought might make a good song: "Return of the Grievous Angel."

By the time Joni Mitchell returned to Los Angeles from British Columbia, David Geffen's Asylum Records had released hit albums by the Eagles, Jackson Browne, and Mitchell (*For the Roses*). When Geffen invited Mitchell to join him on a trip to Paris to stay at the Ritz and eat at the finest restaurants, he also brought along Robbie Robertson and his wife Dominique. Bob Dylan's recording contract was due to be renewed, and Robertson could be a valuable ally in trying to get his old boss to record for Asylum. Joni Mitchell wrote "Free Man in Paris" about Geffen—"nobody was calling me up for favors, no one's future to decide"—but his office was never really closed.

Geffen got his prize when Dylan signed to Asylum and used The Band to record his first album of original material since 1970's *New Morning.* "*Planet Waves* was as good as we could make it in the situation," said Robertson, citing a relatively undistinguished set of Dylan tunes that included one of his most enduring albeit mawkish songs, "Forever Young." The album was cut quickly in order to be in stores when Dylan and The Band set out on a twenty-one-city U.S. tour in January 1974. Dylan hadn't toured since 1966 (with the Hawks), and demand was high, with a mail-order lottery for the half-million available tickets drawing 5.5 million requests. "The tour was damn good for our pocketbooks," said drummer Levon Helm, "but it just wasn't a very passionate trip for any of us." It was business, and in the 1970s, the bank was big. Elton John debuted at the Troubadour in August 1970; two months later, he released *Tumbleweed Connection*, an album highly influenced by The Band. By 1975 John would be playing Dodger Stadium.

Joni Mitchell rose to the commercial occasion with *Court and Spark*, a sublime collection of personal poetics and subtly moving melodies. This wasn't folk or rock but a sophisticated suite of songs recorded with Tom Scott's jazzy group, the L.A. Express. Robbie Robertson played lead guitar on "Raised on Robbery," but it was the heady propulsion of "Help Me" that gave Mitchell her only Top 10 single. Alongside *Blue* and *For the Roses*, *Court and Spark* found the idiosyncratic artist briefly in tune with a mass audience.

That changed with the more experimental *The Hissing of Summer Lawn* (1975), known to have been a particular favorite of Prince. "[Joni] turned left without signaling and the audience went straight on," said Ron Stone, part of her management team. Mitchell would make more remarkable music—*Hejira* (1976) was a meditation on love and wanderlust animated by the lithe electric bass of Jaco Pastorious—and future albums would include collaborations with Charles Mingus and musical contributions by saxophonist Wayne Shorter and jazz guitarist Pat Matheny. In 2008 pianist Herbie Hancock won the Album of the Year Grammy for *River: The Joni Letters*, a collection of her songs performed by, among others, Tina Turner, Nora Jones, and Leonard

Cohen. Mitchell was unique among her pop peers, a genuine artist, and generations of songwriters have gone to school on her transcendent streak of classic albums.

Linda Ronstadt, the sweetheart of the Troubadour, followed her hit-making years with successful albums of pop standards and Mexican folk music; neither the Eagles nor Jackson Browne strayed far from their commercial wheelhouse. Browne found a vital ally in David Lindley, whose slide guitar and violin were integral to songs with lyrics focused on romance ("Jamaica, Say You Will") and the individual's place in society ("For Everyman," "The Pretender"). *Late for the Sky* (1974) was Browne's most artful collection of intimate, personal songs; his support of environmental and liberal political causes anticipated the activism common among Americana artists.

The Eagles focused on solid songs and exquisitely produced records. "The Byrds invented country-rock," said Chris Hillman, "Gram and I refined it in the Burritos, and the Eagles took it to the bank." Parsons took a more critical view. "The Eagles' music is bubblegum," he said. "It's got too much sugar in it. Life is tougher than they make it out to be." Parsons and Harris once played a show headlined by the Eagles and featuring Lester Flatt's band as the opening act. "Lester Flatt had Roland White on guitar," said Bernie Leadon, "and a 15-year-old Marty Stuart on mandolin. I remember Marty told me that that night was when he realized that you could mix country, rock, and bluegrass. He was all excited and went back to tell Lester all about it. Lester just said, 'Aw, it won't amount to shit.'"

The Eagles hit the big time with singles from 1974's *On the Border* ("Already Gone," "Best of My Love") and 1975's *One of These Nights* ("One of These Nights," "Lyin' Eyes"), the latter both the first album totally produced by Bill Szymczyk and the last with Bernie Leadon. The Eagles soon featured two rock guitarists (Don Felder and Joe Walsh) with nary a banjo nor steel guitar to be heard. Frey and Henley came to personify Hollywood hedonism. "They were the horniest boys in town," said a woman in their social circle, "living life without rules or limits. And still they loved to portray themselves in their music as the underdogs, the taken-advantage-of victims. We used to call that song 'Lyin' Guys.'"

The Eagles capped their hit-making years with *Hotel California*; the title song used ringing rock guitars to orchestrate lyrics about where living in the fast lane can lead. But the album that truly reflected the end of the California singer-songwriter and country-rock scene was Jackson Browne's *Running on Empty*, a live album featuring original songs (the hit title track) and cover tunes capturing the seamier side of the rock 'n' roll lifestyle (Danny O'Keefe's "The Road" and a blues standard about the era's drug of choice, "Cocaine"). In the end, the legacy of the Eagles would rest not on their carefully crafted LPs but on a greatest hits collection that became the biggest selling album in history.

Music critics weren't the only people who gave the Eagles no respect. The Dude was an iconic hipster played by Jeff Bridges in the Coen Brothers' 1998 film *The Big Lebowski*. In one scene, a distressed Dude rides in a taxi while "Peaceful Easy Feeling" plays on the radio. "Man, can you change the channel?" said the Dude. "I had a rough night and I hate the fucking Eagles, man." The black cabbie explodes into angry profanities, pulls the taxi to a squealing stop, and throws the Dude to the curb. The polished harmonies and perfectly rendered guitars of the Eagles would come to have a profound effect on commercial country music. As for the Dudes of Americana, they typically dismiss the group while remembering every last hit.

Willie Nelson went back to Texas after his house in Hendersonville, Tennessee, burned to the ground in December 1969. Neither Nelson nor Nashville would ever be quite the same. "I was raised in Texas beer joints," he said, "so I went back to [playing] my old beer joints. I was home again." His daughters returned from the Atlanta Pop Festival excited about seeing Janis Joplin, Creedence Clearwater Revival, and Joe Cocker and wondered if their dad might also appeal to the hippies. Nelson was surprised to learn that Leon Russell, who'd played piano on some of his earliest recordings, had re-created himself as a rock star.

Nelson was thirty-nine when he returned to Texas and was wise to the ways of the music business. "I knew I only had a few years left to do what I was going to do," said Nelson. "I wasn't going down there to quit." Nelson's hair crept over his ears, and he traded his conventional stage wardrobe for blue jeans, tee shirts, and sneakers. But he never denied his past. At his 1972 debut at the Armadillo, the hippest club in Austin, he played to an audience split between longhairs and rednecks and opened with his early classics: "Crazy," "Hello Walls," "Funny How Time Slips Away," and "Night Life." As the show continued, he took more guitar solos and let his harmonica player, Mickey Raphael, strut his stuff. The rich, distinctive sound on the bandstand is what Nelson brought to his Atlantic albums.

The Dripping Springs Reunion, a three-day festival that Nelson helped promote in 1972, anticipated his genre-defying future. The bill placed such mainstream Nashville stars as Roger Miller, Loretta Lynn, and Roy Acuff alongside Willie and his more unorthodox friends Waylon Jennings and Kris Kristofferson. Songwriter Donnie Fritts was at the festival to play keyboards with Kristofferson. "You'd look out there and it'd be hillbillies, cowboy guys, and then you have the hippies, all having fun together," said Fritts. "It was one of the most important gatherings of the seventies, bringing all the different acts and people together in one place. And it happened through Willie Nelson."

Texas was thick with songwriters; Mickey Newbury was one of the most successful, writing songs for everyone from Kenny Rogers and the First Edition ("Just Dropped In [To See What Condition My Condition Was In"]) to Eddy Arnold ("Here Comes the Rain, Baby") and Solomon Burke ("Time Is a Thief"). In 1968 Newbury met a songwriter named Townes Van Zandt in Houston and brought him to Nashville to meet the man who would produce his first record, "Cowboy" Jack Clement; a decade earlier, Clement had helped Johnny Cash shape his signature sound at Sun Records.

"I also took Guy Clark," said Newbury. "Guy only had a couple songs, but I took him to Nashville, signed him with Columbine Music, basically off the strength of... a song called 'Step Inside This House.' If I hadn't taken Townes to Nashville, then there would have been no Guy Clark. Then you think about all the people that said that their major influences were Guy Clark and Townes Van Zandt. Now you're talking about Steve Earle, Lyle Lovett, Nanci Griffith, Joe Ely, all of those people."

Born to a wealthy family with an attentive mother and a corporate lawyer father, Van Zandt was excited to see Elvis Presley on *The Ed Sullivan Show* and got his first guitar the following Christmas. But the smart student and gifted athlete fell into binge drinking and depression at the University of Colorado. Van Zandt was diagnosed with manic depression and underwent three months of insulin shock therapy, which shattered his long-term memory and foretold a lifetime of alcoholism and drug abuse. He quit college in 1967 to become a folk singer.

In Houston, Van Zandt played clubs such as the Jester Lounge and the Old Quarter alongside performers like Guy Clark and Doc Watson; he was especially drawn to the pulsing acoustic blues of Lightnin' Hopkins. "Some people don't know what to think when you tell them your two biggest influ-

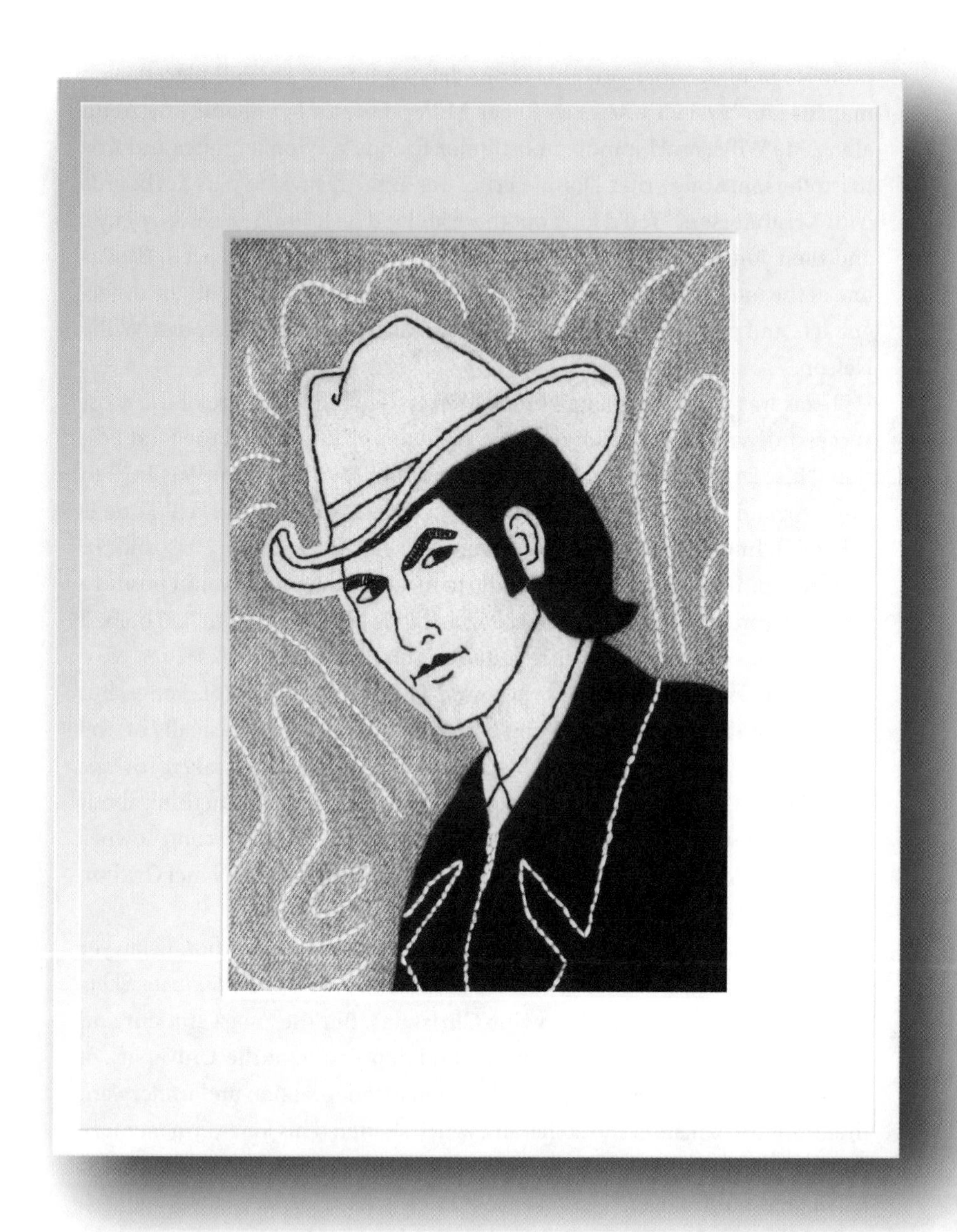

TOWNES VAN ZANDT

ences are Lightnin' Hopkins and Robert Frost," said Van Zandt, but those inspirations are clear in the precision of his language and the fluidity of his fingerpicking. "Townes is the first person I heard who was writing his own songs in a way that made me want to do it, too," said Clark. "Not necessarily in his style, but [with] the care and respect he took with writing."

Van Zandt began recording in 1968, but his albums, released on small independent labels, drew little attention beyond a minor cult following. By 1972, when he recorded a live set at the Old Quarter, he'd already penned some of his most famous and enduring songs including "Pancho and Lefty," "Tecumseh Valley," "Flyin' Shoes," "Kathleen," and "Waiting 'Round to Die." His songs would become country hits for such artists as Willie Nelson and Merle Haggard and perennials in the repertoire of Americana performers. Clark became equally influential. "I see myself as a folksinger and my songs as poetry," he said, adding, "I don't need to prove I'm a poet in every line, and I'm not afraid to speak plainly in my songs.... But it is my obligation as a poet to be faithful to the verse. I write what I know. I write what I see."

Sometimes, that can take time. "It was about four in the morning and I was coming back from a club gig sleeping in the backseat of the car," said Clark of one writing experience. "I woke up to see where we were and said, 'If I could just get off of this L.A. Freeway without getting killed or caught.' Lights started going off in my head with that line, so I got Susanna's eyebrow pencil and a burger sack off the floor and wrote it down." Clark carried the scrap of paper around for a couple of years before completing "L.A. Freeway," which became a hit for Jerry Jeff Walker.

Guy and Susanna Clark were married in 1972; Van Zandt served as best man, and for a time, lived in the couple's East Nashville home. "In the early years we were always together," said Clark. "She and Townes were best friends, and Townes and I were best friends.... And he was always in love with my wife." On one occasion the three were all stricken with the flu and living on antibiotics and cough syrup. "I went to bed and had a dream about being a folksinger," said Van Zandt. "And I was on stage somewhere and I played this song. And it was so vivid that I remembered it, woke up exactly after it finished, turned on the light and reached for this little pad and pencil." In the morning he poured himself a cup of coffee and played the Clarks his new song, "If I Needed You."

"It was fucking Nashville, Tennessee," said Clark, "home of Johnny Cash, and you're a songwriter from Texas. It was top of the world, like Paris in the

Twenties." In this crowd, you had to hold your own. In 1972, Earle played a pass-the-hat gig in Houston to a sparse audience that included Van Zandt, who kept calling out for him to play "The Wabash Cannonball." "I finally had to admit that I didn't know the fuckin' 'Wabash Cannonball,'" said Earle. "And he goes, 'You call yourself a folksinger and you don't know "The Wabash Cannonball?"' So I played this song of his called 'Mr. Mudd and Mr. Gold' that has about 19 million words in it. And he shut up."

Rodney Crowell knew "The Wabash Cannonball" because his parents had met at a Roy Acuff concert. His father worked construction and played small-time music gigs with his own band, J. W. Crowell and the Rhythmaires; Rodney played drums with the group before forming his own teenage combos and taking off for Nashville in 1972. Sleeping in his car, he made ends meet by washing dishes and hung out at a popular folk club, Bishop's Pub. That's where Crowell first met Earle. "Skinny kid with a big black felt cowboy hat," said Crowell. "It was like he stepped right out of a Cormac McCarthy novel."

Crowell caught a break when country singer Jerry Reed heard him play, signed him to his publishing company, and cut his "You Can't Keep Me Here in Tennessee." Freed from his day job, Crowell focused on writing songs worthy of being played at a song circle at Guy and Susanna Clark's house. "Townes Van Zandt was pretty much the alpha male," said Crowell. "He was smart, he was strung out; he'd come into town and be upstairs kicking heroin." Clark was a more stable role model; his 1975 debut, *Old No. 1*, included not only "L.A. Freeway" but "Desperados Waiting for a Train," an enduring classic that had background vocals by Earle, Crowell, and Emmylou Harris. Clark helped Steve Earle get a publishing deal and hired him to play bass in his band. "It all revolved around Guy," said Crowell, "'cause Guy was the curator of all the wild spirits who were really just a group of songwriters trying to figure out how to do it." Crowell and Earle were among the lucky few who honed their craft under Clark's benign tutelage and who got to carve their initials into his wooden dining table.

The Byrds took a slow glide into history after *Sweetheart of the Rodeo*. But with Clarence White on lead guitar, the band also put on the best live shows of its career. The most famous songs from those years were "The Ballad of Easy Rider," which Roger McGuinn composed after Bob Dylan gave him the opening lyric ("The river flows, it flows to the sea / Wherever that river flows, that's where I want to be"), and "Jesus Is Just Alright," which was later a hit for the Doobie Brothers. McGuinn dissolved the current Byrds in 1973 so that the original members could reunite to create a critically dismissed album produced by the ex-Byrd who'd become the biggest star, David Crosby. White did session work while a member of the Byrds, including recordings with Linda Ronstadt, the Everly Brothers, and Jackson Browne. He hit the ground running after the breakup, mounting a reunion tour with the Kentucky Colonels and joining the Muleskinners, a progressive bluegrass group that included Peter Rowan, Davis Grisman, Bill Keith, and Richard Greene.

White was, in a phrase, a working musician, and on the night of July 14, 1973, he and his brothers played the Jack of Diamonds in Palmdale, California. At about 2 a.m. White was loading his equipment into a car, including his B-Bender Telecaster, a unique guitar customized to allow him to emulate a steel guitar by bending its B string as much as a minor third. In a tragic instant, White was struck and killed by a drunk driver. More than a hundred mourners, most of them musicians, gathered for a funeral at St. Mary's Catholic Church. A drunken Gram Parsons joined the mourners for the burial at Joshua Memorial Park. As dirt was thrown onto the coffin, Parsons and Bernie Leadon began to softly sing a traditional gospel tune, "Farther Along," that had been recorded by both the Flying Burrito Brothers and the Byrds. "Farther along we'll know more about it," they sang, joined by others. "Farther along we'll understand why." Chris Ethridge overheard Parsons speaking to Kaufman. "Phil," said Parsons, "if this happens to me, I don't want them doing this to me. You can take me to the desert and burn me. I want to go out in a cloud of smoke."

Parsons nearly got his wish when the Laurel Canyon home he shared with Gretchen burned to the ground. Parsons, in a downward spiral of alcohol and heroin abuse, was due to cut a second album; Harris was excited to get back to work. "*G.P.* was a struggle," she said, "but Gram's singing was so much better after a year on the road." Once more, members of Presley's band were in the studio alongside Bernie Leadon and Byron Berline. "Our singing came together on two songs: 'Love Hurts' and 'Angels Rejoiced [Last Night],'" said Harris. "I finally learned what I was supposed to do. . . . And the fact that his voice sometimes suffered from the hard life that he lived gave it a vulnerable quality."

"The things I like of Gram's were when he was singing with Emmy," said Linda Ronstadt, who added a third voice to one song on the record. "She was very strong and was able to see the uniqueness in what he did. With Gram, most of it was sloppy, but Emmy was able to make it clearer." The album, titled *Grievous Angel* after the tune Parsons wrote using the words of Tom Brown, was Parsons's best work since *Sweetheart of the Rodeo* (reissues included his vocals, which were omitted from the original release) and *The Gilded Palace of Sin*. It also planted the seeds that would make Emmylou Harris the Queen of Americana.

Whereas *GP* was solid but stiff, as if straining to be a true country record, *Grievous Angel* projected a personality of its own. It included superior songs from Parsons's past including "Brass Buttons," which he'd sung as a folk song in 1965, and "$1000 Wedding," which was attempted but abandoned by the Burrito Brothers. "Love Hurts," an Everly Brothers tune by Felice and Boudleaux Bryant, captured the delicate vocal chemistry between Parsons and Harris. "Return of the Grievous Angel" spoke to the allure of love: "Twenty thousand roads I went down, down, down / And they all lead me straight back home to you." Parsons's newest song, "In My Hour of Darkness," written in part as a tribute to Clarence White and sung in close harmony with Harris, closed the album with elegiac grace.

Completed in less than two weeks, the album suggested that Parsons was on his best behavior; Philip Kaufman was said to have acted as something of a babysitter. Parsons considered giving Harris co-billing and putting a photo of them astride a motorcycle on the cover. But those were details to be determined, and with a month before scheduled live dates, Parsons, who'd mentioned plans to divorce his wife, took his new girlfriend, Margaret Fisher, to his spiritual home, Joshua Tree National Park. Hank Williams took his last ride in the back of a blue Cadillac; Parsons drove to Joshua Tree in a new white Jaguar.

During the day, they went to a local bar. "They had one song from Gram's first album on the jukebox," said Fisher, "which he played incessantly." One night, they hit a different bar after supper. "They had a band playing," said Fisher, "and Gram sat in with them. He was singing 'Okie from Muskogee' and he was making up his own words like 'We all smoke marijuana in Muskogee.'" But back at the Joshua Tree Inn Parsons wanted something stronger than pot, and a local dealer obliged not with heroin but with morphine. Parsons, high from the first shot, requested a second, and out went the lights. He was pronounced dead at High Desert Memorial Hospital at 12:15 a.m. on September 19, 1973.

The hospital sent Parsons's body to Los Angeles International Airport for transport to his stepfather's home in New Orleans. Acting on his friend's request, Kaufman and an associate drove a beat-up hearse to the airport, talked their way into possession of the remains, and headed to Joshua Tree, pausing only to buy beer, a bottle of booze, and a five-gallon container of gasoline. They stopped near one of Gram's favorite spots, Cap Rock, and pulled the casket out of the hearse. Opening the lid, Kaufman tucked a "Sin City" jacket into the coffin and soaked everything in gasoline. He then struck a match and sent the grievous angel home in a fireball. A few days later police arrested Kaufman at his home for what one wag called "Grand Theft Parsons." Coincidentally, director Arthur Penn had rented the house as a location for the film *Night Moves*. As the police took Kaufman into custody, Penn said, "I have a feeling I'm directing the wrong movie."

12
THE RED-HEADED ICON

Willie Nelson paid a 1972 visit to Kris Kristofferson in Durango, Mexico, where he was acting in director Sam Peckinpah's *Pat Garrett and Billy the Kid*. Kristofferson had urged Bob Dylan to write a song for the film; he came up with "Knocking on Heaven's Door" and also made his dramatic debut playing a cowboy called Anonymous. He was "a little shy, scared to death," said Nelson. "They had him jumpin' and runnin' on them horses, and he ain't no cowboy." Dylan was more comfortable with six strings than six guns. "Willie ended up serenading the cast and crew all day long at Peckinpah's house," said Kristofferson, "gladly accommodating Dylan's requests to hear more and more."

Nelson, who was now settled outside Austin, Texas, imagined a record that was equally unadorned. He got the chance after he aligned with Neil Reshen, who'd negotiated a new RCA contract for Waylon Jennings that gave him creative control and increased his royalty rate from 5 percent to 8 percent. (Executive and artist Chet Atkins had a long-term pact at 5 percent.) Reshen leveraged the relative success of Nelson's Atlantic releases to get him a comparable deal with Columbia Records.

The inspiration for Nelson's career reinvention came from a song he'd sung as a Fort Worth deejay in the 1950s and to his kids at bedtime, "Tale of the Red

Headed Stranger." Nelson fleshed out the story of the enigmatic cowboy and his black steed with original songs ("Time of the Preacher") and covers of Eddy Arnold's "I Couldn't Believe It Was True" and "Blue Eyes Crying in the Rain," a song written by the man who'd discovered Hank Williams, Fred Rose. But the true revelation of *Red Headed Stranger* (1975) was a stripped-down sound built on Nelson's acoustic guitar, a low-key, often absent rhythm section, and instrumental flourishes by Mickey Raphael on harmonica and Willie's sister Bobbie on piano. Cut and mixed in five days for $4,000 at a studio in Garland, Texas, Nelson used the rest of his $60,000 recording budget for living expenses and to upgrade the band's equipment and tour bus.

Columbia executives were more than skeptical about a submission that sounded like demo recordings in need of a Nashville polish. But Nelson held fast, and *Red Headed Stranger* became both a cultural signifier and a commercial smash, with "Blue Eyes Crying in the Rain" Nelson's first #1 country hit. The country music maverick had hit the big time with an Americana concept album that felt familiar to anyone who'd grown up watching cowboys at the movies and on television. "Texans have known for 15 years what *Red Headed Stranger* finally revealed to the world," said his biographer, Joe Nick Patoski. "That Nelson is simply too brilliant a songwriter, interpreter, and singer—just too damn universal—to be defined as merely a country artist."

It would be another five years before Nelson came up with the song that would define his career, "On the Road Again"; he wrote it for the film *Honeysuckle Rose*, in which Nelson played, well, Willie. But it was the mainstream success of *Red Headed Stranger* that ensured a long and profitable run on the concert circuit; along the way, Nelson would release a steady stream of albums that ranged from the artistically inspired to the amiably workmanlike. Nelson's triumph rubbed off on his musical pals, including Waylon Jennings, with whom Nelson often shared concert bills.

It was Hazel Smith, a publicist for Jennings, who came up with the idea to promote Waylon and Willie as outlaws. "To us," said Jennings, "outlaw meant standing up for your rights, your own way of doing things." Jennings had anticipated the moment with a 1973 album of Billie Joe Shaver songs called *Honky Tonk Heroes*, but its lean, wiry sound hadn't reached much beyond his country fans. That changed in 1976, when RCA catered to the outlaw country hype with a compilation album of previously recorded tracks by Nelson, Jennings, his wife Jessi Colter, and Tompall Glaser. "Waylon was selling, if we were lucky, two hundred and fifty thousand albums," said RCA producer

Jerry Bradley. "Willie comes out with *Red Headed Stranger* and that took off and sold a million records. Jessi Colter put out 'I'm Not Lisa' on Capitol. That damn thing sold half a million, or a million, and set our butt on fire." So RCA put old wine in a new bottle, called it *Wanted! The Outlaws*, and moved more than a million copies while topping the country charts and hitting the pop Top 10.

There's a clear analogy to be made between "outlaw country" and "Americana"; both are terms coined in the interest of marketing music. "You couldn't find two guys who are less like outlaws than Waylon Jennings and Willie Nelson," said their manager, Neil Reshen. "It's all horseshit really. But if the public wants outlaws, we'll give them outlaws." The two men responded differently to mass success. Nelson kept busy on the road, ventured into acting, and repurchased the song copyrights he'd sold during his leaner years. Jennings spent long days (and nights) in the recording studio fueled by a $1,500-a-day cocaine habit, and like all addicts, worried about his supply line. On one occasion his management company in New York arranged for 23 grams of cocaine to be sent via air courier. The DEA detected the suspicious package, removed 22 grams, and sent the rest on its way to Nashville. In his autobiography Jennings said that he escaped arrest thanks to a flawed search warrant, but he neglected to note that Mark Rothbaum, an assistant to Reshen, pled guilty to cocaine distribution to avoid implicating Jennings. Nelson recognized Rothbaum as an outlaw's best friend; he went to work for Willie after serving a brief sentence and later became his manager.

Bob Dylan spent the first two months of 1974 on a U.S. arena tour with The Band that reconfirmed his status as a cultural superstar. Then he devoted two months, five days per week, from 8:30 until 4:30, to a painting class at Norman Raeben's art studio above Carnegie Hall. "He taught you [about] putting your head and your mind and your eye together," said Dylan, "in a way that allowed me to do consciously what I unconsciously felt." Raeben also gave Dylan more concrete ideas. One day, he criticized Dylan's rendering of a blue vase by saying he was "tangled up in blue."

A few days later Dylan had a rough draft of "Tangled up in Blue," which became the lead track of his next album, *Blood on the Tracks*. "I was just trying to make [the song] like a painting where you can see the different parts but then you also see the whole of it," said Dylan. "With that particular song, that's what I was trying to do . . . with the concept of time and the way the characters change from the first person to the third person, and you're never quite sure if the third person is talking or the first person is talking. But as you look at the whole thing, it really doesn't matter."

Dylan titled "Idiot Wind," his most vitriolic song since "Like a Rolling Stone," after another of Raeben's dicta. But Dylan's studies did more than inspire some new songs. "I went home after that and my wife never did understand me ever since that day," said Dylan. "That's when our marriage started breaking up." To be sure, more than adult education contributed to the dissolution of the marriage; although the official divorce was still years away, Dylan spent the summer of 1974 with Ellen Bernstein, a woman he'd met at his new-old label, Columbia Records, at a home he owned alongside the Crow River in Minnesota.

"He was at his best there, at his most comfortable," said Bernstein, "with his brother's house down the road. He had a painting studio out in the field, and the house was far from fancy, out in the middle of nowhere. He was very relaxed, and that's where and when he was writing *Blood on the Tracks*." One of Dylan's most celebrated albums, its meditations on *les histoires de coeur* were assumed to be about the troubled state of his marriage, but these were not like the intimate confessions of Joni Mitchell; they were more like reflections from a lifetime. "Simple Twist of Fate" originally bore the subtitle "Fourth Street Affair," suggesting that it was about Suze Rotolo, while "You're Gonna Make Me Lonesome When You Go" anticipated the end of his relationship with Bernstein.

Dylan polished his lyrics before entering the studio, but recording the music, which he'd composed mainly on a guitar tuned to open D, proved to be a challenge. Dylan played the material for Mike Bloomfield, his guitarist for *Highway 61 Revisited*, who failed to get his arms around songs he heard as long and monochromatic. Eric Weissberg (of "Dueling Banjos" fame) and his band Deliverance joined Dylan in the recording studio, but he used the musicians selectively and enlisted other players for subsequent sessions. "He knew as soon as he heard something whether or not it was what he was going for," said Bernstein. "It was all very immediate and very emotional." Dylan played a test pressing of the album for his brother, David Zimmerman, who was troubled by the minimalist sound and urged him to recut five of the songs with musicians from Minneapolis. This was done over the course of two days in December.

WILLIE NELSON

Columbia released *Blood on the Tracks* in January 1975, the same month it issued Nelson's *Red Headed Stranger*. Critics judged Dylan's album his best since his mid-sixties hot streak, and July saw the commercial release of *The Basement Tapes*, a 2-LP selection of the tunes that Dylan and The Band had recorded in Big Pink. At about that time Dylan started turning up on Greenwich Village stages playing with Muddy Waters, Ramblin' Jack Elliot, and Patti Smith. His buddy Bob Neuwirth also organized jam sessions with such players as Mick Ronson, lead guitarist of David Bowie's glam-rock band, the Spiders from Mars; T-Bone Burnett, an unknown guitarist and singer-songwriter from Texas; and Scarlet Rivera, whom Dylan had invited to play after seeing her walk down Second Avenue carrying a violin case.

"We were all very close," said Dylan. "We had this fire going ten years ago and now we've got it burning again." Dylan might have sought the intimacy of his early years in the Village, but as the Rolling Thunder Revue took shape, with bassist Rob Stoner leading the band, there was no doubt about who was the star of the show. Mounted as a sort of guerilla tour, with an impromptu itinerary that focused on secondary markets, more than seventy were in the troupe when final rehearsals were held at the Sea Crest Beach Motel in Massachusetts, where Dylan serenaded the participants of a mah-jongg tournament with "Simple Twist of Fate" and poet Allen Ginsberg read his elegy for his mother, "Kaddish."

Joan Baez reunited with Dylan for the entire outing, as did Ramblin' Jack Elliott and Roger McGuinn of the Byrds; Joni Mitchell, Arlo Guthrie, and Gordon Lightfoot appeared at a handful of shows. A film crew was on hand to record some of the concerts as well as scenes like Dylan and Ginsberg playing a blues at the grave of Beat writer Jack Kerouac. Despite the presence of playwright Sam Shepard, everything was improvised. "The filming happened in gleeful little happenings," said Baez, who participated alongside Sara Dylan, "enacting whatever dream Dylan had had in the night." Baez had just had a Top 40 hit with an original song, "Diamonds and Rust," about her love affair with the auteur. "Naturally," said Baez, "I was playing a Mexican whore—the Rolling Thunder women all played whores."

The resulting film, *Renaldo and Clara*, clocked in at nearly four hours. Widely panned by critics, it played only a limited run in Los Angeles and New York. Critics were kinder to the live show in which Dylan, wearing feathered hats and mime-style whiteface, performed tunes from *Blood on the Tracks*, debuted new material such as "Isis," and recast old songs in novel arrangements. As if completing a circle, Dylan ended each concert leading the entire cast in singing Woody Guthrie's "This Land Is Your Land." The tour inspired Burnett to form the Alpha Band with two other members of the ensemble, David Mansfield and Steven Soles.

"From a myth-making point of view," said Jon Landau in *Rolling Stone*, "this is all astonishingly effective stuff. . . . This is one rock star who still knows the importance of mystery in creating art and in calling attention to the artist." Landau had recently helped Bruce Springsteen complete *Born to Run*, an album that landed the singer on simultaneous covers of *Time* and *Newsweek* in September 1975. A few months later, Springsteen saw the Rolling Thunder Revue in New Haven and went backstage to meet the maestro. "Hey," said Dylan, "I hear you're the new me."

Emmylou Harris was at her parents' home in Maryland when she learned that Gram Parsons had died; she then spent a weekend with Barry Tashian and others (including banjo virtuoso Bill Keith) at a cabin in Connecticut. Playing a tape of her last session with Parsons, she wept as he sang "Brass Buttons." "When Gram died," said Harris, "I felt like I'd been amputated, like my life had been whacked off. I'd only been with him a short time, but it was like everything had become clear to me in that short period."

Grievous Angel was released in January 1974. At the insistence of Gretchen Parsons, the cover photo of Gram and Emmylou was scuttled for a ghostly image of Parsons against a pale blue sky. Despite the album's poor sales, Warner Brothers offered Harris a solo deal with an advance sufficient to hire the same Presley-honed musicians. *Pieces of the Sky* amounted to an Americana sampler with songs by Parsons ("Sleepless Night"), Merle Haggard ("The Bottle Let Me Down"), Dolly Parton ("Coat of Many Colors"), and a Top 5 country single (sung with Herb Pederson) of the Louvin Brothers' "If I Could Only Win Your Love." "Blueberry Wine," the LP's opening track, was written by an unknown from Houston named Rodney Crowell.

"The first time I laid eyes on her," said Crowell, "she was playing a show at a folk club in Washington D.C. There was talk of her recording one of my songs, so I had gone to meet her. Afterwards, we went to the house of one of her friends and sat until the wee hours with guitars talking about songs. I would sing an obscure Townes Van Zandt song, or a Louvin Brothers song, and she would say, 'I know that.'" Music cemented the bond. "It was great to find a new writer who was of my generation," said Harris. "He was like a kid brother. If we had grown up together we would have been making music together all our lives."

Harris, like Parsons, made country music with an album-rock sensibility. "After Gram died," said Harris, "I wanted to carry on his music in some small way. I also felt I could speak to some people like me who'd sort of looked down on country music. . . . I was kind of an ex-hippie—I was one of them. I also brought to it more than a love for traditional country; I could get really excited by a Louvin Brothers song, and I'd also cut a Beatles song. I was genuinely affected by both of these things."

On tour with the same musicians who'd recorded her album—now called the Hot Band—Harris reconnected with Crowell in Austin, where he sat in at the Armadillo World Headquarters. At the end of the evening, Harris offered Crowell a gig as the Hot Band's rhythm guitarist. He left the next day for Los Angeles. "It wasn't my musicianship at all," said Crowell, who was thrilled to play guitar alongside James Burton. "It was the conversation that Emmy and I were having about songs . . . I was part of the discussion about the material that was being done."

Elite Hotel, released in December 1975, consolidated the success of Harris's debut, becoming a #1 country album on the strength of hit singles identified with Patsy Cline ("Sweet Dreams") and Buck Owens ("Together Again"). The eclectic repertoire included tunes by Hank Williams ("Jambalaya [On the Bayou]"), Lennon-McCartney ("Here, There, and Everywhere"), and more selections by Parsons ("Sin City," "Ooh Las Vegas," and "Wheels"). Harris sang Crowell's "Till I Gain Control Again" and co-wrote a song with him called "Amarillo."

In the space of twelve months, Harris had become the kind of hipster country artist that Parsons had hoped to be. "I'm influenced by the real Old Guard country music," said Harris. "George Jones and Webb Pierce and the real stone-hard country. But I can't pretend to be that kind of artist." Instead, she became the kind of interpreter who'd also perform songs by Crowell and his songwriting heroes, Guy Clark and Townes Van Zandt. Crowell blossomed while playing in the Hot Band and harmonizing with Harris on songs such as the Louvin Brothers' "You're Running Wild." By now, everybody wanted to sing with Emmylou, including Bob Dylan, who invited her to sessions for *Desire*, the follow-up to *Blood on the Tracks.*

Dylan wrote most of the album with Jacques Levy, a theater director known for the controversial *Oh! Calcutta*, and eschewed the personal in favor of narrative songs about boxer Hurricane Carter ("Hurricane") and gangster Joey Gallo ("Joey"). Dylan attempted to record *Desire* with a large ensemble, but the final album, one of his most commercially successful, featured a small group. "I'd never heard the songs before, and we did most of them in one or two takes," said Harris. "His phrasing changes a lot, but Gram did that a lot, too . . . I watched him all the time, so I did just the same thing with Dylan."

"Those first royalty checks we got almost killed some of us," said The Band's Rick Danko, who earned a couple of hundred thousand dollars from "This Wheel's on Fire," which he co-wrote with Dylan. "Suddenly we had all the money we needed, and people were falling over themselves to make us happy, which meant giving us all the dope we could stand."

"After *The Band*," said Robertson, "something threw us off track. . . . Mentally, health wise, success was not the best thing for The Band." The five musicians were never less than world-class, but their next two studio efforts, *Stage Fright* and *Cahoots*, lacked the cohesive artistry that distinguished the group's first two albums. Those had followed years of playing with Ronnie Hawkins and a wild ride with Bob Dylan. Now they were rock stars living in a world of distractions. The albums also lacked new songs by, most crucially, Manuel, as well as Danko and Helm. That brought another issue into focus: money. Helm, who was taking heroin while Manuel was increasingly lost to alcoholism, complained about Robertson's writing the group's material without sharing his publishing income with the other members.

"Levon was influenced by a more recent model," said John Simon. "Songwriters in [some] bands would show up in the studio with their songs only in fragmentary form. Then the other players in the group would contribute a little bit, often only their parts, and claim partial authorship for their efforts. But what those players did is not writing. Writing is the creating of melody and lyrics. . . . And though I completely understand and sympathize with Levon's anger about it, all in all I have to side with Robbie on the traditional definition of authorship."

Rock of Ages, a live album recorded during a series of concerts at the Academy of Music in New York at the end of 1971, captured the group at its musical peak. A five-piece horn section playing arrangements by Allen Toussaint, a master of New Orleans rhythm & blues, iced the cake. "I was determined to maintain their original sound," said Toussaint, who traveled to Woodstock to do the job, and in the process, experienced his first snowstorm. "If I didn't spoil anything they'd already achieved, then it was a good job." After midnight on New Year's Eve, Bob Dylan, who'd only recently begun to step back out into the spotlight, joined his old group to welcome in 1972.

After *Rock of Ages*, The Band's albums became less consequential—*Moondog Matinee* was an amiable collection of rock 'n' roll oldies, while *Northern Lights—Southern Cross* was crucially enhanced by Garth Hudson's instrumental expertise. The musicians had relocated to Los Angeles, with homes scattered around Malibu and music made at a leased recording compound dubbed "Shangri-La." But Shangri-La wasn't Big Pink, and the brotherhood of old was gone. "We were drifting further apart, we weren't putting our hearts into it," said Richard Manuel, who lived in a converted stable on the compound and drank endless bottles of Grand Marnier.

"I walked out of my house," said Robertson, "and the first thing I saw was Keith Moon lying unconscious on the beach with the tide coming in and lapping around his body. I remember thinking, 'Hey, this is taking things a little too close to the edge.'" It was the mid-'70s peak of rock-star decadence. "That was the first sense I had of Robbie's slight alienation from the whole thing," said Jonathan Taplin, who worked as The Band's road manager before producing such Martin Scorsese films as *Mean Streets* and *Taxi Driver*. "He didn't want to be a baby sitter anymore." That's when Robertson came up with the notion of *The Last Waltz*, a concert extravaganza that would essentially mark the end of The Band.

Scorsese, who'd been a cameraman for the movie *Woodstock*, was engaged to film a concert that would find The Band backing significant figures from their musical past, including Ronnie Hawkins, Muddy Waters, Dr. John, and Paul Butterfield. Rock star colleagues like Van Morrison, Joni Mitchell, Neil Young, and Eric Clapton were also on the bill. It was held on Thanksgiving Day in 1976 at the Winterland Ballroom in San Francisco, where promoter Bill Graham provided a turkey dinner for the audience. The stage was dressed with scenery borrowed from the San Francisco Opera's production of *La Traviata*. Warner Brothers put up $1.5 million for a movie and soundtrack with the proviso that Bob Dylan would perform with his original backing group.

The Last Waltz was an artful concert movie that captured a musical performance polished in post-production. "Rick's bass was generally out of tune," said John Simon, who was the event's musical director, "and Richard hit a lot of the cracks between the piano keys. Garth always looked for opportunities to improve his parts and Robbie was a perfectionist who wanted to fix his parts too. . . . So everyone re-did their parts—except for Levon."

To complete the film and to illustrate the group's roots in country and rhythm & blues, the five original members of The Band assembled for the last time on a Hollywood soundstage. Scorsese filmed "The Weight" with verses sung by Pops and Mavis Staples of the Staple Singers and a new Robertson song, "Evangeline," that was derived from a poem by Henry Wadsworth Longfellow. The Band performed that song with a gifted singer whose career had come a long way in a short time, Emmylou Harris.

Walking the beach in Malibu in 1977, Willie Nelson met Booker T. Jones, the keyboardist of Booker T. and the MG's, a band best known for its instrumental hit "Green Onions." They became fast friends, and Nelson asked Jones to write him an arrangement of a pop song from the 1940s, "Moonlight in Vermont." Nelson was very comfortable in his musical skin after the success of the *Red Headed Stranger*, and now he had a notion to do an album drawn from the Great American Songbook. "I remember the first night I sang [Hoagy Carmichael's] 'Stardust' with my band at the Austin Opera House,'" said Nelson. "There was a kind of stunned silence in the crowd for a moment and then they exploded with cheering and whistling and applauding. The kids in the crowd thought 'Stardust' was a new song I had written. The older folks remembered the song well and loved it as much as I did."

"We had a lot of common influences," said Jones, who ended up producing and arranging an album that came to be called *Stardust*. "Ray Charles was a big influence of mine and he was a big influence on Willie. I had heard Bob Wills and his Texas country jazz. Willie just loved jazz." Nelson also appreciated great songs. Besides the title tune, the album included Duke Ellington's "Don't Get Around Much Anymore," George and Ira Gershwin's "Someone to Watch over Me," and Kurt Weill's "September Song."

Stardust was recorded at the home studio of Brian Ahern, who'd used the facility to produce records by the woman who became his wife, Emmylou Harris. Mickey Raphael, who'd recorded with Emmylou, already knew that recording his harmonica in the bathroom provided natural reverb. Bobbie Nelson and Booker T. handled the keyboards; Chris Ethridge, the former

Burrito Brother who was now a member of Willie's band, played bass. The album's cover featured a painting by Susanna Clark, the wife of another Lone Star songwriter, Guy Clark.

Columbia Records predictably balked at the prospect of selling an album of standards by a singer they'd already promoted as an outlaw. Then *Stardust* became a multi-platinum #1 country album with two chart-topping singles, Hoagy Carmichael's "Georgia on My Mind" and Irving Berlin's "Blue Skies." Critical reaction was positive. "These tunes have become part of the folk music of exurban America," wrote Ariel Swartley in *Rolling Stone*. "And that's the way Nelson plays them—spare and simple, with a jump band's verve and a storyteller's love of a good tale."

"I'm a melody man," said Nelson. "I like stating the melody plain and simple. Simplicity is always the key. . . . My kind of singing isn't meant to be perfect. It's meant to reflect the imperfections of a human being like me." Booker T. Jones recognized a kindred spirit. "He's more special because he's a journeyman musician," said Jones. "He comes from where I come from in the music, and making six dollars a night playing to four a.m."

Ray Charles knew of those late-night gigs, and with the success of *Stardust*, Willie Nelson joined Charles among a handful of American music icons (including Louis Armstrong) that transcended musical genres. Charles had done that when the rhythm & blues pioneer embraced country music with *Modern Sounds in Country and Western Music* (1962). "I wasn't trying to broaden a damn thing," said Charles. "I was just singing songs I've always loved." Nelson knew that he had another link with Charles. "All the artists I loved the most," said Nelson, "from Hank Williams to Django Reinhardt to Ernest Tubb to Ray Charles, played the blues."

Nelson and Charles would appear together on a television special and duet on a 1984 #1 country hit, "Seven Spanish Angels." Ray also challenged Willie to a friendly game of chess that was played in a dark room with nondescript pieces identified in braille. And together they sang "It Was a Very Good Year," a song identified with another exceptional American singer, Frank Sinatra. Charles died in 2004 after a very good life, and the Red-Headed Icon was at the funeral to sing the song that they'd both made their own, "Georgia on My Mind."

13

PUNKS, GOD, AND URBANE COWBOYS

In the wee hours of November 22, 1976, Jerry Lee Lewis drove his Lincoln Continental to the home of Elvis Presley. Lewis had been drinking at the Vapors, a club where he often played impromptu shows, and where a sheriff had just presented him with a .38 caliber derringer pistol. The loaded gun was on the dashboard when Lewis cracked a window trying to throw an empty champagne bottle to the side of the road. Then he crashed into the gates of Graceland. "He was out of his mind," said Harold Loyd, who was guarding the entrance. "Get on the goddamn phone," said Jerry Lee. "Tell him the Killer's here to see him." Elvis, watching over a closed-circuit camera, said to call the police. "Tell 'em to lock his butt up, and throw the goddamn key away." Jerry Lee looked nonplussed on the mug shot seen around the world.

It had been a long twenty years since the impromptu meeting of the Million Dollar Quartet. Elvis and Jerry Lee were now both patients of Dr. George Nichopoulos; in the first eight months of 1977 "Dr. Nick" wrote prescriptions for more than ten thousand doses of sedatives, amphetamines, and narcotics for Elvis. On the morning of August 16, 1977, the King of Americanaland collapsed. He was due to leave for another tour later in the day. Instead, the world learned that he'd died of "cardiac arrest." Fourteen different drugs were found in his broken forty-two-year-old body.

Word traveled fast. Steve Earle was spending the day with Townes Van Zandt. They planned to stay sober until they heard the news and then got seriously smashed. "I went over my whole life," said Bob Dylan. "I went over my whole childhood. I didn't talk to anyone for a week." That night, Willie Nelson played a show at the Mid-South Coliseum in Memphis, with Emmylou Harris and the Hot Band as the opening act. At the end of the concert, Jerry Lee joined Willie for an encore of gospel songs dedicated to the first-born son of Sun. But the Killer didn't shed a tear. "Looked to me like he was celebrating," said Rodney Crowell, a guitarist in the Hot Band. "*He's* the king now."

But Jerry Lee had faded on the country charts, and each marriage was worse than the last; one wife's drug-related death inspired a *Rolling Stone* story that essentially called Lewis a literal killer. In 1979 the IRS auctioned off his possessions to settle back taxes. Meanwhile, his cousins were hitting it big, with Mickey Gilley having hits that sounded more than a little like Jerry Lee and Jimmy Swaggart selling gospel albums through a television ministry that would ultimately collapse after he was arrested for consorting with prostitutes. In 1981 Lewis nearly died of a perforated stomach; painkillers, sometimes injected directly into his stomach, had replaced amphetamines as his drug of choice.

Lewis wasn't the only legend in decline. George Jones and Tammy Wynette divorced in 1975; she left with both their band and the bus. Jones now chased his liquor with cocaine. "I missed more personal engagements than I kept from 1975 through 1980," said Jones, who earned a new nickname, "No Show Jones." A history of bad investments, including such ill-fated projects as the George Jones Rhythm Ranch, led to bankruptcy in the late 1970s. Then 1980's "He Stopped Loving Her Today" became his first #1 hit in six years. Jones hated the ballad in which the singer, swaddled in lavish strings and the lonely peel of a steel guitar, is reunited with his lost love at his own funeral. Producer Billy Sherrill pieced together Jones's vocal from multiple drunken takes; the result was a country classic that shamelessly embraced the genre's worst clichés.

Johnny Cash was another legend living in the cultural shadows. In 1980 he invited Marty Stuart, twenty-two, to join his band. Stuart had spent his teens playing mandolin and other stringed instruments with Lester Flatt and Doc Watson. "Johnny Cash and the Tennessee Three were my Beatles," said Stuart. “I knew every record they did, and I was a little torn to see what he had become. I was hoping to work with the guy who was at Folsom Prison . . . but I found myself in the middle of this kind of family show. It wasn’t as rock ’n’ roll as I thought it would be.” Stuart spent five years playing with Cash.

“I felt he was a little lost in this world,” said Stuart. “He had a lifestyle that was huge. He and June had houses upon houses; they had kids upon kids; employees upon employees; it was really a cumbersome lifestyle.” Stuart married Cash’s daughter Cindy in 1983. They divorced in 1987, but he remained close to the Man in Black. “Every December, [Johnny] and I would go to the graveyard to visit Luther [Perkins, Cash’s original guitarist] and bring him a cigarette,” said Stuart. “We would lie down on the grave, smoke, and talk to Luther, telling him what a lazy son of a bitch he was for lying there while we were out touring, killing ourselves to promote him.”

Emmylou Harris was now a major country star and a world-class bandleader. When James Burton left the Hot Band she recruited a British guitar star, Albert Lee, who would later play with a reunited Everly Brothers. (The Everlys’ career had foundered during the 1960s; they broke up in 1972 when Phil famously smashed his guitar and walked off the stage at Knott’s Berry Farm in California.) When Rodney Crowell left the group for a solo career, Harris found another instrumental and vocal foil, Ricky Skaggs.

Born in Kentucky, Skaggs started playing mandolin at the age of five; a year later, he jammed with Bill Monroe. As a teenager Skaggs played with Ralph Stanley’s Clinch Mountain Boys and in 1976 formed Boone Creek, a progressive bluegrass group that included dobro virtuoso Jerry Douglas. Skaggs brought his understanding of mountain music to Emmylou’s bluegrass album *Roses in the Snow*, singing harmony and playing guitar, mandolin, banjo, and fiddle. He was a traditionalist who understood history. “I was influenced by the Beatles and the Stones,” he said. “The Beatles sounded like the Everly Brothers, who sounded like the Louvin Brothers, who sounded like the Stanley Brothers, who sounded like the Monroe Brothers. It just goes right back all the way to the Delmore Brothers.”

Crowell had honed his talents performing with Harris, and his profile rose when his songs were included on her albums. One night he and Emmylou went to a party thrown by Waylon Jennings; Crowell took the opportunity to play one of his new songs, “Leaving Louisiana in the Broad Daylight.” “I was stunned," said Rosanne Cash, who was a student at Vanderbilt University. "I thought it was just about the best song I had ever heard." Susanna Clark made the introductions. Cash later asked Crowell to help cut demos for a record that was to be released in Europe, a strategy that she thought would allow her to escape the shadow of her father. The Ariola release went nowhere until her father played it for the head of Columbia's Nashville division, who signed Cash's eldest daughter to cut an album that would be produced by Crowell.

Rosanne Cash was wary of show business, having grown up with an absent father who cheated on her mother. But she was drawn to the art of songwriting, and after high school she travelled with her father's road show. Along the way, he introduced her to his canon of essential country and folk songs. Crowell was soon courting Rosanne and had occasion to borrow her dad's Cadillac; he cracked up the car and was quick to pay for the repairs. They married while recording *Right or Wrong* in Los Angeles with musicians from Emmylou's band. The album was a hit, but a pregnant Rosanne was unable to promote it with a concert tour. Her breakout moment came a year later with *Seven Year Ache*.

Rosanne was a different kind of country star. Whereas Emmylou was seen as an interpretive singer, Rosanne was considered a singer-songwriter. She was also suddenly selling more records than her father. "When I was having hit records," said Cash, "my dad and I felt competitive with each other. He admitted it later. I mean, he would ask me about my contract and how many points I was getting. . . . But when he felt that I was pulling away from him, he gave me a lot of space. I think it probably hurt him some."

Crowell's albums weren't big sellers, but Waylon Jennings had a hit with "Ain't Living Long Like This," and then Michigan rocker Bob Seger took his "Shame on the Moon" to #2 on the pop charts. The song featured a harmony vocal by Glenn Frey of the Eagles, who knew Seger from his days in Detroit. Having songs recorded by others was how Nashville songwriters typically made a living. Singer-songwriter John Hiatt moved to town from his native Indianapolis in 1970 at the age of 18; within a few days he had a publishing deal for $25 per week. "I couldn't believe it," said Hiatt. "I walked out of there four feet off the ground. It was like, 'Holy crap. I'm a songwriter.'"

Harris, her marriage to Brian Ahern failing, moved to Nashville in 1982. "Rodney and Rose had moved here," said Harris. "And through Rodney, I'd met Guy and Susanna [Clark] and gotten to know them." There were also new kids in town. "There was a little handwritten sign in the window [of the

Bluebird Café] that said 'Steve Earle and the Dukes,'" said Harris. "I'm thinking, 'That has to be a made-up name.' And so we walk in there and there's Steve with a drummer and a bass player. And one of the first songs he did was 'The Devil's Right Hand.' And I turned to Paul [Kennerley, her new producer and next husband] and said, 'This was the right move.'"

Popular music began to splinter during the 1970s, with the rise of punk rock and disco reflecting the increased bifurcation of the mass audience. Steve Earle saw the Sex Pistols, the safety-pinned icons of British punk, at Randy's Rodeo in San Antonio. "Sid [Vicious] got hit by a bottle and probably lost half a pint of blood," said Earle. "If it hadn't been such a shitty, short show he probably would have died! I didn't think they were very good but . . . it had a big effect on me, and this is the point of it all; hey, this is supposed to be fucking *fun*."

Punk rock was a conscious response to the slick professionalism of popular bands like the Eagles and Fleetwood Mac. Though the musical elements of punk can be traced from Chuck Berry and rockabilly through such 1960s rock bands as the Who and the Rolling Stones, the music pointedly embraced politics, anger, and irony. British punk met Americana when singer-songwriter Joe Ely from Lubbock, Texas, toured with the Clash. The unlikely alliance was struck when the Clash arranged to meet Ely, whose 1977 debut caused a buzz in England with its rocky spin on country, blues, and folk. In London to promote the album, Ely couldn't identify the strangers at his sound check. "We didn't think they were a band," said Ely. "We thought they were probably trying to steal our gear."

Ely and Joe Strummer of the Clash bonded over Buddy Holly, Eddie Cochran, and the Everly Brothers; Sonny Curtis, a Lubbock musician who'd played with Holly, had written "I Fought the Law," the band's first British hit. The short U.S. tour included a show in Monterey and, said Ely, "some of the places [Strummer] wanted to play in Texas that were the names of Marty Robbins songs." The show drew a big audience in Lubbock, where Ely and his band joined the Clash for an encore of their "I'm So Bored with the U.S.A." "It was such a full onslaught of power chords that the meaning of the song completely flipped," said Ely. "All of a sudden it's, 'I'm rocking out in the U.S.A.'"

When punk bands dabbled in country, critics called it "cowpunk," and it was often delivered with an ironic wink. The biggest punk band in Los

Angeles, X, put off-kilter folkie harmonies atop loud guitars; later, some of the members turned down the volume to record country and folk songs as the Knitters. Rank and File, comprised of members from two San Francisco punk bands, the Dils and the Nuns, wrote stripped-down country & western songs. The band's Alejandro Escovedo later became an acclaimed solo artist. The Long Ryders played country rock with a nod to Gram Parsons, a musical hero of band member Sid Griffin; Green on Red gave the world another talented solo artist, Chuck Prophet. In Nashville, Jason and the Scorchers played originals alongside songs by Hank Williams ("Lost Highway") and Bob Dylan ("Absolutely Sweet Marie").

The Blasters influenced Americana with their superior roots-rock musicianship and their influential support of Los Lobos (a Latino roots-rock band) and Dwight Yoakam (a country singer from Kentucky-via-Ohio). Los Lobos (Spanish for "the wolves") had a #1 hit in 1987 with a cover of Richie Valens's "La Bamba" and spent subsequent decades making albums that artfully mixed a variety of styles from north and south of the border. Yoakam played honky-tonk country with the passion of a punk and the discipline of a pro. "I look to John [Prine] as a benchmark," said Yoakam. "His first album had the song 'Paradise,' about his family migrating to Chicago from western Kentucky. . . . What that meant to me as a songwriter was, 'Hey, I can do exactly this, the things that are from my musical legacy, and my family's culture and the culture I was born into, and have it still remain pertinent for a contemporary audience of my generation.'"

Yoakam stood out in the Los Angeles music scene. "It was shocking to see bodies slamming," he said of punk rock's mosh pits. "It was crazy. We were slammin', but we were in tune." He was also sharp in a bolo tie and Stetson hat atop his tight jeans and cowboy boots. When Yoakam met guitarist Pete Anderson, it was akin to when Buck Owens found Don Rich. That was when Dave Alvin of the Blasters saw Yoakam play the Palomino in North Hollywood. "There were maybe thirty people there," said Alvin, "including the band, and I just sat at the bar and watched this guy deliver a totally complete, professional show, as if there were a thousand people. . . . They sounded like they would three years later when he was a star."

Robbie Robertson was already a rock star, but after *The Last Waltz* he saw a lot more of director Martin Scorsese than he did of his colleagues in The Band. "There was a period there where Robbie and Marty saw the sun come up every day for at least six months, maybe longer," said Jonathan Taplin.

But the odd couple weren't cruising the rock clubs; instead, they were snorting cocaine and screening classic movies at Scorsese's house on Mulholland Drive. This unique albeit debauched film school prepared Robertson to serve as the music supervisor for such Scorsese films as *Raging Bull* and *The King of Comedy*.

Bob Dylan, who was born with the cantankerous attitude of a punk rocker, surprised everybody by becoming a born-again Christian. A few years after his divorce from Sara, an actress girlfriend brought Dylan to church at the Vineyard Christian Fellowship. Musicians from the Rolling Thunder Revue were in the congregation. "T-Bone was the first one to go through this [born again] experience and Steve [Soles] sort of followed him, and I eventually did, too," said David Mansfield. "And T-Bone has more than a bit of preacher in him and was probably hammering at all of his friends in the way that he could be most effecting—arguing. . . . Bob would be way in the back [of the church] incognito, but T-Bone, Steven and I were all playing in the church band."

Dylan approached his newfound devotion to Jesus Christ with the same dedication that he'd shown to painting, taking a three-month, four-day-a-week course at the Vineyard Fellowship. The evangelical church embraced an apocalyptic vision wherein the wicked would wither during the coming battle of Armageddon and the second coming of Christ would usher in a millennium of peace. Dylan's songs, most notably those on *John Wesley Harding,* had long included biblical allusions, but his new songs stunned fans whom he'd once told "Don't follow leaders, watch the parkin' meters."

Slow Train Coming was produced by Jerry Wexler and keyboardist Barry Beckett and recorded at a citadel of southern soul, Muscle Shoals Sound Studio in Sheffield, Alabama. Wexler hired guitarist Mark Knopfler of Dire Straits, instructing him to play like Albert King, and was initially caught off guard by the fundamentalist tenor of Dylan's new material. "I had no idea he was on this born-again Christian trip," said Wexler, "until he started to evangelize me. I said, 'Bob, you're dealing with a sixty-two-year-old confirmed Jewish atheist. I'm hopeless. Let's just make an album." Critics were stunned by Dylan's dogmatic lyrics but pleased by the soulful sound of *Slow Train Coming*. Dylan's touring band was similarly praised for making some of the best live music of his performing career. But Dylan's hellfire preaching also alienated fans. "I told you 'The Times They Are A-Changin',' and they did," he told one concert audience in 1979. "I said the answer was 'Blowin' in the

Wind,' and it was. I'm telling you now Jesus is coming back, and He is! And there is no other way of salvation. . . . There's only one way to believe, there's only one way—the Truth and the Life."

Britain's Richard Thompson, who was raised a Presbyterian, had his own religious conversion after leaving Fairport Convention: He became a follower of Sufism, a form of Islamic mysticism that encourages introspection in order to forge a spiritual connection with God. "I had been waiting as long as I could remember for an appropriate way to thank God," said Thompson. Praying, he said, allowed him "to stop using [his] brain for thinking and to start using it for reflecting."

Thompson the guitar player had always aimed to play with individuality. "At some point, I said, 'No blues,'" said Thompson, who was well schooled in the licks of B. B. King and Chuck Berry. "It was a conscious decision to really turn away from the blues, and if I used bent notes on guitar, it was to make them more Celtic than blues." Joe Boyd recognized this when he produced Fairport Convention. "In his playing you can hear the evocation of the Scottish piper's drone and [the] melody of the chanter as well as echoes of Barney Kessel's and James Burton's guitars and Jerry Lee Lewis's piano," said Boyd. "But no blues clichés."

During the 1970s Thompson recorded as a duo with his wife Linda, and for a time, the couple and their two young children lived in a Sufi commune. Their albums were well received but sold poorly. The couple's fortunes took an ironic turn when Boyd proposed recording an album in a couple of days and using the rest of the budget to finance a U.S. tour. The result was 1981's *Shoot Out the Lights*, a critically acclaimed collection about a relationship on the rocks that suggested Dylan's *Blood on the Tracks* with better guitar solos. By the time the Thompsons finished the U.S. tour their marriage was over, and Richard had secured a devoted following that would allow him to cut albums and tour both with an electric band and as a solo acoustic performer.

Dylan and Thompson were too set in their ways to care much about punk rock; Neil Young responded by bookending his 1979 *Rust Never Sleeps* with acoustic and electric versions of "Hey Hey, My My (Into the Black)." "It's better to burn out than to fade away," sang Young, who the previous year had found success with a largely acoustic album, *Comes a Time*. All told, the early mating of punk and country didn't result in much enduring music, but punk's do-it-yourself philosophy helped inspire what came to be called alt-country. Jeff Tweedy, who would form both Uncle Tupelo and Wilco, was a punk rock fan from Belleville, Illinois. Shopping at Target with his mother, he hesitated to put the Clash's *London Calling* in the shopping cart because of a sticker that read "Parental Advisory: Explicit Content, Strong Language." On subsequent visits to the store, Tweedy carefully scraped the label off the record's cover, which he'd protectively filed under "Z." Mission finally accomplished, Mrs. Tweedy bought her son the Clash.

No longer just a country star, Dolly Parton was a household name. "Here You Come Again" (1977) was a huge pop hit, and in 1980 she starred alongside Jane Fonda and Lily Tomlin in the film *9 to 5*, for which she also wrote and sang the #1 title tune. Then came "Islands in the Stream," her chart-topping duet with Kenny Rogers on a tune written and produced by the Bee Gees. But nothing defined country music in the early eighties more than *Urban Cowboy*, a film in which John Travolta courted Debra Winger on the back of a mechanical bull at Gilley's, a Texas honky-tonk run by Jerry Lee's cousin Mickey Gilley. The soundtrack included a hit by Johnny Lee ("Lookin' for Love"), and popular not-exactly-country songs by Gilley, the Eagles, Bonnie Raitt, Boz Scaggs, and Linda Ronstadt. The film positioned country music as the sound of the suburbs, where couples did line dances wearing polyester cowboy shirts and well-polished boots.

The seeds of Americana lived at clubs and song circles in Austin, Nashville, and New York, not at Gilley's. Lucinda Williams was the daughter of Miller Williams, a widely published poet and college professor. A single father, he took his three children on a tour of the southland; by the time Lucinda was in the tenth grade she'd lived in Mississippi (Vicksburg and Jackson), Georgia (Atlanta and Macon), Louisiana (Lake Charles, Baton Rouge, and New Orleans), and Santiago, Chile. Wherever the family landed, writers gathered, and Lucinda spent time with James Dickey, Charles Bukowski, and Flannery O'Connor. "Those were the best parties in the world," she said. "Everybody was there—talking, drinking—and there I was, playing my songs on the guitar." She got started at the age of twelve, taking her cues from the Hank Williams and Bob Dylan albums in her dad's collection. (Lucinda's father had seen Hank play, and after the show, bought him a drink.)

Williams was thrown out of high school for protesting the Vietnam War by refusing to stand for the pledge of allegiance. She was accepted into college anyway but dropped out to play coffeehouses in Austin and Houston, where she rubbed shoulders with Townes Van Zandt and Steve Earle and jockeyed for gigs alongside Nanci Griffith and Lyle Lovett. Williams made two records for Folkways. Her 1979 debut, *Ramblin'*, featured blues and folk with multiple songs by Robert Johnson and A. P. Carter, as well as tunes by Memphis Minnie ("Me and My Chauffeur") and Hank Williams ("Jambalaya [On the Bayou]"). Williams wrote original songs for her *Happy Woman Blues* (1980), and while she didn't come into her own as a songwriter until the late eighties, she already understood the elements of her style. "It's American roots music," said Williams. "It's coming from different sounds, including country, but also blues and traditional folk. I think Gram Parsons and I are coming from a lot of the same places."

Nanci Griffith played folk clubs as a teenager in Austin and continued doing gigs while studying at the University of Texas and teaching kindergarten. After winning a songwriting competition at the Kerrville Folk Festival she recorded for tiny independent labels. Lyle Lovett, a student at Texas A&M University, interviewed Griffith for the campus newspaper. Lovett graduated with degrees in German and journalism but intended to pursue a life in music. "When we met," said singer-songwriter Robert Earl Keen, who shared a house with Lovett, "Lyle was a lot more advanced in making music a career than I was. I didn't want to hang around with the old men playing fiddle tunes till I was 70. I wanted to write and play music I wrote. Lyle was already doing that."

Griffith met Jim Rooney at a barbecue and believed that he was the producer to take her career to the next level. When she arrived in Nashville to record, she brought Lovett along to add background vocals. Rooney's path to Nashville was filled with bohemian connections. As a student at Amherst College in the late 1950s he met banjoist Bill Keith, and they began playing as a duo; one of their first gigs was opening for Joan Baez at Dartmouth College (Rooney sings and plays guitar). While attending graduate school at Harvard University, he and Keith performed weekly at Club 47. Rooney eventually left school to book a who's who of musical artists at the venerable folk and blues venue; in the summertime he worked for George Wein at the Newport Folk Festival.

In 1969 Rooney formed the Blue Velvet Band with Keith, violinist Richard Greene, and multi-instrumentalist Eric Weissberg; the group released one album, *Sweet Moments with the Blue Velvet Band*. Rooney wrote a book called *Bossmen* about two very different bandleaders, Bill Monroe and Muddy Waters and later collaborated with Eric Von Schmidt on an oral history of the Cambridge folk scene, *Baby, Let Me Follow You Down*. He spent time in Woodstock, New York, overseeing the building of Bearsville Studios for Dylan's manager Albert Grossman and played in the Woodstock Mountain Revue with John Herald, Happy Traum, and Bill Keith. Relocating to Nashville in the mid-1970s, he fell in with the songwriting circle that revolved around Guy Clark and Townes Van Zandt and worked at a studio owned by Jack Clement, who'd gotten his start working at Sun with Jerry Lee Lewis and Johnny Cash.

By the time Rooney met Griffith he was also working with John Prine, whose 1978 album *Bruised Orange*, produced by his friend Steve Goodman, was the best he'd made since his debut. Prine subsequently formed his own record label (Oh Boy!) and discovered that selling fifty thousand albums as an independent was more profitable than selling hundreds of thousands for a major label. Rooney met Prine at a music festival in Maine. "We had some quality time in the bar where we got acquainted," said Rooney, who struck Prine as a latter-day Huckleberry Finn. "I had a motor home instead of a raft, but I was certainly floating freely down the river of life." Along the way, Rooney produced Townes Van Zandt's *At My Window*.

Griffith's *Once in a Very Blue Moon* (1985) included originals as well as a song by Lyle Lovett ("The Woman I Am") and a title tune by Pat Alger. Players included veteran steel guitarist Lloyd Green and a pair involved in expanding the vocabulary of bluegrass, Bela Fleck and Mark O'Connor. Griffith's next Rooney-produced album, *The Last of the True Believers*, included her most famous composition, "Love at the Five and Dime." Griffith then signed with MCA, which required her to use an in-house producer. It was a tough lesson for Rooney, who learned another when he advised Lovett to take his promising collection of songs to a Nashville publisher. Rooney soon became a partner in a new publishing company, Forerunner; payday came a few years later when the firm's most successful songwriter, Pat Alger, started writing tunes with a newcomer named Garth Brooks.

In the early 1980s future figures of Americana were gigging in, of all places, New York City. The Buddy Miller Band played regularly at the Lone Star Café, the Fifth Avenue club with a giant iguana on its roof. Miller, who'd grown up in New Jersey, was a soulful singer and guitarist who came to the city from Austin, Texas, where he'd fallen in love with Julie Griffin, the singer in a band for which he played guitar. Buddy and Julie soon met Larry Campbell, who

BUDDY MILLER

joined the band to play fiddle and guitar. Campbell had grown up in the city and gigged around the country before playing with John Herald (of the Greenbriar Boys) and working recording sessions in New York. (Herald also hired Cindy Cashdollar, a Woodstock native, to play dobro and lap steel; she later joined Asleep at the Wheel and played with Van Morrison and Ryan Adams.) Working musicians are happy (and economically obliged) to play with a lot of people. "At the time," said Campbell, "I was also working with Soozie Tyrell and Patti Scialfa, from way before Patti [and Soozie] got together with Bruce [Springsteen]."

The Buddy Miller Band played country gigs at City Limits and other clubs while backing headliners at the Lone Star. "Since we loved that music so much," said John Leventhal, another musician on the scene, "we would really listen to the great country records, and analyze them—Ray Price records of the fifties, Merle and Buck records of the sixties, or George Jones records from any period—to really understand not only the songwriting, but what the musicians played, and how it was all put together."

Jim Lauderdale came to New York to play the clubs and write songs after attending college in North Carolina. "Doc Pomus lived in my building," said Lauderdale of the celebrated songwriter who wrote "Save the Last Dance for Me." "He was always very encouraging, but wouldn't work with me until I had a deal. . . . He'd have great visitors—Dr. John in the lobby—and great birthday parties." Lauderdale bonded with the other urbane cowboys. "In the same way that British kids listened to blues records or rock & roll in the late fifties," he said, "for this group there was something about country that affected us all deeply, made us pore over those records deeply, and share a real passion for it."

The Buddy Miller Band attracted the interest of record labels, but Julie, who'd grown up with an abusive father, was hesitant. "Like many people, I had a lot of unresolved, crippled parts of myself," said Julie, "but I wasn't one of these people who were good at denial. I lived it out, every gig, have a few drinks, a few drugs, and go a little crazy." "We got out of the Lone Star one morning around 4 a.m.," said Larry Campbell, "and I brought her to the hospital, Bergen Pines in New Jersey, and unwittingly got her committed. So there was this [opening for] Muddy Waters gig the next day, and Buddy pulled this *One Flew over the Cuckoo's Nest* maneuver to get her out." On stage, Julie was an open book. "Her heart was right on her sleeve," said Campbell, "this primal emotional thing that would come out of her, sounding exactly like you would hear her today—totally unfiltered. And what else could you want for somebody singing this music?"

Then Julie left for good. "Yeah," said Julie, "you might say that Buddy, being Jewish and all, was quite surprised. He and the band were at this bar that we were playing, and they were wondering where I'd gone, and I called them at this bar and said, 'Buddy, you're not going to believe this, but I've just met some Christians and I've given my life to Jesus and I can't come back." Miller, with a calendar full of upcoming gigs, called a singer who'd impressed him in Austin, Shawn Colvin. She'd played in a country swing band and performed as a solo folk singer, and was more than happy to come to New York in December 1980 to join a working band.

But Buddy had a broken heart, and he soon left New York, as did Campbell, who went on the road with Doug Sahm. It was now the Shawn Colvin Band and, in need of a lead guitarist, she reached out to John Leventhal, who'd seen her play with Buddy. "I liked Buddy and the whole band," said Leventhal, "but Shawn kind of blew me away." Colvin and Leventhal collaborated on songs—and a romance. Buddy joined Julie in Texas. "It was weird enough for me," said Julie, "but then six months later, Buddy became a Christian too. I'll never get over it. He read that Bible that I left that was under the sofa. It was like God said, 'Okay, Buddy, time to meet me.'" God, as is said, works in mysterious ways.

14
HARD-CORE TROUBADOURS

Emmylou Harris's tour bus pulled into a truck stop near Oklahoma City. "Hey," said Harris to Tony Brown, her keyboard player, "go to the jukebox and play [George Jones's] 'He Stopped Loving Her Today.' It's going to kill you!" Touring with the Hot Band was a musical education for Brown, who had never listened to popular music as a kid in North Carolina because he played in his preacher father's family gospel group. Gospel music won Brown an audience with Elvis Presley, and the Lord blessed him with a job playing keyboards in the King's band.

"He was Elvis the celebrity, not Elvis the King of Rock 'n' Roll," said Brown, who was there at the end. "I was just as excited about playing with James Burton and [drummer] Ronnie Tutt as I was playing with Elvis." The Hot Band schooled Brown about country music and about how Emmylou, Rodney, and Rosanne Cash were crazy for the Beatles. "These people were like musicologists," said Brown. "They showed me how [my gospel piano playing] fit into this big important picture of American music making. . . . With Emmy I found out about that whole country-rock scene and about Gram Parsons."

Rodney Crowell formed the Cherry Bombs to back both himself and Rosanne Cash; the first-call guitarists were Vince Gill, Richard Bennett, and

Albert Lee. Tony Brown played keyboards, but he really wanted to produce records, so he took a job at RCA, where he signed Alabama and his pal Vince. Jimmy Bowen of MCA hired Brown away in the mid-1980s. Bowen was riding high as the producer of two of the day's biggest country stars, George Strait and Reba McEntire; both were dubbed "new traditionalists" because they had hits without trying to cater to the pop audience. Ricky Skaggs, who was also in that school, hit it big after playing in the Hot Band, scoring eleven #1 country hits in five years. At MCA Brown signed artists whom he might have met backstage at an Emmylou show, including a trio of singer-songwriters from Texas: Nanci Griffith, Lyle Lovett, and the wild card of the bunch, Steve Earle.

Earle had bounced in and out of Nashville for a decade. A singer-songwriter who grew up on rock, he cut a rockabilly record for Epic that went unreleased until his MCA debut became a hit. "I was way into Creedence [Clearwater Revival], the Beatles, and the Stones," said Earle, "but when I started writing and playing coffeehouses, I couldn't make my guitar sound like theirs. But I could make my guitar sound like Tim Buckley or Tim Hardin." Townes and Guy were major influences, but rock was still the root. "The turning point for me," said Earle, "was seeing Springsteen's *Born in the U.S.A.* tour, and watching him turn a 20,000-seat arena into a coffeehouse. I went home and literally started writing *Guitar Town* the next day." On a beach-house weekend on the Gulf Coast Earle met Tony Brown, who was bowled over when Earle played him a ballad called "My Old Friend the Blues."

Earle travelled to Los Angeles to write with guitarist Richard Bennett bringing along a cassette of new songs like "Guitar Town," "Hillbilly Highway," and "Fearless Heart." Earle and Bennett wrote "Good Ol' Boy," and Bennett's snaky electric guitar provided an instrumental foil akin to Pete Anderson's work with Dwight Yoakam. Bennett relocated to Nashville to help record *Guitar Town* (1986), a mixture of country twang and rock 'n' roll that remains a defining album of Americana. Brown thought it important that Earle have a backing group just as Emmylou had her Hot Band; Emory Gordy Jr. left her combo to play bass, and Harry Stinson joined to play drums and sing harmony.

Tony Brown credits Bennett for informing the album's elemental sound, but there was no mistaking that Earle was the auteur. "I thought Steve was writing the real stuff and I felt like he was the guy he was writing about," said Stinson. "It felt like his experience." And since he'd grown up as a fan of rock 'n' roll, Earle made a country record that could also appeal to rockers.

Guitar Town reached the top of the country charts—in the end, Earle's only real country hit—but his raspy vocals and working-class lyrics also reminded many of Bruce Springsteen.

A decade earlier, Bob Dylan had teased Springsteen about being "the new me." Now Earle and midwestern rocker John Mellencamp found themselves in the shadow of Bruce, who'd become a star with *Born to Run* (1975) and kept his songs focused on working-class characters with 1978's *Darkness on the Edge of Town* (1978). "I wanted to write about the way people lived and the possibilities of life," said Springsteen. "Country asked all the right questions. It was concerned with how you go on living after you reach adulthood. I was asking those questions myself. Everything after *Born to Run* was shot full with a lot of country music—those questions." On *The River* (1980) Springsteen achieved a new sense of lyrical rigor; every word counted. And on *Nebraska* (1982), a dark, minimalist album that Springsteen recorded at home, he made music that was firmly in the folk tradition. He was soon singing Woody Guthrie's "This Land Is Your Land" during his concerts.

Born in the U.S.A. (1984) applied these lessons to a rock album that sold in the multi-millions and established Springsteen as mainstream rock's biggest star. Earle sang Springsteen's "State Trooper" in concert, and critics noticed when Mellencamp started writing lyrics about the workingman's blues. The songs on Mellencamp's *Scarecrow* depicted rural troubles, and he helped Willie Nelson launch Farm Aid, an annual benefit devoted to supporting family farms struggling to compete with industrial operations. (Bob Dylan invented the idea of Farm Aid during a ramshackle appearance in 1985 at Live Aid with Keith Richards and Ronnie Wood of the Rolling Stones; performing at a benefit to help victims of famine in Africa, Dylan said that somebody should also help the American farmer.) Featuring socially conscious songs with a band that now featured fiddle, mandolin, and dobro, *The Lonesome Jubilee* (1987) anticipated the sound of Americana. "These instruments," said Mellencamp, "almost give the music a timeless feel. Nobody's going to say that sounds like 1987, because it was a conscious effort to look at the music of today and try to get 180 degrees away from it."

The country crowd knew nothing of Mellencamp, whose albums sold in the millions. But a photo of Springsteen carrying a copy of *Guitar Town* gave Earle credibility with a rock audience with which he had much in common. The same went for Griffith and Lovett, the other Texas singer-songwriters signed and produced by Tony Brown. Griffith had cut stylish independent albums produced by Jim Rooney; with a more lavish recording budget, Brown put a flattering focus on Griffith's angelic voice and finger-style guitar, a combination that placed her in the folk-pop lineage of Judy Collins.

But country stardom proved elusive; Griffith's most celebrated original song, "Love at the Five and Dime," was a Top 5 country hit only after it was sung by Kathy Mattea; "From a Distance," by Julie Gold, helped Griffith establish a loyal audience in Ireland, but the Grammy-winning U.S. hit was sung by Bette Midler. Still, Griffith was pleased. "My role models for what I wanted out of my career were Townes Van Zandt, Guy Clark and Jerry Jeff Walker," she said. "I really expected to spend my life driving myself around America, playing small clubs and following in the footsteps of my heroes."

Lyle Lovett, with a high-rise haircut that recalled David Lynch's *Eraserhead*, was a nimble singer and guitar picker with a wry way with words; his songs drew not only from country but also from blues, swing, folk, and gospel. His eclectic style made him and Griffith appealing to baby boom singer-songwriter fans but a tough sale to country radio. Steve Earle got more coverage in the rock press, but Lovett sold more records, beginning a run of gold albums with *Pontiac* (1988). Brown, who found big-time country success producing Vince Gill, Patty Loveless, and Wynonna Judd, came to recognize that Griffith and Lovett fundamentally appealed to a different audience.

"Artists who are singer-songwriters," said Brown, "if they can have commercial success on their terms, when the commercial success is over, they can still succeed on their terms. To this day Guy Clark and Lyle Lovett can play all kinds of places and make good money performing their music to an audience that really appreciates their work, as opposed to playing empty houses to fans who have moved on to . . . whomever the latest artist du jour is in country music." Performing songwriters such as John Prine and Townes Van Zandt enjoyed similarly scaled careers.

Kathryn Dawn Lang, known professionally as k. d. lang, was another exceptional talent who rattled Nashville in the 1980s. Born in Canada, lang was drawn to country by the music of Patsy Cline; her U.S. debut, *Angels with a Lariat* (1987), included a cover of Cline's "Three Cigarettes in an Ashtray." That song inspired an unlikely collaboration with Cline's producer, Owen Bradley, for *Shadowland* (1988), a collection steeped in "countrypolitan" orchestrations. But Nashville remained wary of a self-consciously artful mezzo-soprano who would soon come out as gay and who won a Grammy for a duet with Roy Orbison on his "Crying." Lang found pop success in 1992 with *Ingénue* (and its hit single "Constant Craving"), cut an album with Tony Bennett, and on *Hymns of the 49th Parallel* (2004), fashioned an Americana album composed of songs written by Canadians.

Among the musicians of the mid-1980s, only one became a true country star: Dwight Yoakam. "I was around for Rank and File and all the cowpunk movement," said record executive Bill Bentley, "and from a million miles away you could tell that Dwight wasn't part of that. He played those shows with them and the Blasters and got in with that crowd pretty good. But it was apples and oranges." Yoakam's 1986 debut album, *Guitars, Cadillacs, Etc., Etc.*, included a #3 country hit, a cover of Johnny Horton's "Honky Tonk Man." When Yoakam first met guitarist-producer Pete Anderson he had twenty-one original songs, all of which appeared on one of his first three million-selling albums.

"We were definitely the same graduating class," said Steve Earle, "but different. I was making a singer-songwriter record, and what Dwight did was based on honky-tonk music as a specific art form." But that wasn't the whole story. "We made our records from a rock, West Coast perspective," said Anderson, "not from a Nashville perspective. We made them like we were rock and roll guys." And though he and Anderson were clearly creating an amped-up version of Buck Owens's Bakersfield sound, Yoakam also cited the influence of a California rock band. "I was really inspired by Creedence Clearwater Revival illustrating that country-hyphen-rock/pop could be pertinent for a young audience," said Yoakam. "The Byrds were folk rock, but country rock is John Fogerty. 'Cause you can't get any harder rockin', and in some places more country, than Creedence—a real hybrid that was a commercial success."

Owens had stopped performing live after his musical partner, singer-guitarist Don Rich, died in a motorcycle accident in 1974. In 1988 Yoakam arranged to pay Buck his respects when he played a concert in Bakersfield. "I didn't know that he had not sang [*sic*] with anyone live in years and never had gotten up and sat in with anyone in Bakersfield until he got to the fairgrounds," said Yoakam. "And I said, 'We know a few of your songs if you wanna get up.' And he did." Yoakam and Owens then collaborated on a song Buck had recorded in 1973, "Streets of Bakersfield." The song became Yoakam's first #1 hit and Buck's biggest record since he'd begun hosting *Hee Haw*.

A less likely intergenerational encounter involved Nick Lowe, a British musician who'd produced records by Graham Parker and Elvis Costello, the latter of whom travelled to Nashville to make *Almost Blue*, an album of country covers (with a handful of original songs) with producer Billy Sherrill. (Costello later recorded his "Stranger in the House" with George Jones.) Lowe married into country royalty when he wed singer Carlene Carter. "You're always a little nervous about your in-laws," said Lowe, "but Johnny Cash and June Carter gave it a whole new twist."

Lowe had Cash in mind when he wrote a song called "The Beast in Me." "John was the most charismatic man I've ever met," he said. "But he was in a lot of pain, physical and emotional. He was a flawed man but I adored him." Johnny and June would stay with Nick and Carlene when in London. "We used to get sloshed together and listen to old records," said Lowe, with Cash introducing him to some of his country and gospel favorites. "I'd get up in the morning and he'd be sitting in his dressing gown strumming a guitar in my tiny kitchen while June would be there in a bejeweled turban frying some eggs. It was brilliant!"

Bob Dylan was bored. "During one show in Australia we were supposed to do 'When the Night Comes Falling from the Sky,'" said Mike Campbell, lead guitarist for Dylan's latest backing band, Tom Petty and the Heartbreakers, "and he didn't feel like doing it. He turned to me and said, 'You know the chords for "All Along the Watchtower," don't you?' And we'd never rehearsed it. I said, 'There's only three, right?' And he said, 'Yeah, let's go!'"

The 1980s were something of a lost decade for Dylan. He'd come out of his born-again period, but his records were mediocre, and few of the new songs could compete with the best of his songbook. The excitement surrounding *Biograph* (1985), a career overview seeded with unreleased performances, suggested that his renown was rooted as much in the past as in whatever might be next. But Dylan still sold concert tickets, and in 1986 he toured the world with Tom Petty and the Heartbreakers, who played their own hits and backed the Bard. "We'd all been huge Dylan fans," noted Petty, "and we were very intrigued by the idea of playing with Bob. So off we went."

The preparation was a blast for a band that counted the Byrds as one of its original inspirations. "The times I remember the fondest are the rehearsals where Bob might start playing some songs that we didn't know," said Petty, "and you'd discover something new." Now and then it was hard to tell the new from the old. "He knows a million songs, old Delta blues songs and stuff like that," said keyboardist Benmont Tench. "Sometimes, I wasn't sure if they were blues songs or a new arrangement of 'It's Alright Ma (I'm Only Bleeding).'"

The Grateful Dead were Dylan's backing band for six stadium shows in the summer of 1987. "It was one of those things [where] we'd always thought, 'Wow, that'd be far out'—Bob Dylan and the Grateful Dead," said Jerry Garcia. Maybe that's why the Dead agreed to a 70–30 financial split with Dylan, whose rehearsals with the band were more about the roots of Americana than about Bob's back pages. "We talked about people like Elizabeth Cotten, Mississippi Sheiks, Earl Scruggs, Bill Monroe, Gus Cannon," said Garcia. "I showed Bob some of those songs: 'Two Soldiers', 'Jack-A-Roe', 'John Hardy.' Trouble was, Bob seemed to prefer to do these rather than rehearse his songs."

The Grateful Dead had become big business, and Garcia, a diabetic drug addict, was the bankable star of the show. No wonder he relished playing acoustic music with his old pal David Grisman; their deep bond and musical synchronicity are captured in the film *Grateful Dawg*. As they played folk and bluegrass, sea shanties and modal instrumentals, their improvisations anticipated the acoustic side of Americana. Other bluegrass players were drawn to the electric jams of the Dead and the jazz-rock fusion of Weather Report. Bela Fleck, an innovator on the banjo during his years with New Grass Revival, went even further with Bela Fleck and the Flecktones. Featuring Howard Levy on harmonica, Victor Wooten on bass, and Roy Wooten on synthesizer-based percussion, Fleck's *Flight of the Cosmic Hippo* (1991) topped Billboard's contemporary jazz chart.

Garcia died of a heart attack in 1995 at the age of fifty-three; his music, with and without the Grateful Dead, inspired a school of "jamgrass" bands including Leftover Salmon and the Yonder Mountain String Band. "I didn't know anybody who listened to bluegrass," said Vince Herman of Leftover Salmon, "but because of Jerry Garcia, I got into it. Talk to anyone on the jam scene, or bluegrassers who didn't grow up with bluegrass, and most everyone will tell you that Old and In the Way got their attention. Grisman did as well. If you listened to his quintet, you heard Tony Rice and turned on to J. D. Crowe and the New South." If Americana music has roots in the past, Captain Trips helped tip it into the future.

George Harrison, in Los Angeles, needed a new tune for the B side of a single from his 1987 album *Cloud Nine*. He called the record's co-producer, Jeff Lynne of the Electric Light Orchestra, who was making a record with Roy Orbison. Lynne suggested that maybe they could use the studio in Dylan's Malibu garage. "We phoned up Bob," said Harrison. "He said, 'Sure, come on over.' Tom Petty had my guitar, and I went to pick it up; he said, 'Oh, I was wondering what I was going to do tomorrow!' And Roy Orbison said, 'Give us a call tomorrow if you're going to do anything—I'd love to come along." (Orbison, who'd gotten his start at Sun Records, went on to record hits like "Oh, Pretty Woman" and "Only the Lonely" in the 1960s. He enjoyed a late-life renaissance when his "In Dreams" was prominently featured in David Lynch's 1987 movie *Blue Velvet*.)

Dylan joined the jam, and when Warner Brothers told Harrison that "Handle with Care" was just too good to use as a B side, the Beatle formed his second group, the Traveling Wilburys. "We'd go to Bob's house and we'd just sit outside," said Orbison, "and there'd be a barbecue, and we'd all just bring guitars, and everyone would be throwing something in here and something in there, and then we'd just go to the garage studio, and put it down." The sessions taught Petty about Dylan's methods. "I had never written more words than I needed," said Petty, "but he tended to write lots and lots of verses, then he'll say, this verse is better than that, or this line. . . . He was very good in The Traveling Wilburys; when somebody had a line, he could make it a lot better in big ways."

The Traveling Wilburys was an international hit, selling more than five million copies, but its convivial alchemy felt strained on the inevitable follow-up, recorded after the death of Orbison. The fun, and massive sales, occurred as Dylan recorded his best album of the decade. At the suggestion of Bono, he met with Daniel Lanois, a producer who'd worked with U2 and specialized in crafting unique musical atmospheres; Dylan was particularly impressed by his production of the Neville Brothers' *Yellow Moon*. "The recording studio is very foreign to me," said Dylan, who by now had been making records for nearly three decades. "You need somebody there who knew you, who could push you around a little bit. Daniel got me to do stuff that wouldn't have entered my mind." The resulting album, *Oh Mercy*, was yet another comeback for Dylan, and it anticipated his even greater collaboration with Lanois on 1997's *Time out of Mind*.

The Traveling Wilburys weren't the only impromptu supergroup of the late 1980s; the three women who recorded 1987's *Trio* didn't even bother to cook up a name. That's because everybody already knew Dolly Parton, Emmylou Harris, and Linda Ronstadt. Harris met Parton in 1975 when her debut album became a hit. "So I come to Nashville," said Harris, "and the first day

I'm there I meet Dolly Parton and George Jones and I throw up. Not because I was drinking or anything; it was just so overwhelming." Back in Los Angeles, Emmylou invited Dolly to her house and then telephoned her friend Linda. "I jumped in my car," said Ronstadt, "and pushed it as fast as I dared.... Emmy and Dolly were sitting on the sofa, trading stories and laughing together." Emmylou soon picked up a guitar and the trio sang its first song, the Carter Family's "Bury Me Beneath the Willow."

The women sang on Parton's mid-1970s television show, *Dolly!*, and went into the studio in 1979 for sessions that were ultimately abandoned, though some of the tracks appeared on albums by Harris ("Mister Sandman," "Evangeline") and Ronstadt ("My Blue Tears"). Feeling that their previous sessions were too pop-oriented, the trio reconvened in 1987 with a different strategy. "We wanted to bring that part of her voice, that part of Dolly back into Appalachia," said Harris. "And using it to our purposes, too, having Dolly's voice there, and just Dolly's presence there, made us authentic." For Parton, the collaboration offered something else. "Linda Ronstadt and Emmylou for Dolly were street cred," said Rodney Crowell. "Really intense street cred."

"[*Trio*] hit Nashville like a bomb," said the album's producer, George Massenburg. "They loathed it." Then it topped the country charts (and reached #6 on the pop chart) on the way to selling more than four million copies. The album's first hit single was "To Know Him Is to Love Him," a song written by Phil Spector about his father that was a #1 hit for his group the Teddy Bears in 1958. *Trio* later won a Grammy and was the 1987 Academy of Country Music award winner for Album of the Year. It was neither the first nor the last time that traditional music that went against Nashville's contemporary grain would be so honored.

Trio II didn't come out until 1999 because the recording sessions ended in acrimony when Parton requested that the release be timed to accommodate her schedule. "It got into a power play," said Parton. "I was made to feel hurt, insulted, burdened with guilt.... Finally, I just said, 'The hell with it, sue me.'" Parton demanded that her vocals be stripped from the recordings. Ronstadt's 1995 album, *Feels Like Home*, ended up including three tracks from the sessions, one featuring all three voices and two with just Linda and Emmylou. *Trio II* ultimately won a Grammy for the three women's interpretation of Neil Young's "After the Goldrush."

Young had signed with Geffen Records and spent the 1980s releasing albums in a dizzying array of styles, including electronic music (*Trans*, 1982)

DOLLY PARTON

and, after Geffen rejected a country album (*Old Ways*), a rockabilly record (*Everybody's Rockin'*, 1983). David Geffen sued Young for producing albums that were "unrepresentative" and "uncharacteristic" of his rock-y oeuvre. Young countersued, and the matter was resolved with an apology to the artist and the release of *Old Ways*. The album included a single, "Are There Any More Real Cowboys?," that was promoted with a video featuring Young's new best friend, Willie Nelson.

"I remember the first time he came back from Willie's," said Joel Bernstein, a photographer and archivist who worked for Young, "he literally looked like Charlton Heston down from the mountain." Young had grown a beard, and when he started wearing a headband some of those in his road crew took to calling him "Willie Neil." The delayed release of *Old Ways* put fire in Young's belly; he told Geffen, "Back off or I'm going to play country music forever. . . . I'll turn into George Jones." When Young returned to his old label, Reprise, he made his most characteristic album of the decade, *Freedom*, which included "Rockin' in the Free World." In 1992 he released *Harvest Moon*, the mid-life follow-up to *Harvest* that was recorded with many of the same musicians. "The real sense of the album," said Young, "is how do you keep going? How can you keep an old relationship new? How do you make love last?"

"*Guitar Town* made us all feel redundant," said Rosanne Cash. "I remember the reporter coming up to me at the record release party . . . and say[ing] 'Do you think [Steve Earle] has the potential to be a star?' And I said, 'Doesn't matter. He's already changed everything.'" Cash enjoyed hit singles and a Grammy for her 1985 album *Rhythm and Romance*, but now found its country-pop sound lacking. She had also taken to cocaine the way her father had to pills. Rodney Crowell was also in a slump; Warner Brothers had rejected his *Street Language* album and wanted a more country-oriented effort. He retooled the album for Columbia, but it still bombed. Both albums included songs written by John Hiatt, who'd been kicking around Nashville and recording since 1972. In 1987 Hiatt recruited an all-star band (Ry Cooder on guitar, Nick Lowe on bass, and Jim Keltner on drums) and found critical and commercial success with *Bring the Family*. Bonnie Raitt then scored with his "That Thing Called Love." That's how things worked in Music City. Hipsters knew about Lucinda Williams, but the business knew her as the writer of a hit by Mary Chapin Carpenter called "Passionate Kisses."

Rodney advised Rosanne to try something different for *King's Record Shop* (1987). "He described a more rootsy sounding record," said Cash, "not just in reaction to the heavy pop vibe of *Rhythm and Romance*, but as something fresh and more suited to my natural instincts. I studied Bob Dylan's *Writings and Drawings* (a book of lyrics and sketches) as if it were the Dead Sea Scrolls, and dissected Guy Clark and Townes Van Zandt songs as exercises to better myself as a songwriter. I should, I thought, make a record that reflected those sensibilities." But it was the album's stunning vocal and instrumental performances that made *King's Record Shop* a career milestone with four #1 country singles, including one by Hiatt ("The Way We Make a Broken Heart") and another by Johnny Cash ("Tennessee Flat Top Box") that had hit #11 in 1961. When Rosanne recorded the tune, which featured her old friend Randy Scruggs, another child of a country legend, playing the song's flat-top guitar solos, she thought it was in the public domain; its success made her father proud.

Producing a modern yet traditional collection for his wife inspired Crowell (with co-producer Tony Brown) to make one of his own, *Diamonds and Dirt* (1988). The confident swing of Crowell's cover of Buck's "Above and Beyond" was reflected in his own "I Couldn't Leave You If I Tried." Crowell wrote "She's Crazy for Leavin'" with Guy Clark and three other songs with Will Jennings, best known for his work with the British rock musician Steve Winwood. But Crowell's ace in the hole was a studio band that included Barry Beckett on keyboard, Paul Franklin on steel guitar, and Mark O'Connor on fiddle and mandolin. Vince Gill and Rosanne Cash, who dueted with her husband on "It's Such a Small World," provided background vocals. Like *Guitar Town* and *King's Record Shop*, *Diamonds and Dirt* was a hit country album (it contained five #1 songs) made by people who'd grown up with rock 'n' roll.

In 1988 Tony Brown also co-produced Steve Earle's most overtly rocking album, *Copperhead Road*, the first record that didn't include Richard Bennett on guitar. (Bennett never toured with Earle because he played far more lucrative concert dates with Neil Diamond. More recently, he has recorded and played live with Mark Knopfler, who has also collaborated with Emmylou Harris.) Brown said that when he played *Copperhead Road* for Jimmy Bowen, MCA's Nashville chief, "he said the album was a piece of shit." The company's pop division would subsequently market the label's so-called renegades—Earle, Lyle Lovett, and Nanci Griffith.

STEVE EARLE

Earle released *Guitar Town* when he was thirty-one years old. Sudden success can kill a young star, but Earle was no innocent; he'd been toying around with heroin since he was thirteen. "I started traveling," said Earle, speaking of his tours behind *Guitar Town* and its follow-up, *Exit 0*, "which brought me to places where there was good cheap heroin. Suddenly I was going to New York, and I was going to L.A. and Amsterdam. . . . I had a pretty steady habit going. . . . Usually before tours I would kick. But I would usually come back off a tour strung out, depending on where we played."

Robbie Robertson broke up The Band because of his fear of dying on the road. Initially, the members of The Band pursued solo careers, with Helm and Danko cutting solo albums and Hudson playing sessions. Helm found a second calling as an actor and made a vivid debut alongside Sissy Spacek in the 1980 movie about the life of Loretta Lynn, *Coal Miner's Daughter*. He also had a role in Philip Kaufman's 1983 film *The Right Stuff*, adapted from Tom Wolfe's book about America's first astronauts. That same year, The Band reformed minus Robertson and hit the road without recording new music.

In January 1986 Albert Grossman died of a heart attack while flying to Europe on the Concorde. Richard Manuel, one of Grossman's troubled charges, sang "I Shall Be Released" at his Bearsville funeral. A little more than a month later, The Band played the Cheek to Cheek Lounge in Winter Park, Florida. After the show Manuel spent time with Helm, telling him it was a drag doing club gigs after playing big shows and jetting around the country with Bob Dylan. "We're just musicians," Helm told Manuel. "We're just working for the crowd. It's the best we can do." Manuel returned to his room in the Quality Inn and finished a bottle of Grand Marnier. Then he went into the bathroom and used a leather belt to hang himself. At his funeral in Canada, Garth Hudson played "I Shall Be Released" on the organ.

Steve Earle's drug use was flagrant by the time he was recording *Copperhead Road*; Tony Brown was surprised but said nothing when he began snorting heroin in the studio. "Copperhead Road" was about the son of a bootlegger who comes home from Vietnam and starts growing pot. The music mixed a droning bagpipe with mandolin and hard-driving drums and guitars. Earle described it as a cross between heavy metal and bluegrass; it sure wasn't country music. Ignored by country radio and embraced by rock critics, *Copperhead*

Road became Earle's best-selling album; Waylon Jennings had a Top 5 hit with the collection's second-best song, "The Devil's Right Hand."

In the song, the devil's right hand is a handgun. One time, Earle was to open a concert for Rosanne Cash but was late because he was arrested trying to board a plane with a .45 Colt automatic. Earle closed the show, and Cash was not amused. "You don't have to create drama in your life," she said. "You embody it." While in Memphis Earle obtained prescriptions for Tussionex, a narcotic cough suppressant, from Dr. George Nichopolous. "For me," he said, "going to see Dr. Nick was just like going to Graceland. I went for the same reason. Then I got the cough mixture, too, which was a bonus."

The tours became increasingly toxic. "I felt like [Steve] was lost and I wasn't speaking to him anymore," said drummer Harry Stinson. "And so I had enough. . . . It took awhile for me to recover from being on the road with all that going on." Stinson, who would later play with Marty Stuart and His Fabulous Superlatives, had been there before. "I remember being with Etta James, and you know, you're living the blues," he said. "You might be doing a show and getting paid for it, but when you're traveling with Etta, it's the blues lifestyle, and it rubs off on you."

Townes Van Zandt knew all about the highs and lows of life on the road. In 1987 Robert Palmer wrote a review in the *New York Times* that compared Van Zandt to Hank Williams. "Their songwriting craft and vocal musicianship are exceptional," said Palmer, "but what you hear is beyond all that; it seems to be the direct, untrammeled expression of a man's soul. You can hear the South and Southwest in the accents, the casually mentioned names of towns and rivers, the music's unforced swing. But the highway runs from one end of America to the other, and for men like these the highway is heritage and home."

Earle traveled those roads, and along the way the music took a back seat to dope. Since he needed to finance his habit and the $8,000 per month he owed in alimony and child support, his guitars started showing up for sale in Nashville music shops. "Towards the end," said Earle, "I had to have some heroin in my system or I couldn't sing, I'd just throw up. At the very end, I did heroin just to get straight. That's why I started smoking cocaine, to get high, because I was using heroin or methadone just to stop from getting sick." Townes Van Zandt tried to counsel his friend. "I must be bad if they're sending you," said Earle. Then the two old friends poured themselves drinks.

Earle was ultimately saved by a traffic stop. He was on a drug run when he got arrested for driving with a suspended license and for being in possession of a crack pipe, three rocks of cocaine, and ten syringes. Around the time Van Zandt nearly died after entering Vanderbilt Hospital in a dire, "late-stage" alcoholic state, Earle was sentenced to a year in jail; he was released to a drug rehab program after three months. He wrote two songs while behind bars, the rocking "Hard-Core Troubadour" and a poignant ballad, "Goodbye." "There's probably women all over the world that think 'Goodbye' was written for them," said his singer-songwriter son Justin Townes Earle, who had his own struggles with addiction. "But I guarantee you, 'Goodbye' was written for junk." In August 2020 a sober father spoke by telephone to the son he'd named after an old friend. "I said, 'Do not make me bury you,'" said Steve to Justin. "And he said, 'I won't.'" Later that night, he died of an accidental drug overdose.

15
THE "BIRTH" OF AMERICANA

Alison Krauss began playing classical violin at the age of five and turned to bluegrass after winning her first fiddle contest at eight. Her father had emigrated from Germany in 1952, and she grew up not in a rural mountain holler but in the college town of Champaign, Illinois. "My grandmother played the piano, my mother played the guitar and we listened to Hank Williams and classical music," said Krauss. She was naturally drawn to folk music that featured the fiddle. "I was really into the second-generation bluegrass people," said Krauss, citing Lester Flatt and Earl Scruggs. "But my hero was Ralph [Stanley]," she said, "that kind of real mountain singing."

Krauss was named Most Promising Fiddle Player by the Society for the Preservation of Bluegrass Music at the age of twelve; while playing at bluegrass festivals she learned to modulate her voice to intimate effect and met the players who would form her group, Union Station. At sixteen Krauss went to Nashville to record her 1987 debut album for Rounder Records. The players were the cream of the acoustic crop and included Sam Bush, Bela Fleck, Tony Trischka, and Jerry Douglas, who would join Union Station in 1998.

"At one point, Jack Clement brought Johnny Cash upstairs," said Jim Rooney, the record's engineer. "Johnny volunteered to put a bass harmony on one song (which [producer] Ken Irwin chose not to use). Alison was young enough that her parents were still with her, and you wouldn't have blamed her if she'd let all of this throw her, but it didn't. She kept her focus. You could tell she was going somewhere." Krauss won her first Grammy Award for the title song of her 1990 album *I've Got That Old Feeling*. By 2019 she'd won twenty-seven Grammys, fourteen of them with Union Station.

Krauss's success was an anomaly in the relatively cloistered world of bluegrass, where the big time meant a contract with an independent label such as Rounder or Sugar Hill and gigs at the Telluride Bluegrass Festival (started in 1974) and Merlefest, an annual roots music event in North Carolina launched by Doc Watson in 1988. Festival attendees often bring their own instruments for campground jam sessions, while the pros network backstage. That's how Krauss became acquainted with Nickel Creek, a young bluegrass trio consisting of Chris Thile (mandolin) and siblings Sara Watkins (fiddle) and Sean Watkins (guitar). Krauss produced the trio's self-titled 2000 album, an influential success that, though grounded in bluegrass, also incorporated elements of jazz, classical, folk, and rock. Americana lived in this music, and the young players would become stars of the new genre.

Gillian Welch took a more circuitous path to find her musical home. She was adopted at birth (literally delivered to her new parents via a Manhattan taxi) by a showbiz couple who did comedy and wrote songs; when she was three, the family moved to Los Angeles when her parents got a job writing music for *The Carol Burnett Show*. She studied photography at the University of California before the untrained guitarist (she'd played bass in a Goth rock band) enrolled in the Berklee College of Music, where she shared a house with members of a string band. "I discovered bluegrass music," said Welch, "and it was like an electric shock. . . . I hadn't heard people playing the music I had sung as a kid [at a progressive school], and it made me think, I know these songs, and I sound good singing them." Welch (like Krauss) adored Ralph Stanley.

Welch studied songwriting at Berklee and left without a degree. "I looked at my record collection," she said, "and saw that all the music I loved had been made in Nashville—Bill Monroe, Dylan, the Stanley Brothers, Neil Young—so I moved there. Not ever thinking I was thirty years too late." Welch and David Rawlings met at Berklee and played music alongside other talented students. But they found their sound in the kitchen of his Nashville apartment when their voices and guitars fused on "Long Black Veil."

Gillian and David played open mike nights in Nashville, where Welch honed an original repertoire that was as leanly artful as the duo's performances. Denise Stiff, who was managing Alison Krauss, got Welch a publishing deal. At the Station Inn, T-Bone Burnett saw her play and said, "Do you want to make a record?" Burnett has a gift for producing new artists with a résumé that includes debut recordings by Los Lobos, Counting Crows, the BoDeans, and Joe Henry. He also produced one of Elvis Costello's best records, *King of America*, and hired Presley's guitar player, James Burton, and drummer Jim Keltner to play the sessions. Both musicians appeared on Welch's first album, *Revival*.

Burnett "had a deep and abiding concern that I find my way as an artist," said Welch, and "that my first record should show the world what I wanted to talk about and what I wanted to sound like." Burnett kept the focus on Gillian and David's harmonies, which built on country music's rich history of duets. Ann Powers, reviewing *Revival* for *Rolling Stone*, said that Welch and Rawlings created "settings they could only know from reading James Agee and listening to Folkways recordings." After mentioning Welch's Hollywood background, she continued: "Concentrate only on the sound, and these songs will haunt you; Welch's musical precision is eerie, the mark of a true obsessive so deeply wedded to her subject that she has become it. Ultimately, though, Welch's gorgeous testimonies manufacture emotion rather than express it."

Krauss, a fan of the rock band Foreigner, fielded few complaints about her authenticity, and Bob Dylan was one of many who studied the songs of Harry Smith's *Anthology*. No matter. Emmylou Harris cut Welch's "Orphan Girl" for her *Wrecking Ball* before it appeared on *Revival*. "One of the things that Gillian did very well was sing the song rather than the notes," said Pat Pattison, her songwriting teacher at Berklee. "You have singers who have a really great instrument, but you don't feel they're inside the song. When Gillian sings, it's about the presentation of emotion. Even back then, she didn't sing notes; she sang feelings and ideas."

Other musicians approached roots music from a different perspective. "We'd all been involved in rock bands, and punk rock, which is fun to listen to but doesn't always age well," said Gary Louris of the Jayhawks. "When we stumbled on country music, it sounded rebellious to us. It was definitely outsider music." Both the Jayhawks, based in Minneapolis, and Uncle Tupelo, a band from Belleview, Illinois, developed their sound far from the scrutiny of coastal critics. "Most of these bands were like us," said Rob Miller of Bloodshot

Records in Chicago, "discovering the music as they were creating it. Terms like 'alternative country' are now standard critical fare, but back then no one had any idea of what to do with it."

"We were conscious of the juxtaposition of putting a loud electric guitar next to acoustic folk-oriented songs, but at the time we didn't feel like we were really doing anything that different," said Jay Farrar of Uncle Tupelo. "It just seemed like more of a continuum[,] really," said Farrar on another occasion, "following bands like the Byrds and the Burrito Brothers." Farrar met Jeff Tweedy in high school and they played 1960s rock 'n' roll and punk covers in a band called the Primitives. "It wasn't like we were ever intentionally trying to merge punk and country," said Tweedy. "That's just what came out." Uncle Tupelo and the Jayhawks embraced the do-it-yourself ethos of punk, recording for small labels and sleeping on couches during club tours entailing long hours in dilapidated vans.

"If there was a class on how to start an alt.country band," said BJ Barham of the group American Aquarium, "this is your syllabus on Day One. You're talking Gram Parsons and then you're talking about Uncle Tupelo. This was punk-rock kids from the Midwest who listened to Iggy Pop and the Stooges, who decided to pick up mandolins and acoustic guitars and fiddles and start playing their own kind of music. It's paramount that you mention Uncle Tupelo when you mention this genre, because without them kind of paving that way between the late-Eighties scene and the early Nineties rock scene, you don't have what we call Americana now, what we called alt.country in the late Nineties."

In 1993 Uncle Tupelo opened for Johnny Cash in a California club. Tweedy said that Cash let out a cheer when they played "No Depression," a Carter Family song by June's uncle A. P. "I don't remember saying much," said Tweedy. "What was there to say to Johnny Cash? It was like talking to the Empire State Building or a bald eagle." *No Depression* was the title of Uncle Tupelo's 1990 debut; early in the decade, the name would be used for an AOL message board populated by Tupelo fans. In 1995 *No Depression* became the name of an influential publication covering a style of music that was mutating from alt.country to Americana.

In an era dominated by the grunge rock of Nirvana and Pearl Jam, the alt-country crowd embraced a different sort of alternative rock. Uncle Tupelo had two singer-songwriters: Farrar, who sang in a deep, resonant voice and whose lead guitar was influenced by Neil Young, and Tweedy, who played bass (and guitar) and whose vocals owed more to folk-rock than to blues. Both wrote songs about an industrial Midwest that had seen better days. On a lark, Uncle Tupelo played occasional acoustic shows as Coffee Creek, performing country classics by Buck, Cash, and Haggard.

Farrar and Tweedy shared a band, a van, and an apartment in Belleville; by the time they'd recorded three indie albums (including *March 16–20, 1992*, an acoustic record produced by R.E.M.'s Peter Buck) and Uncle Tupelo's major label debut (*Anodyne*), they barely spoke. So Farrar left the group. Tweedy renamed the band Wilco, and Farrar formed Son Volt. But before then, Uncle Tupelo contributed a song to *Arkansas Traveler*, a 1992 collection in which the folk singer Michelle Shocked recruited a veritable who's who of Americana. Besides Tupelo, Shocked's guests included Levon Helm and Garth Hudson of The Band, Pops Staples of the Staple Singers, the Red Clay Ramblers, Alison Krauss and Union Station, fiddler Mark O'Connor, and such powerful pickers as Doc Watson, Norman Blake, Jerry Douglas, and Bernie Leadon.

Uncle Tupelo never made it big, but it cast a large shadow. Patterson Hood's band Adam's House Cat opened for the group in "a small, little punk-rock dive bar" in Memphis. Hood was no stranger to country music. "A friend of mine," he said, "made me this mix tape of all this old-timey country stuff, the kind of stuff I'd hear at my great uncle's farm, or he would play, that I didn't embrace at all growing up. But now I heard it with fresh ears." He heard that music reflected in Uncle Tupelo's *March 16–20, 1992*. Hood and Mike Colley would soon form a punk-inflected roots band of their own, Drive-By Truckers.

"Uncle Tupelo's influence wasn't as musical innovators," said writer Peter Blackstock, "but they were very influential in galvanizing a fan base and a base of artists interested in this kind of music. It's a smaller version of what R.E.M. did for alternative rock in the '80s." Peter Buck played guitar for R.E.M. "They were the right band at the right time," said Buck, "and maybe just as important, they broke up at the right time. Just when a lot of stuff that was influenced by them was starting to break through to the mainstream, and older artists doing the same thing—like Steve Earle and Lucinda Williams—were starting to get recognized, the bright young hope called it quits. It reminds me a lot of bands like the Velvet Underground and Big Star, who made great music and were playing to audiences of like eight people, and it was only years later that a larger audience figured out how great they were."

When Blackstock and Grant Alden launched *No Depression* it was a quarterly; the first cover featured Son Volt. The Americana chart created in the early 1990s didn't last long, but in 1999 the genre inspired the creation of the Americana Music Association. By then, *No Depression* was a bi-monthly and considered to be the Bible of Americana, though it persisted in calling itself "A magazine about alt.country (whatever that is)." (*No Depression* ceased print publication in 2008 and subsequently maintained an online presence; in 2014 it was bought by FreshGrassLLC, a nonprofit company that also promotes an annual music festival.)

Whiskeytown was Americana's first big band. Ryan Adams played punk in the Patty Duke Syndrome but never forgot the country music that he'd heard growing up in North Carolina. "I started this damn country band," sings Adams on the title track of Whiskeytown's indie-label debut, *Faithless Street*, "because punk rock is too hard to sing." Jim Scott produced Whiskeytown's second album and major label debut, *Strangers Almanac*, and gave the band's music clarity and crunch (Scott had engineered Tom Petty's *Wildflowers*). The repertoire was eclectic; Adams touched on classic country ("Excuse Me While I Break My Own Heart Tonight"), country rock ("16 Days"), and folk rock (Turn Around"); acoustic songs evoked his singer-songwriter side. "By listening to a bunch of great songs, [Adams had] taught himself to be a great songwriter—across all genres," said Thomas O'Keefe, Whiskeytown's road manager.

Adams made the cover of *No Depression*, and *Strangers Almanac* was modestly successful, selling 150,000 copies. But an Americana star was a mainstream nobody, and Adams hated it when Whiskeytown opened a tour for John Fogerty of Creedence Clearwater Revival. Before Whiskeytown's subsequent demise, the band appeared on a television tribute to Gram Parsons on *Sessions at West 54th Street*. Musicians appearing on the show included Emmylou Harris, Steve Earle, Gillian Welch and David Rawlings, Wilco, Chris Hillman, Jim Lauderdale, and Buddy Miller. The high regard in which Adams was held in the world of Americana was reflected by the fact that he opened the show singing "Return of the Grievous Angel" with Emmylou. After the taping, musicians gathered at an East Village bar where Welch and Adams were at the center of a song swap. "We ended up playing music until four or five a.m.," said Welch. "Ryan seemed kinda burnt on Manhattan [where he was living] and he kept saying, 'Nobody ever does this up here, just play for fun.' We mostly did old covers—George Jones, Hank Williams, the usual fare."

Welch was enlisted by T-Bone Burnett to help create a soundtrack for Joel and Ethan Coen's 2000 film *O Brother, Where Art Thou?*, a Depression-era musical nominally based on Homer's *Odyssey*. For inspiration, and before the script was completed, they burned compilation CDs of country, blues, and bluegrass music from the 1930s. Burnett and the filmmakers then gathered a roomful of musicians including Welch, Alison Krauss, Emmylou Harris, and Norman Blake. "Everyone's sort of hanging out and playing, picking, and then Ralph [Stanley] walked in," said Ethan Coen. "It was like they'd wheeled in one of the heads from Mount Rushmore. The whole room just kind of fell silent."

The film starred George Clooney, who lip-synched "Man of Constant Sorrow," a folk song recorded in the 1950s by the Stanley Brothers and in the 1960s by Bob Dylan. Dan Tyminki of Union Station sang the song for *O Brother*, and his wife said, "Your voice coming out of George Clooney's body? This is my fantasy come true." The lively rendition was ear candy compared to the soundtrack's other indelible tune, "O Death." Burnett first had Ralph Stanley cut the song while playing the banjo, but then had him sing it a cappella because "it was much more terrifying that way." The *O Brother* soundtrack sold more than eight million copies and won five Grammys, including Album of the Year, a producer award for Burnett, and Best Male Country Vocal for Stanley.

"[Burnett] said he understood what I'd been doing all these years," said Stanley, "sticking with my old-time mountain music when everybody else was going uptown. I told him it wasn't a strategy. More like an instinct." Burnett said he wasn't surprised at the success of *O Brother*, which also included songs by Jimmie Rodgers ("In the Jailhouse Now") and the Carter Family ("Keep on the Sunny Side"). "To me it just sounded like a really good record," he said. "I had high hopes for it because we had a broadcast medium that wasn't dependent on the power structure in Nashville. We had this movie—a movie starring George Clooney at that—and I thought, if people hear this music they'll like it, because it's good."

"Johnny was one of the few people who wrote me when I was locked up," said Steve Earle. "He sent me a very encouraging letter saying how everybody was pulling for me, and that he and June were praying for me." Earle knew that he'd walked right up to the edge. "I probably would have died," he said. "I'm not about to thank the judge or anybody, but he probably saved my life. I went into treatment not to get clean but to get out of jail. But something happened in treatment, and I can't talk about it very much. One thing about me that's not very unique is this fucking disease I have, and somehow, this program [Alcoholics Anonymous] is helping me keep it under control."

Music also helped. Shortly after he was released from rehab, Earle cut an acoustic album with Norman Black on guitar and fiddle, Peter Rowan on mandolin, and Roy Huskey Jr. on acoustic bass. "We were all in the room playing with each other," said Rowan. "The acoustic music tradition has a sense of the moment and the rough edges are still there." Intimacy is the key. "Everybody can hear each other," said Blake. "Just really listening to what's going down and getting it to where you've got a real good recording to start with before you get to the point of 'we can fix it in the mix.'"

Train a-Comin' included songs Earle had written but never recorded and covers such as "I'm Looking Through You" by the Beatles and "Tecumseh Valley" by Townes Van Zandt. Hoping to get Emmylou Harris to add some harmonies, Earle sent her a tape of the sessions. She was moved to tears by "Goodbye," the ballad he'd written in jail, and asked Earle for permission to record the song for *Wrecking Ball*, inviting him to play on the track. Guitarist Richard Bennett, who hadn't seen Earle in years, was also on the date. "Out of the corner of my eye," said Bennett, "I saw this mountain of a redneck in these overalls . . . and I thought, 'Who the fuck is this in here with Emmy?' And he came up and said, 'Richard, it's Steve.'"

Bennett agreed to help produce the electric album that Earle was already planning and which is now considered one of his very best. "It's a modern, mid-90s *Guitar Town*," said Bennett, "in that it's back to being very simple. . . . It's a great rock album without trying to be 'rock.' In that sense, some kind of circle had closed." *I Feel Alright* included the hard-rocking title song; "Hard-Core Troubadour," which echoed Van Morrison's "Brown-Eyed Girl" and referenced Bruce Springsteen's "Rosalita"; "Now She's Gone," a song that evoked the sound of *Rubber Soul*; and a duet with Lucinda Williams, "You're Still Standin' There."

Earle issued another album, *El Corazon*, a year later, and hired Buddy Miller to play lead guitar on the subsequent tour; Miller did double duty by opening some shows with his wife Julie. Earle found both solace and purpose in writing "Ellis Unit One" for a Tim Robbins film about a convict's execution, *Dead Man Walking*. "You're kind of a new person when you're sober," said Earle, "and I'd yet to write something that I felt real serious about in a topical slash political vein. So when I wrote it, there was something of a catharsis for me;

it was as if now the picture was complete." While recording "Ellis Unit One," he ran into another contributor to the soundtrack, Johnny Cash.

"When I got to the studio, nobody was there but John and the engineer," said Earle. "I walk in and there's this old-fashioned picnic basket sitting in the middle of the pool table—you know, gingham tablecloth, the whole bit. John's got his hand in that picnic basket, and he looks up and says, 'Steve, would you like a piece of tenderloin on a biscuit that June made this morning?' I was really hungry so I said, 'Yeah,' and he said, 'I knew you would.' We could have talked about our shared demons—I'd been clean probably a year and a half—but he knew that sometimes it's better to leave some things private and just talk about tenderloin and biscuit."

Earle then agreed to produce Lucinda Williams's 1998 album *Car Wheels on a Gravel Road*. Williams had already discarded a nearly complete version of *Car Wheels* that she'd recorded with her longtime guitarist and producer, Gurf Morlix. "Steve Earle and I," said Williams, "write with a contemporary point of view but with reference to traditional music forms." But they ended up butting heads, and Roy Bittan, a keyboardist for Bruce Springsteen's E Street Band, completed the album. Musicians playing on the record include Buddy Miller on guitar and Jim Lauderdale and Emmylou Harris on background vocals.

Car Wheels was a hit with critics, topping the *Village Voice*'s annual "Pazz and Jop" poll and winning the Grammy for Best Contemporary Folk. "The album turns that much-maligned genre—call it American roots rock—into a heady, soul-baring and, would you believe, unabashedly sexy art form," said Gavin Martin of Britain's *New Music Express*. "What she has over all the other girls with guitars is a masterful sense of pace and rhythm, deliciously tailored tunes and a big, warm, enveloping voice with a burnished edge." Lucinda's songs smelled of the South and were thick with love, regret, and the urge for going. Williams would continue to make noteworthy music, but *Car Wheels* remains both her best-selling album and an enduring masterpiece.

Earle's fellow Texans, Nanci Griffith and Lyle Lovett, sustained successful, low-key careers. Griffin reunited with producer Jim Rooney to cut *Other Voices, Other Rooms*, a collection of songs written by artists who'd inspired her, including Townes Van Zandt, Dylan, John Prine, Gordon Lightfoot, and Jerry Jeff Walker. Griffith sang the Carter Family's "Are You Tired of Me, Darling?" with Emmylou and Iris DeMent. Rooney had produced DeMent's 1992 debut,

Infamous Angel, and her striking voice and songs of rural life and emotional introspection created such a buzz that Warner Brothers bought out her contract with Rounder Records and rereleased the album. DeMent later sang the title song of John Prine's 1999 album of duets, *In Spite of Ourselves.*

Lovett was encouraged to curb his offbeat instincts and tailor songs for the radio. Instead, he brought horns into his band to add a little swing and acted in two films by Robert Altman, *Short Cuts* and *The Player*. (It was on the set of the latter that Lovett met actress Julia Roberts; they married and amicably divorced two years later.) "I want to be successful enough to keep my job," said Lovett, "but somehow make the records the way I want to, without outside influence, with freedom of thought. . . . And that attitude comes from those nights at the Anderson Fair Retail Restaurant in Houston, where, after the gig was over . . . we would play songs till four in the morning and tell stories about Guy and Townes."

Lovett would honor the Texas school with *Step Inside This House* (1998). The title song was Guy Clark's first original song, which the notoriously self-critical songwriter never recorded; the album also included Van Zandt's "If I Needed You" ("If I needed you . . . Would you come to me and ease my pain?") and "Sailing Shoes" ("Days full of rain / Sky's comin' down again / I get so tired / Of the same old blues"). Van Zandt was by now, to borrow the title of one of his songs, waiting around to die. Live shows kept him solvent but were apt to run off the rails. "He started doing some of his songs," said musician Jim Calvin of a gig in Dallas, "except for half of it was in tongues, half of it was just howling." Sonic Youth drummer Steve Shelley offered him a deal to cut a record for Geffen, but before sessions commenced in Memphis near Christmas 1998, Van Zandt took a drunken tumble; declining medical attention, he arrived at the recording studio in a wheelchair.

"He hadn't shaved in a few days, and he was gaunt," said writer Robert Gordon. "He was a very heavy drinker and I remember when he took a shot during the sessions, you could hear . . . it moving through his blood going into his body and then out again." The sessions went nowhere. At his ex-wife Jeanene's insistence, Van Zandt finally went to the hospital and discovered that he'd broken his hip. The next morning, against doctor's orders but at Van Zandt's request, Jeanene took him home. It was New Year's Day 1997, forty-four years to the day after Hank died in the back of his Cadillac. Townes would join him before sunset. The funeral was at Belmont Church, just off Music Row in Nashville. Steve Earle, sober as a judge, introduced tributes in the form of spoken words and musical performances by Lyle, Emmylou, Nanci, and Guy Clark, who said, "I booked this gig thirty-something years ago."

"What records do I listen to?" said Bob Dylan to Bono of U2. "I still listen to those records that I listened to when I was growing up—they really changed my life. They still change my life. Robert Johnson, the Louvin Brothers, Hank Williams, Muddy Waters, Howlin' Wolf, Charlie Patton." In 1992, thirty years after releasing his first album, Dylan used his acoustic guitar and harmonica to record *Good as I Been to You* in the garage of his Malibu home. The album contained the kind of folk ("Frankie and Albert") and blues (Blind Boy Fuller's "Step It Up and Go") that he might have played opening for John Lee Hooker at the Gaslight Café. Dylan repeated the format a year later with *World Gone Wrong*. Revisiting the repertoire of his youth led to *Time out of Mind* (1997), the first of a series of outstanding late-career recordings that were suffused with the blues.

Dylan made the album with Daniel Lanois, who'd produced his 1989 album *Oh Mercy* and co-produced U2 albums with Brian Eno. Dylan read Lanois the lyrics he'd written for *Time out of Mind* and advised him to listen to records by Charlie Patton, Little Walter, and Arthur Alexander for inspiration. Dylan made demos with Lanois at Teatro, the studio he'd built in an old theater in Oxnard, California, but the album was recorded in Miami. The assembled musicians included a pair of drummers (Jim Keltner and Brian Blade), two keyboardists (Augie Meyers and Jim Dickinson), multiple guitarists (including Lanois and Duke Robillard), and Cindy Cashdollar on slide guitar. "There was a lot of heart in the room," said Dickinson, "and a lot of people of a certain age. There was a lot of mortality there."

"My years with Eno had provided me with an appetite for innovations," said Lanois, "and so my time in Miami was all about providing Bob with a futuristic way of looking at his work." Lanois established the proper pulse by feeding pre-recorded rhythms into the drummer's headphones and ran Dylan's vocal through a Gretsch guitar amplifier to get an old-fashioned sound. The dense, spectral arrangements complemented Dylan's autumnal songs. "Love Sick," a title that alluded to Hank Williams's "Love Sick Blues," set the album's tone with its opening line: "I'm walking through streets that are dead." Things lighten up, nominally, on "Not Dark Yet" ("It's not dark yet, but it's getting there"). Dylan won a rock vocal Grammy for "Cold Irons Bound," in which his voice floats within a lattice of guitars, distorted keyboards, and rattling drums.

A decade earlier Robbie Robertson had hired Lanois to co-produce his first new music since leaving The Band. "Robbie and the Band made a great impression on me as a kid coming up in Canada," said Lanois. Recording Robertson while also working on U2's *Joshua Tree*, he encouraged his new client to come to Ireland to record a pair of songs with the group. Whereas the music of The Band seemed removed from the calendar, the album *Robbie Robertson* was saturated in the sound of the day; its best song, "Fallen Angel," a eulogy to the late Richard Manuel, featured Peter Gabriel and sounded as if it could have been on his own Lanois-produced album, *So*.

In 1995 Harris sent Lanois a tape of songs that she planned to record. "The simplicity of her recording touched me," said Lanois. "I heard the frailty inside the confidence of this master singer's voice." Lanois asked U2's Larry Mullen to play drums and had Malcolm Burns bounce honky-tonk piano against his own electric guitar, mandolin, and dulcimer (which he'd found in Emmylou's house). "The multiple strings of these instruments ringing in unison created a harmonic cohesion," he said, "a sort of choral group, moving with every chord change."

Harris has always been a curator of superior songs, and *Wrecking Ball* included material by such Americana figures as Julie Miller ("All My Tears"), Dylan ("Every Grain of Sand"), Lucinda Williams ("Sweet Old World"), Steve Earle ("Goodbye"), Gillian Welch ("Orphan Girl"), and Jimi Hendrix ("May This Be Love"). Neil Young, who would record an album (*Le Noise*) with Lanois in 2010, added a harmony vocal to his song "Wrecking Ball." Harris also recorded "Goin' Back to Harlan" by Anna McGarrigle, who sang on the record with her sister Kate. "These great Canadian singers have a beautiful and special blend, a sort of warbling bird sound," said Lanois of the folk duo.

Wrecking Ball won the Grammy for Best Contemporary Folk Recording and sold 250,000 copies, a healthy figure that nonetheless paled alongside sales of Emmylou's earlier country albums. But she now thrived in the incipient genre of Americana, and when she put together a new band, she hired Buddy Miller. "The first thing we sang after I got the gig was 'Love Hurts,'" said Miller of the Everly Brothers song that Harris had once performed with Gram Parsons. "At that point I told her manager that he didn't really have to pay me."

In 1998 Lanois and Emmylou met Willie Nelson in Las Vegas and rode his tour bus to Oxnard to record an album called *Teatro*. Nelson was coming off of

EMMYLOU HARRIS

Spirit, an intimate album that he'd recorded with a small ensemble; Lanois's strategy was to frame Nelson's Gypsy jazz guitar style with Latin accents. A late-night ambiance was established when Willie and his sister Bobbie (on electric piano) opened the album with a Django Reinhardt classic, "Ou Es-Tu, Mon Amour?" Nelson's Spanish-inflected guitar then introduced "I Never Cared for You," a song Nelson first recorded in 1964 (it was a hit in Texas). *Teatro* exists somewhere between country and folksy Latin jazz, with pianist Brad Mehldau making an appearance and Mickey Raphael anchoring some of the tracks with a bass harmonica.

Teatro is utterly unique in Nelson's voluminous catalog and sits comfortably alongside Latin Americana recordings by Los Lobos, the Mavericks, and the Texas Tornados. The Mavericks, led by Cuban American singer Raul Malo, enjoyed Top 40 country hits in the 1990s ("What a Crying Shame," "Here Comes the Rain") and continues to play music that mixes elements of Tex-Mex, Latin, and rock 'n' roll. The Texas Tornados were a Lone Star supergroup that included Doug Sahm and Augie Meyers of the Sir Douglas Quintet, country star Freddy Fender ("Wasted Days and Wasted Nights"), and a master of the conjunto accordion, Flaco Jimenez. Recording in both English and Spanish, the Tornados spiked rock and country songs with a variety of Mexican and Latin styles.

Daniel Lanois recognized something when he recorded Dylan and Nelson. "There is a similarity between [them]," said Lanois, "both tireless troubadours, both relying on the call of the road." While Willie lived to be on the road again, Dylan had begun what became known as the "Never Ending Tour." "Bob considers himself a simple man who performs a trade," said his road manager, Victor Maymudes. "Like a plumber, carpenter, or stone mason . . . Bob sees himself as a musician, that's his trade, and musicians play concerts."

"I had just had this huge record with *King's Record Shop*," said Rosanne Cash. "I had a ton of leverage with the record label, but I just felt like I veered off the track of my life. . . . When you think of yourself as a songwriter, and then you make a record that's truly successful, and there's only a couple of yours on there, I was a little shaken." So she wrote *Interiors* (1990), a quietly intense record she produced by herself. "Somebody wrote a review [of *Interiors*] and said it was a 'divorce record,'" said Cash, "and I was shocked. . . . And then, of course, later on, I realized that he was right."

Country radio ignored *Interiors*, and at Cash's request promotion of the album was shifted to Columbia's pop division. Rodney Crowell similarly struggled to meet the commercial expectations generated by *Diamonds & Dirt*. "It was different in the nineties," he recalled. "I made a couple of records for MCA that I wasn't proud of." So Crowell began releasing more personal albums on smaller labels. In one respect, however, he never left mainstream country music. "As a songwriter," said Crowell, "every couple of years, something I write, somebody else will cover it and it'll be a hit, and it subsidizes the art."

Crowell and John Leventhal co-produced an album in the early 1990s by Jim Lauderdale, who'd moved from New York to Los Angeles and reconnected with Buddy Miller, who played lead guitar in his band while helping his wife Julie record albums for the Christian market. In the years since Buddy and Julie had left New York, Shawn Colvin and Leventhal had become romantically involved and had begun collaborating on songs. "John would give me these rhythm and blues type things that he had put on tape," said Colvin, "and I'd make it into a Richard Thompson kind of thing on my guitar. I wrote the first verse and chorus of 'Diamond in the Rough,' and I called John thinking that he'd hate it. But he didn't, and encouraged me to keep on going. So I finished it, and discovered that I'd found something that seemed to be unique to me." Colvin was part of the New York Fast Folk scene that launched Suzanne Vega. Colvin sang on Vega's hit song "Luka" and toured Europe in her band; she then got a deal with Columbia Records. Leventhal produced Colvin's *Steady On*, and though the couple's romance didn't last, their record won the Contemporary Folk Grammy.

Leventhal had also co-written songs with Lauderdale. "For about a year and a half, we had this magical thing going," said Lauderdale of the collaboration, "with many of the songs ending up on *Planet of Love*." Colvin sang backup on that album (as well as those by Julie Miller), but for "King of Broken Hearts," a song written about Gram Parsons, Crowell called in his old boss. "Emmylou was like the Queen," said Julie. "Nobody could imagine actually knowing her personally!" Few people heard *Planet of Love*, but those who did mattered. "I think nine out of ten tracks of that album have been recorded by others," said Lauderdale. Country star George Strait heard and cut both "King of Broken Hearts" and "Where the Sidewalk Ends" on the same day. Lauderdale has enjoyed a long career as a recording artist, but it's songwriting royalties that has kept him comfortably solvent.

Crowell, Cash, and Harris had ended the 1980s at the top of the country heap, but that all changed in the 1990s. Dwight Yoakam had his biggest record with a modern take on the Bakersfield sound, *This Time* (1993), but mislaid his audience with *Lost* (1995). "It wasn't a slow decline," said Yoakam's producer, Pete Anderson. "We went from a triple platinum record [three million sold] to a record that sold three hundred and fifty thousand copies." Mainstream country had changed with the arrival of Garth Brooks, whose arena-rock version of country crushed everybody this side of Shania Twain, whose country-pop albums were produced by her husband Mutt Lange, who also recorded AC/DC and Def Leppard.

Rosanne Cash divorced her husband and moved to New York. "It was a matter of trying to figure out how not to destroy my kids' lives," she said. "How to unleash myself from a 6,000-square-foot house and a big diamond ring and a marriage that everybody had elevated to this kind of, I don't know, iconic entertainment." Cash settled in Greenwich Village and reinvented herself as the bohemian daughter of a country legend who wrote prose as well as songs. When it came time to write and produce her next album (*The Wheel*), she turned to John Leventhal, a Manhattan neighbor whom she'd met through Crowell.

Shawn Colvin recorded her second album (*Fat City*) with bassist Larry Klein, who was married to Joni Mitchell. "There was this whole incestuous minidrama going on where Rosanne was now dating, and working with, John Leventhal, I was working with [Rosanne's previous guitar player] Steuart Smith and Larry had just finished producing an album for Rodney Crowell, Rosanne's ex-husband, using Steuart and John on guitars." By the time Colvin collaborated with Leventhal on *A Few Small Repairs* (1996), he would be married to Rosanne. Colvin's "Sunny Came Home" won the 1998 Grammy Awards for both Song and Record of the Year. During the broadcast, Ol' Dirty Bastard of the Wu-Tang Clan interrupted her acceptance speech to declare "Wu-Tang is for the children!" But that wasn't the weirdest thing that happened. When Bob Dylan, who won Album of the Year for *Time out of Mind*, was performing "Love Sick," a bare-chested man with "Soy Bomb" written on his chest bounded onto the stage to do a spastic dance alongside Dylan, who played a guitar solo as the trespasser was hustled off the stage. Looking on with bemused concern was a new member of Dylan's group, Larry Campbell, who once played with Colvin in the Buddy Miller Band.

At the turn of the century, the Americana genre was coalescing as the music business was falling apart. The CD boom was over, and digital file sharing was both crushing profits and anticipating a future that would see physical products replaced by internet streams. But it wasn't just a business model that was changing; it was the music itself. The genre of rock 'n' roll, aside from heritage acts such as Bruce Springsteen, U2, and the Rolling Stones, was now a sliver of a music market dominated by dance, hip-hop, and other styles that most grown-ups don't know. Anemic record sales meant that artists increasingly made their money from live performances, and Americana emerged as a natural refuge for rock bands, singer-songwriters, and roots musicians.

Americana was also helpful to artists whom country radio had kicked aside in favor of younger performers. In 2000 Merle Haggard released his last great record, *If I Could Only Fly*, named after the Blaze Foley title song, on Anti, a subsidiary of the punk rock label Epitaph. The same label released Porter Wagoner's *Wagonmaster*, an old-school country album produced by Marty Stuart and featuring his band, the Fabulous Superlatives. Loretta Lynne attracted a new crop of hipster fans when Jack White of the White Stripes produced her *Van Lear Rose.* But nothing compared to the late-career renaissance of Johnny Cash albums engineered by a producer who practiced transcendental meditation and sported the long beard of a guru.

Rick Rubin co-founded Def Jam Records while living in a New York University dorm and producing hits by LL Cool J and the Beastie Boys. After making records with Tom Petty and the Red Hot Chili Peppers, Rubin approached Cash with a proposition. "You'll come to my house, take a guitar and start singing," he said. "You'll sing every song you love, and somewhere in there we'll find a trigger song that will tell us we're headed in the right direction." The odd couple clicked. Cash recorded *American Recording* (1994) in Rubin's living room with only his guitar (save two tracks from the Viper Room in Los Angeles). The repertoire included folk evergreens ("Delia's Gone") and songs by Leonard Cohen ("Bird on a Wire"), Loudon Wainwright III ("The Man Who Couldn't Cry"), and Nick Lowe ("The Beast in Me"). Before releasing the album, Cash asked the opinion of a trusted friend. "I can't see nothing wrong with this," said Marty Stuart. "This is as pure as it gets." The stark, intimate recording proved to be the most critically and commercially successful music Cash had made in decades.

"Rick came along at exactly the right time," said Rosanne Cash. "Before Rick, Dad was depressed, discouraged. It was a powerful thing that happened between them, and Dad was completely revitalized and back to his old enthusiastic self." *Unchained* (1996) was largely recorded with Tom Petty and the Heartbreakers at a studio in a seedy neighborhood of Los Angeles. One day Cash arrived with a smile on his face. "He was laughing, so I said, 'Hey, where you been?'" said Petty. "He said, 'June and I thought it would be fun to just sit on the bus bench across the street for a while. I met the most interesting people over there.'" *Unchained* won the Grammy for Country Album, rankling Nashville music executives, who successfully lobbied the National Academy of Recording Arts and Sciences to protect their franchise by creating new Grammy categories in Contemporary Folk and, in 2009, Americana.

Cash's work with Rubin reached its emotional epiphany when he sang "Hurt" by Trent Reznor of Nine Inch Nails. "What have I become, my sweetest friend," sang Cash in a voice that exposed his increasingly fragile health. "Everyone I know goes away in the end." A video for the song juxtaposed triumphant scenes from his past with shots of June looking at her husband with deep, loving concern. Cash showed his daughter the video before approving its release. "I told him, 'You have to put it out,'" said Rosanne. "'It's so unflinching and brave and that's what you are.'" The father and daughter had a complicated history. Shortly after Cash started working with Rubin, Rosanne reluctantly accepted her father's request to join him at Carnegie Hall to perform a song that he'd recorded in 1958, "I Still Miss Someone." "As we sang together," said Rosanne, "all the old pain dissolved and the old longing to connect was completely satisfied under the lights and the safety of a few thousand people who loved us, thus achieving something I'd been trying get since I was six years old."

As a boy in Dyess, Arkansas, Cash loved listening to the Carter Family on the radio; years later, he married June and joined the clan. In early 2003 John Leventhal put music to "September When It Comes," lyrics that his wife had written and put away in the mid-1990s; he encouraged her to make it a duet with her father. Cash recorded three vocal takes. "I cannot be who I was then," he sang. "In a way, I never was." The song was released in the spring of 2008 on Rosanne's *Rules of Travel*. Johnny lost June in May and followed her home the following September.

16
ACROSS THE GREAT DIVIDE

"If you'll be my dixie chicken, I'll be your Tennessee lamb," go the lyrics of Little Feat's "Dixie Chicken," the song that gave the Dixie Chicks their name. Martie and Emily Robinson were multi-instrumentalists (fiddle, banjo, mandolin, bass) who formed the group in 1989 with bassist Laura Lynch and guitarist Robin Lynn Macy; the ensemble reorganized as a trio in 1995 when singer-guitarist Natalie Maines joined the sisters. The repertoire was an Americana mix of country, bluegrass, folk, and pop. But when their first two albums (*Wide Open Spaces* [1998] and *Fly* [1999]) each sold an astonishing ten million copies, they became country stars instead of the darlings of Americana. Songs by Buddy Miller, Jim Lauderdale, Marty Stuart, and singer-songwriter Patty Griffin supplemented the band's original tunes.

Then the group released *Home* and traveled to London in March 2002 to start its "Top of the World Tour." At the time, the United States was preparing to attack Iraq because Saddam Hussein was said to possess weapons of mass destruction. "We do not want this war, this violence," said Natalie Maines while introducing "Travelin' Soldier" during the band's first London show. "We're ashamed that the President of the United States is from Texas." In the blink of a news cycle, the music of country music's most popular group disappeared from country radio, and the career of the Dixie Chicks was carved up like a Tennessee lamb.

The country audience is reliably conservative, and after the terrorist attack of 9/11, airwaves crackled with songs like Toby Keith's "Courtesy of the Red, White, & Blue (The Angry American)" and "This Ain't No Rag, It's a Flag" by the Charlie Daniels Band. Maines tried to clarify her remarks and personally apologized to President George W. Bush, but the die was cast, and the naked Chicks soon appeared on the cover of *Entertainment Weekly* tattooed with the epithets cast upon the group ("Traitors," "Hero," "Saddam's Angels"). The Dixie Chicks returned in 2006 with *Taking the Long Way*, produced by Rick Rubin. The album debuted atop both the pop and country charts, but the Chicks were now cultural totems and no longer country stars. They won Grammys for Album of the Year and Song of the Year ("Not Ready to Make Nice"), but then did not release new music until *Gaslighter* (2020). Before its release, the trio responded to heightened racial sensitivity by officially dropping "Dixie" from its name.

The Chicks wouldn't have been banished from Americana, which has been called "country music for Democrats." Steve Earle wrote "John Walker's Blues" about the young American who travelled to Afghanistan and joined the Taliban, and though the song generated some outrage on the right, the brouhaha had little effect on Earle's more modest audience and didn't prevent him from winning a Contemporary Folk Grammy for his highly political 2004 album, *The Revolution Starts Now*.

Bruce Springsteen never hid his liberal leanings, and the rocker won the Traditional Folk Grammy for *We Shall Overcome: The Seeger Sessions* (2006). Though few of the selections from Pete Seeger's repertoire were overtly political, devoting an album to songs associated with a once-blacklisted artist was a statement in itself. The recording was made at Springsteen's New Jersey home with musicians gathered by the E Street Band's fiddle player, Soozie Tyrell. Springsteen subsequently toured with "The Sessions Band" and joined Joan Baez, Emmylou Harris, Steve Earle, John Mellencamp, and Roger McGuinn at the Clearwater Concert, a (what else?) benefit held at Madison Square Garden to celebrate Seeger's ninetieth birthday. The musicians commemorated a singular life bookended by riding the rails with Woody Guthrie and singing "This Land Is Your Land" at the presidential inauguration of Barack Obama. Seeger sang and played the banjo in pursuit of peace, equal rights, and a healthy environment. He knew that his work would never be done, and on almost every Saturday until the day he died in January 2014, he would stand on the shoulder of Route 9 near his home in Beacon, New York, and hold up a placard that said "Peace."

Wilco's *Yankee Foxtrot Hotel* was to be released on September 11, 2001. Then Warner Brothers rejected it. Tensions had been building between the band and a label once known to be supportive of artists like Randy Newman and Ry Cooder who made artful records that sold relatively few copies. Relations with the label were cordial at the time of the band's debut, *A.M.*, which was of an alt.country piece with Tweedy's work with Uncle Tupelo. But that changed when Tweedy began working with multi-instrumentalist Jay Bennett to create the densely layered rock of *Being There* (1996) and *Summerteeth* (1999).

Executives would have preferred the folk rock found on *Mermaid Avenue* (1998), a collaboration between Wilco and British folk singer Billy Bragg for which he and Tweedy put music to never-used lyrics by Woody Guthrie. The collection included "California Stars," a winsome shuffle that has remained in Wilco's concert repertoire for decades. But Tweedy was no dustbowl folkie. "*Summerteeth* was partly a reaction to how defined the band had become by the alt.country tag," said Tweedy, "or roots rock, or No Depression, whatever they were calling it that month." *Summerteeth* was more concerned with rock 'n' roll and electronic experimentation. "It was a great record, but it was Jeff as pop genius rather than alt.country guy," said Gary Briggs, a product manager at the label. "That alt.country audience accounted for 70 percent of Wilco's sales base, and it still does. But that record shut the door on the *No Depression* era of Wilco."

That was okay with Wilco, which by the turn of the century was earning more than a million dollars a year on the road and maintained a rehearsal-and-recording space on the north side of Chicago. So when Warner rejected *Yankee Foxtrot Hotel*, which had more in common with Britain's Radiohead than with the Burrito Brothers, Wilco posted the music on its web site and let fans stream it for free. (By the end of the album's troubled gestation, Tweedy had fired Jay Bennett; both men were struggling with opioid addictions.) Wilco then played a sold-out show at Town Hall in New York to an audience already familiar with its new songs. Labels now jockeyed to release an album that had already been paid for by Warner Brothers. Nonesuch won the prize, which meant that a single recording conglomerate paid Wilco twice for the same album.

In the new century, dance-oriented pop stars and hip-hoppers had the hits while many who played rock or alt.country gathered under the accommodating umbrella of Americana. *Heartbreaker*, the 2001 solo debut of Ryan Adams, was the most popular record ever released by the independent label Bloodshot Records. This was Adams the singer-songwriter nursing a romantic breakup; Adams and David Rawlings wrote the opening song, "To Be Young (Is to Be Sad, Is to Be High)," which sounded like mid-1960s Dylan, and Emmylou added a harmony to "Oh My Sweet Carolina." The album sold more than three hundred thousand copies, including one to music fan Elton John. "I was completely and utterly floored by the simplicity and beauty of the songs," said John, who was inspired to streamline the sound of his own records.

Adams made *Gold* (2001) for Lost Highway, a boutique label of Universal Records that marketed such Americana artists as Lucinda Williams. The album highlighted both the balladeer ("La Cienega Just Smiled") and the rocker ("New York, New York") and included a song written with Gillian Welch ("Enemy Fire"). Adams's most successful release (four hundred thousand copies in the United States and an equal amount worldwide), the album also included a ballad ("When the Stars Go Blue") that became a country hit for Tim McGraw. *Gold* was produced by multi-instrumentalist Ethan Johns, the son of Glyn Johns, who'd produced the Eagles; in 2011 Adams would record *Ashes & Fire* with Ethan's father.

"The kid's so prolific it's unreal," said Luke Lewis, who ran Lost Highway, and hoped that "somewhere in the middle of it all, a radio hit pops out." Adams formed the Cardinals (which for a time included Cindy Cashdollar on lap steel) to play a jam-band style of country rock reminiscent of the Grateful Dead. In 2006 Adams produced and the Cardinals played on *Songbird*, an album by Willie Nelson; Ryan and Willie also appeared in an ad for the Gap singing Hank's "Move It On Over." But Adams could be his own worst enemy. His numerous and inconsistent records confused his audience, and substance abuse made him an erratic and sometimes cantankerous live performer.

"My behavior was getting extreme," said Adams. "I was running the risk of becoming one of those people who talks to himself all the time." He went through a cold-turkey withdrawal (with the help of Valium) and was diagnosed with an inner-ear disorder, Meniere's disease. Traditional rock stardom remained elusive. "The part of me that's missing self-respect would have thought: 'I am something,'" said Adams. "But I don't write a song with that in mind. I write a song to be a better song—200,000 sales is an honest living."

It's also a big deal in the world of Americana. That's what many learned from John Prine, who had long operated his own label, Oh Boy! Adams established Pax Americana and leased his more commercially oriented recordings to major labels. Wilco created its own dBpm Records, while Gillian Welch and David Rawlings formed the Acony label (Gillian also helps her partner make records as the David Rawlings Machine). But in a world where streaming music sites have cannibalized record sales, revenue from live shows became increasingly vital.

"For years we were devoutly unsigned," said Patterson Hood of the Drive-By Truckers, "playing hundreds of shows a year and often saying as we were about to go on stage in some dive bar in Ames, Iowa or Columbia, Missouri or Fort Worth, Texas that 'Tonight we were going to get signed!'" Hood grew up in Muscle Shoals, Alabama. His father David was a successful studio musician at Muscle Shoals Sound Studio and played bass on albums by, among many others, Aretha Franklin, Bob Dylan, and Paul Simon. Patterson was a child when the Staple Singers recorded "I'll Take You There." "I would hear it on the radio and Mavis would call out his name—'David, little David,'" said Patterson. "Before that, I knew he played on records but I think that made me realize just how special it was." David Hood's record collection became his son's college of musical knowledge.

Hood formed Adam's House Cat with Mike Cooley in 1985, but the band broke up before it could release an album. In 1996 they launched the Drive-By Truckers; the band struggled in obscurity until it made *Southern Rock Opera* (2001), a concept album about the South in general and Lynyrd Skynyrd in particular. When the group lost a guitar player, Hood and Cooley recruited a local talent, Jason Isbell. "This chubby kid—he was 22 but looked like he was 15," said Hood of Isbell, a guitarist who also wrote songs. Drive-By Truckers were soon named *No Depression*'s "Band of the Year."

For *Decoration Day* (2003) and *The Dirty South* (2004), Hood, Cooley, and Isbell wrote rock and country songs about hard lives lived far from the glittery coasts. Frequent tours led to better-sounding records and shows, but the lifestyle could be a challenge, a reality noted by Isbell's "Danko/Manuel,"

JASON ISBELL

which referenced two late members of The Band. When the Truckers lost their bass player, the band hired Isbell's wife, Shonna Tucker. But the marriage suffered because Isbell was having too much rock star fun with drugs and Jack Daniels. "Some people get drunk and become kind of sweet," said Hood. "Jason wasn't one of those people." With the band about to implode, and Isbell refusing to take a hiatus, he got a call from Cooley, who said, "That isn't going to work for us." Isbell and Tucker divorced, and for a time, she stayed with the band.

Drive-By Truckers held it together, barely, by going on an acoustic tour that included keyboardist Spooner Oldham, a studio colleague of Hood's father. Isbell fronted his own group, the 400 Unit, until the bottle finally let him down. In 2012 his musician girlfriend, Amanda Shires, reached out to family and Isbell's friend Ryan Adams to help encourage him to go into rehab. Isbell emerged a couple of weeks later and was soon sharing bills with Adams. "It was nice to be on the road with someone who had been through the recovery process," said Isbell, who on another occasion added, "I don't remember a lot of the good times from my days with the Truckers. This time I want to remember it all."

"In the Pines" is a folk song that's as old as the hills; the most famous interpretations are by Lead Belly and Bill Monroe and His Bluegrass Boys. Kurt Cobain of Nirvana sang the song under the title "Where Did You Sleep Last Night?" on the group's 1994 album *MTV Unplugged in New York*. In 2004 Robert Plant and Alison Krauss met to rehearse for a Lead Belly tribute at the Rock & Roll Hall of Fame. The first song they sang was "In the Pines," and though Krauss couldn't help but be tickled to be singing with the lead singer of Led Zeppelin, she had something to teach the rock star. Plant says that she asked him, "'Is there any chance you can sing the same thing twice, so I could find out how to sing a harmony on it?' I said, 'Oh! A light came on. . . . I had to learn to sing with somebody else.'"

Plant proposed making an album together, and Krauss suggested enlisting T-Bone Burnett, the producer with whom she'd worked on *O Brother, Where Art Thou?* Choosing a repertoire was the first step. "[T-Bone] knows so many obscure songs," said Burnett's recording engineer, Mike Piersante, "so he'll pull together these lists and then he'll pare them down and . . . end up with CDs of original versions of suggested songs." The final set list was an Americana sampler that included songs by the Everly Brothers, Townes Van Zandt, Tom Waits, Allen Toussaint, Doc Watson, and Gene Clark of the Byrds.

"It was very scary because both of us were out of our comfort zones," said Krauss. "We were away from our usual environments so we just had to go with what we felt. I vividly remember calling [Robert] before we started *Raising Sand* and saying, 'I'm worried,' and he said, 'That's good, because I am too.'" Released on Rounder, the independent roots label that was home to Krauss, *Raising Sand* sold 2.5 million copies and won five Grammy Awards including Album of the Year and Record of the Year. When Burnett looked for a guitarist to join the touring band, he hired Americana's go-to guy, Buddy Miller.

Buddy and Julie Miller had moved to Nashville in the mid-1990s after Julie, with Buddy's assistance, had released four albums for the Christian market. "We toured a little," said Julie of those years, "and it was as different as it could possibly be. I started out as a honky tonk girl so I wasn't used to playing to strictly Christian audiences"—which is not to say that Miller wasn't serious about her faith and her songs. "There was a small, hardcore, wounded little pocket of Christians," she said, "who seemed to really find some comfort in my songs." The tunes could be equally moving for a secular audience. Emmylou Harris sang background vocals on Miller's 1993 recording of "All My Tears" and included the song on her own *Wrecking Ball*. Miller knew she was painting outside the rigid lines of Christian music. "It wasn't like anything contemporary Christian at all," she said. "That song really had come from my internalization . . . but even more so of Ralph Stanley, who is my Elvis."

Buddy released his solo debut, *Your Love and Other Lies*, in 1995, and Julie made her first secular album, *Blue Pony*, in 1997. They're natural collaborators. "If I'm working on a record," said Buddy, "she'll just write some great country songs. But if it's for her record, my role is to get her to finish it, and maybe add something musically. If I have some music and need some help, she'll help me, and if she won't, I'll go find Jim Lauderdale." In 1999 friends surrounded Julie when she recorded her best record, *Broken Things*, including Buddy, Emmylou, Steve Earle, Larry Campbell, and Patty Griffin. The title song was a ballad reprised from one of her Christian albums. "I didn't have enough songs when we started playing and opening for Steve Earle," said Julie. "I was almost embarrassed to play ['Broken Things'] there, but people were saying, 'What's that song?'" In 2002 *Buddy and Julie Miller*, the couple's first duo recording, was named Album of the Year at the Americana Music Association's first Americana Music Honors and Awards ceremony.

By the time Burnett called Buddy to join the *Raising Sand* tour, he'd already served as the lead guitarist for Harris and Earle and played on the "Down from the Mountain" tour spawned by the success of *O Brother.* Miller also produced numerous records at the ground-floor studio of his and Julie's Nashville home, including works by Richard Thompson (*Electric*), the Carolina Chocolate Drops (*Leaving Eden*), Jimmie Dale Gilmore (*One Endless Night*), and Solomon Burke (*Nashville*). The "Three Girls and Their Buddy" tour found Miller in an acoustic song swap with Emmylou, Shawn, and Patty Griffin. After a performance in Baltimore, Miller complained of acute indigestion; the women insisted that he go to Johns Hopkins Hospital. Miller had suffered a heart attack, and the next morning he underwent triple bypass surgery.

Buddy had seen Led Zeppelin at the Fillmore East in the late 1960s, and the guitarist was quick to bond with Plant. "Buddy Miller is everybody's dream date," said Plant, who asked him to co-produce an Americana record to be named *Band of Joy* after the group Plant shared with drummer John Bonham before they joined Led Zeppelin. Miller suggested that Patty Griffin add a second voice to a repertoire that included songs by Richard Thompson, Los Lobos, and Townes Van Zandt. Griffin was a gifted singer-songwriter—her gospel album, *Downtown Church*, had been produced by Miller—and was quick to sign on. "Robert was one of my vocal inspirations early on," said Griffin. "I got to sing in so many styles singing with him [on tour]. I used all my paint." Griffin and Plant became a couple and later shared a house in South Austin, while Buddy took up Burnett's offer to produce songs written by Griffin, Gillian Welch, Lucinda Williams, and others, for the television show *Nashville.*

"Any way you slice it, Plant is the biggest rock star ever to live within Austin city limits," wrote *Texas Monthly*. "The hospitality and friendships and initiation into Americana—not just the music—was marvelous," said Plant. When the pair played a benefit at the Continental Club, the bill read "Patty Griffin & Her Driver." Griffin opened the show with her quiet, intimate songs; then her boyfriend, in a chauffeur's cap, came out to play a set that included such Zeppelin songs as "Black Dog" and "Going to California." But Plant's celebrity proved problematic. "It was my own inability to deal with the rabid attention that was paid to me," Plant noted, "and there was no way to hide it." The pair broke up, and Plant moved back to the United Kingdom. "It was one of the most rewarding, classic periods of my life," he said of his time in

Americanaland. But it was over, at least until he and Krauss decide to finish the record they abandoned: *Raising Hell.*

Larry Campbell was twelve when he saw Bob Dylan and The Band play the 1967 Woody Guthrie tribute concert at Carnegie Hall. Thirty years later, Campbell began a seven-year tenure playing in Dylan's band. "There are times when I found myself on stage," said Campbell, "playing certain tunes with certain people and I just think, 'How the hell did I get here?'" One of those moments was during a particularly good Dylan concert. "At the end of the show, we did, for the first time that I played with him, a version of 'Blowin' in the Wind.' It was done in such an emotional way on everybody's part—Bob and everyone in the band. It sort of left the audience stunned. And we finish the tune and I'm just thinking, 'Man, I have arrived.' This is the completion of a circle for me . . . I'm at the source."

When Campbell got the job, they spent a few days playing old rock 'n' roll and country tunes that never appeared on the set list. "It was a very amorphous existence," said Campbell of life in Dylan's group. "There was no set way to do anything until there was, and then that was the only way to do it, but then the next day it wasn't anymore." Campbell played guitar, banjo, mandolin, and violin on Dylan's *Love and Theft*, which was released on September 11, 2001. Produced by Dylan (using the pseudonym Jack Frost), the album drew on American roots music including jump blues, country swing, and the ballads of Tin Pan Alley. The albums that followed, *Modern Time* and *Together Through Life*, which featured accompaniment by David Hidalgo of Los Lobos and Mike Campbell of the Heartbreakers, continued Dylan's critically acclaimed ramble through Americana. Some accused Dylan of improperly lifting lyrics and melodies from old blues songs and obscure literary sources; he shrugged off the criticisms and said that it was part of the folk tradition.

Larry Campbell left Dylan's Never-Ending Tour with an enhanced reputation and a literal suitcase full of cash because he'd saved most of his per diems by basing his diet on the backstage buffet. He immediately played Manhattan's Bowery Ballroom with Buddy and Julie Miller as well as the opening act, Olabelle, a group that included Levon Helm's daughter Amy. She also played at her father's "Midnight Ramble" concerts in Woodstock, events that helped Levon with the medical bills that came with throat cancer. Shows were held in the barn that also housed Helm's recording studio; Levon played drums while nursing vocal chords ravaged by radiation treatments.

"When he got sick I used to visit and we'd play together a lot," said guitarist Jimmy Vivino, who was in the house band of *The Conan O'Brien Show* and plays in the Fab Faux, a band that re-creates the music of the Beatles. "Locking into that snare drum is like when you get into a classic car and really enjoy the ride." Helm's voice slowly began to recover. "He and I started to sing a little bit with each other," said Amy. "I remember one day he taught me the words to a few of the old hymns, and I recorded him with a little hand-held tape recorder so I could learn the tunes. I was excited when I listened to it back, because his voice was getting stronger." By the time Campbell joined the troupe with his wife, singer Teresa Williams, Helm had regained most of his vocal abilities.

"I remember early on when I was playing with Bob," said Campbell, "and there were something like fifty thousand people out there, and we were doing 'Forever Young' at the end of the show and I thought, 'Man, this is pretty cool.' But this Ramble is something else, like the audience is invited guests, like friends or family. There's no pressure, and it's just about enjoying playing the music. I read some Eastern philosophy book years ago that asked, 'What is music?' And the explanation was that the first thing is that music is 'joy.' And I went, 'sure,' but now, I finally get what that means, and it's very profound, because more than anything else, even if you're playing the blues, it's the joy of self expression."

"Levon is ground zero of the Americana genre to me," Campbell continued. "All the music that means anything to me, the genuine American music—blues, rock 'n' roll, country, bluegrass, gospel—Levon can perform and sing it with complete authority. He does it all. That's what The Band did back in the day—they took all these relatively disparaged genres and blended them all into one unique thing." It's no wonder that artists identified with Americana came to perform at the Midnight Rambles including Emmylou, Gillian, Elvis Costello, Dr. John, Mavis Staples, Kris Kristofferson, and Allen Toussaint. When the Drive-By Truckers opened a Ramble, David Hood joined his son Patterson's band to play "I'll Take You There." Later, father and son sang along to "The Weight."

In 2007 Campbell and Amy Helm turned on the recording gear to produce *Dirt Farmer*, Levon's first studio album since 1982. The idea was to make a largely acoustic album and present rhythmic tunes such as Paul Kennerley's

"Got Me a Woman" and J. B. Lenoir's "Feelin' Good" alongside string band songs like the Carter Family's "Single Girl, Married Girl." Contemporary Americana was represented by Steve Earle's "The Mountain" and Buddy and Julie Miller's "Wide River to Cross." Helm's comeback won the Grammy for Best Traditional Folk Album. In 2009 Campbell produced the more urbane *Electric Dirt*, which won the Grammy in a brand-new category, Americana.

By then Helm was taking his Ramble on the road. "Playing the Ryman with Levon was almost like a Nashville *Last Waltz*," said Campbell. "It felt really triumphant for him. For musicians, especially on the singer-songwriter side of Nashville, the non-commercial side, the people who are there because they're artists, Levon holds a high level of respect. And it's understandable, because he and The Band pretty much represent the whole Americana genre." Amy Helm was thrilled to play with her dad in Nashville. "It was like I had died and gone to some kind of heaven," she said. "I mean, I was singing background for Emmylou Harris!"

But then the cancer returned; Helm's last concert was at the Tarrytown Music Hall in New York, where the set list included "When I Go Away," a song from *Electric Dirt* that Campbell had originally written for the Dixie Hummingbirds. "We were still playing it live," said Campbell, "and I'd sing it, but I missed his voice in there. We did it that night, and I sang the first verse, I'm about to come in on the second, and from the drums, clear as a bell with strength I couldn't imagine, here comes Levon. It just gave me chills, and the whole place exploded. Oh God, the emotion I was going through. It was like this incredible sadness that he couldn't do this anymore, and the joy that he'd just *done* it, and the hope that maybe it meant something and maybe he was coming back again . . . and the despair of the knowledge that he couldn't."

Helm drummed at one more Ramble, but his time had come. "I got a message that Levon was in the hospital," said Robbie Robertson, his estranged friend and bandmate, "and he was dying. I got on a plane and I went to the hospital." But there would be no reconciliation; by the time he arrived, Levon had lost consciousness, and on April 19, 2012, he crossed the great divide. Helm was buried a couple of miles from his barn at the local cemetery; after the interment, Larry Campbell and Jimmy Vivino led a second line parade thick with drummers into the heart of Woodstock.

17
YESTERDAY AND TODAY

Roger McGuinn and Chris Hillman went on tour in 2018 to celebrate the fiftieth anniversary of *Sweetheart of the Rodeo*, the pioneering country-rock album that introduced the world to Gram Parsons. Emmylou Harris had already curated *Return of the Grievous Angel* (1999), a tribute album that featured a who's who of Americana. Parsons was also the subject of multiple biographies and documentaries, as well as a feature film about his unorthodox cremation at Joshua Tree National Park (*Grand Theft Parsons*). Marty Stuart and His Fabulous Superlatives accompanied the two Byrds. The Superlatives are drummer Harry Stinson (from Steve Earle's *Guitar Town*), guitarist Kenny Vaughan (who's toured with Lucinda Williams), and bassist and pedal steel player Chris Scruggs (Earl's grandson).

Stuart played mandolin with Lester Flatt as a teenager. After joining Johnny Cash's band he started collecting country music artifacts. "When I first arrived in Nashville in 1972," said Stuart, "it was a sight to behold when the stars gathered. It truly was Hillbilly Hollywood. Rhinestone suits, Cadillacs, fancy guitars, pompadours and beehive hairdos gave those hard hitting country songs even deeper impact." Stuart's collection, which he plans to display at a museum in his hometown of Philadelphia, Mississippi, includes recordings, photographs, stage outfits, and musical instruments. Marty has a railroad lantern that belonged to Jimmie Rodgers, one of A. P. Carter's cancelled checks, and handwritten lyrics by Hank Williams. He has Johnny Cash's Sun-era "Man in Black" suit and guitars that belonged to Lester Flatt and Pops Staples. "My father was Marty's godfather," said Mavis Staples. "My sisters and I took him in as our brother.... When he's playing guitar, he sounds like Pop."

Stuart also owns the sunburst B-Bender Telecaster that Clarence White played as a member of the Byrds. In the early 1980s White's widow Susie had asked Stuart if he'd be interested in buying her late husband's 1954 Stratocaster. While looking at the Strat, Stuart played the B-bender. "She said, 'That's what you really came to see, wasn't it? Well, I might consider selling,'" said Stuart. "There were those two guitars, some Nudie suits, and some Byrds memorabilia." Stuart took out a blank check and asked her to name a price (he was prepared to pay between $50,000 and $60,000). She wrote in the amount of $1,450. "I said, 'Susie, the E string alone is worth that.' She said, 'I know exactly what it's worth, but I think Clarence would want you to have it. I know you will take care of it.'" There was history in White's guitar, and Stuart didn't put it behind glass but, rather, played it on the *Sweetheart* tour.

"We had this 10-year-old Ford Econoline and we pulled a trailer and we just did it," said Patterson Hood of the years when the Drive-By Truckers all but lived on the road. "Even though we may not have been pulling enough people for some of the rooms we were playing, the people who came would drink so much that the club was happy and would have us back." David Hood played bass on countless records and toured with Traffic, so it wasn't crazy for his son to harbor classic rock dreams. But by the time the Truckers first peaked during their years with Jason Isbell (2002–2007), all but the most popular rock bands played to a more limited audience. Bands can create a community, however, and in that sense, Hood realized his dream. In February 2020, for the twentieth consecutive year, fans from around the country traveled to Athens, Georgia, to attend the Drive-By Truckers' three-night "Heathens Homecoming" at the town's premiere rock club, the 40 Watt.

In 2015 Hood wrote an op-ed essay for the *New York Times* arguing that people should stop flying the Confederate "Stars and Bars" flag. "If we want to truly honor our Southern forefathers," he said, "we should do it by moving on from the symbols and prejudices of their time and building on the diversity, the art and the literary traditions we've inherited from them." Then the songs on *American Band* (2016) took aim at racially tinged police encounters, school shootings, and immigration. "I have a feeling people are going to look back on this moment in time as a very pivotal turning point," said Hood of the era of Donald Trump. Most country or rock bands (indeed, most popular artists) avoid being overtly political. By contrast, the self-proclaimed "dance band of the resistance" released a confrontational 2020 album called *The Unraveling*. Then the Covid-19 pandemic canceled an election year full of tour dates.

Since playing with the Drive-By Truckers, Jason Isbell had become a superstar of Americana; *Something More Than Free* (2016) and *The Nashville Sound* (2018), swept all the applicable Grammy and Americana awards. "I definitely don't feel like I would be the musician that I am, or the type of songwriter, had I not come from that particular place," said the guitarist of growing up in Muscle Shoals, Alabama. "The soul music that came out of there, and a lot of the soul-influenced rock and roll and country music that came out of the studios in north Alabama in the '60s and '70s had a big influence on me." Those roots were in evidence on his 2020 album, *Reunions*.

Isbell's wife Amanda Shires makes her own albums while playing in her husband's band, the 400 Unit. In 2019 Isbell closed the last of seven sold-out shows at the Ryman Auditorium by playing one of southern rock's greatest hits, the Allman Brothers Band's "In Memory of Elizabeth Reed." Ryan Adams is also a rock fan, and his most popular track on Spotify is his cover of "Wonderwall" by the British band Oasis. He continued to produce music in a variety of genres, including a rock album (*Ryan Adams* [2014]), a re-creation of Taylor Swift's *1989*, and a live collection of solitary singer-songwriter performances recorded at Carnegie Hall.

Adams was married to Mandy Moore, a singer and an actress on television's *This Is Us*. The couple's 2016 divorce informed his next release, *Prisoner*, with "To Be Without You" nominated for Song of the Year at the Americana Music Awards. In early 2019 Adams announced that before December he would release three studio albums. Then the *New York Times* reported that numerous women (including his ex-wife) had accused Adams of seeking sexual favors through manipulative and emotionally abusive behavior. He was also said to have had improper online contact with a minor. Adams lost endorsements, canceled concert tours, and released no new music until December 2020 (*Wednesdays*).

"If I picture what playing well into my 60s or 70s would look like," said Jeff Tweedy, who turned fifty-three in 2020, in a 2004 interview, "it would be more like John Prine or Leonard Cohen—people who have been allowed to grow old." (Prine, who'd survived bouts with cancer, died in April 2020 from complications related to Covid-19. Cohen passed in 2016 at the height of his fame.) Tweedy's band Wilco is the most enduring and critically acclaimed band born in the days when alt-country morphed into Americana. Wilco has had a consistent lineup since guitarist Nels Cline became its sixth member in 2004. Cline's background included playing jazz and experimental music, which complemented Tweedy's wide-ranging interests and added instrumental spice to compositions typically built on lyrical wordplay and folk-styled rhythm guitar.

Besides recording with Wilco, Tweedy has cut a collection (*Sukierae*) with his son Spencer and made solo albums. During the pandemic, Tweedy recorded *Love Is the King* (2020). "At the beginning of the lockdown I started writing country songs to console myself," said Tweedy, "folk and country type forms being the shapes that come most easily to me in a comforting way." Working at Wilco's headquarters, Tweedy has also produced an album by Richard Thompson (2015's *Still*) and worked with Mavis Staples on three records. Since 2010 Wilco has curated the Solid Sound Festival at a Massachusetts art museum, MASS MoCA; the band also promotes an annual music festival, "Wilco's Sky Blue Sky," in Mexico.

"I have a great life," said Tweedy, "but it's an uncool life. It was a wonderful revelation to move to Chicago and make music and just be normal [albeit with migraine headaches and, for a time, an addiction to opioids]. So many artists reach a certain level of success, and then they cross over. They surrender everything to the service of their persona. . . . Even with Bob Dylan, there was clearly a point early in his career where he was completely able to immerse himself into that persona."

Wilco toured with Dylan and My Morning Jacket on a 2013 package called the Americanarama Festival of Music. One night Tweedy peeked out of the dressing room door as Dylan's group passed on its way to the stage. "As they got to our door I heard what sounded like a Bob Dylan impression," said Tweedy. "'Hey, Jeff, how's it going, man? Good to see you!' Without breaking stride. And I was left in his wake trying to play it cool, but I could feel all of the other folks around us looking at me. It was impossible to play it cool. 'Dylan talked to me. Did you guys see that?!'"

On another occasion Dylan said to Tweedy, "Tell Mavis she should have married me!" (In the 1960s Dylan and the Staple Singers sang at civil rights rallies, and the writer of "Chimes of Freedom" asked Pops Staples for his daughter's

JEFF TWEEDY

hand.) When Tweedy passed along this comment to Mavis, she said to tell Bob that she was still available. "Yeah?" said Dylan. "I wish." Staples later opened shows for Dylan. "I felt," she said, "like a sixteen-year-old girl again."

In 2017 Rosanne Cash was the resident artistic director of SFJAZZ in San Francisco. After performing concerts with Emmylou Harris and Lucinda Williams, Rosanne called Ry Cooder, who'd recently toured with country-turned-bluegrass star Ricky Skaggs. "I offered a few ideas," said Cash. "He brushed off my initial thoughts and said, 'What springs to mind is a show of your dad's songs.' I've spent almost 40 years avoiding that very thing, but when Ry suggested it, oddly, I didn't even hesitate. I said, 'Okay, let's do Johnny.'"

Since her father's death, Cash has made two albums that referenced him: *The List*, a collection of covers drawn from the one hundred essential songs he taught her on his tour bus, and *The River and the Thread,* an artful song cycle about her family's southern roots written by the daughter who'd become a New Yorker. At Carnegie Hall Rosanne performed with Ry and a band led by her husband, John Leventhal. Preparing for the short run of shows, Cooder discovered that Rosanne's half-brother John owned a Telecaster played by Luther Perkins in the Tennessee Three. Cooder held the guitar up to the audience like a talisman and used it to play the boom-chicka-boom rhythm of "I Walk the Line" and "Folsom Prison Blues."

Artists absorb musical history on their way to individual styles. Brandi Carlile grew up outside Seattle and quit high school to busk on the street and pursue music gigs. She formed a group with twin brothers Phil (bass) and Tim Hanseroth (guitar); they performed songs written by Carlile and one or both of the brothers and agreed to split everything three ways. Carlile attracted notice with her second album, *The Story* (2007), produced by T-Bone Burnett, who insisted that the band trade their everyday gear for vintage instruments. "He took our confidence away and replaced it with vulnerability, discomfort and tension," said Carlile, who five years earlier had come out as a lesbian. "And those three things are what essentially made the performance happen."

Sales spiked when "The Story" and other tunes were played on episodes of the television program *Grey's Anatomy*. "After years of trying to get somewhere," said Carlile, "my music is now all over TV, I'm selling records, and Elton John sent me flowers and a bottle of wine from the year of my birth."

Elton performed a duet with Carlile on her next album, *Give up the Ghost*, which was produced by Rick Rubin, who'd recorded Johnny Cash's autumnal records and championed another popular Americana act, the Avett Brothers. In 2015 Carlile appeared with the Avett Brothers on *Late Night with David Letterman* singing the Carter Family's "Keep on the Sunny Side."

Carlile hit it big when *By the Way, I Forgive You* swept the Americana awards at the 2018 Grammy; a star was born when she sang her song of empowerment, "The Joke," on the telecast. Carlile then appeared on a PBS program titled *Joni 75: A Birthday Celebration*, joining Kris Kristofferson for a duet and then soloing on Mitchell's "Down to You." The performance turned out to be a prelude for a 2019 concert performance of Mitchell's deepest, most resonant album, *Blue*. Carlile had married Catherine Shepherd in 2012, and they're the parents of two daughters. Now Hollywood stars were in the orchestra seats, and Joni was sitting next to Elton.

The week of Mitchell's seventy-fifth birthday, Chris Thile offered a fifteen-minute tribute on his weekly National Public Radio show, *Live from Here*. Thile is a mandolin player who found success with an acoustic trio, Nickel Creek, and later played in a folk and bluegrass quartet called the Punch Brothers. He's recorded with a wide variety of musicians including jazz pianist Brad Mehldau and classical cellist Yo-Yo Ma. Thile, a 2012 MacArthur Fellow, was a frequent guest on the public radio program *A Prairie Home Companion*, which regularly featured roots-oriented acoustic musicians; he won the program's hosting job upon the retirement of Garrison Keillor. (The name of the program was changed to *Live from Here* when Keillor's behavior was called out by the Me Too movement.) For the Joni Mitchell tribute, Thile enlisted Aoife O'Donovan to sing "Coyote" and "A Case of You."

O'Donovan, who sang in the progressive bluegrass band Crooked Still, now records solo albums and performs with I'm With Her, a trio that shows how far string band music has come since the Carter Family left Poor Valley. The group, who became acquainted at bluegrass festivals, consists of Sara Watkins (violin, guitar), who played with Nickel Creek, Sarah Jarosz (banjo, mandolin, guitar), and O'Donovan (keyboards and guitar). Both Jarosz and O'Donovan studied at the New England Conservatory of Music; Jarosz was in her dorm room when she learned that "Mansinneedof," an instrumental track from her 2009 debut album *Song Up in Her Head*, was nominated for a Grammy. "I grew up appreciating musicians that were kind of on the edge," said Jarosz, "coming from acoustic folk and bluegrass backgrounds, but also pushing the envelope." Jarosz won two Grammy Awards for her fourth album, *Undercurrent* (2016). Her 2020 album, *World on the Ground*, was made with one of Americana's go-to producers, John Leventhal.

I'm With Her, which won the best group award at the 2019 Americana Awards, performs around a single microphone and plays music that touches on folk, pop, and jazz. Alone or together, all are regulars on *Live from Here*, and along with Thile himself, personify a public radio aesthetic that has embraced Americana. They all play smart, roots-based music for the kind of grown-up music fans who might also listen to *All Things Considered*. (*Live from Here* was cancelled in 2020, a victim of the pandemic.) The same goes for Rhiannon Giddens, who studied opera at the Oberlin Conservatory and gained notice as a member of the Carolina Chocolate Drops, a string band in which she played the banjo. Her 2015 solo debut, *Tomorrow Is My Turn*, produced by T-Bone Burnett, found Giddens singing songs associated with Nina Simone and Patsy Cline and others written by Dolly Parton and Sister Rosetta Tharpe. "It all came from a common well," said Giddens, whose work won her a MacArthur Fellowship. "I just want to talk about the banjo and American music, the voices that have been lost, this rich tapestry that we keep trying to thin out. That's why I'm on this planet." Giddens had a recurring role on the television show *Nashville* and recorded *Songs of Our Native Daughters*, a 2019 album that explored the lingering impact of slavery, with Amythyst Kiah, Allison Russell, and Leyla McCalla.

Amanda Shires lives in a public radio world but was still annoyed about "tomatogate," a controversy that roiled Nashville when a radio consultant advised country deejays to limit the airplay of female artists and to think of them as the tomatoes in a male musical salad. Shire approached Brandi Carlile with the idea of creating a group that would come to include Natalie Hemby and another emerging star, Maren Morris. They called themselves the Highwomen after the Highwaymen, the late-career quartet of Willie Nelson, Waylon Jennings, Johnny Cash, and Kris Kristofferson. Carlile and Shire put new words to the Jimmy Webb song that gave the Highwaymen its name, and the original outlaw tale became a song about women challenged by immigration, sexism, and racism. "My existence is political," said Carlile. "I was married before it was legal in the states. I don't know how to not write that into my music. The plight of displaced peoples is fundamental to me and to my faith." That is why even though the Highwomen's album debuted at the top of the country charts, they are really citizens of Americanaland.

"In many ways I don't really feel as if I'm in the music business anymore," said Shawn Colvin. "What I do is kind of archaic. I don't belong at a label that's going to want a million-selling record. That's just not me, and aside from one song and one record ['Sunny Came Home' and *A Few Small Repairs*], it never really was. I go and play shows with a voice and a guitar, and people come to see me because that is what they want to hear." In 2016 Colvin reunited with producer John Leventhal to co-write all but one of the original songs on *These Four Walls*.

When Colvin went on tour she recruited guitarist Buddy Miller, who had hired her in 1980 and who produced her next album, *All Fall Down* (2012). "When we played Town Hall in New York," said Colvin, "both Larry Campbell and John Leventhal sat in. The circle had come around. We were all still playing and doing well. It was such a moment of pride and satisfaction." Shawn and Steve Earle collaborated on a 2012 album called *Colvin & Earle* that was produced by Miller. She teaches alongside Earle at Camp Copperhead, an annual songwriting seminar that he hosts at the Full Moon Resort in the Catskill Mountains. Colvin has also taught at Richard Thompson's Frets & Refrains music camp.

Earle borrowed the name of a Hank Williams song, "I'll Never Get Out of This World Alive," for both the title of his first novel and an album produced by T-Bone Burnett. Earle has also published a book of short stories (*Doghouse Roses*), produced an album by Joan Baez (*Day After Tomorrow*), and acted in and contributed music to two HBO dramas, *The Wire* and *Treme*. He hosts a radio show (*Hardcore Troubadour*) on SiriusXM's "Outlaw Country" channel; Buddy Miller and Jim Lauderdale, who recorded an album of duets, offer *The Buddy and Jim Show* on the same channel. These and other Americana artists are regulars on such seafaring music festivals as the Cayamo Cruise and the Outlaw Country Cruise.

Earle made two albums in honor of his heroes: *Townes* (2009) and *Guy* (2019). "I knew when Guy [Clark] died that I'd have to make a record," said Earle, "because I don't want to run into that motherfucker on the other side having made Townes's record and not made his." "Old Friends" closed *Guy* with Earle and Emmylou Harris harmonizing on a wistful chorus ("Old friends, shine like diamonds"), and included spoken recitations by Emmylou, Rodney Crowell, and Jerry Jeff Walker. Before Clark died in 2016 of lymphoma, he'd asked singer-songwriter and visual artist Terry Allen to incorporate his ashes into one of his sculptures. That's how Clark, who had a special fondness for crows, ended up in the belly of a bird. But before that, Earle, Crowell, and other friends gathered for a private wake in Nashville. They then boarded a bus for Santa Fe, where Emmylou, Lyle Lovett, and Joe Ely joined them in the Land of Enchantment to sing the songs of their old friend around a campfire.

Emmylou and Rodney are old friends. "We have a rich, rewarding friendship," said Harris, who made two albums with Crowell, *Old Yellow Moon* (2013) and *The Traveling Kind* (2015). "So many other friends and so much great music has come from it." Crowell concurs. "Our conversation hasn't changed much over 40 years," he said. "It's about our faith and passion when it comes to music, and our sense of wonder that these songs that we love even exist." Crowell followed his brief run as a mainstream country star with a string of more personal albums. "I had my 15 minutes of fame," he remarked. "And if I stayed on that path, I wouldn't be on the path I'm on now." Crowell's trail led to *Texas* (2019), an album on which he shared the microphone with such other Lone Star musicians as Willie, Lyle, and Steve Earle.

When he was a young child, Crowell's parents took him to a concert by Johnny Cash and Jerry Lee Lewis; in 1991, he introduced his mother to Roy Acuff backstage at the Grand Ole Opry House. "She told the most popular country musician of her generation that she'd met the love of her life at his concert in the Buchanan High School gymnasium," said Crowell. "My mother floated out of Mr. Acuff's dressing room, an eighteen-year-old girl again. 'Why, Rodney, he was just like I always knew he'd be.... And didn't his hair remind you of your daddy's?'"

"Country music could only have happened in America," said Emmylou. "Country music is the product of so many separate cultures of people coming together to create something else. It used to be that everybody wanted to get off the farm and get to the big city. In music you make it because you're a country boy or a country girl. Then you go get sophisticated pretty fast. Nowadays, everybody has cable television."

Welcome to Americanaland. Turn on the television and you see Americana acts guesting on late-night talk shows and a fourteen-hour history of country music by Ken Burns. On Netflix, *Heartstrings* presents vignettes based on Dolly Parton songs. (In recent years, Parton has mostly recorded acoustic mountain music. "I had to get rich in order to afford to sing like I was poor again," said Dolly, who in 2020 gave Vanderbilt University $1 million for research into a vaccine for Covid-19.) Independent filmmakers have made documentaries on everybody from Townes Van Zandt and Guy Clark (*Heartworn Highways*) to Wilco (*I Am Trying to Break Your Heart*) and Drive-By Truckers (*The Secret to a Happy Ending*). Gillian Welch and David Rawlings performed their Oscar-nominated song "When a Cowboy Trades His Spurs for Wings" at the 2019 Academy Awards; it was included in *The Ballad of Buster Scruggs*, a film by the Coen Brothers, who also made a movie about the early-1960s folk revival, *Inside Llewyn Davis*.

Bob Dylan once camouflaged his history with tall tales; more recently he's curated a more factual past with a memoir (*Chronicles: Volume One*), a pair of documentaries produced by Martin Scorsese (*Bringing It All Back Home* and *Rolling Thunder Revue*), and an expanding library of both new recordings and archival releases from his exceedingly well-documented career. Dylan was awarded the Nobel Prize in Literature in 2016 "for having created new poetic expressions within the great American song tradition." Dylan collected his million-dollar prize after delivering the required Nobel lecture, during which he referenced his myriad inspirations, including Buddy Holly, Lead Belly, *Moby Dick*, *Don Quixote*, the *Odyssey*, and "ragtime blues, work songs, Georgia sea shanties, Appalachian ballads and cowboy songs."

Dylan, who turned seventy-nine in 2020, released an album in that year called *Rough and Rowdy Ways*. It included everything from a rocking blues ("Goodbye Jimmy Reed") to "Murder Most Foul," a seventeen-minute recitation about both the assassination of President John F. Kennedy and the rich musical culture of the nation that he led. Dylan had lately taken an extended turn singing tunes from the Great American Songbook, many of them associated with Frank Sinatra. He recorded these albums with a small combo that used a fiddle and pedal steel guitar to suggest Sinatra's orchestrations. Bob was no stranger to this music. "'Ebb Tide,'" he said, has "never failed to fill me with awe.... When Frank sang that song, I could hear everything in his voice—death, God and the universe." Dylan the folk musician admired the musical sophistication of these songs, and there's a moving, autumnal quality to his late-life walk in this world.

Dylan was among the stars of a 1995 television tribute on the occasion of Sinatra's eightieth birthday. When Sinatra invited the performers to a dinner party at his home, the guest list included both Dylan and Bruce Springsteen. In 2019 Springsteen made *Western Skies*, with original songs reminiscent of the late-1960s country-pop hits that Jimmy Webb wrote for Glen Campbell. But on this night Springsteen left the singing to his wife, Patti Scialfa. "Sometime after dinner," said Springsteen, "we find ourselves around the living room piano with Steve [Lawrence] and Eydie Gorme and . . . I get to watch my wife beautifully serenade Frank Sinatra and Bob Dylan." At one point during the evening, Dylan found himself alone on the patio with the Chairman of the Board. "'You and me, pal, we got blue eyes, we're from up there," said Sinatra, pointing to the stars. "These other bums are from down here."

Willie Nelson, whose eyes are hazel, also made two albums of Sinatra songs, *My Way* (2018) and *That's Life* (2021). "I learned a lot about phrasing listening to Frank," said Nelson. "He didn't worry about behind the beat or in front of the beat, or whatever—he could sing it either way, and that's the feel you have to have." Bob and Willie have a lot more than Frank in common. They, like most musicians, live to play. In Woodstock, New York, Bill Keith and Eric Weissberg (both now passed) were regulars at a weekly bluegrass jam. When producer Jim Rooney started spending part of the year in Ireland, he made a point to enlist his musician friends to play as Rooney's Irregulars whenever he returned to Nashville. And country star Vince Gill, who after the death of Glenn Frey became a member of the Eagles, is a Monday night regular with the Time Jumpers, a Western swing band filled with session players.

Bob and Willie are also both entrepreneurs. Dylan shocked many in 2020 when he sold the rights to his catalog of more than six hundred songs to Universal Music Publishing Group for a price said to be more than $300 million. Dylan also sells original paintings and iron works in art galleries and markets a line of premium whiskey under the name Heaven's Door. Nelson sells Willie's Reserve marijuana products and makes a political point of operating his tour bus (named Honeysuckle Rose after one of his movies) on biodiesel fuel. But the bus really runs on music. "When Willie plays the jazzy Django Reinhardt classic 'Nuages,'" said musician Marshall Chapman, who was a late-night passenger, "Bobbie never misses a chord or a beat. The bond between these two runs deeper than deep. I'm thinking the whole 'Willie Nelson & Family' phenomenon begins right here with those two siblings." And the tradition continues: Willie's son Lukas plays country rock with a band called Promise of the Real that has toured as Neil Young's backing band.

Imagine Willie and Bob boarding the Honeysuckle Rose with a couple of acoustic guitars. It's the Traveling Willieburys, on the road (again) and singing the songs of America in the long dark winter of the 2020 pandemic. They roll through Alabama playing Hank's "Howlin' at the Moon" and trade blue yodels as they approach Meridian, Mississippi. Thinking of Memphis to the north, they toast Cash with "Big River" and Elvis with "Mystery Train" and pay tribute to the Black Lives Matter demonstrators not with Woody's "This Land Is Your Land" but the Carter Family song that gave him the melody, "When the World's on Fire." They're two old men, wise to the ways of a wicked world and grateful to share the songs of a century. They roll past roadhouses that will once again be filled with fiddles and Telecasters and quiet cafés where songwriters will debut new songs at open mikes. They reach Texas, and like a couple of kids, break into Buddy Holly's "Not Fade Away." Bob and Willie, trading tunes, and living in the heart of Americanaland.

LAST CALL

Thanks to the musicians, past and present, who give voice to these pages. I'm grateful to the Woodstock Library and the Mid-Hudson Library System for providing a steady stream of pertinent books. Additional items were obtained from the New York Public Library for the Performing Arts. Please use and support your local library, one of our most valuable public resources.

I offer grateful appreciation to the biographers of the principal musicians in *Americanaland*: Rick Bragg, David Cantwell, Eddie Dean, Colin Escott, Chet Flippo, Ben Fong-Torres, Holly George-Warren, Peter Guralnick, Robert Earl Hardy, Paul Hemphill, Clinton Heylin, Robert Hilburn, Christopher Hjort, Eddie Huffman, Bob Kealing, Rich Kienzle, Greg Kot, Mark Lewisohn, Barry Mazor, Jimmy McDonough, David McGee, Don McLeese, David Menconi, David N. Meyer, Philip Norman, Joe Nick Patoski, David Ritz, Johnny Rogan, Lloyd Sachs, Robert Shelton, Richard D. Smith, Lauren St. John, Nick Tosches, Elijah Wald, Sean Wilentz, and Mark Zwonitzer.

Other authors offered helpful insights in broader works about country, folk, bluegrass, country rock, and songwriters. Among these are Joe Boyd, John Einarson, Sid Griffin, David Hadju, Craig Harris, Barney Hoskyns, Bill C. Malone, Greil Marcus, William McKeen, Alana Nash, Tom Piazza, Jim

PATSY CLINE

Rooney, Daryl Sanders, John Simon, Michael Streissguth, Dave Thompson, Eric von Schmidt, and Paul Zollo. Amid all this reading, one book stood apart for its informative sweep and artful prose: Nicholas Dawidoff's *In the Country of Country: A Journey to the Roots of American Music*.

For nearly twenty-five years, I've had the pleasure of singing and playing with two roots-oriented Hudson Valley bands, the Comfy Chair and the Sunburst Brothers. Thanks to the talented friends who've given me a world of fun and made me both a better musician and a more informed writer: Baker Rorick, Josh Roy Brown, Steve Burgh, Chuck Cornelis, Jake Guralnick, Steve Mueller, Larry Packer, Eric Parker, and Doug Wygal. Members of my writer's group, Laura Claridge and Richard Hoffman, offered insightful critiques during the preparation of my manuscript.

My agent Carol Mann helped get *Americanaland* signed not once, but twice. Stephen P. Hull, who published our earlier book, *Crossroads*, originally bought the proposal, but then the University Press of New England went out of business; thanks to Laurie Matheson and the University of Illinois Press for picking up a work in progress. I'm tickled by the synchronicity that during my first week as the rock critic of the *Chicago Daily News*, I wrote the obituary for the King of Americanaland, Elvis Presley. Thanks as well to Tim Geaney for photographing the artwork, Jennifer Comeau for editorial advice, Dustin Hubbart for the cover design, Jane Zanichkowsky for the conscientious copyediting, and Robert Pruter for attention to detail while creating the index.

Finally, thanks to Margie Greve for finding a way to use fabric and embroidery floss to make her portraits sing. Love you, Margie. We'd make a great team even if we weren't married.

NOTES

Introduction

1 "I originally wanted": Fox and Ching, *Old Roots, New Routes*, 39.
1 "That one stuck with me": ibid.
1–2 "Contemporary music": Cain, *Americana Revolution*, 61.
2 "I've been bleeding outside the lines": Fiona Sturges, "Emmylou Harris: 'I smoked country music but I didn't inhale,'" *Independent*, April 17, 2001.
4 "You don't get limos": Fox and Ching, *Old Roots, New Routes*, 43.
6 "Where I come from": Michael Ross, "Marty Stuart Interview," *Guitar Player*, November 2010.
6 "The blues is": Jann Wenner, "The Rolling Stone Interview: John Lennon," *Rolling Stone*, January 1971.

Chapter 1. Will You Miss Me When I'm Gone?

7 "When we made the record": MacMahon and McGorty, *American Epic*, 65.
8 "[The Carter Family's] style": Mazor, *Meeting Jimmie Rodgers*, 187.
8 "It's arguable": ibid., 112.
10 "We'd get together": MacMahon and McGorty, *American Epic*, 64.
10 "I'd gone to Sara": Zwonitzer and Hirshberg, *Will You Miss Me When I'm Gone?*, 67.
11 "If you believe": Mazor, *Meeting Jimmie Rodgers*, 260.

12 “Man, you don’t know”: Gordon, *Can’t Be Satisfied*, xv.
14 “Charlie and I”: Rosenberg and Wolfe, *Music of Bill Monroe*, 26.
14 “He hit the bandstand”: Patoski, *Willie Nelson*, 36.
14 “Right across the street”: Dawidoff, *In the Country of Country*, 225.
15 “The first hint”: Zollo, *More Songwriters on Songwriting*, 21.
15 “I learned a lot”: ibid., 18.
15 “Woody said, ‘Wait’”: Pete Seeger on NPR’s *Fresh Air*, January 28, 2014.
16 “The first time”: Zwonitzer and Hirshberg, *Will You Miss Me When I’m Gone?*, 7.
16 “I was his tape recorder”: ibid., 131.
16 “You don’t have to”: ibid., 132.
18 “Maybelle was kind of like a second mama”: Dawidoff, *In the Country of Country*, 47.
18 “I’d lay my head”: Zwonitzer and Hirshberg, *Will You Miss Me When I’m Gone?*, 273.
19 “The old, weird America”: Greil Marcus, liner notes to *Anthology of American Folk Music*, Smithsonian Folkways Recordings, 1997, 5.
19 “We knew every word”: Dave Van Ronk, ibid.
19 “I’m glad to say”: Harry Smith, ibid., 68.
19 “I owe everything”: Zwonitzer and Hirshberg, *Will You Miss Me When I’m Gone?*, 286.

Chapter 2. The Lost Highway

20 “Hank said, ‘Jake’”: Michael Kosser, “Don Helms: Add Some Steel Guitar; Don Helms and the Songwriting of Hank Williams, Sr.,” *American Songwriter*, January 2009.
20–21 “When you paid”: Hemphill, *Lovesick Blues*, 36.
21 “All the training”: Escott, Merritt, and MacEwen, *I Saw the Light*, 6.
21 “It’s Roy Acuff”: Flippo, *Your Cheatin’ Heart*, 105.
21 “You’ve got a million-dollar voice”: Hemphill, *Lovesick Blues*, 39.
21–22 “I booked Hank”: Flippo, *Your Cheatin’ Heart*, 45.
22 “Real spiritual qualities”: Masino, *Family Tradition*, 29.
22–23 “When a hillbilly sings”: Rufus Jarman, “Country Music Goes to Town,” *Nation’s Business*, February 1953.
23 “Characteristic of Williams”: Pleasants, *Great American Popular Singers*, 233.
23 “I’ll tell you”: Hemphill, *Lovesick Blues*, 81.
25 “Hank had the same look”: Escott, Merritt, and MacEwen, *I Saw the Light*, 82.
25 “One Sunday morning”: Hemphill, *Lovesick Blues*, 136.
26 “Hank’s recorded songs”: Bob Dylan, *Chronicles: Volume 1*, 96.
26 “Nobody notices this”: Marcus and Sollors, *New Literary History of America*, 845.
26 “I was sort of a tune pimp”: Broven, *Record Makers and Breakers*, 89.

26 "When I heard": Escott, Merritt, and MacEwen, *I Saw the Light*, 156.
27 "He had a way": Hemphill, *Lovesick Blues*, 130.
27 "Oh no, I ain't": ibid., 121.
27 "I was embarrassed": Zwonitzer and Hirshberg, *Will You Miss Me When I'm Gone?*, 294.
28 "When I was about eight": Ralph Gleason, "Hank Williams, Roy Acuff and Then God!!," *Rolling Stone*, June 1969.
28 "I was shinin' shoes": ibid.
28 "When you got to San Pablo": ibid.
28 "And he had that *thing*": ibid.
28 "No one could handle": Frizzell, *I Love You a Thousand Ways*, 1.
29 "It's good to have": Escott, Merritt, and MacEwen, *I Saw the Light*, 171.
29 "Don't call me 'Mama'": Zwonitzer and Hirshberg, *Will You Miss Me When I'm Gone?*, 297.
30 "I realized": Hemphill, *Lovesick Blues*, 154.
30 "I introduced him": Carlton Stowers, "Price He's Paid," *Dallas Observer*, October 12, 2000.
30 "We recorded": Escott, Merritt, and MacEwen, *I Saw the Light*, 215.
31 "Heaven": ibid., 265.

Chapter 3. Sunrise

34 "It was like everything": Miller, *Million Dollar Quartet*, 122.
34 "It was a time": Piazza, *Devil Sent the Rain*, 97.
34 "When I heard": Segrest and Hoffman, *Moanin' at Midnight*, 87.
34–35 "He would sit there": ibid., 89.
35 "We were broke": Guralnick quoted in Miller, *Rolling Stone Illustrated History of Rock 'n' Roll*, 23.
35 "I also dug": Terkel, *And They All Sang*, 288.
35 "The reason I taped Elvis": Pleasants, *Great American Popular Singers*, 267.
36 "Elvis picked up his guitar": Guralnick, *Sam Phillips*, 212.
36 "Bill jumped up": ibid., 214.
36 "'That's All Right' is in": Miller, *Million Dollar Quartet*, 81.
36 "We worked many a show": Zwonitzer and Hirshberg, *Will You Miss Me When I'm Gone?*, 305.
36–37 "The thing is": ibid., 311.
37 "Well": ibid.
37 "He was the first boy": Piazza, *Devil Sent the Rain*, 98.
37 "Get down close to it": Perkins and McGee, *Go, Cat, Go!*, 13.
37 "We were set up and picking": Guralnick, *Sam Phillips*, p 228.
37 "When I'd jump around": Perkins and McGee, *Go, Cat, Go!*, 106.
39 "Hillbilly rock and roll": Tosches, *Country: Living Legends*, 55.
39 "When the song was popular": Piazza, *Devil Sent the Rain*, 95.

43 "I can remember": Zollo, *More Songwriters on Songwriting*, 617.
43 "Buddy played the music": Dylan, Nobel Prize lecture, https://www.nobelprize.org/prizes/literature/2016/dylan/lecture/.
44 "It has already": Guralnick, *Sam Phillips*, 285.
44 "Most of the record-buying public": Jones and Carter, *I Lived to Tell It All*, 35.
44 "We were having trouble": Bill Friskics-Warren, "Ray Price, Groundbreaking, Hit-Making Country Singer, Dies at 87," *New York Times*, December 16, 2013.
44–45 "I took Willie": Michael Corcoran, "Ray Price Changed Country Music While Staying True to His Own Sound," *Statesman*, December 17, 2013.
45 "I wanted to sound": Dawidoff, *In the Country of Country*, 203.
45 "A country singer": Jones and Carter, *I Lived to Tell It All*, 54.
45 "It makes you sad": Dawidoff, *In the Country of Country*, 206.
45 "We knew when to switch": ibid.,143.
46 "Driving back to Nashville": Kurt Loder, "The Everly Brothers: The Rolling Stone Interview," *Rolling Stone*, May 8, 1986.
47 "A natural born blues singer": Bragg, *Jerry Lee Lewis*, 70.
47 "The worst singer": ibid.
47 "It's where I got my juice": ibid., 78.
47 "Mr. Paul knew": ibid., 123.
47 "We sat down at the little spinet": Tosches, *Hellfire*, 103.
47 "I did notice": Bragg, *Jerry Lee Lewis*, 163.
49 "I felt like we ought to get off of it": Tosches, *Hellfire*, 122.
49 "He came off": Guralnick, *Feel Like Going Home*, 183.
50 "One night we parked": Bragg, *Jerry Lee Lewis*, 238.
51 "Follow that": Vallee, *Rancid Aphrodisiac*, 80.
51 "He's a great artist": Bragg, *Jerry Lee Lewis*, 283.
51–52 "He hid her in his house": ibid., 284.
52 "Hello, I'm Johnny Cash": Zwonitzer and Hirshberg, *Will You Miss Me When I'm Gone?*, 346.
52 "From the time": Hilburn, *Johnny Cash*, 190.
52 "There was a little bit of drugs": ibid., 191.
53 "If Elvis Presley": Guralnick, *Rolling Stone History of Rock 'n' Roll*, 30.
53 "Everything was all happening": Guralnick, *Sam Phillips*, 455.

Chapter 4. Blowin' in the Wind

54 "There was a halo": Jonathan Cott, "The Last Days of Buddy Holly," *Rolling Stone*, February 2009.
55 "Late at night": Wald, *Dylan Goes Electric!*, 35.
55 "We gave Bob": Shelton, *No Direction Home*, 54.
55 "I first met Bob": ibid., 66.
55 "In 1959": ibid., 151.
56 "There were little pockets": David Grisman, *Grateful Dawg*, Sony Pictures, 2001.
56 "We'd go out": Hajdu, *Positively 4th Street*, 10.

57 "Do you know": Van Ronk and Wald, *Mayor of MacDougal Street*, 58.
57 "From Odetta": Ron Rosenbaum, "The Playboy Interview: Bob Dylan," *Playboy*, March 1978.
57 "The sight of her": Dylan, *Chronicles: Volume 1*, 254.
58 "They were screaming": Bragg, *Jerry Lee Lewis*, 307.
58 "He started havin' a lot of goons": Tosches, *Hellfire*, 191.
58 "If the son of a bitch don't die": Dawidoff, *In the Country of Country*, 145.
58 "It's been thirty years": ibid., 147.
58 "That tunnel of light": Mike Boehm, "A Blue-Tinged Life for the Silver Screen: Story of Rock Survivor Carl Perkins Could Be Sobering, Uplifting Movie," *Los Angeles Times*, August 6, 1989.
59 "Get so drunk": Hilburn, *Johnny Cash*, 296.
59 "When I was six": ibid., 246.
59 "Me and you": Dawidoff, *In the Country of Country*, 189.
59 "I'd watched": Anthony DeCurtis, "Johnny Cash Won't Back Down," *Rolling Stone*, October 26, 2000.
59 "We were the original": Jennings and Kay, *Waylon*, 110.
60 "I will never forget": Zwonitzer and Hirshberg, *Will You Miss Me When I'm Gone?*, 342.
60 "The next day": Michael Streissguth, "Merle Haggard's Lost Interview," *Rolling Stone*, January 2017.
60 "I remember always saying": liner notes, *The Buck Owens Collection (1959–1990)*, Rhino, 1992.
61 "I'm driving": Dawidoff, *In the Country of Country*, 241.
61 "Don and I": Halpin, *Experiencing the Beatles*, 214.
61 "My songs are quite alike": liner notes, *The Buck Owens Collection*.
61 "Buck was wild": Dawidoff, *In the Country of Country*, 241.
61 "I got two hits": ibid., 29.
62 "If I could write": Patoski, *Willie Nelson*, 79.
63 "From the songwriter's viewpoint": Nassour, *Honky Tonk Angel*, 135.
63 "[Patsy] went out there": Patoski, *Willie Nelson*, 3.
63 "No one should try": Nelson and Ritz, *It's a Long Story*, 144.
63 "She understood": ibid.
63 "Even though her style": Jon Dolan, "Fifty Country Abums Every Rock Fan Should Own," *Rolling Stone*, September 22, 2019.
63–64 "I can't recall": Charles and Ritz, *Brother Ray*, 43.
65 "I could do country": ibid., 88.
65 "The words to country songs": Ben Fong-Torres, "Ray Charles: The Rolling Stone Interview," *Rolling Stone*, January 1973.
65 "I came up": Nassour, *Honky Tonk Angel*, 365.
65 "Greenwich Village": Petrus and Cohen, *Folk City*, 156.
65–66 "Washington Square": Ron Rosenbaum, "The Playboy Interview: Bob Dylan," *Playboy*, March 1978.
66 "Playing stuff": Dylan, *Chronicles: Volume 1*, 94.

66 “His influence”: Shelton, *No Direction Home*, 82.
66 “Everything I needed”: McKeen, *Everybody Had an Ocean*, 154.
67 “Lightnin’ would stay with me”: Bob Ruggiero, “John Sebastian and Lightnin’ Hopkins: The Odd Couple,” *Houston Press*, September 25, 2014.
67 “Ralph and I”: John Herald, author interview, June 10, 1999.
67 “I was learning”: ibid.
67 “Ralph told me once”: Doc Watson, author interview, June 18, 1999.
67 “My first acquaintance”: ibid.
68 “There’s only one”: Smith, *Can’t You Hear Me Callin’*, 176.
68 “Before he came along”: Bill Friskics, “Bill Keith, Who Uncovered Banjo’s Melodic Potential, Dies at 75,” *New York Times*, October 26, 2015.
68 “If not for every taste”: Robert Shelton, “Bob Dylan: A Distinctive Folk-Song Stylist,” *New York Times*, September 29, 1961.
68 “It seemed like eons ago”: Dylan, *Chronicles: Volume 1*, 279.
70 “Half of the cuts”: ibid., 262.
70 “I tend to base”: Rosenbaum, “Playboy Interview: Bob Dylan.”
70 “I did see”: Dylan, *Chronicles: Volume 1*, 283.
70 “I took the song apart”: ibid., 275.
70 “If I hadn’t heard”: ibid., 287.
71 “I had to get out”: Petrus and Cohen, *Folk City*, 274.
71 “They were kindred spirits”: Goodman, *Mansion on the Hill*, 95.
71 “You could look”: ibid., 96.
71 “When I heard”: Hadju, *Positively 4th Street*, 147.
71–72 “When he was on tour”: ibid., 173.
72 “He came on my radio show”: ibid., 75.
72 “To the old left”: ibid., 210.
72 “I think of that”: ibid., 166.

Chapter 5. Turn! Turn! Turn!

73 “[America] is where the music came from”: *Speaking of Everything*, ABC Radio, October 6, 1974, https://www.youtube.com/watch?v=LfMLRW9nxbo&t=315s.
73 “We’d never heard”: WPLJ-FM interview, September 10, 1971.
73 “Little Richard was”: BBC Radio 2 interview, May 11, 2001.
73–74 “Practically every Buddy Holly song”: Lewisohn, *Tune In*, 11.
74 “First of all”: BBC Radio 1 interview, December 6, 1974.
74 “I liked Elvis”: Richards and Fox, *Life*, 71.
74 “Paul would be doing”: Lewisohn, *Tune In*, 366.
76 “If the Beatles”: ibid., 587.
76 “Right from the start”: Ono, *Memories of John Lennon*, HarperCollins, 219.
77 “All my songs”: Wald, *Dylan Goes Electric!*, 287.
77 “He [Dylan] practically jumped”: Hajdu, *Positively 4th Street*, 197.
77 “They were doing”: Rogan, *The Byrds*, 53.

77 "I played all the folk songs": Cameron Crowe, liner notes to *Bob Dylan: Biograph*, Columbia Records, 1985.
77 "His singing style": Wald, *Dylan Goes Electric!*, 70.
77 "There aren't any": Nat Hentoff, "Bob Dylan, the Wanderer," *New Yorker*, October 24, 1964.
78 "The political folkies": Hajdu, *Positively 4th Street*, 210.
78 "You seem to be": Irwin Silber, "An Open Letter to Bob Dylan," *Sing Out!*, November 1964.
79 "We wound up": Harry, *Ultimate Beatles Encyclopedia*, 517.
79 "It was a magic time": ibid.
79 "I first saw the Beatles": Hjort, *So You Want to Be a Rock 'n' Roll Star*, 16.
79 "We learned faster": ibid., 17.
79–80 "A lot of bands": ibid.
80 "I can remember": Crosby and Gottlieb, *Long Time Gone*, 19.
80 "Wow, man": Rogan, *The Byrds*, 55.
80 "We tried by editing": Heylin, *Bob Dylan: The Recording Sessions*, 34.
82 "I remember working": author interview, Woodstock, NY, May 15, 2000.
83 "I remember that we didn't": Hajdu, *Positively 4th Street*, 233.
83 "It's from Chuck Berry": Robert Hilburn, "Rock's Enigmatic Poet Opens a Long-Private Door," *Los Angeles Times*, April 4, 2004.
84 "You haven't worked": Hjort, *So You Want to Be a Rock 'n' Roll Star*, 17.
84 "The first thing": Marcus, *Like a Rolling Stone*, 110.
84 "There was a clear generation and cultural gap": Boyd, *White Bicycles*, 42.
85 "Today you've heard": Von Schmidt and Rooney, *Baby, Let Me Follow You Down*, 253.
85 "We were boogying": ibid., 253.
85 "Lomax walked down": ibid., 258.
85 "What we played": Ward, *Mike Bloomfield*, 44.
85 "We just learned": Mike Bloomfield, "Impressions of Bob Dylan," *Hit Parader*, June 1968.
86 "We had been playing": Van Ronk and Wald, *Mayor of McDougal Street*, 241.
86 "Yeah, sure you could": ibid.
86 "Highway 61": Dylan, *Chronicles: Volume 1*, 240.
86 "We did 20": Hjort, *So You Want to Be a Rock 'n' Roll Star*, 39.
86–87 "After finishing": Polizzotti, *Highway 61 Revisited*, 2006.
88 "Long live ze king": "The Beatles meet Elvis Presley," https://www.beatlesbible.com/1965/08/27/the-beatles-meet-elvis-presley/.
88 "He was our greatest idol": ibid.

Chapter 6. White Line Fever

89 "His songs hit me": Cantwell, *Merle Haggard*, 48.
89–90 "Relaxed, warm and rugged": ibid., 68.

90 "If there was anything": Haggard and Russell, *Sing Me Back Home*, 203.
90 "It's amazing": Dawidoff, *In the Country of Country*, 257.
92 "I Shall Sing": "Pledge to Country Music," *Music City News*, March 1965.
92 "That's me trying a rewrite": Gould, *Can't Buy Me Love*, 262.
92 "Man! Those boys": Von Schmidt and Rooney, *Baby, Let Me Follow You Down*, 244.
92 "He thought": Lynn and Cox, *Still Woman Enough*, 8.
92 "I remember": Lynn and Vecsay, *Coal Miner's Daughter*, 97.
93 "The way most": ibid., 117.
93 "A little girl": Zollo, *More Songwriters on Songwriting*, 140.
93 "The country music jamboree": Shelton quoted in Jones and Carter, *I Lived to Tell It All*, 98.
94 "That was the first time": Sanders, *Thin, Wild Mercury Sound*, 24.
94 "I don't know": Hoskyns, *Across the Great Divide*, 97.
94 "Because they'd read": ibid.
94 "It was like": Sounes, *Seventies*, 122.
94 "I'd watch": Hoskyns, *Across the Great Divide*, 100.
94–95 "It was like thunder": ibid., 102.
95 "It was so in your face": Sanders, *Thin, Wild Mercury Sound*, 29.
95 "There were hardly": Hoskyns, *Across the Great Divide*, 112.
95 "He'd teach me": Doggett, *Are You Ready for the Country*, 22.
95–96 "Johnston came to us": Sanders, *Thin, Wild Mercury Sound*, 94.
96 "I saw Dylan": Sean Wilentz, "Mystic Nights," *Oxford American*, October 13, 2016.
96 "After five or six minutes": Doggett, *Are You Ready for the Country*, 22.
96 "It was one": Sander, *Thin, Wild Mercury Sound*, 115.
96 "This is the definitive version": ibid., 117.
96 "He was really impressed": ibid., 128.
96–97 "The time we spent": ibid., 169.
97 "That thin": Ron Rosenbaum, "Bob Dylan: The Playboy Interview," *Playboy*, March 1978.
97 "We'd look at one another": Heylin, *Behind the Shades*, 236.
97 "By the time": ibid., 246.
97 "He was what you call": Hadju, *Positively 4th Street*, 280.
97 "In those hotel rooms": Robertson, *Testimony*, 232.
97 "It was a little bit": Heylin, *Behind the Shades*, 259.
97 "I remember his saying": John Kruth, "On 'Revolver' the Beatles Quit Being Cute and Become True Artists," *Observer*, August 10, 2016.
97 "Paul was obviously": Heylin, *Behind the Shades*, 259.
98 "Bob and Johnny": Robertson, *Testimony*, 232.
98 "And with that": ibid.
98 "The concerts": Williams, *Bob Dylan: Performing Artist*, 1:214.

98 "Something is happening here": Williams, *Bob Dylan Live 1966*, Columbia Records, 1998.
98 "Come, come, boy": Hajdu, *Positively 4th Street*, 291.
98 "We laid him down": ibid.
99 "I was drivin'": J. Hughes, *Invisible Now*, 164.

Chapter 7. Something in the Air

100 "Of course": Rogan, *Timeless Flight Revisited*, 163.
100 "The Rick by itself": Noe Gold, "7 Class Axes & the Guitarists Who Wielded Them," *Best Classic Bands*, https://bestclassicbands.com/best-rock-guitarists-part-1-10-8-15/.
101 "Joni [Mitchell] was singing": https://jonimitchell.com/library/view.cfm?id=747.
103 "One song especially": McKeen, *Everybody Had an Ocean*, 274.
103 "I went up": Chris Morris, "Elliot Roberts, Neil Young's Longtime Manager, Dies at 76," *Variety*, June 21, 2019.
103 "It sucks": ibid.
103–4 "When I heard": Chris LeDrew, "Joni Mitchell's Skewered Perceptions of Bob Dylan," *Onstage*, June 2013.
104 "I heard Bob Dylan": Bert van de Kamp, "Leonard Cohen—All culture is nail polish," *OOR* magazine no. 21, October 23, 1974.
104 "He turned": Zollo, *More Songwriters on Songwriters*, 533.
104 "I really can't imagine": "Bob Dylan: The Paul Zollo Interview," *American Songwriter*, January 2012.
104 "He was going": Hoskyns, *Hotel California*, 38.
104 "She was very important": McKeen, *Everybody Had an Ocean*, 300.
104 "David and I": ibid.
104 "Oh, beware, my lord": William Shakespeare, *Othello*, act 3, scene 3.
104–5 "I never worked so hard": Guralnick, "Jerry Lee Lewis: Lust of the Blood," https://www.peterguralnick.com/post/43480661142/jerry-lee-lewis-lust-of-the-blood.
105 "We didn't rehearse it": Randy Lewis, "Looking Back at the 1968 TV Special That Made Elvis Presley Matter Again," *Los Angeles Times*, November 21, 2018.
106 "We talked": Guralnick, *Careless Love*, 341.
106 "It might have taken": Jones and Carter, *I Lived to Tell It All*, 112.
106 "Because I love her": ibid., 125.
106 "When I came to Nashville": Patoski, *Willie Nelson*, 220.
107 "I was always sick": D'Ambrosio, *Heartbeat and a Guitar*, 205.
107 "That very night": George-Warren, *Janis*, 277.
107–8 "I had the sound": Nelson and Ritz, *It's a Long Story*, 186.
108 "The turning point": Griffin, *Million Dollar Bash*, 55.

109 "With the covers": Heylin, *Behind the Shades*, 274.
109 "[He'd] pull out some": ibid.
109 "Bob would": Marcus, *Invisible Republic*, 235.
109 "We played": Griffin, *Million Dollar Bash*, 153.
110 "You know": Heylin, *Recording Sessions*, 57.
110 "It amazed me": Griffin, *Million Dollar Bash*, 150.
110 "Bob just made me think": Hoskyns, *Across the Great Divide*, 120.
110 "It was the Summer of Love": Steve Thomas, "Bob Dylan Talks Basement Tapes," https://www.youtube.com/watch?v=OuCRNNo8wBc.
111 "Listening back": Griffin, *Million Dollar Bash*, 308.
111 "There was something": ibid., 284.
111 "Every artist in the world": Sounes, *Down the Highway*, 226.
111 "The songs were written": Jim Beviglia, "The Ballad of Frankie Lee and Judas Priest," *American Songwriter*, May 2012.
112 "Some of it": "John Wesley Harding," http://www.bobdylancommentaries.com/in-progress/.
112 "I realized quickly": Simon, *Truth, Lies and Hearsay*, 126.
112 "These guys were accustomed": ibid., 129.

Chapter 8. Sweetheart of the Rodeo

113 "I asked Gram": Geoff Edgers, "It Was the Byrds Album Everyone Hated in 1968. Now, 'Sweetheart of the Rodeo' Is a Classic." *Washington Post*, August 16, 2018.
113 "He started singing": Einarson and Hillman, *Hot Burritos*, 59.
114 "I wanted to crawl": Meyer, *Twenty Thousand Roads*, 236.
115 "[When recording] with Buck Owens": ibid., 238.
115 "I learned something": ibid.
115 "McGuinn was reluctant": Hjort, *So You Want to Be a Rock 'n' Roll Star*, 174.
115 "Wandering around": Hillman, *Time Between*, 110.
115 "He couldn't have things": Fong-Torres, *Hickory Wind*, 96.
117 "He taught me": Bockris, *Keith Richards*, 147.
117 "Clarence White's brother": Randy Lewis, "Two Original Byrds Salute the Band's Country-Rock Classic 'Sweetheart of the Rodeo' 50 Years Later," *Los Angeles Times*, July 20, 2018.
117 "I remember buying *Sweetheart*": ibid.
117 "It was my gateway record": ibid.
118 "I wanted to discover": liner notes, *Music from Big Pink*, Capitol Records, 2000.
118 "I didn't want": ibid.
118 "Many levels above": Simon, *Truth, Lies and Hearsay*, 125.
118 "You make the drum": Helm and Davis, *This Wheel's on Fire*, 166.
118 "Robbie had obviously learned": Simon: *Truth, Lies and Hearsay*, 126.

118 "Gave Robbie": ibid., 140.
119 "The characters": Helm and Davis, *This Wheel's on Fire*, 166.
119 "They were seasoned": Simon, *Truth, Lies and Hearsay*, 174.
119 "When we were up": liner notes, *Music from Big Pink*.
119 "There are people": Al Kooper, review of *Music from Big Pink*, *Rolling Stone*, August 10, 1968.
119 "These guys were": Hjort, *Stranger Brew*, 202.
119–20 "When 'The Weight' came on": Robertson, *Testimony*, 310.
120 "He alone of them": Helm and Davis, *This Wheel's on Fire*, 183.
120 "Charming and attractive": ibid., 184.
120–21 "[Gram] had this sort": Einarson, *Desperados*, 138.
121 "We drove to a modern": Fong-Torres, *Hickory Wind*, 103.
121 "They were harmonies": Einarson, *Desperados*, 140.
121–22 "I was going through": Fong-Torres, *Hickory Wind*, 105.
122 "We were consciously welding": Einarson, *Desperados*, 141.
122 "The three-fingered dumb hum": John Milward, "Old Souls: Dan Penn and Spooner Oldham find sweet inspiration in country R&B," *No Depression*, January–February 2009.
122–23 "We were always wanting": Gordon, *It Came from Memphis*, 162.
123 "I met Miss Audrey": McDonough, *Soul Survivor*, 140.
123 "Every R&B record": ibid., 141.
123 "I cannot recall": Einarson, *Desperados*, 137.
123 "I was the taskmaster": Einarson and Hillman, *Hot Burritos*, 141.
124 "We started listening": "Turning Back the Clock—Mudcrutch Interview," posted May 29, 2009, mudcrutch.com.
124 "Glen Frey": Einarson, *Desperados*, 163.
124 "I always thought": ibid., 164.
124 "Gram was very": Doggett: *Are You Ready for the Country*, 84.
124 "Gram was one of the few": Meyer, *Twenty Thousand Roads*, 303.
124 "Gram was as knowledgeable": ibid., 305.
125 "I think the Burritos" Einarson and Hillman, *Hot Burritos*, 179.
125 "Woodstock was": Echols, *Scars of Sweet Paradise*, 264.
125 "When we went": Jagger, Richards, Watts, and Lane, *According to the Rolling Stones*, 146.
125 "Gram was there": Meyer, *Twenty Thousand Roads*, 316.

Chapter 9. American Tune

126 "Soldiers started": Martin Chilton, "Merle Haggard: 'Sometimes I Wish I Hadn't Written Okie from Muskogee,'" *Telegraph* (UK), April 8, 2016.
126 "We wrote it": ibid.
127 "Many Americans": Malone and Neal, *Country Music, U.S.A.*, 317.
127 "An in-depth study": Guralnick, *Careless Love*, 416.

127 "I don't know": Bill Demain, "The Time Johnny Cash Met Richard Nixon," https://www.mentalfloss.com/article/30142/when-johnny-cash-met-richard-nixon.

128 "Some little woman": Michael Kruse, "The TV Interview That Haunts Hillary Clinton," *Politico*, September 23, 2016.

129 "You can feel the wood": liner notes, *The Band*, reissue, 2007.

129 "We took great care": ibid.

129 "With 'Rag Mama Rag'": ibid.

129 "We called Garth 'H. B.'": Helm, *This Wheel's on Fire*, 188.

129 "Everybody played": Robertson, *Testimony*, 313.

129–30 "Mostly [Richard] would": liner notes, *The Band*.

130 "I could relate": Hoskyns, *Across the Great Divide*, 194.

130 "Make General Robert E. Lee": Helm, *This Wheel's on Fire*, 188.

130 "Instead of keeping": ibid., 188.

130 "It was like": liner notes, *The Band*.

130 "High-school fat girl": Helm, *This Wheel's on Fire*, 186.

130 "The, tall, silver-haired hypnotist": ibid., 191.

130 "The hypnotist": "'He really couldn't play': Elliott Landy remembers hypnotizing night for the Band's Robbie Robertson," https://somethingelsereviews.com/2014/01/24/he-really-couldnt-play-elliott-landy-remembers-robbie-robertsons-hypnotizing-night/.

130–32 "My drums": Helm, *This Wheel's on Fire*, 193.

132 "Me and a bunch": Hoskyns, *Across the Great Divide*, 186.

132 "Fairport had been": ibid., 281.

132 "The Band had": Griffin, *Million Dollar Bash*, 311.

132 "Bob Dylan, a Jewish bloke": ibid., 311.

132 "It was very family oriented": Hoskyns, *Small Town Talk*, 91.

133 "He was hiding": Campbell Stevenson, "Frozen in Time: Bob Dylan at Home with His Son," *Guardian*, May 15, 2016.

133 "I used to think": Mikal Gilmore, "Bob Dylan's Lost Years," *Rolling Stone*, September 2013.

133 "Now there's no way": ibid.

133 "He hardly said": Heylin, *Behind the Shades*, 295.

134 "No one ever counted off": Gilmore, "Bob Dylan's Lost Years."

134 "The songs reflect": Doggett, *Are You Ready for the Country*, 14.

134 "We started playing": Heylin, *Recording Sessions*, 75.

135 "They looked": Hilburn, *Johnny Cash: The Life*, 350.

135 "*Nashville Skyline* achieves": Paul Nelson, "Nashville Skyline," *Rolling Stone*, May 31, 1969.

135 "It's cast": Doggett, *Are You Ready for the Country*, 15.

135 "An enthusiastic Nixon supporter": ibid.

135–36 "When I told": Marshall Chapman, *They Came to Nashville*, 24.

136 "Joni Mitchell sang": "Johnny Cash's 'Million Dollar Songwriter Circle,'" SavingCountryMusic.com, July 28, 2013.

136 "I couldn't justify": Edward Morris, "Buck Owens' Autobiography Is Unsparingly Candid," *CMT News*, January 2014.

Chapter 10. Troubadours

137 "The Troubadour": Eliot, *To the Limit*, 40.
137 "The first day": Einarson, *Desperados*, 164.
137 "Had this legendary": Hoskyns, *Hotel California*, 17.
137 "Linda Ronstadt cheered": Boyd, *White Bicycles*, 228.
138 "The beginnings": Hoskyns, *Hotel California*, 49.
138 "Joni writes": ibid., 122.
140 "My style at that time": Hoskyns, *Waiting for the Sun*, 205.
140–41 "I was at my most defenseless": Hoskyns, *Hotel California*, 125.
141 "The ultimate irony": ibid.
141 "My production values": ibid., 111.
141 "One night": Doggett, *Are You Ready for the Country*, 140.
142 "When Steve brought Kris": Eals, *Steve Goodman*, 216.
142 "I started shuffling": Huffman, *John Prine*, 39.
142–43 "We had an early wake-up": liner notes, *John Prine*, Atlantic, 1971.
143 "It must've been": ibid.
143 "He offered me": Huffman, *John Prine*, 14.
143 "In my songs": ibid., 45.
143 "He [Berry] told a story": Zollo, *More Songwriters on Songwriting*, 435.
143 "So we come over": ibid., 456.
143–44 "So he showed up": ibid.
144 "[Willie] got on the stool": Streisguth, *Outlaw*, 110.
144 "Your phrasing": Nelson and Ritz, *It's a Long Story*, 224.
144 "I witnessed": Chet Flippo, "Nashville Skyline: Willie's Outlaw Roots Shown in Retrospective," http://www.cmt.com/news/1531607/nashville-skyline-willies-outlaw-roots-shown-in-retrospective/.
144–45 "If I'm going to look": Chet Flippo, "The Rolling Stone Interview: Dolly Parton," *Rolling Stone*, August 1977.
145 "I said, 'Well'": Jim Jerome, "One Tough Dolly," *Ladies' Home Journal*, July 1995.
145 "I got turned on": Doggett, *Are You Ready for the Country*, 113.
145 "Bluegrass bands": ibid., 114.
147 "After hearing Dylan's country": ibid., 114.
147 "Crosby and those guys": ibid., 115.
147 "We used to go see": Shaugn O'Donnell, https://shaugn.com/workingmans-dead.
147 "Bluegrass music": David Grisman, http://www.chiefnoda.com/intvw/dgr.html.
148 "There was definitely": ibid., 103.
149 "Uh, well, it's kind of Appalachian": McEuen, *Life I've Picked*, 87.
149 "Hell! It ain't nothing but country": ibid., 87.
149 "Acuff made a couple": Tosches, *Living Legends*, 145.

149 "You know, John": ibid., 145.
149 "Well, I never knew," "Would you boys": McEuen, *Life I Picked*, 89.
149 "I said, 'You'll make millions'": Eliot, *To the Limit*, 63.
150 "We did four sets": Doggett, *Are You Ready for the Country*, 158.
150 "They were doing Chuck Berry stuff": Eliot, *To the Limit*, 72.
150 "Somebody picked up": ibid.
150 "Joni and Jackson": Hoskyns, *Hotel California*, 229.
150–51 "We'd watched bands": Hoskyns, *Waiting for the Sun*, 227.
151 "The Eagles were made": ibid., 226.
151 "Another thing": Robert Christgau, "Trying to Understand the Eagles," *Newsday*, June 1972.
151 "It's no accident": ibid.
151 "I saw through": Doggett, *Are You Ready for the Country*, 188.
152 "Asylum was": Eliot, *To the Limit*, 91.
152 "I was saying, 'OK'": Hoskyns, *Hotel California*, 147.
152 "More than any artist": McDonough, *Shakey*, 364.
152 "His rhythm playing": ibid.
152 "We wound up": ibid.
152–53 "I don't think": ibid.
153 "This song put me": Neil Young, liner notes of *Decade*, 1977.
153 "The only time": "Bob Dylan: Not Like a Rolling Stone Interview," *Spin*, December 1985.

Chapter 11. Grievous Angels

154 "Engineers and technicians": "Keith Richards and Gram Parsons 1971: Summer in Exile," https://selvedgeyard.com/2009/08/13/keith-richards-gram-parsons-1971-summer-in-exile-villa-nellcote/.
154 "The three of us": ibid.
155 "Mick, I think": ibid.
155 "A lot of *Exile*": from the film *Stones in Exile*, dir. Stephen Kijak, Eagle Rock Entertainment, 2010.
155 "[Producer] Jimmy Miller was not": Danny Dutch, "The Stones and the True Story of Exile on Main St," https://www.dannydutch.com/post/the-stones-and-the-true-story-of-exile-on-main-st.
155 "I got this call": Meyer, *Twenty Thousand Roads*, 357.
155 "We went down": Doggett, *Are You Ready for the Country*, 149.
155 "I was the jaded": Frank Thompson, "The Grievous Angel," https://allthingswildlyconsidered.blogspot.com/2009/10/grievous-angel-people-have-never-heard.html.
156 "It really turned my head around": Dawidoff, *In the Country of Country*, 282.
156 "It's always intriguing": ibid., 279.
156 "I thought he was": Fong-Torres, *Hickory Wind*, 169.
156 "One day his voice": ibid., 173.
156 "When I looked": from *Gram Parsons: Fallen Angel*, dir. Gandulf Hennig.
156 "I was the audience": Meyer, *Twenty Thousand Roads*, 372.

157 "When I heard *GP*": Doggett, *Are You Ready for the Country*, 179.
157 "We had the most": Hennig, *Gram Parsons: Fallen Angel*.
157 "After that we decided": Einarson, *Desperados*, 244.
157 "Gram's first solo record": Meyer, *Twenty Thousand Roads*, 388.
157 "That was the first time": Einarson, *Desperados*, 246.
158 "*Planet Waves* was": Heylin, *Behind the Shades*, 357.
158 "The tour was": Helm and Davis, *This Wheel's on Fire*, 241.
158 "[Joni] turned left": Hoskyns, *Hotel California*, 243.
159 "The Byrds invented": Einarson and Hillman, *Hot Burritos*, 277.
159 "The Eagles' music": Doggett, *Are You Ready for the Country*, 156.
159 "Lester Flatt had": Einarson and Hillman, *Hot Burritos*, 311.
159 "They were the horniest": Hoskyns, *Hotel California*, 225.
160 "Man, can you change": *The Big Lebowski*, dir. Joel Coen, Working Title Productions, 1998.
160 "I was raised": Patoski, *Willie Nelson*, 217.
160 "I knew I only had": Streissguth, *Outlaw*, 106.
161 "You'd look out there": ibid., 135.
161 "I also took Guy Clark": Clifford and Hillis, *Pickers and Poets*, 27.
161–63 "Some people don't know": ibid., 29.
163 "Townes is the first": ibid., 43.
163 "I see myself": ibid., 48.
163 "It was about four": ibid., 41.
163 "In the early years": Doug Freeman, "We Were from Texas," *Austin Chronicle*, July 19, 2013.
163 "I went to bed": Zollo, *Songwriters on Songwriting*, 446.
163–64 "It was fucking Nashville": Freeman, "We Were from Texas."
164 "I finally had": McGee, *Steve Earle*, 35.
164 "Skinny kid": ibid., 54.
164 "Townes Van Zandt": ibid., 56.
164 "It all revolved around Guy": ibid.
165 "Phil, if this happens": Fong-Torres, *Hickory Wind*, 191.
165 "*G.P.* was a struggle": Meyer, *Twenty Thousand Roads*, 413.
165 "Our singing came together": ibid., 414.
165–66 "The things I like": Hoskyns, *Hotel California*, 208.
166 "They had one song": Meyer, *Twenty Thousand Roads*, 419.
166 "They had a band": ibid., 419.
167 "I have a feeling": ibid., 438.

Chapter 12. The Red-Headed Icon

168 "A little shy": Patoski, *Willie Nelson*, 224.
168 "Willie ended up": ibid., 224.
169 "Texans have known": Joe Nick Patoski, "Redneck Rock in Austin," *Mother Jones*, June 1976.
169 "To us": Jennings and Kay, *Waylon*, 223.
169–70 "Waylon was selling": Streissguth, *Outlaw*, 189.

170 “You couldn’t find”: ibid., 192.
170 “He taught you”: Wilentz, *Bob Dylan in America*, 139.
170 “Tangled up in blue”: ibid.
170–71 “I was just trying”: ibid., 140.
171 “I went home”: Heylin, *Behind the Shades*, 368.
171 “He was at his best”: ibid., 371.
171 “He knew as soon as he heard”: Heylin, *Recording Sessions*, 105.
173 “We were all”: Shelton, *No Direction Home*, 450.
173 “The filming happened”: Heylin, *Behind the Shades*, 425.
173 “Naturally, I was playing”: ibid.
174 “From a myth-making”: Jon Landau, “Dylan the Mythmaker Makes It Real,” *Rolling Stone*, January 15, 1976.
174 “Hey, I hear”: Heylin, *Behind the Shades*, 336.
174 “When Gram died”: Meyer, *Twenty Thousand Roads*, 440.
174–75 “The first time”: Fiona Sturges, “How We Met: Emmylou Harris and Rodney Crowell,” *New York Times*, February 24, 2013.
175 “It was great”: ibid.
175 “After Gram died”: Dawidoff, *In the Country of Country*, 289.
175 “It wasn’t my musicianship”: Streissguth, *Outlaw*, 177.
175 “I’m influenced”: Nash, *Behind Closed Doors*, 207.
176 “I’d never heard”: Heylin, *Behind the Shades*, 402.
176 “Those first royalty checks”: John Milward, “Levon Helm: Midnight Rambler,” *No Depression*, November–December 2007.
176 “After *The Band*”: Hoskyns, *Across the Great Divide*, 399.
176 “Levon was influenced”: Simon, *Truth, Lies and Hearsay*, 250.
177 “I was determined”: Hoskyns, *Across the Great Divide*, 264.
177 “We were drifting”: ibid., 258.
177 “I walked out”: ibid., 325.
177 “That was the first”: ibid.
177–78 “Rick’s bass was”: Simon, *Truth, Lies and Hearsay*, 247.
178 “I remember the first night”: Streissguth, *Outlaw*, 235.
178 “We had a lot”: Patoski, *Willie Nelson*, 337.
179 “These tunes”: Ariel Swartley, *Stardust* album review, *Rolling Stone*, June 29, 1978.
179 “I’m a melody man”: Nelson and Ritz, *It’s a Long Story*, 323.
179 “He’s more special”: Patoski, *Willie Nelson*, 464.
179 “I wasn’t trying”: Nelson and Ritz, *It’s a Long Story*, 252.
179 “All the artists”: ibid., 327.

Chapter 13. Punks, God, and Urbane Cowboys

180 “He was out”: “Jerry Lee Lewis, Arrested at the Gates of Graceland,” https://www.elvis.com.au/presley/jerry-lee-lewis-arrested-at-the-gates-of-graceland.shtml.
180 “Tell ’em to lock”: ibid.

181 "I went over my whole life": Heylin, *Behind the Shades*, 456.
181 "Looked to me": Streissguth, *Outlaws*, 218.
181 "I missed more personal engagements": ibid., 177.
181–82 "Johnny Cash and the Tennessee Three": Hilburn, *Johnny Cash*, 478.
182 "I felt he was a little": ibid., 478.
182 "Every December": Editors of *Rolling Stone*, *Cash*, 211.
182 "I was influenced": Doggett, *Are You Ready for the Country*,197.
182–83 "I was stunned": Cash, *Composed*, 70.
183 "When I was having": Editors of *Rolling Stone*, *Cash*, 163.
183 "I couldn't believe": Chapman, *They Came to Nashville*, 260.
183 "Rodney and Rose had moved": ibid., 75.
183–84 "There was a little": ibid., 78.
184 "Sid [Vicious] got hit": St. John, *Hardcore Troubadour*, 83.
184 "We didn't think": Joe Ely and Alex Rawls, "Texas Calling," *Oxford American*, Winter 2004.
184 "Some of the places": ibid.
184 "It was such a full onslaught": ibid.
185 "I look to John": Lynne Margolis, "Dwight Yoakam: Outlier Country," *American Songwriter*, March–April 2017.
185 "It was shocking": McLeese, *Dwight Yoakam*, 14.
185 "There were maybe thirty": ibid., 60.
185 "There was a period": Hoskyns, *Across the Great Divide*, 359.
186 "T-Bone was the first": Heylin, *Behind the Shades*, 405.
186 "I had no idea": ibid., 502.
186–87 "I told you": Wilentz, *Bob Dylan in America*, 178.
187 "I had been waiting": Tim Adams, "Why Richard Thompson Is Keeping the Faith," *Guardian*, April 10, 2010.
187 "To stop using [his] brain": ibid.
187 "At some point": Zollo, *More Songwriters on Songwriting*, 604.
187 "In his playing": Boyd, *White Bicycles*, 167.
188 "Those were the best": Darcy Frey, "Lucinda Williams Is in Pain," *New York Times Magazine*, September 14, 1997.
189 "It's American roots music": Dawidoff, *In the Country of Country*, 286.
189 "When we met": Andy Langer, "A Long Way from Church Street but Still in Sync," *New York Times*, May 25, 2013.
190 "We had some quality": Huffman, *John Prine*, 125.
192 "At the time": author interview, Woodstock, NY, August 22, 2007.
192 "Since we loved that music": Barry Mazor, "Where the Twang Finally Met: How New York's Short-Lived Country Craze Spawned the Stars of Americana," *Journal of Country Music* 24, 2004.
192 "Doc Pomus lived": author interview, New York, NY, August 21, 1999.
192 "In the same way": Mazor, "Where the Twang Finally Met."
192 "Like many people": ibid.
192 "We got out of the Lone Star": author interview, Woodstock, NY, July 21, 2007.

193 "Her heart": ibid.
193 "Yeah, you might say": John Milward, "Free and Kindred Spirits," *Los Angeles Times*, March 31, 2000.
193 "I liked Buddy": Mazor, "Where the Twang Finally Met."
193 "It was weird enough": Milward, "Free and Kindred Spirits."

Chapter 14. Hard-Core Troubadours

194 "Hey, go to the jukebox": Kienzle, *Grand Tour*, 186.
194 "He was Elvis": McGee, *Steve Earle*, 73.
194 "These people": ibid., 73.
195 "I was way into Creedence": John Milward, "As in His Song, He's Been to Hell and Back," *New York Times*, April 14, 1996.
195 "The turning point": Holly Gleason, "Paying Tribute to His Mentors, Steve Earle Still Stands Tall," *Vineyard Gazette*, July 4, 2019.
195 "I thought Steve": St. John, *Hardcore Troubadour*, 124.
196 "I wanted to write": Dawidoff, *In the Country of Country*, 311.
196 "These instruments": author telephone interview, New York, NY, June 22, 1987.
197 "My role models": Michael Hall, "You Can't Go Home Again," *Texas Monthly*, January 1999.
197 "Artists who are": McGee, *Steve Earle*, 88.
198 "I was around": McLeese, *Dwight Yoakam*, 63.
198 "We were definitely": ibid., 46.
198 "We made our records": ibid., 186.
198 "I was really inspired": ibid., 33.
198 "I didn't know": Craig Shelburne, "Dwight Yoakam Shares Stories of Buck Owens," *CMT News*, October 2007.
199 "You're always a little nervous": author interview, New York, NY, April 22, 1996.
199 "John was the most": Adrian Deevoy, "Whitney Houston Made Me a Million," *Mail Online* (UK), May 18, 2019.
199 "We used to get sloshed together": ibid.
199 "I'd get up in the morning": Jem Asway, "Nick Lowe on 'Peace, Love and Understanding,' His Former Father-in-Law Johnny Cash, and Being an Indie Icon," *Variety*, June 28, 2017.
199 "During one show": Heylin, *Behind the Shades*, 588.
199 "We'd all been": Paul Zollo, "From the Archives: Tom Petty on Bob Dylan," *American Songwriter*, October 2017.
199 "The times I remember": ibid.
199 "He knows a million songs": Heylin, *Behind the Shades*, 583.
200 "It was one of those things": ibid., 612.
200 "We talked about people": ibid.
200 "I didn't know anybody": Harris, *Bluegrass, Newgrass*, 323.
201 "We phoned up Bob": Heylin, *Behind the Shades*, 625.

201 “We’d go to Bob’s house”: ibid., 626.
201 “I had never”: Mat Snow, “The Mojo Interview,” *Mojo*, January 2010.
201 “The recording studio”: Heylin, *Behind the Shades*, 629.
201–2 “So I come to Nashville”: Chapman, *They Came to Nashville*, 72.
202 “I jumped in my car”: Holly George-Warren, liner notes to *Complete Trio Sessions*, Rhino, 2016.
202 “We wanted to bring”: *Sisters in Country: Dolly, Linda and Emmylou*, BBC Four, 2016.
202 “Linda Ronstadt and Emmylou”: ibid.
202 “[Trio] hit Nashville like a bomb”: ibid.
202 “It got into a power play”: Chet Flippo, “The Unsinkable Dolly Parton,” *Rolling Stone*, December 1980.
204 “I remember the first time”: McDonough, *Shakey*, 586.
204 “Back off”: ibid., 292.
204 “The real sense of the album”: ibid., 662.
204 “*Guitar Town* made us”: McGee, *Steve Earle*, 106.
205 “He described”: Cash, *Composed*, 105.
205 “He said the album”: McGee, *Steve Earle*, 145.
207 “I started traveling”: ibid., 119.
207 “We’re just musicians”: John Milward, “Midnight Rambler,” *No Depression*, November–December 2007.
208 “You don’t have to”: St. John, *Hardcore Troubadour*, 180.
208 “For me, going to see Dr. Nick”: ibid., 200.
208 “I felt like [Steve] was lost”: McGee, *Steve Earle*, 121.
208 “I remember being”: ibid.
208 “Their songwriting craft”: Robert Palmer, “A Hard Road, Seldom Taken,” *New York Times*, June 7, 1987.
208 “Towards the end”: John Milward, “As in His Song, He’s Been to Hell and Back,” *New York Times*, April 14, 1996.
208 “I must be bad”: St. John, *Hardcore Troubadour*, 285.
209 “There’s probably women”: ibid., 312.
209 “I said, ‘Do not make’”: Ben Sisario, “The Album Steve Earle Never Wanted to Make: A Tribute to His Son,” *New York Times*, December 29, 2020.

Chapter 15. The “Birth” of Americana

210 “My grandmother”: Paul Sexton, “Alison Krauss Interview for the Release of *Essential Alison Krauss*,” *Telegraph* (London), July 22, 2009.
210 “I was really”: ibid.
210–11 “At one point”: Rooney, *In It for the Long Run*, 166.
211 “I discovered bluegrass”: Alec Wilkinson, “The Ghostly One: How Gillian Welch and David Rawlings Rediscovered Country Music,” *New Yorker*, September 12, 2004.
211 “I looked at my record collection”: ibid.

212 “Do you want”: Zack Harold, “How Gillian Welch Created an Americana Touchstone in ‘Revival,’” *Rolling Stone*, November 9, 2016.

212 “Had a deep”: Billy Altman, “A Music Maker Happy to Be Just a Conduit,” *New York Times*, February 24, 2002.

212 “Settings that could”: Powers quoted in Harold, “How Gillian Welch Created.”

212 “Concentrate only”: ibid.

212 “One of the things”: Wilkinson, “Ghostly One.”

212 “We’d all been involved”: Kot, *Wilco*, 48.

212–13 “Most of these bands”: ibid., 99.

213 “We were conscious”: ibid., 45.

213 “It just seemed like”: Lee Zimmerman, “Interview with Jay Farrar,” *No Depression*, January 2017.

213 “It wasn’t like”: Jason Fine, “Heart of the Country,” *Option*, November–December 1993.

213 “If there was a class”: Jim Beaugez, “Uncle Tupelo’s ‘Anodyne’ at 25: An Oral History,” *Rolling Stone*, October 5, 2018.

213 “I don’t remember”: Tweedy, *Let’s Go (So We Can Get Back)*, 261.

214 “A small, little”: Beaugez, “Uncle Tupelo’s ‘Anodyne.’”

214 “A friend of mine”: ibid.

214 “Uncle Tupelo’s influence”: Kot, *Wilco*, 102.

214 “They were the right band”: ibid., 100.

215 “I started”: Ryan Adams, “Faithless Street,” on *Faithless Street*, Outpost, 1998.

215 “By listening”: O’Keefe and Oestreich, *Waiting to Derail*, 126.

215 “We ended up playing”: Menconi, *Ryan Adams*, 124.

216 “Everyone’s sort of”: Jim Ridley, “Brothers in Arms: Talking with Joel and Ethan Coen About ‘O Brother, Where Art Thou?,’” *Nashville Scene*, May 22, 2000.

216 “Your voice”: Daniel Menaker, “Arts in America: A Film Score Odyssey Down a Quirky Country Road,” *New York Times*, November 30, 2000.

216 “It was much more terrifying”: interview by Terry Gross, *Fresh Air*, NPR, January 13, 2010.

216 “[Burnett] said he understood”: Sachs, *T Bone Burnett*, 133.

216 “To me it just sounded”: Altman, “Music Maker.”

216 “Johnny was one”: Editors of *Rolling Stone*, *Cash*, 215.

216 “I probably would have died”: author interview, New York, NY, March 20, 1996.

217 “We were all”: McGee, *Steve Earle*, 180.

217 “Everybody can hear”: ibid., 179.

217 “Out of the corner”: St. John, *Hardcore Troubadour*, 308.

217 “It’s a modern”: John Milward, “As in His Song, He’s Been to Hell and Back,” *New York Times*, Aril 14, 1996.

217–18 “You’re kind of a new person”: ibid.

218 "When I got to the studio": Editors of *Rolling Stone*, *Cash*, 215.
218 "Steve Earle and I": Dawidoff, *In the Country of Country*, 285.
218 "The album turns": Gavin Martin, review of *Car Wheels on a Gravel Road*, *New Musical Express*, November 2011.
219 "I want to be successful": Geoffrey Himes, "Lyle Lovett, Feel Like Going Home," *No Depression*, September 2003.
219 "He started doing": Hardy, *Deeper Blue*, 249.
219 "He hadn't shaved": Matt Hanks, "Townes Van Zandt—A Gentleman and a Shaman," *No Depression*, January 1999.
220 "I booked this gig": Hardy, *Deeper Blue*, 266.
220 "What records": "The Bono Vox Interview," *Hot Press*, July 8, 1984.
220 "There was a lot": Damien Love, "Bob Dylan Special: The Complete Tell Tale Signs," https://www.uncut.co.uk/features/bob-dylan-tell-tale-signs-special-mark-howard-37964/.
220 "My years with Eno": Lanois, *Soul Mining*, 159.
221 "Robbie and the Band": ibid., 86.
221 "The simplicity": ibid., 133.
221 "The multiple strings": ibid., 136.
221 "These great Canadian singers": ibid., 138.
221 "The first thing": John Milward, "Free and Kindred Spirits," *Los Angeles Times*, March 31, 2000.
223 "There is a similarity": Lanois, *Soul Mining*, 198.
223 "Bob considers": Maymudes and Maymudes, *Another Side of Bob Dylan*, 220.
223 "I had just had": Chuck Reece, "Rosanne Cash: The Bitter Southerner Interview," *Bitter Southerner*, November 2018.
223 "Somebody wrote a review": ibid.
224 "It was different": Michael Roberts, "Vintage Q&A with Rodney Crowell," *Westword*, March 4, 2008.
224 "As a songwriter": ibid.
224 "John would give me": Colvin, *Diamond in the Rough*, 101.
224 "For about a year": author interview, New York, NY, August 21, 1999.
224 "Emmylou was like the Queen": Milward, "Free and Kindred Spirits."
224 "I think nine out of ten": author interview, New York, NY, August 21, 1999.
225 "It wasn't a slow decline": McLeese, *Dwight Yoakam*, 149.
225 "It was a matter": Reece, "Rosanne Cash."
225 "There was this whole": Colvin, *Diamond in the Rough*, 139.
226 "You'll come to my house": Editors of *Rolling Stone*, *Cash*, 47.
226 "I can't see nothing": Hilburn, *Johnny Cash*, 550.
227 "Rick came along": ibid., 555.
227 "He was laughing": Editors of *Rolling Stone*, *Cash*, 216.
227 "I told him": Hilburn, *Johnny Cash*, 603.
227 "As we sang": Cash, *Composed*, 29.

Chapter 16. Across the Great Divide

228 "We do not want": "The Dixie Chicks Backlash Begins," https://www.history.com/this-day-in-history/the-dixie-chicks-backlash-begins.

230 "*Summerteeth* was": Tweedy, *Let's Go*, 160.

230 "It was a great record": Kot, *Wilco*, 164.

231 "I was completely": "Sir Elton Meets Ryan Adams at the 'Crossroads,'" http://www.mtv.com/news/1453256/sir-elton-meets-ryan-adams-at-the-crossroads/.

231 "The kid's so prolific": Neil Strauss, "A Future So Bright, He's Already Seen It," *New York Times*, June 17, 2001.

231 "My behavior": Anthony DeCurtis, "Ryan Adams Didn't Die. Now the Work Begins," *New York Times*, June 17, 2007.

232 "The part of me": Dave Simpson, "Ryan Adams: Things Got Broken and I Couldn't Fix Them," *Guardian*, September 22, 2011.

232 "For years we were": liner notes, *It's Great to Be Alive* by Drive-By Truckers, ATO Records, 2015.

232 "I would hear": Monica Collier, "David and Patterson Hood: Something Special," *Times Daily* (Florence, AL), June 18, 2017.

232 "This chubby kid": Dwight Garner, "Jason Isbell, Unloaded," *New York Times Magazine*, May 31, 2013.

234 "Some people get drunk": ibid.

234 "That isn't going to work": ibid.

234 "It was nice": Jason P. Woodbury, "Jason Isbell on His 'Bromance' with Ryan Adams and Powerful Recovery Album, Southeastern," *Phoenix New Times*, September 18, 2013.

234 "I don't remember": Garner, "Jason Isbell, Unloaded."

234 "'Is there any chance'": Martin Kielty, "How Robert Plant Won a Grammy in the 'Alison Krauss Category,'" https://ultimateclassicrock.com/robert-plant-alison-krauss-grammy/.

234 "[T-Bone] knows": Blair Jackson, "Robert Plant and Alison Krauss: An Unlikely But Fruitful Musical Union," *Mix*, December 1, 2007.

235 "It was very scary": Piers Hernu, "The World According to Alison Krauss," https://www.dailymail.co.uk/home/moslive/article-1378857/Alison-Krauss-Robert-Plant-asked-wrong-him.html.

235 "We toured a little": John Milward, "Free and Kindred Spirits," *Los Angeles Times*, March 31, 2000.

235 "There was a small": ibid.

235 "It wasn't like anything": Hight, *Right by Her Roots*, 50.

235 "If I'm working": Milward, "Free and Kindred Spirits."

235 "I didn't have enough songs": ibid.

236 "Buddy Miller": Brian Mansfield, "Robert Plant Loves to Dig in America's Rich Musical Soil," *USA Today*, September 14, 2010.

236 "Robert was one": Andy Langer, "The Patty Griffin Effect," *Texas Monthly*, April 2013.

236 "Any way you slice it": ibid.

236 "The hospitality": Jonathan Ringen, "Robert Plant, Party of One (With Friends, Too)," *New York Times*, October 11, 2017.

236 "It was my own inability": ibid.

236–37 "It was one of the most rewarding": ibid.

237 "There are times": Jeff Giles, "Larry Campbell Shares Memories of Bob Dylan, Phil Lesh, Hot Tuna, Paul Simon and More," *Ultimate Classic Rock*, May 14, 2015.

237 "At the end of the show": ibid.

237 "It was a very amorphous": author interview, Woodstock, NY, July 21, 2007.

238 "When he got sick": author telephone interview, Woodstock, NY, July 29, 2007.

238 "He and I started": John Milward, "Midnight Rambler," *No Depression*, November–December 2007.

238 "I remember early on": author interview, Woodstock, NY, July 21, 2007.

238 "Levon is ground zero": ibid.

239 "Playing the Ryman": Milward, "Midnight Rambler."

239 "It was like I had died": author telephone interview, Woodstock, NY, July 25, 2007.

239 "We were still playing": Giles, "Larry Campbell Shares Memories."

239 "I got a message": from the film *Once Were Brothers: Robbie Robertson and The Band*, dir. Daniel Roher, Magnolia, 2020.

Chapter 17. Yesterday and Today

240 "When I first arrived": "The Marty Stuart Collection," http://www.martystuart.com/Collection.htm.

241 "My father was": Chuck Dauphin, "Mavis Staples Talks Las Vegas Shooting & Reasserting Herself as a Voice for Change," *Billboard*, October 10, 2017.

241 "She said, 'That's'": "The Marty Stuart Collection."

241 "I said, 'Susie'": ibid.

241 "We had this": Steven Hyden, "Drive-By Truckers Carry On," *Grantland*, March 4, 2014.

241 "If we want": Patterson Hood, "The South's Heritage Is So Much More Than a Flag," *New York Times*, July 9, 2015.

242 "I have a feeling": Tyler Coates, "How Drive-By Truckers' American Band Reclaimed Rock for the Anti-Trump South," *Esquire*, September 2016.

242 "I definitely don't": Rachel Bailey, "Jason Isbell: That New Southern Style," *Flagpole*, November 2012.

242–43 "If I picture": Chuck Klosterman, "Wilco: Interview with Jeff Tweedy," *Spin*, July 2004.

243 "At the beginning": Lindsay Zoladz, "The Playlist: Jeff Tweedy, 'Gwendolyn,'" *New York Times*, October 9, 2020.

243 "I have a great life": ibid.

243 "As they got to our door": Tweedy, *Let's Go*, 263.
243 "Tell Mavis": ibid.
245 "Yeah": ibid.
245 "I felt like": Dauphin, "Mavis Staples Talks Las Vegas."
245 "I offered a few ideas": Jeff Tamarkin, "Cash and Cooder on Cash," Carnegie Hall Playbill, 2019–2020 season.
245 "He took our confidence": Aaron Aye, "The Story," *Harp*, June 2007.
245 "After years of trying": Nick Duerden, "Close-up: Singer Brandi Carlile," *Independent*, April 20, 2008.
246–47 "I grew up appreciating": Andy Langer, "Singer, Songwriter, Prodigy, All at 19," *New York Times*, May 7, 2001.
247 "It all came from": Harris, *Bluegrass, Newgrass*. 320.
247 "I just want": ibid., 321.
247 "My existence is political": Natalie Weiner, "Country Music Is a Man's World. The Highwomen Want to Change That," *New York Times*, September 3, 2019.
248 "In many ways I don't": Colvin, *Diamond in the Rough*, 173.
248 "When we played Town Hall": ibid., 188.
248 "I knew when Guy": Amanda Petrusich, "Steve Earle's Winsome Tribute to Guy Clark," *New Yorker*, March 25, 2019.
249 "We have a rich": Fiona Sturges, "How We Met: Emmylou & Rodney Crowell," *New York Times*, February 24, 2013.
249 "Our conversation hasn't changed": ibid.
249 "I had my 15 minutes": Henry Carrigan, "Sharing the Stage: Rodney Crowell and Vince Gill on Four Decades of Friendship," *No Depression*, August 2019.
249 "She told the most": Crowell, *Chinaberry Sidewalks*, 259.
249 "Country music": Dawidoff, *In the Country of Country*, 287.
249 "I had to get": D. Jones, *Wichita Lineman*, 195.
250 "Ragtime blues": Bob Dylan, Nobel Lecture, https://www.nobelprize.org/prizes/literature/2016/dylan/lecture/.
250 "'Ebb Tide' has": Dylan, *Chronicles: Volume 1*, 81.
251 "Sometime after dinner": Melinda Newman, "10 Revelations from Bruce Springsteen's New Memoir," *New Jersey Monthly*, October 2016.
251 "You and me, pal": Bob Dylan interview by Bill Flanagan, https://www.bobdylan.com/news/qa-with-bill-flanagan/.
251 "I learned a lot": Patrick Doyle, "A Brief History of Willie Nelson and Frank Sinatra's Bromance," *Rolling Stone*, August 27, 2018.
251 "When Willie plays": Chapman, *They Came to Nashville*, 209.

BIBLIOGRAPHY

Bockris, Victor. *Keith Richards: The Biography*. Poseidon, 1992.

Boyd, Joe. *White Bicycles: Making Music in the 1960s*. Serpent's Tail, 2007.

Bragg, Rick. *Jerry Lee Lewis: His Own Story*. HarperCollins, 2014.

Broven, John. *Record Makers and Breakers: Voice of the Independent Rock 'n' Roll Pioneers*. University of Illinois Press, 2009.

Cain, Michael Scott. *The Americana Revolution: From Country and Blues Roots to the Avett Brothers, Mumford and Sons, and Beyond*. Rowman and Littlefield, 2017.

Cantwell, David. *Merle Haggard: The Running Kind*. University of Texas Press, 2013.

Cash, Rosanne. *Composed: A Memoir*. Viking, 2010.

Chapman, Marshall. *They Came to Nashville*. Vanderbilt University Press, 2010.

Charles, Ray, and David Ritz. *Brother Ray*. Da Capo, 2004.

Clifford, Craig E., and Craig Hillis. *Pickers and Poets: The Ruthlessly Poetic Singer-Songwriters of Texas*. Texas A&M University Press, 2016.

Colvin, Shawn. *Diamond in the Rough*. William Morrow, 2012.

Cooper, Daniel. *Lefty Frizzell: The Honky Tonk Life of Country Music's Greatest Singer*. Little, Brown, 1995.

Corcoran, Michael. *All over the Map: True Heroes of Texas Music*. University of North Texas Press, 2017.

Crosby, David, and Carl Gottlieb. *Long Time Gone: The Autobiography of David Crosby*. Doubleday, 1987.

Crowell, Rodney. *Chinaberry Sidewalks*. Knopf, 2011.

D'Ambrosio, Antonino. *A Heartbeat and a Guitar: Johnny Cash and the Making of Bitter Tears*. Nation Books, 2009.

Dawidoff, Nicholas. *In the Country of Country: A Journey to the Roots of American Music*. Random House, 1997.

Dean, Eddie. *Pure Country: The Leon Kagarise Archives*. Process Media, 2008.

Doggett, Peter. *Are You Ready for the Country: Elvis, Dylan, Parsons and the Roots of Country Rock*. Penguin, 2000.

Dylan, Bob. *Chronicles: Volume One*. Simon and Schuster, 2004.

Eals, Clay. *Steve Goodman: Facing the Music*. ECW, 2012.

Echols, Alice. *Scars of Sweet Paradise: The Life and Times of Janis Joplin*. Henry Holt, 1999.

Editors of *Rolling Stone*. *Cash*. Crown, 2004.

Einarson, John. *Desperados: The Roots of Country Rock*. Cooper Square, 2001.

Einarson, John, with Chris Hillman. *Hot Burritos: The True Story of the Flying Burrito Brothers*. Jawbone, 2008.

Eliot, Marc. *To the Limit: The Untold Story of the Eagles*. Little, Brown, 1998.

Ellison, Jim, ed. *Younger Than That Now: The Collected Interviews with Bob Dylan*. Da Capo, 2004.

Escott, Colin, with George Merritt and William MacEwen. *I Saw the Light: The Story of Hank Williams*. Little, Brown, 2004.

Flippo, Chet. *Your Cheatin' Heart: A Biography of Hank Williams*. Simon and Schuster, 1981.

Fong-Torres, Ben. *Hickory Wind: The Life and Times of Gram Parsons*. St. Martins Griffin, 1991.

Fox, Pamela, and Barbara Ching, eds. *Old Roots, New Routes: The Cultural Politics of Alt.Country Music*. University of Michigan Press, 2008.

Frizzell, David. *I Love You a Thousand Ways: The Lefty Frizzell Story*. Santa Monica, 2011.

George-Warren, Holly. *Janis: Her Life and Music*. Simon and Schuster, 2019.

———. *Public Cowboy No. 1: The Life and Times of Gene Autry*. Oxford University Press, 2007.

Goodman, Fred. *The Mansion on the Hill: Dylan, Young, Geffen, Springsteen, and the Head-on Collision of Rock and Commerce*. Vintage, 1998.

Gordon, Robert. *Can't Be Satisfied: The Life and Times of Muddy Waters*. Little, Brown, 2002.

———. *It Came from Memphis*. Atria, 2001.

Gould, Jonathan. *Can't Buy Me Love: The Beatles, Britain, and America*. Harmony, 2007.

Gray, Michael. *The Bob Dylan Encyclopedia*. Bloomsbury Academic, 2006.

Gray, Timothy. *It's Just the Normal Noise: Marcus, Guralnick, No Depression, and the Mystery of Americana Music*. University of Iowa Press, 2001.

Green, Douglas B. *Classic Country Singers*. Gibbs Smith, 2008.

Griffin, Sid. *Million Dollar Bash: Bob Dylan, The Band, and the Basement Tapes*. Jawbone, 2007.
Guesdon, Jean-Michel, and Margotin, Phillippe. *All the Songs: The Story Behind Every Beatles Release*. Black Dog and Leventhal, 2013.
Guralnick, Peter. *Careless Love: The Unmaking of Elvis Presley*. Little, Brown, 1999.
———. *Feel Like Going Home: Portraits in Blues and Rock 'n' Roll*. Outerbridge and Dienstfrey, 1971.
———. *Last Train to Memphis: The Rise of Elvis Presley*. Little, Brown, 1994.
———. *Sam Phillips: The Man Who Invented Rock 'n' Roll*. Little, Brown, 2015.
Hadju, David. *Positively 4th Street: The Lives and Times of Joan Baez, Bob Dylan, Mimi Baez Fariña, and Richard Fariña*. Picador, 2011.
Haggard, Merle, with Peggy Russell. *Sing Me Back Home: My Life*. Times Books, 1981.
Halpin, Brook. *Experiencing the Beatles: A Listener's Companion*. Rowman and Littlefield, 2018.
Hardy, Robert Earl. *A Deeper Blue: The Life and Music of Townes Van Zandt*. University of North Texas Press, 2008.
Harris, Craig. *Bluegrass, Newgrass, Old-Time, and Americana Music*. Pelican, 2018.
Harry, Bill. *The Ultimate Beatles Encyclopedia*. Hyperion, 1982.
Haslam, Gerald, Alexandra Haslam Russell, and Richard Chon. *Workin' Man Blues: Country Music in California*. University of California Press, 1999.
Helm, Levon, with Stephen Davis. *This Wheel's on Fire: Levon Helm and the Story of The Band*. Morrow, 1993.
Hemphill, Paul. *Lovesick Blues: The Life of Hank Williams*. Viking, 2005.
———. *The Nashville Sound: Bright Lights and Country Music*. Simon and Schuster, 1970.
Heylin, Clinton. *Bob Dylan: Behind the Shades*. Summit, 1991.
———. *Bob Dylan: The Recording Sessions*. St. Martin's, 1995.
Hickey, Dave. *Air Guitar: Essays on Art and Democracy*. Art Issues Press, 1997.
Hight, Jewly. *Right by Her Roots: Americana Women and Their Songs*. Baylor University Press, 2001.
Hilburn, Robert. *Johnny Cash: The Life*. Little, Brown, 2013.
Hillman, Chris. *Time Between: My Life as a Byrd, Burrito Brother, and Beyond*. BMG, 2020.
Hjort, Christopher. *So You Want to Be a Rock 'n' Roll Star: The Byrds Day-by-Day, 1965–1973*. Jawbone, 2008.
———. *Strange Brew: Eric Clapton and the British Blues Boom, 1965–1970*. Outline, 2007.
Hoskyns, Barney. *Across the Great Divide: The Band and America*. Hyperion, 1993.
———. *Hotel California*. Wiley, 2006.
———, ed. *Joni: The Anthology*. Picador, 2016.
———. *Small Town Talk*. Faber and Faber, 2017.
———. *Waiting for the Sun: A Rock 'n' Roll History of Los Angeles*. Viking, 1996.
Huffman, Eddie. *John Prine: In Spite of Himself*. University of Texas Press, 2015.

Hughes, Charles L. *Country Soul: Making Music and Making Race in the American South*. University of North Carolina Press, 2015.
Hughes, John. *Invisible Now: Bob Dylan in the 1960s*. Routledge, 2013.
Hume, Martha. *Martha Hume's Guide to the Greatest in Country Music: You're So Cold I'm Turnin' Blue*. Viking, 1982.
Jagger, Mick, Keith Richards, Charlie Watts, and Ronnie Lane. *According to the Rolling Stones*. Chronicle Books, 2003.
Jennings, Waylon, with Lenny Kay. *Waylon: An Autobiography*. Warner Books, 1996.
Jones, Dylan. *The Wichita Lineman: Searching in the Sun for the World's Greatest Unfinished Song*. Faber and Faber, 2019.
Jones, George, with Tom Carter. *George Jones: I Lived to Tell It All*. Villard, 1996.
Kealing, Bob. *Gram Parsons and the Roots of Country Rock*. University Press of Florida, 2015.
Kienzle, Rich. *The Grand Tour: The Life and Music of George Jones*. William Morrow, 2016.
Kot, Greg. *Wilco: Learning How to Die*. Broadway Books, 2004.
Lanois, Daniel. *Soul Mining: A Musical Life*. Faber and Faber, 2010.
Lewisohn, Mark. *Tune In: The Beatles; All These Years*. Crown Archetype, 2013.
Lomax III, John. *Nashville: Music City USA*. Harry N. Abrams, 1985.
Lynn, Loretta, and Patsi Bale Cox. *Still Woman Enough: A Memoir*. Hyperion, 2002.
Lynn, Loretta, with George Vecsay. *Loretta Lynn: Coal Miner's Daughter*. Bernard Geis Associates, 1976.
MacMahon, Bernard, and Allison McGorty. *American Epic: The First Time America Heard Itself*. Atria Books, 2017.
Malone, Bill C. *Sing Me Back Home: Southern Roots and Country Music*. University of Oklahoma Press, 2017.
Malone, Bill C., and Jocelyn R. Neal. *Country Music, U.S.A.* University of Texas Press, 2010.
Marcus, Greil. *Invisible Republic: Bob Dylan's Basement Tapes*. Henry Holt, 1997.
———. *Like a Rolling Stone: Bob Dylan at the Crossroads*. Public Affairs, 2005.
———. *Mystery Train: Images of America in Rock 'n' Roll Music*. Dutton, 1976.
Marcus, Greil, and Werner Sollors, eds. *A New Literary History of America*. The Belknap Press of Harvard University Press, 2009.
Masino, Susan. *Family Tradition: Three Generations of Hank Williams*. Backbeat Books, 2011.
Maymudes, Victor, and Jacob Maymudes. *Another Side of Bob Dylan: A Personal History on the Road and off the Tracks*. St. Martin's, 2014.
Mazor, Barry. *Meeting Jimmy Rodgers: How America's Original Roots Music Hero Changed the Pop Sounds of a Century*. Oxford University Press, 2012.
———. *Ralph Peer and the Making of Popular Roots Music*. Chicago Review Press, 2015.
McCoy, Charlie. *Fifty Cents and a Box Top: The Creative life of Nashville Session Musician Charlie McCoy*. West Virginia University Press, 2017.
McDonough, Jimmy. *Shakey: Neil Young's Biography*. Anchor, 2003.

———. *Soul Survivor: A Biography of Al Green*. Da Capo, 2017.

McEuen, John. *The Life I've Picked: A Banjo Player's Nitty Gritty Journey*. Chicago Review Press, 2018.

McGee, David. *Steve Earle: Fearless Heart, Outlaw Poet*. Backbeat, 2005.

McKeen, William. *Everybody Had an Ocean: Music and Mayhem in 1960s Los Angeles*. Chicago Review Press, 2017.

McLeese, Don. *Dwight Yoakam: A Thousand Miles from Nowhere*. University of Texas Press, 2012.

Menconi, David. *Ryan Adams: Losering, a Story of Whiskeytown*. University of Texas Press, 2012.

Meyer, David N. *Twenty Thousand Roads: The Ballad of Gram Parsons and His Cosmic American Music*. Villard, 2008.

Miller, Jim. *The Rolling Stone Illustrated History of Rock & Roll*. Random House/Rolling Stone Press, 1980.

Miller, Stephen. *The Million Dollar Quartet: Jerry Lee, Carl, Elvis and Johnny*. Omnibus, 2013.

Milward, John. *Crossroads: How the Blues Shaped Rock 'n' Roll (And Rock Saved the Blues)*. Northeastern University Press, 2013.

Nash, Alanna. *Behind Closed Doors: Talking with the Legends of Country Music*. Knopf, 1988.

Nassour, Elis. *Honky Tonk Angel: The Intimate Story of Patsy Cline*. Chicago Review Press, 2008.

Nelson, Willie, with David Ritz. *It's a Long Story: My Life*. Little, Brown, 2015.

Norman Philip. *Rave On: The Biography of Buddy Holly*. Simon and Schuster, 2014.

O'Keefe, Thomas, with Joe Oestreich. *Waiting to Derail: Ryan Adams and Whiskeytown, Alt-Country's Brilliant Wreck*. Skyhorse, 2018.

Ono, Yoko. *Memories of John Lennon*. HarperCollins, It Books, 2005.

Patoski, Joe Nick. *Willie Nelson: An Epic Life*. Little, Brown, 2008.

Perkins, Carl, and David McGee. *Go, Cat, Go! The Life and Times of Carl Perkins, the King of Rockabilly*. Hyperion, 1996.

Petrus, Stephen, and Ronald D. Cohen. *Folk City: New York and the American Folk Music Revival*. Oxford University Press, 2015.

Petrusich, Amanda. *It Still Moves: Lost Songs, Lost Highways, and the Search for the Next American Music*. Faber and Faber, 2008.

Piazza, Tom. *Devil Sent the Rain: Music and Writing in Desperate America*. Harper Perennial, 2011.

Pleasants, Henry. *The Great American Popular Singers*. Simon and Schuster, 1974.

Polizzotti, Mark. *Highway 61 Revisited*. Bloomsbury, 2006.

Richards, Keith, and James Fox. *Life*. Little, Brown, 2010.

Robertson, Ray. *Lives of the Poets (with Guitars): Thirteen Outsiders Who Changed Modern Music*. Biblioasis, 2016.

Robertson, Robbie. *Testimony*. Crown, 2016.

Rogan, Johnny. *The Byrds: Timeless Flight Revisited (The Sequel)*. Rogan House, 2001.

Rooney, Jim. *Bossmen: Bill Monroe and Muddy Waters*. Da Capo, 1991.

———. *In It for the Long Run: A Musical Odyssey*. University of Illinois Press, 2014.

Rosenberg, Neil V., and Charles K. Wolfe. *The Music of Bill Monroe*. University of Illinois Press, 2007.

Sachs, Lloyd. *T Bone Burnett: A Life in Pursuit*. University of Texas Press, 2016.

Sanders, Daryl. *That Thin, Wild Mercury Sound: Dylan, Nashville, and the Making of* Blonde on Blonde. Chicago Review Press, 2019.

Schmidt, Randy L. *Dolly on Dolly: Interviews and Encounters*. Chicago Review Press, 2017.

Segrest, James, and Mark Hoffman. *Moanin' at Midnight: The Life and Times of Howlin' Wolf*. Pantheon, 2004.

Shelton, Robert. *No Direction Home: The Life and Music of Bob Dylan*. Beech Tree, 1986.

Simon, John. *Truth, Lies and Hearsay: A Memoir of a Musical Life in and out of Rock and Roll*. Amazon, 2018.

Sisk, Eileen. *Buck Owens: The Biography*. Chicago Review Press, 2010.

Skaggs, Ricky, with Eddie Dean. *Kentucky Traveler: My Life in Music*. HarperCollins, 2013.

Smith, Richard D. *Can't You Hear Me Callin': The Life of Bill Monroe, Father of Bluegrass*. Little, Brown, 2000.

Sounes, Howard. *Down the Highway: The Life of Bob Dylan*. Doubleday, 2001.

———. *Seventies: The Sights, Sounds and Ideas of a Brilliant Decade*. Simon and Schuster, 2006.

St. John, Lauren. *Hardcore Troubadour: The Life and Near Death of Steve Earle*. Fourth Estate, 2003.

Stanley, Ralph, and Eddie Dean. *Man of Constant Sorrow: The Life and Times of a Music Legend*. Gotham, 2009.

Streissguth, Michael. *Always Been There: Rosanne Cash, "The List," and the Spirit of Southern Music*. Da Capo, 2009.

———. *Outlaw: Waylon, Willie, Kris, and the Renegades of Nashville*. HarperCollins, 2013.

Tchi, Cecelia. *High Lonesome: The American Culture of Country Music*. University of North Carolina Press, 1994.

Terkel, Studs. *And They All Sang: Adventures of an Eclectic Disc Jockey*. Granta Books, 2006.

Thompson, Dave. *Hearts of Darkness: James Taylor, Jackson Browne, Cat Stevens and the Unlikely Rise of the Singer-Songwriter*. Backbeat, 2012.

Tosches, Nick. *Country: The Biggest Music in America*. Stein and Day, 1977.

———. *Country: Living Legends and Dying Metaphors in America's Biggest Music*. Scribner, 1985.

———. *Hellfire: The Jerry Lee Lewis Story*. Delacorte, 1982.

———. *Unsung Heroes of Rock 'n' Roll: The Birth of Rock in the Wild Years Before Elvis*. Da Capo, 1999.

Tweedy, Jeff. *Let's Go (So We Can Get Back)*. Dutton, 2018.

Vallee, Mickey. *Rancid Aphrodisiac: Subjectivity, Desire, and Rock 'n' Roll*. Bloomsbury Academic, 2016.
Van Ronk, David, and Elijah Wald. *The Mayor of MacDougal Street: A Memoir*. Da Capo, 2005.
Von Schmidt, Eric, and Jim Rooney. *Baby, Let Me Follow You Down: The Illustrated Story of the Cambridge Folk Years*. University of Massachusetts Press, 1994.
Wald, Elijah. *Dylan Goes Electric! Newport, Seeger, Dylan, and the Night That Split the Sixties*. HarperCollins, 2015.
Ward, Ed. *Mike Bloomfield: The Rise and Fall of an American Guitar Hero*. Chicago Review Press, 2016.
Weissman, Dick. *Which Side Are You On? An Inside History of the Folk Music Revival in America*. Continuum, 2005.
Wexler, Jerry, and David Ritz. *Rhythm and the Blues: A Life in American Music*. Knopf, 1993.
Wilentz, Sean. *Bob Dylan in America*. Doubleday, 2010.
Williams, Paul. *Bob Dylan: Performing Artist*, vol. 1: *The Early Years, 1960–1973*. Omnibus, 2004.
Zimmerman, Lee. *Americana Music: Voices, Visionaries and Pioneers of an Honest Sound*. Texas A&M University Press, 2019.
Zollo, Paul. *Songwriters on Songwriting*. Da Capo, 1997.
———. *More Songwriters on Songwriting*. Da Capo, 2016.
Zwonitzer, Mark, with Charles Hirshberg. *Will You Miss Me When I'm Gone? The Carter Family and Their Legacy in American Music*. Simon and Schuster, 2002.

INDEX

JOHN MILWARD has written about popular music for more than forty years; he was the chief pop music critic for the *Chicago Daily News* and *USA Today* and has written for *Rolling Stone*, the *New York Times*, and *No Depression*. He is the author of *Crossroads: How the Blues Shaped Rock 'n' Roll (and Rock Saved the Blues)*.

MARGIE GREVE's work has appeared in *Rolling Stone* and the *New Yorker* and has been shown in galleries in New York City and the Hudson Valley.

MUSIC IN AMERICAN LIFE

Only a Miner: Studies in Recorded Coal-Mining Songs *Archie Green*
Great Day Coming: Folk Music and the American Left *R. Serge Denisoff*
John Philip Sousa: A Descriptive Catalog of His Works *Paul E. Bierley*
The Hell-Bound Train: A Cowboy Songbook *Glenn Ohrlin*
Oh, Didn't He Ramble: The Life Story of Lee Collins, as Told to Mary Collins *Edited by Frank J. Gillis and John W. Miner*
American Labor Songs of the Nineteenth Century *Philip S. Foner*
Stars of Country Music: Uncle Dave Macon to Johnny Rodriguez *Edited by Bill C. Malone and Judith McCulloh*
Git Along, Little Dogies: Songs and Songmakers of the American West *John I. White*
A Texas-Mexican *Cancionero*: Folksongs of the Lower Border *Américo Paredes*
San Antonio Rose: The Life and Music of Bob Wills *Charles R. Townsend*
Early Downhome Blues: A Musical and Cultural Analysis *Jeff Todd Titon*
An Ives Celebration: Papers and Panels of the Charles Ives Centennial Festival-Conference *Edited by H. Wiley Hitchcock and Vivian Perlis*
Sinful Tunes and Spirituals: Black Folk Music to the Civil War *Dena J. Epstein*
Joe Scott, the Woodsman-Songmaker *Edward D. Ives*
Jimmie Rodgers: The Life and Times of America's Blue Yodeler *Nolan Porterfield*
Early American Music Engraving and Printing: A History of Music Publishing in America from 1787 to 1825, with Commentary on Earlier and Later Practices *Richard J. Wolfe*
Sing a Sad Song: The Life of Hank Williams *Roger M. Williams*
Long Steel Rail: The Railroad in American Folksong *Norm Cohen*
Resources of American Music History: A Directory of Source Materials from Colonial Times to World War II *D. W. Krummel, Jean Geil, Doris J. Dyen, and Deane L. Root*
Tenement Songs: The Popular Music of the Jewish Immigrants *Mark Slobin*
Ozark Folksongs *Vance Randolph; edited and abridged by Norm Cohen*
Oscar Sonneck and American Music *Edited by William Lichtenwanger*
Bluegrass Breakdown: The Making of the Old Southern Sound *Robert Cantwell*
Bluegrass: A History *Neil V. Rosenberg*
Music at the White House: A History of the American Spirit *Elise K. Kirk*
Red River Blues: The Blues Tradition in the Southeast *Bruce Bastin*
Good Friends and Bad Enemies: Robert Winslow Gordon and the Study of American Folksong *Debora Kodish*

Fiddlin' Georgia Crazy: Fiddlin' John Carson, His Real World, and the World of His Songs *Gene Wiggins*
America's Music: From the Pilgrims to the Present (rev. 3d ed.) *Gilbert Chase*
Secular Music in Colonial Annapolis: The Tuesday Club, 1745–56 *John Barry Talley*
Bibliographical Handbook of American Music *D. W. Krummel*
Goin' to Kansas City *Nathan W. Pearson Jr.*
"Susanna," "Jeanie," and "The Old Folks at Home": The Songs of Stephen C. Foster from His Time to Ours (2d ed.) *William W. Austin*
Songprints: The Musical Experience of Five Shoshone Women *Judith Vander*
"Happy in the Service of the Lord": Afro-American Gospel Quartets in Memphis *Kip Lornell*
Paul Hindemith in the United States *Luther Noss*
"My Song Is My Weapon": People's Songs, American Communism, and the Politics of Culture, 1930–50 *Robbie Lieberman*
Chosen Voices: The Story of the American Cantorate *Mark Slobin*
Theodore Thomas: America's Conductor and Builder of Orchestras, 1835–1905 *Ezra Schabas*
"The Whorehouse Bells Were Ringing" and Other Songs Cowboys Sing *Collected and Edited by Guy Logsdon*
Crazeology: The Autobiography of a Chicago Jazzman *Bud Freeman, as Told to Robert Wolf*
Discoursing Sweet Music: Brass Bands and Community Life in Turn-of-the-Century Pennsylvania *Kenneth Kreitner*
Mormonism and Music: A History *Michael Hicks*
Voices of the Jazz Age: Profiles of Eight Vintage Jazzmen *Chip Deffaa*
Pickin' on Peachtree: A History of Country Music in Atlanta, Georgia *Wayne W. Daniel*
Bitter Music: Collected Journals, Essays, Introductions, and Librettos *Harry Partch; edited by Thomas McGeary*
Ethnic Music on Records: A Discography of Ethnic Recordings Produced in the United States, 1893 to 1942 *Richard K. Spottswood*
Downhome Blues Lyrics: An Anthology from the Post–World War II Era *Jeff Todd Titon*
Ellington: The Early Years *Mark Tucker*
Chicago Soul *Robert Pruter*
That Half-Barbaric Twang: The Banjo in American Popular Culture *Karen Linn*
Hot Man: The Life of Art Hodes *Art Hodes and Chadwick Hansen*
The Erotic Muse: American Bawdy Songs (2d ed.) *Ed Cray*
Barrio Rhythm: Mexican American Music in Los Angeles *Steven Loza*
The Creation of Jazz: Music, Race, and Culture in Urban America *Burton W. Peretti*
Charles Martin Loeffler: A Life Apart in Music *Ellen Knight*
Club Date Musicians: Playing the New York Party Circuit *Bruce A. MacLeod*
Opera on the Road: Traveling Opera Troupes in the United States, 1825–60 *Katherine K. Preston*

The Stonemans: An Appalachian Family and the Music That Shaped Their Lives *Ivan M. Tribe*
Transforming Tradition: Folk Music Revivals Examined *Edited by Neil V. Rosenberg*
The Crooked Stovepipe: Athapaskan Fiddle Music and Square Dancing in Northeast Alaska and Northwest Canada *Craig Mishler*
Traveling the High Way Home: Ralph Stanley and the World of Traditional Bluegrass Music *John Wright*
Carl Ruggles: Composer, Painter, and Storyteller *Marilyn Ziffrin*
Never without a Song: The Years and Songs of Jennie Devlin, 1865–1952 *Katharine D. Newman*
The Hank Snow Story *Hank Snow, with Jack Ownbey and Bob Burris*
Milton Brown and the Founding of Western Swing *Cary Ginell, with special assistance from Roy Lee Brown*
Santiago de Murcia's "Códice Saldívar No. 4": A Treasury of Secular Guitar Music from Baroque Mexico *Craig H. Russell*
The Sound of the Dove: Singing in Appalachian Primitive Baptist Churches *Beverly Bush Patterson*
Heartland Excursions: Ethnomusicological Reflections on Schools of Music *Bruno Nettl*
Doowop: The Chicago Scene *Robert Pruter*
Blue Rhythms: Six Lives in Rhythm and Blues *Chip Deffaa*
Shoshone Ghost Dance Religion: Poetry Songs and Great Basin Context *Judith Vander*
Go Cat Go! Rockabilly Music and Its Makers *Craig Morrison*
'Twas Only an Irishman's Dream: The Image of Ireland and the Irish in American Popular Song Lyrics, 1800–1920 *William H. A. Williams*
Democracy at the Opera: Music, Theater, and Culture in New York City, 1815–60 *Karen Ahlquist*
Fred Waring and the Pennsylvanians *Virginia Waring*
Woody, Cisco, and Me: Seamen Three in the Merchant Marine *Jim Longhi*
Behind the Burnt Cork Mask: Early Blackface Minstrelsy and Antebellum American Popular Culture *William J. Mahar*
Going to Cincinnati: A History of the Blues in the Queen City *Steven C. Tracy*
Pistol Packin' Mama: Aunt Molly Jackson and the Politics of Folksong *Shelly Romalis*
Sixties Rock: Garage, Psychedelic, and Other Satisfactions *Michael Hicks*
The Late Great Johnny Ace and the Transition from R&B to Rock 'n' Roll *James M. Salem*
Tito Puente and the Making of Latin Music *Steven Loza*
Juilliard: A History *Andrea Olmstead*
Understanding Charles Seeger, Pioneer in American Musicology *Edited by Bell Yung and Helen Rees*
Mountains of Music: West Virginia Traditional Music from *Goldenseal* *Edited by John Lilly*
Alice Tully: An Intimate Portrait *Albert Fuller*
A Blues Life *Henry Townsend, as told to Bill Greensmith*

Long Steel Rail: The Railroad in American Folksong (2d ed.) *Norm Cohen*
The Golden Age of Gospel *Text by Horace Clarence Boyer; photography by Lloyd Yearwood*
Aaron Copland: The Life and Work of an Uncommon Man *Howard Pollack*
Louis Moreau Gottschalk *S. Frederick Starr*
Race, Rock, and Elvis *Michael T. Bertrand*
Theremin: Ether Music and Espionage *Albert Glinsky*
Poetry and Violence: The Ballad Tradition of Mexico's Costa Chica *John H. McDowell*
The Bill Monroe Reader *Edited by Tom Ewing*
Music in Lubavitcher Life *Ellen Koskoff*
Zarzuela: Spanish Operetta, American Stage *Janet L. Sturman*
Bluegrass Odyssey: A Documentary in Pictures and Words, 1966–86 *Carl Fleischhauer and Neil V. Rosenberg*
That Old-Time Rock & Roll: A Chronicle of an Era, 1954–63 *Richard Aquila*
Labor's Troubadour *Joe Glazer*
American Opera *Elise K. Kirk*
Don't Get above Your Raisin': Country Music and the Southern Working Class *Bill C. Malone*
John Alden Carpenter: A Chicago Composer *Howard Pollack*
Heartbeat of the People: Music and Dance of the Northern Pow-wow *Tara Browner*
My Lord, What a Morning: An Autobiography *Marian Anderson*
Marian Anderson: A Singer's Journey *Allan Keiler*
Charles Ives Remembered: An Oral History *Vivian Perlis*
Henry Cowell, Bohemian *Michael Hicks*
Rap Music and Street Consciousness *Cheryl L. Keyes*
Louis Prima *Garry Boulard*
Marian McPartland's Jazz World: All in Good Time *Marian McPartland*
Robert Johnson: Lost and Found *Barry Lee Pearson and Bill McCulloch*
Bound for America: Three British Composers *Nicholas Temperley*
Lost Sounds: Blacks and the Birth of the Recording Industry, 1890–1919 *Tim Brooks*
Burn, Baby! BURN! The Autobiography of Magnificent Montague *Magnificent Montague with Bob Baker*
Way Up North in Dixie: A Black Family's Claim to the Confederate Anthem *Howard L. Sacks and Judith Rose Sacks*
The Bluegrass Reader *Edited by Thomas Goldsmith*
Colin McPhee: Composer in Two Worlds *Carol J. Oja*
Robert Johnson, Mythmaking, and Contemporary American Culture *Patricia R. Schroeder*
Composing a World: Lou Harrison, Musical Wayfarer *Leta E. Miller and Fredric Lieberman*
Fritz Reiner, Maestro and Martinet *Kenneth Morgan*
That Toddlin' Town: Chicago's White Dance Bands and Orchestras, 1900–1950 *Charles A. Sengstock Jr.*
Dewey and Elvis: The Life and Times of a Rock 'n' Roll Deejay *Louis Cantor*

Come Hither to Go Yonder: Playing Bluegrass with Bill Monroe *Bob Black*
Chicago Blues: Portraits and Stories *David Whiteis*
The Incredible Band of John Philip Sousa *Paul E. Bierley*
"Maximum Clarity" and Other Writings on Music *Ben Johnston, edited by Bob Gilmore*
Staging Tradition: John Lair and Sarah Gertrude Knott *Michael Ann Williams*
Homegrown Music: Discovering Bluegrass *Stephanie P. Ledgin*
Tales of a Theatrical Guru *Danny Newman*
The Music of Bill Monroe *Neil V. Rosenberg and Charles K. Wolfe*
Pressing On: The Roni Stoneman Story *Roni Stoneman, as told to Ellen Wright*
Together Let Us Sweetly Live *Jonathan C. David, with photographs by Richard Holloway*
Live Fast, Love Hard: The Faron Young Story *Diane Diekman*
Air Castle of the South: WSM Radio and the Making of Music City *Craig P. Havighurst*
Traveling Home: Sacred Harp Singing and American Pluralism *Kiri Miller*
Where Did Our Love Go? The Rise and Fall of the Motown Sound *Nelson George*
Lonesome Cowgirls and Honky-Tonk Angels: The Women of Barn Dance Radio *Kristine M. McCusker*
California Polyphony: Ethnic Voices, Musical Crossroads *Mina Yang*
The Never-Ending Revival: Rounder Records and the Folk Alliance *Michael F. Scully*
Sing It Pretty: A Memoir *Bess Lomax Hawes*
Working Girl Blues: The Life and Music of Hazel Dickens *Hazel Dickens and Bill C. Malone*
Charles Ives Reconsidered *Gayle Sherwood Magee*
The Hayloft Gang: The Story of the National Barn Dance *Edited by Chad Berry*
Country Music Humorists and Comedians *Loyal Jones*
Record Makers and Breakers: Voices of the Independent Rock 'n' Roll Pioneers *John Broven*
Music of the First Nations: Tradition and Innovation in Native North America *Edited by Tara Browner*
Cafe Society: The Wrong Place for the Right People *Barney Josephson, with Terry Trilling-Josephson*
George Gershwin: An Intimate Portrait *Walter Rimler*
Life Flows On in Endless Song: Folk Songs and American History *Robert V. Wells*
I Feel a Song Coming On: The Life of Jimmy McHugh *Alyn Shipton*
King of the Queen City: The Story of King Records *Jon Hartley Fox*
Long Lost Blues: Popular Blues in America, 1850–1920 *Peter C. Muir*
Hard Luck Blues: Roots Music Photographs from the Great Depression *Rich Remsberg*
Restless Giant: The Life and Times of Jean Aberbach and Hill and Range Songs *Bar Biszick-Lockwood*
Champagne Charlie and Pretty Jemima: Variety Theater in the Nineteenth Century *Gillian M. Rodger*
Sacred Steel: Inside an African American Steel Guitar Tradition *Robert L. Stone*

Gone to the Country: The New Lost City Ramblers and the Folk Music Revival *Ray Allen*
The Makers of the Sacred Harp *David Warren Steel with Richard H. Hulan*
Woody Guthrie, American Radical *Will Kaufman*
George Szell: A Life of Music *Michael Charry*
Bean Blossom: The Brown County Jamboree and Bill Monroe's Bluegrass Festivals *Thomas A. Adler*
Crowe on the Banjo: The Music Life of J. D. Crowe *Marty Godbey*
Twentieth Century Drifter: The Life of Marty Robbins *Diane Diekman*
Henry Mancini: Reinventing Film Music *John Caps*
The Beautiful Music All Around Us: Field Recordings and the American Experience *Stephen Wade*
Then Sings My Soul: The Culture of Southern Gospel Music *Douglas Harrison*
The Accordion in the Americas: Klezmer, Polka, Tango, Zydeco, and More! *Edited by Helena Simonett*
Bluegrass Bluesman: A Memoir *Josh Graves, edited by Fred Bartenstein*
One Woman in a Hundred: Edna Phillips and the Philadelphia Orchestra *Mary Sue Welsh*
The Great Orchestrator: Arthur Judson and American Arts Management *James M. Doering*
Charles Ives in the Mirror: American Histories of an Iconic Composer *David C. Paul*
Southern Soul-Blues *David Whiteis*
Sweet Air: Modernism, Regionalism, and American Popular Song *Edward P. Comentale*
Pretty Good for a Girl: Women in Bluegrass *Murphy Hicks Henry*
Sweet Dreams: The World of Patsy Cline *Warren R. Hofstra*
William Sidney Mount and the Creolization of American Culture *Christopher J. Smith*
Bird: The Life and Music of Charlie Parker *Chuck Haddix*
Making the March King: John Philip Sousa's Washington Years, 1854–1893 *Patrick Warfield*
In It for the Long Run *Jim Rooney*
Pioneers of the Blues Revival *Steve Cushing*
Roots of the Revival: American and British Folk Music in the 1950s *Ronald D. Cohen and Rachel Clare Donaldson*
Blues All Day Long: The Jimmy Rogers Story *Wayne Everett Goins*
Yankee Twang: Country and Western Music in New England *Clifford R. Murphy*
The Music of the Stanley Brothers *Gary B. Reid*
Hawaiian Music in Motion: Mariners, Missionaries, and Minstrels *James Revell Carr*
Sounds of the New Deal: The Federal Music Project in the West *Peter Gough*
The Mormon Tabernacle Choir: A Biography *Michael Hicks*
The Man That Got Away: The Life and Songs of Harold Arlen *Walter Rimler*
A City Called Heaven: Chicago and the Birth of Gospel Music *Robert M. Marovich*
Blues Unlimited: Essential Interviews from the Original Blues Magazine *Edited by Bill Greensmith, Mike Rowe, and Mark Camarigg*

Hoedowns, Reels, and Frolics: Roots and Branches of Southern Appalachian Dance *Phil Jamison*
Fannie Bloomfield-Zeisler: The Life and Times of a Piano Virtuoso *Beth Abelson Macleod*
Cybersonic Arts: Adventures in American New Music *Gordon Mumma, edited with commentary by Michelle Fillion*
The Magic of Beverly Sills *Nancy Guy*
Waiting for Buddy Guy *Alan Harper*
Harry T. Burleigh: From the Spiritual to the Harlem Renaissance *Jean E. Snyder*
Music in the Age of Anxiety: American Music in the Fifties *James Wierzbicki*
Jazzing: New York City's Unseen Scene *Thomas H. Greenland*
A Cole Porter Companion *Edited by Don M. Randel, Matthew Shaftel, and Susan Forscher Weiss*
Foggy Mountain Troubadour: The Life and Music of Curly Seckler *Penny Parsons*
Blue Rhythm Fantasy: Big Band Jazz Arranging in the Swing Era *John Wriggle*
Bill Clifton: America's Bluegrass Ambassador to the World *Bill C. Malone*
Chinatown Opera Theater in North America *Nancy Yunhwa Rao*
The Elocutionists: Women, Music, and the Spoken Word *Marian Wilson Kimber*
May Irwin: Singing, Shouting, and the Shadow of Minstrelsy *Sharon Ammen*
Peggy Seeger: A Life of Music, Love, and Politics *Jean R. Freedman*
Charles Ives's *Concord*: Essays after a Sonata *Kyle Gann*
Don't Give Your Heart to a Rambler: My Life with Jimmy Martin, the King of Bluegrass *Barbara Martin Stephens*
Libby Larsen: Composing an American Life *Denise Von Glahn*
George Szell's Reign: Behind the Scenes with the Cleveland Orchestra *Marcia Hansen Kraus*
Just One of the Boys: Female-to-Male Cross-Dressing on the American Variety Stage *Gillian M. Rodger*
Spirituals and the Birth of a Black Entertainment Industry *Sandra Jean Graham*
Right to the Juke Joint: A Personal History of American Music *Patrick B. Mullen*
Bluegrass Generation: A Memoir *Neil V. Rosenberg*
Pioneers of the Blues Revival, Expanded Second Edition *Steve Cushing*
Banjo Roots and Branches *Edited by Robert Winans*
Bill Monroe: The Life and Music of the Blue Grass Man *Tom Ewing*
Dixie Dewdrop: The Uncle Dave Macon Story *Michael D. Doubler*
Los Romeros: Royal Family of the Spanish Guitar *Walter Aaron Clark*
Transforming Women's Education: Liberal Arts and Music in Female Seminaries *Jewel A. Smith*
Rethinking American Music *Edited by Tara Browner and Thomas L. Riis*
Leonard Bernstein and the Language of Jazz *Katherine Baber*
Dancing Revolution: Bodies, Space, and Sound in American Cultural History *Christopher J. Smith*
Peggy Glanville-Hicks: Composer and Critic *Suzanne Robinson*
Mormons, Musical Theater, and Belonging in America *Jake Johnson*
Blues Legacy: Tradition and Innovation in Chicago *David Whiteis*

Blues Before Sunrise 2: Interviews from the Chicago Scene *Steve Cushing*
The Cashaway Psalmody: Transatlantic Religion and Music in Colonial Carolina *Stephen A. Marini*
Earl Scruggs and Foggy Mountain Breakdown: The Making of an American Classic *Thomas Goldsmith*
A Guru's Journey: Pandit Chitresh Das and Indian Classical Dance in Diaspora *Sarah Morelli*
Unsettled Scores: Politics, Hollywood, and the Film Music of Aaron Copland and Hanns Eisler *Sally Bick*
Hillbilly Maidens, Okies, and Cowgirls: Women's Country Music, 1930–1960 *Stephanie Vander Wel*
Always the Queen: The Denise LaSalle Story *Denise LaSalle with David Whiteis*
Artful Noise: Percussion Literature in the Twentieth Century *Thomas Siwe*
The Heart of a Woman: The Life and Music of Florence B. Price *Rae Linda Brown, edited by Guthrie P. Ramsey Jr.*
When Sunday Comes: Gospel Music in the Soul and Hip-Hop Eras *Claudrena N. Harold*
The Lady Swings: Memoirs of a Jazz Drummer *Dottie Dodgion and Wayne Enstice*
Industrial Strength Bluegrass: Southwestern Ohio's Musical Legacy *Edited by Fred Bartenstein and Curtis W. Ellison*
Soul on Soul: The Life and Music of Mary Lou Williams *Tammy L. Kernodle*
Unbinding Gentility: Women Making Music in the Nineteenth-Century South *Candace Bailey*
Punks in Peoria: Making a Scene in the American Heartland *Jonathan Wright and Dawson Barrett*
Homer Rodeheaver and the Rise of the Gospel Music Industry *Kevin Mungons and Douglas Yeo*
Americanaland: Where Country & Western Met Rock 'n' Roll *John Milward, with Portraits by Margie Greve*

The University of Illinois Press
is a founding member of the
Association of University Presses.

Text designed by Lisa Connery
Composed in 10.25/14 Athelas
with Birch and BarberinoRG display
at the University of Illinois Press
Manufactured by Versa Press, Inc.

University of Illinois Press
1325 South Oak Street
Champaign, IL 61820-6903
www.press.uillinois.edu